SPORT COACHING CONCEPTS

Coaching is a vital factor for success in sport at all levels. *Sport Coaching Concepts* offers a comprehensive introduction to the theoretical issues that underpin sport coaching practice. Now in a fully revised and updated new edition, it explains why a conceptual approach to sport coaching is more important than ever before, using practice-oriented analysis to help students develop a full understanding of coaching theory and practice.

Drawing on more than a decade's worth of research, the book reflects upon the profound changes that have transformed coach education and development. It covers all the key topics of the sport coaching curriculum and includes six new chapters on the evolution of coaching theory, coaching expertise, decision making, social perspectives on the coach–athlete relationship, social inclusion and principles of coach development. Each chapter contains a full range of pedagogical features to aid learning, including discussion questions, practical projects, guides to further reading, case studies and insights from practising coaches.

Sport Coaching Concepts is essential reading for all students of sport coaching and any serious coaches looking to develop their own coaching practice.

John Lyle is Professor of Sport Coaching at Leeds Beckett University, UK, and previously Dean of the School of Psychology and Sport Sciences at Northumbria University, UK. He has had a long and successful career in higher education, first in physical education and later specialising in sport coaching studies. He established the first professional diploma in sport coaching and played a significant role in the development of sport coaching as an academic field of study. He is the author of *Sports Coaching Concepts: First Edition*, and co-editor of *The Coaching Process* and *Sports Coaching: Professionalisation and Practice*.

Chris Cushion is Professor of Coaching and Pedagogy at Loughborough University, UK. His research interests focus on understanding coach learning, coaching practice and coach behaviour, within a framework of developing a sociology of coaching. He has worked on projects with a number of governing body organisations and professional clubs, as well as developing coaching and coach education in non-sporting contexts such as the police and the military. He is Associate Editor of the journal *Sports Coaching Review* and has co-edited two recent books: *Sports Coaching: Professionalisation and Practice* and *The Sociology of Sports Coaching*.

SPORT COACHING CONCEPTS

A FRAMEWORK FOR COACHING PRACTICE

SECOND EDITION

JOHN LYLE AND CHRIS CUSHION

Routledge
Taylor & Francis Group

LONDON AND NEW YORK

Second edition published 2017
by Routledge
2 Park Square, Milton Park, Abingdon, Oxon OX14 4RN

and by Routledge
711 Third Avenue, New York, NY 10017

Routledge is an imprint of the Taylor & Francis Group, an informa business

First edition published 2003 by Routledge

British Library Cataloguing-in-Publication Data
A catalogue record for this book is available from the British Library

Library of Congress Cataloging in Publication Data
Names: Lyle, John, author. | Cushion, Chris, author.
Title: Sport coaching concepts: a framework for coaching practice /
John Lyle and Chris Cushion.
Description: Second edition. | Abingdon, Oxon; New York, NY:
Routledge, 2017. | Includes bibliographical references and index.
Identifiers: LCCN 2016021540| ISBN 9780415675765 (hardback) |
ISBN 9780415675772 (pbk.) | ISBN 9780203126424 (ebook)
Subjects: LCSH: Coaching (Athletics)—Great Britain.
Classification: LCC GV711 .L95 2017 | DDC 796.07/70941—dc23
LC record available at https://lccn.loc.gov/2016021540

ISBN: 978-0-415-67576-5 (hbk)
ISBN: 978-0-415-67577-2 (pbk)
ISBN: 978-0-203-12642-4 (ebk)

Typeset in Melior
by Keystroke, Neville Lodge, Tettenhall, Wolverhampton
Printed by Ashford Colour Press Ltd.

CONTENTS

FIGURES

FIGURES

TABLES

NOTES ON THE AUTHORS

John Lyle is Professor of Sport Coaching at Leeds Beckett University, UK, and prior to that was Dean of the School of Psychology and Sport Sciences at Northumbria University, UK. This was the culmination of a long and successful career in higher education, first in physical education and thereafter specialising in sport coaching studies. He established the first professional diploma in sports coaching and the first Master's degree in coaching studies in the UK. He has played a significant role in the development of sport coaching as an academic field of study, and is the author of *Sports Coaching Concepts*, and co-editor of *The Coaching Process* and *Sports Coaching: Professionalisation and Practice*. He combines his role as an academic with a role as research consultant. John's academic experience is complemented by considerable personal experience as a coach, and engagement in the delivery of high-performance coach education and development. He has coached and played volleyball at international level, including the European club championships, European Championships and World University Games. He was also a professional soccer player.

Chris Cushion is Professor of Coaching and Pedagogy at Loughborough University, UK. His research interests are in understanding coach learning, coaching practice and coach behaviour, within a framework of developing a sociology of coaching. He has worked on projects with a number of governing body organisations and professional clubs, and also developed coaching and coach education in non-sporting contexts such as the police and the military. He has published widely on sport coaching, with over 100 articles and book chapters. He is Associate Editor of the journal *Sports Coaching Review* and has co-edited two recent books, *Sports Coaching: Professionalisation and Practice* and *The Sociology of Sports Coaching*. Chris is a UEFA-qualified football coach and has worked as a coach and coach educator in professional football in the UK and in collegiate football in the US.

INTRODUCTION TO THE SECOND EDITION

The invitation to consider a second edition of *Sports Coaching Concepts* was received with some trepidation. First, the original text was published in 2002, and there have been significant changes and developments in the landscape of coaching science as an academic field of study. This has included a plethora of undergraduate-directed textbooks and academic journals dedicated to sport coaching research and commentary. Second, the horizons of researchers and authors have broadened. The field is over-reliant on secondary application of theoretical insights from other academic domains, which are not always accompanied by convincing insights into the realities of coaching practice. Nevertheless, behavioural observation studies and questionnaire-based leadership studies have been supplanted by social and educational theories, cognitive psychology, ethnographic studies and much more. Third, the quantity of published research has vastly increased. However, as we will elaborate in this edition, many of the shortcomings identified in 2002 are still evident today. Fourth, an element of specialisation is evident in recent publications, although some textbooks maintain an attempt at comprehensive coverage. However, in both the specialist and generalist texts, we feel that there has been a rather limited attempt to identify or adhere to a coherent conceptual framework. This subsequently becomes evident in a failure to address challenging issues of role, domain specificity, professionalisation, social esteem, coach accountability, quali-fication structures and expertise. In general, there is a lack of self-criticism in the writing and of a critical approach to stated and unspoken assumptions about coaching more generally.

A number of factors weighed heavily in the decision to go ahead:

1. Despite the increase in research and dissemination, basic conceptual issues were not being addressed. The concept of sport coaching itself was rarely treated as problematical; indeed, the clear domain distinctions within the social phenomenon that is sport coaching and their implications for coaches' education, development, behaviour and expertise were often ignored in the search for a generalisable and homogeneous landscape. Research and policy making were slow to reflect these distinctions. Despite the universal acceptance of the centrality of context in both understanding and operationalising coaching, the conceptual context was rarely acknowledged. Sport coaching continues to be

treated as a unidimensional construct, with an assumed hierarchy of practice levels. We recognise sport coaching to be a convenient term for a family of roles in which coaches create and deliver (albeit with various levels of contribution from athletes) interventions designed to improve sporting performance. The recognition that sport coaching per se is an umbrella term and that researchers and policy makers need to specify practice contexts and goal climates is perhaps the most important message to be taken from this edition.

2. The 2002 edition was a success, albeit benefitting greatly from being one of the first textbooks in the UK in this field. Not only was it widely distributed, it became established reading in almost all undergraduate and postgraduate courses, and was very well received by academic peers. A recent citation network analysis (using the years 2007 and 2008) found that the 2002 edition could be considered the biggest 'hub' in the coaching science field (Rangeon *et al.* 2012). Naturally, it is our intention that the new edition should continue to make a contribution to the study of sport coaching.

3. The first edition of the book had a number of objectives: comprehensive coverage, textbook format and a focus on the concepts that underpin our understanding of sport coaching. Importantly, the first edition has to be appreciated in its time and space: it was the first attempt in the UK to put together a non-sport-specific analysis of the coaching process. However, the first edition was quite explicit in its intended approach. First, it sought to identify the concepts that constituted the building blocks of the coaching process in its social manifestation and operational functioning, and thereby were necessary for analysis, research and education. Second, the book offered a conceptual framework, a vocabulary and a number of suppositions, which the reader, student or researcher was invited to challenge, refute, extend and supplant. The first edition's intended role as a starting point for the furtherance of the academic study of sport coaching was quite deliberate. What is our judgement on how these two approaches have fared?

In so far as there were few alternative sources, the content has been widely referenced and has permeated the vocabulary of the field. For many authors it has been a reference point against which, often in critical terms, to situate their own work and alternative perspectives. It would be invidious to invite criticism and then cavil when it happens. Nevertheless, there were some fundamental issues about coaching domains, coaching effectiveness, research quality, coaching expertise and model building that we feel have not adequately been challenged or resolved since its publication.

There was also a quite specific issue about the 'ideal' model of the coaching process that was presented in Chapter 6 of the first edition and with which the book has, to some extent, become synonymous. This has variously been described as overly systematic, rational, linear and context-free, and used as an example of how not to represent the complexity and inherent interaction within the coaching process. We will have much more to say about the potential for a generic model of the coaching process in this edition. However, the criticism is a little disappointing – and it would be fair to say the model has been, at times, misunderstood and criticised for things it never set out to do. The text explicitly

Introduction to the second edition

states that the various elements of the model (which itself merely situates these elements) should be elaborated by researchers for 'how they may be operationalised' in practice. It is disappointing that the two examples of elaborations are never, or rarely, referenced. The limitations of all models are clearly stated, and we still await robust examples of practice models or theory-driven models that can be operationalised.

We do accept that the analytical approach and the attempt to situate the various elements of the process give the presentation a 'clarity' that was not intended to replicate practice. Although the first edition pointed out and emphasised that there was a planned, systematic and goal-directed character to much of coaching, we take the opportunity to remind the reader of what was written:

> the coaching process is characterised by uncertainty, complexity and uniqueness . . . this makes it difficult to describe and analyse . . . coaching practice has to deal with a continuum from the controllable and predictable to the unpredictable, the latter requiring more contingency and possibly crisis management.
>
> (Lyle 2002, p. 118)

Overall, it has been a matter of some disappointment that various parts of the book have not been used as catalysts for further research, but have been ossified and thus treated as 'finished products'.

4. As we demonstrate in Chapter 1 (and Chapter 15) there has been a significant expansion in the literature available to support the study of coaching. These new disciplinary insights are a very welcome addition and draw us closer to becoming a mature field of study. In particular, there has been considerable attention to the social dimension of sport coaching practice and interaction. However, our interpretation of the literature suggests that the centrality of performance enhancement is missing from much of the work. We believe that this needs to be redressed. In addition, the attempt to generalise from research findings or to create generic models founders on the issue of sport specificity. Even if it were possible to identify a core process, there is a subsequent layer of sport specificity that needs to be superimposed on it. Research papers will identify the sport from which research populations are selected but will very rarely discuss how the characteristic practice of coaches and the cultural nuances in that sport have impacted on the results. There is also a tendency for the trinity of researcher, method and sport to coalesce around certain themes. We consider this another reason why there needs to be recourse to a conceptual framework – a language and meaning that transcends sport specificity.

5. Professionalisation of sport coaching has been a constant theme in the literature and there have been policy imperatives to further this process (sports coach UK 2008; ICCE *et al.* 2013). Increased funding for high-performance sport has created a remunerated occupational grouping with some career progression, but the majority of coaches are minimally trained volunteers, working to introduce young people to sport. We do not, at this time, detect any public support or drive for the professionalisation process. An alternative approach is needed, and we

believe that a conceptual appreciation of sport coaching is required to understand fully the parameters that impact on the professionalisation process.

6. There is no doubt that formal coach education is much improved since 2002, and, in our experience, there are more effective coach development programmes for high-performance coaches. Nevertheless, the formal structures continue to perpetuate a mistaken hierarchy of roles and qualifications, and, more importantly, coach education in general is not based on a consensual view about coach expertise or a widely shared model of coach development. In short, once again there is a need to approach our understanding of and ideas for improvements in coach education from a conceptual perspective.

STRUCTURE OF THE NEW EDITION

It will immediately be obvious that we have adopted the use of the term 'sport coaching' rather than the more-familiar 'sports coaching'. This is not accidental. We believe that the use of the latter is simply a taken-for-granted continuation of a historical usage that maintains and implies a more generalisable process than we believe it to be. The emphasis should be on the 'coaching process in a sport context' (to distinguish it from other coaching realms, such as business or drama), rather than the 'sports' referring to specific examples such as badminton, boxing or basketball. This may seem pedantic, but it is an example of conceptual thinking applied to the discourse and specificity of language necessary to delineate appropriately the field of study. Our view is that there is a set of core principles that describe the coaching process, but that its application across domains, sports and individual contexts is very particular. It is not helpful to imply that coaching applies to all sports, in the same way that physical education teachers in schools will use the medium of different sports to achieve their educational goals. In simpler terms, the adjective 'sport' qualifies the realm, with all the nuances, domains, development stages, social, cultural and institutional dimensions, and distinctive roles that this implies, and not merely a list of specific sports.

We were faced with a number of options in designing and creating the content for the new edition. We could tinker with the content and retain the existing chapter structure. This would be merely an updating process that would be inappropriate given the changes highlighted above. It was considered appropriate, therefore, to incorporate more extensive changes that would not only take into account the extended time period and changes in the academic discourse since the first edition, but would also permit us to incorporate our own changes in thinking about sport coaching since that time. The result might more appropriately be considered a new book. The chapter structure and the contents have been completely rewritten. Of course, we have retained much of the text and the ideas that were novel at that time.

- There is a continued emphasis on the creation of a conceptual framework that will help to understand sport coaching, and this is a constant theme throughout the book.
- We have been more selective than in the first edition: conceptually focused content has been retained, and some themes incorporated into new chapters.

4

There is a focus on those issues that we considered would benefit most from conceptual analysis.

- Increased emphasis has been given to coaching domains, coaching expertise, professionalisation, operationalising coaching practice and social context.

The most significant and welcome change was an invitation to Professor Chris Cushion to collaborate on the new edition. Chris and I had collaborated on previous occasions and we shared similar, although certainly not identical, views on sport coaching. This was designed to strengthen the writing team by offering complementary insights and distinctive expertise. I was delighted to have him join me in producing this second edition.

We intend this book to act as a catalyst to thinking more deeply about sport coaching. We are quietly confident that it will make a valued contribution to the field of study, but are realistic about its impact as a study companion and stimulus to research. We have enjoyed writing it, and we hope that readers will enjoy immersing themselves in a conceptual framework for sport coaching.

Professor John Lyle
May 2016

REFERENCES

ICCE, ASOIF, & LMU (2013). *International sport coaching framework v1.2.* Champaign, IL: Human Kinetics.

Lyle, J. (2002). *Sports Coaching Concepts.* London: Routledge.

Rangeon, S., Gilbert, W. D., & Bruner, M. (2012). Mapping the world of coaching science: A Citation Network Analysis. *Journal of Coaching Education,* 5(1), 83–108.

sports coach UK (2008). *The UK Coaching Framework.* Leeds: sports coach UK.

CHAPTER 1

DEVELOPMENTS IN THE FIELD

INTRODUCTION

One of the primary reasons for initiating a second edition of the book was the significant expansion of academic writing since the publication of the first edition in 2002. As we will demonstrate, the academic study of sport coaching has increased in depth, breadth and quality. This is evident in the number of academic departments and staff in universities, the range of disciplinary lenses being applied to the subject and the number of dissemination avenues open to the researcher. The number of postgraduate programmes, PhD completions and peer-reviewed publications is testament to a rapidly evolving field of study. It is important, therefore, to begin by charting some of the developments that have taken place. We do this, not only to provide context, but because we believe that an adequate interpretation of the field of coaching science requires a measure of conceptual appreciation. Our belief is that the diversity of academic enquiry is in danger of creating a rather fragmented and polemical field of study, without an understanding of the conceptual framework that could bind it together. The aim of the second edition is to provide just such a conceptual framework.

The purpose of this short introductory chapter is to provide an overview of the principal developments in academic 'thinking' about sport coaching in the past 15 years. Clearly, the scope for a descriptive account of each 'school' or disciplinary approach is endless. This is not our intention, however. Some selective readings are offered, but readers can easily follow-up each of these approaches in detail. Rather, our purpose is to identify the major schools of thought as they apply to sport coaching and to offer a critical interpretation of their 'positioning' in relation to the conceptual framework. Therefore, the issues that will be raised relate to definitions, boundaries, domains, modelling, key questions, place of performance objectives and the role of the coach. We hope to demonstrate that attention to a consensual conceptual framework would allow better communication, a reconciliation of positions and a unifying mechanism for aggregating academic contributions to education and development.

We take the view that the distinctive disciplinary positions, with their concomitant methodological paradigms, are not inimical but take different perspectives and merely address different questions – a question of focus and scope rather than validity. Nevertheless, we are also aware that academic writing in our field is often unnecessarily adversarial in nature; perhaps more concerned to identify the shortcomings of other perspectives rather than highlighting the strengths of their own. We invite you to consider whether the practical implications for change and evolution in coaching practice are as evident as the identification of limitations in existing practice. The developments in academic writing and theoretical scaffolding have taken place alongside much enhanced coaching provision in schools, high-performance development programmes, talent development pathways and coach education programmes. Nevertheless, our own experience as coach developers suggests to us that earlier warnings that there is a theory–practice divide have not yet been overcome. It is our hope that greater attention to the conceptual framework for sport coaching will facilitate greater communication between academics and developers.

Rather than be overwhelmed by the mass of published work on sport coaching, we have adopted a more pragmatic approach of identifying the key categories and offering a critical interpretation of their relationship to some of the conceptual framework constructs that were introduced in the first edition and elaborated in this. In one sense, we are attempting to raise the profile of these concepts, which we will then deal with at much greater length in subsequent chapters. Useful theoretical and philosophical categories are identified by Gilbert and Trudel (2004), Gilbert and Rangeon (2011) and North (2013). One option available to us was to group writings under thematic headings, and we would commend this to you as a useful exercise – such themes as expertise, planning, goal-setting, pedagogy, career development/socialisation and effectiveness. We have selected a balance of thematic and discipline-based approaches and have categorised recent academic approaches in the following way: behavioural, cognitive, complexity, social and conceptual (a much fuller account of theoretical approaches is provided in Chapter 9).

RECENT DEVELOPMENTS IN THE LITERATURE

Behavioural approaches

Many of the references cited in the first edition were based on behavioural research. In general, such an approach looks for regularities in coaches' behaviours through observation instruments that identify observable behaviours. These are quantified and categorised according to constructs such as praise, negative feedback, questioning, instruction and so on. Such an approach can be criticised as being positivistic and

7

insufficiently sensitive to contextual variation. In addition, the search for 'correct' or 'appropriate' behaviours that lead to effective coaching may be criticised as perpetuating a 'one way' approach to coaching and coach education.

This approach continues to be used with more technologically advanced instrumentation (Cushion *et al.* 2012) and an attempt to provide more contextual background (Horn 2008) or reinforcement from coach interviews. There has also been some attempt to model appropriate behaviours (Jowett 2007) and a considerable literature on coaching efficacy (Feltz *et al.* 2008).

It seems clear that attention to the conceptual framework in terms of expertise, effectiveness, role of the coach and coaching domains (which would include process boundaries) would enhance interpretation of this type of research. Criticisms are largely based on the methodological paradigm adopted, but it is important not to criticise this approach beyond what it claims to achieve. In our view, the search for regularities in behaviour continues to be useful, but a more nuanced contextual siting is required, particularly if related to performance outcomes.

Cognitive approaches

The first edition of the book paid particular attention to decision making as an important feature of coaches' behaviour and practice, building on some earlier work (Lyle 1992, 1996, 1999; Côté *et al.* 1995), and introduced Naturalistic Decision Making as an appropriate paradigm to explain coaches' decision making. Since publication in 2002, the cognitive approach to conceiving of and understanding sport coaching has become a major school of thought in this field. We conceive of coaching expertise and operational coaching as a cognitive exercise. This means

8

that there is a need to identify, understand and develop the cognitive structures, organisation and processes that facilitate the coach's behaviour. This is evidenced in the work of Abraham and Collins (2011a, 2011b), Lyle (2003, 2010), Vergeer and Lyle (2007, 2009), Debanne (Debanne & Fontayne 2009; Debanne *et al.* 2014), Nash and Collins (2006) and Harvey *et al.* (2015).

A good deal of attention has been focused on Naturalistic Decision Making (Lipshitz *et al.* 2001; Ross *et al.* 2006) as an appropriate means of accounting for coaches' decision making, particularly in situations characterised as dynamic and uncertain. Experts make decisions in such circumstances in an apparently intuitive manner. This experiential decision making relies on recognition and interpretation of situations, and rapid matching to stored solutions. This may be particularly useful in contexts such as interactive training sessions and management of competition (Lyle 2010; Abraham & Collins 2011b). Of interest is how coaches mix and blend this less-deliberative decision making with more-deliberative decision making, for example in planning, and the balance of more-routinised behaviour with more-conscious

---

INTERPRETATION

- Writing to date has been more concerned to establish the validity of the approach than to provide detail of the substance of coaches' cognitions.
- The recourse to 'expert decision making' and the need for developed knowledge bases may mean that Naturalistic Decision Making is more relevant in performance coaching.
- There is an assumption of goal-directed behaviour that facilitates the relevance to particular coaching goals.
- There is a strong element of sport-specificity (team/individual, open/contested performance) because of the role of the coach in training and competition.
- Expertise is about efficient and effective access to appropriate cognitions. The mechanism for describing the necessary alignment of goals and cognitions is yet unresolved (see Jones *et al.* 2010; Jones & Corsby 2015).
- The academic writing has an element of prescription about it as yet. Although the implications for coach education and development are often identified, there are few, if any, examples of educational interventions.
- The cognitive approach deals with individual coaches' cognitions, and focuses on personal bias, catalysts, heuristics and types of knowledge; the how and what. Although it is acknowledged to be contextual, there is a need to layer in the social context and the institutional context to decision making.
- Particular attention has been paid to mental models and their role in facilitating decision making. However, this remains as yet at the level of presumption.

9

deliberation. Coaches' knowledge and access to reasoning is thought to be largely tacit (Nash & Collins 2006), and this means that research has recourse to innovative ways of accessing coaches' cognitions (Lyle 2003; Debanne *et al.* 2014).

It will be clear from the references cited that this is an approach with which we find favour. Our subsequent explication of expertise owes much to this goal-driven cognitive approach to conceptualising the coaching process. It provides a bridge to sport performance-related decision making that is missing from other approaches. Nevertheless, there is a good deal of empirical work required to 'populate' the emerging assumptions about how coaches' cognitions operate.

Complexity approaches

The identification of the sport coaching milieu as exhibiting a dynamic complexity has become an influential and enduring theme in the sport coaching literature. Initiated by the earlier work of Saury and Durand (1998) and d'Arripe-Longueville *et al.* (1998, 2001), the period since the publication of *Sports Coaching Concepts* in 2002 has witnessed a consolidation of this approach, particularly by Robyn Jones, arguably the most influential and prolific writer in the field (Bowes & Jones 2006; Jones & Wallace 2005, 2006; Jones *et al.* 2010, 2013, 2016). Coaching moments have to be understood as the product of a construction between the coach and the athlete, but taking place within layers of socio-cultural expectations, practices and priorities.

The identification of the complexity of interaction and operationalisation is perhaps a response to the limitations of the more rational and linear conceptions of the coaching process and recognition of the social and cultural context within which coaching takes place. Coaches are aware that the operationalisation of practice requires a 'juggling' of many factors. However, the expertise required to 'manage' the process (the focus here is often on micro-management) – orchestration, alignment, accommodation – remains speculative (Jones *et al.* 2010, 2013).

There is no doubt that the coaching process exhibits a dynamic complexity, and this needs to be accounted for in the conceptual framework. Complexity approaches are strong on theoretical underpinning, but, as yet, weak on translation to education and development. Such approaches acknowledge the process nature of coaching (sometimes by default), but can underplay the role of goal-directed structure in the operationalisation process. There are occasions when goals are ill-defined or taken for granted. However, in some domains, performance goals are absolutely central to coaches' practice. If you ask the question 'how difficult is it to achieve goals and maintain progression and momentum in the world of (team) coaching?', then these difficulties need to be addressed. If you ask the question, in the real world of acknowledged complexity, 'how is it that coaches manage to cope with this and maintain momentum towards quite precise goals and performance targets – while remaining sane and achieving the cooperation and engagement of athletes?', a different set of answers is required.

INTERPRETATION

- The issue is less about the obvious complexity of implementation and more about the polemical juxtaposition with more goal-directed practice. It has been argued (Lyle 2007) not that the complexity is overstated, but that the influence of goal-directed and routinised practice is understated – and this relationship needs more exploration.
- There is a strong sport-specific feature in the work. Given that the social and cultural context is emphasised, it is surprising that the developmental team sport context that characterises much of the empirical work, with often less well-defined goals, is not contrasted with other more 'structured' coaching contexts.
- The micro-management of the coaching moment is portrayed as a shared interaction, but there is a distinction between social theory (socially generated meaning through interaction) and the performance-related knowledge that (often) the coach has greater access to and then has to try to share/convince the athlete to engage with. Those who coach know that (in high-performance contexts) there is usually an eventual cooperation and mutual generation of understanding – but it is generally coach-directed.
- Although cognitive approaches are criticised, it seems clear that coaches rely on fluid and flexible cognitions to micro-manage the coaching moment. The place of 'coaching strategy or craft' (admittedly contested terms) is not obvious.
- The emphasis on the coaching moment is said to reduce the value of 'coaching domains'. Given their impact on socio-cultural expectations of both coach and athlete, we find this surprising.
- The very nature of complexity means that there are no successful attempts to model this approach, as portraying it currently presents insurmountable difficulties. Other attempts to model the coaching process are criticised for their lack of incorporation of complexity.

Social approaches

There is no doubt that sport coaching is a social phenomenon; it has a social dimension through the interaction of various actors, and a social presence in layers of institutions and organisations. The work of authors such as Jones, Cushion and Potrac stresses the absence of a critical awareness of social context in understanding coaching practice and delivering coaching education. The early work of Jones (Jones 2000; Jones *et al.* 2002) has been superseded by a sociological analysis of sport coaching (Cushion & Jones 2006; Jones *et al.* 2011; Piggott 2012) in which the perspectives of well-known social theorists have been applied to sport coaching.

11

There has also been a significant emphasis on the shortcomings of coaching education (Nelson & Cushion 2006; Cushion 2011).

The basic premise is twofold: (1) that the coaching process is presented (largely in coach education) as de-contextualised, being too simplistic and rational; and (2) that conscious agency is supplemented by the unchallenged internalisation of accepted practice. Those adopting this approach offer a critical analysis of knowledge forms, scientism and passive learning. There is a particular emphasis on understanding power hierarchies.

This is an approach that tests the boundaries of the conceptual framework. There is little attempt to engage with the performance-enhancement features of sport coaching or to weigh the coach's conscious application of knowledge and expertise on a day-to-day basis with a social critique of the unquestioned social determinants of behaviour. To some extent there is a sense that the theorists are saying 'we can see something that you cannot' – and there is a danger that critical social theory can appear like an arrogant club in which members have penetrated an ideologically obscured reality that is inaccessible to 'ordinary' people. However, if my intention as a coach (and athlete) is to improve performance and compete with success, a more sophisticated social critique of my practice may not be the most immediate answer

– that said, no practice is neutral and all practice serves or supports some interests and opposes others and is worthy of critical analysis. Arguably, the critical analyses of coach education are very appropriate and this is where such approaches have most value, although the practical recommendations for changing educational practice need to be bolder in challenging the situated realities of coach education structures and opportunities.

Conceptual approaches

We have taken this to include not only the approach adopted in this book and similar writings (Cushion 2007; Lyle 2007, 2011a, 2011b; Lyle & Cushion 2010; Cushion & Lyle 2013), but also those in which sport coaching practice is identified in greater detail (Lynn 2010; Stafford 2011; Navin 2011; Nash 2015) and/or in which authors offer prescriptions for better practice (Côté & Gilbert 2009; Gilbert & Côté 2013). We include in this the contributions of Abraham *et al.* (2006) and Abraham and Collins (2011a, 2011b), which we consider to be most relevant to conceptual discourse.

Not surprisingly, there is no unifying theme or disciplinary approach in this category. Writers tend to draw upon other published works to provide a rationale for their arguments; indeed, the level of 'prescriptive' writing is worthy of comment. We have identified (admittedly selectively) a number of themes that are addressed by our conceptual framework in subsequent chapters. These include the professionalisation of coaching (Taylor & Garratt 2010a, 2010b, 2013), expertise (Schempp & McCullick 2010), ethical issues (Telfer & Brackenridge 2011), career trajectories (Erickson *et al.* 2007; Mallett 2010), gender issues (Norman 2010, 2013) and pedagogy (Jones 2006; Cassidy 2010; Armour 2013; Cushion & Nelson 2013). This category will also include prescriptive or normative 'models' of coaching (Côté *et al.* 2010; Abraham & Collins 2011a; Muir *et al.* 2011).

We have not included an interpretation box for this category as it is so diverse; comments are incorporated in the summary. In general, we find that there is limited attention to conceptual issues. It is rare to find that writers attend to coaching domains, or identify coaches by the specifics of their coaching practice. Much of the work is prescriptive and greater clarity is required to distinguish between translation of empirical findings or accumulated research into conceptual schemas or diagrams that represent practice, and normative 'models' intended to influence coach developers.

SUMMARY

There is no doubt that the expansion of academic writing research and dissemination in the past 15 years has brought us closer to becoming a mature field of study. The greater diversity of disciplinary approaches has added to this. Nevertheless, the preponderance of literature from a social perspective perhaps hides the fact that the field is much weaker in the detail of a number of areas:

- coaching expertise;
- micromanagement of progression and momentum in performance programmes;
- linkages between coaching behaviour and practice and performance outcomes and other goals;
- contextual differences across coaching domains;
- the particularity of these contextual differences on interpersonal interactions;
- the nature and degree of coaching as a conscious collective endeavour.

We perceive there to be an unfortunate trend in much of the literature in which academics adopt a polemical stance that appears to be more concerned to identify the shortcomings of alternative approaches, rather than to be clear about the contribution of their own. We suggest that the field would be stronger for a degree of humility in accepting the contribution of each disciplinary or thematic lens. It is important for the development of coaching not to disregard existing accumulated and useful knowledge, and a challenge is the integration of these different perspectives to develop a more sophisticated knowledge base. In simplistic terms, ontology is a preferred way of asking questions about the world and how it works. An epistemology identifies the kind of evidence that would provide answers to these preferred questions. Our interpretation of the growing field of coaching science is that we have yet to acknowledge the complementary rather than contradictory contributions of different approaches and 'schools' of thinking about sport coaching.

Coaching practice comprises coaching moments and interventions, social interaction, plans and programmes, institutional and organisational structures and layers of meaning and history – some conscious and much unconscious. Academics differ in what they find interesting about sport coaching or how they perceive that it can best be explained and understood. However, we stress that there is a reality of coaching practice to be found in the everyday experience of sport coaching throughout the different domains. This does not change as a result of different modes of academic enquiry. For example, there may be a legitimate criticism that some writers conceive of coaching as too rational, linear and systematic, and that its assumptions are unchallenged. For others, coaches are engaged in a continuous process of collective re-creation of innovative practice within broad goal-led parameters. However, coaches' practice remains as it is – it is the interpretation and explanation that differs. For change to occur within sport coaching, there needs to be a focus on coach education and development, on policy makers and on the transformational practice of some coaches. Unfortunately, the literature is much less specific about how such change should be achieved. Much of it strays into prescription and aspiration.

We identify the following trends and issues:

- There is much common ground. We know that both the coaching moment/ intervention and the coaching process/practice within which it is sited are layered and complex. We also know that it is goal-directed, planned and has a combination of reactive, contingent practice alongside routine and well-tried methods. These behaviours are sport-specific, domain-specific and contested. The issue is one of balance and emphasis.

Developments in the field

- Much of the literature presents a critical interpretation of coaching practice. There is a danger that sport coaches are portrayed as unaware, unconcerned, unreflective and subject to taken-for-granted assumptions that develop within occupations and serve to reinforce particular ideologies or power hierarchies. We are in no doubt that there is some truth in this, but it will not and should not be applied to all coaches. There are many sophisticated, reflective coaches who are innovative and challenge their own and traditional practice. Such generalisations require far greater contextualisation.
- We are surprised by the absence of 'like comparisons' in much of the writing. The literature is critical of sport coaching and sport coaches, but the expectations against which this criticism is measured rarely situate it in the context of mini-mally trained volunteer coaches with limited engagement with athletes. Would the criticisms and shortcomings be appropriate in other similar occupations? What are these? The borrowed theories and exemplars applied to sport coaching need to be applied with a much greater appreciation of a conceptual framework that differentiates coaching roles.
- A good deal of criticism is directed to the limitations of coaching education, and much of this is warranted. However, writers must take care to situate their just criticisms in a greater awareness of the conceptual framework. Criticisms of the mass education system that characterises the early stages of formal coach education programmes should be tempered by realistic expectations of what can be achieved with such minimal intervention. It might be more helpful to consider whether such interventions constitute coach education and preparation at all. In our experience there is a very welcome improvement in coach development for high-performance coaches in the UK.
- In reviewing the literature, it would be expected that research methods would mirror the disciplinary lens adopted. However, we are disappointed by (1) the unproblematic approach to the selection of research populations, and (2) the limited extent of research into *in situ* coaching practice. There should be a much greater acknowledgement of the particularity of the coaching practice and context of research populations chosen to reinforce the researchers' view of coaching.

The purpose of sport coaching is to improve sport performance within a set of sporting goals and environments. There are other complementary developmental goals, but it is the performance element (differing in nature, scope and ambition) that defines it and gives it meaning. We feel that this needs to be put much closer to the focus of academic study, including a better complementarity between social context and operationalisation. Much of the literature has become focused on a critical interpretation of coaching (treated as an unproblematic term) as a social phenomenon and the challenges of implementation, and appears to be divorced from the reality of athlete aspirations and coaches' practice.

We acknowledge, of course, that athletes engage in, and contribute to, a collective process. They may choose to adopt a passive role in decision making (which sociologists will recognise to be socially engineered), but this does not mean they are unaware of this. Coaches, in practice, adopt 'directive' leadership and pedagogical strategies and this may reflect their (often) greater knowledge and awareness of performance needs and capacity to gather relevant information. Academics who choose to focus on practical/pragmatic intervention are not unaware of the social dimension; they are asking different questions. Indeed, this may reflect a similar criticism that writers who omit any reference to performance enhancement are not necessarily unaware of its centrality to coaching practice. We also point to the need for less talking about what should be done in coach education and more empirical and experiential work on attempts to improve it. Less evidence that it's broken and more evidence of how to fix it!

To sum up: how has thinking changed and is there consensus in the literature? From our perspective, there is a good deal of common ground (Abraham & Collins 2011b; Jones *et al.* 2016):

- Sport coaching has an observable and tacit dimension in behaviour, reasoning and values. This creates methodological challenges for research.
- Sport coaching is contextual – even to the point of particularity (it can only be understood in its particular context). It has a layered social, cultural, psychological, environmental and performance dimension. Coaches cope with this, but how they do so requires much greater attention.
- Sport coaching is goal-directed. The debate is only one of degree – structured improvisation versus instrumental accommodation.
- Sport coaching expertise has a knowledge dimension (multidisciplinary, sport-specific technical and sport science/performance foundation) and an 'orchestration, accommodation, coping' dimension. There is no disagreement, but the translation into effective education and development practice is much less evident.
- Sport coaching depends on cognition. For some this is manifest in various forms of decision making; for others, it is an ill-defined process that accommodates the various layers of context within which coaches operate.

We remain convinced that the first edition of the book was modestly successful in establishing the value of a consensual conceptual framework, and that this review of recent thinking merely highlights the need for greater attention to conceptual issues.

REFERENCES

Abraham, A., & Collins, D. (2011a). Effective skill development: How should athletes' skills be developed? In D. Collins, A. Button, & H. Richards (Eds) *Performance Psychology: A Practitioner's Guide.* Edinburgh: Churchill Livingstone, 207–229.

Abraham, A., & Collins, D. (2011b). Taking the next step: Ways forward for coaching science. *Quest, 63,* 366–384.

Abraham, A., Collins, D., & Martindale, R. (2006). The coaching schematic: Validation through expert coach consensus. *Journal of Sports Science, 24*(6), 549–564.

Armour, K. (Ed.) (2013). *Sport Pedagogy: An Introduction for Teaching and Coaching.* Abingdon: Routledge.

Bowes, I., & Jones, R. L. (2006). Working at the edge of chaos: Understanding coaching as a complex interpersonal system. *The Sport Psychologist, 20*, 235–245.

Cassidy, T. (2010). Understanding athlete learning and coaching practice: Utilising 'practice theories' and 'theories of practice'. In J. Lyle & C. Cushion (Eds) *Sports Coaching: Professionalisation and Practice.* Edinburgh: Churchill Livingstone, 177–191.

Côté, J., Bruner, M., Erickson, K., Strachan, L., & Fraser-Thomas, J. (2010). Athlete development and coaching. In J. Lyle & C. Cushion (Eds) *Sports Coaching: Professionalisation and Practice.* Edinburgh: Churchill Livingstone, 63–83.

Côté, J., & Gilbert, W. D. (2009). An integrative definition of coaching effectiveness and expertise. *International Journal of Sports Science & Coaching, 4*, 307–323.

Côté, J., Salmela, J., Trudel, P., & Russell, S. (1995). The coaching model: A grounded assessment of expert gymnastics coaches' knowledge. *Journal of Sport and Exercise Psychology, 17*(1), 1–17.

Cushion, C. J. (2007). Modelling the complexities of the coaching process. *International Journal of Sports Science & Coaching, 2*(4), 395–401.

Cushion, C. J. (2011). Coaches' learning and development. In I. Stafford (Ed.) *Coaching Children in Sport.* Abingdon: Routledge, 57–69.

Cushion, C. J., & Jones, R. L. (2006). Power, discourse, and symbolic violence in professional youth soccer: The case of Albion Football Club. *Sociology of Sport Journal, 23*, 142–161.

Cushion, C., & Lyle, J. (2013). Sport coaching: Some key questions and issues. In R. Wegener, A. Fritze, A., & M. Loebbert (Eds) *Coaching-Praxisfelder: Forschung und Praxis im Dialog.* Online-Teil. Wiesbaden: Springer VS, 115–134.

Cushion, C. J., & Nelson, L. (2013). Coach education and learning: Developing the field. In P. Potrac, W. D. Gilbert, & J. Dennison (Eds) *The Routledge Handbook of Sports Coaching.* London: Routledge, 359–374.

Cushion, C. J., Harvey, S., Muir, B., & Nelson, L. (2012). Developing the Coach Analysis and Intervention System (CAIS): Establishing validity and reliability of a computerised systematic observation instrument. *Journal of Sports Sciences, 30*(2), 201–216.

d'Arripe-Longueville, F., Fournier, J. F., & Dubois, A. (1998). The perceived effectiveness of interactions between expert French judo coaches and elite female athletes. *The Sport Psychologist, 12*, 317–332.

d'Arripe-Longueville, F., Saury, J., & Fournier, J. F. (2001). Coach–athlete interaction during elite archery competitions: An application of methodological frameworks used in ergonomics to sport psychology. *Journal of Applied Sport Psychology, 13*, 275–299.

Debanne, T., & Fontayne, P. (2009). A study of a successful experienced elite handball coach's cognitive processes in competition situations. *International Journal of Sports Science & Coaching, 4*(1), 1–16.

Debanne, T., Fontayne, P., & Bourbousson, J. (2014). Professional handball coaches management of players' situated understanding during official games. *Psychology of Sport and Exercise, 15*(6), 596–604.

17

Erickson, K., Côté, J., & Fraser-Thomas, J. (2007). Sport experiences, milestones, and educational activities associated with high performance coaches' development. *The Sport Psychologist*, *21*, 302–316.

Feltz, D. L., Short, S. E., & Sullivan, P. J. (2008). *Self-Efficacy in Sport*. Champaign, IL: Human Kinetics.

Gilbert, W. D., & Côté, J. (2013). Defining coaching effectiveness: A focus on coaches' knowledge. In P. Potrac, W. D. Gilbert, & J. Denison (Eds) *Routledge Handbook of Sports Coaching*. London: Routledge, 147–159.

Gilbert, W. D., & Rangeon, S. (2011). Current directions in coaching research. *Revista De Iberoamericana De Psicología Del Ejercicio Y El Deporte*, *6*(2), 217–236.

Gilbert, W. D., & Trudel, P. (2004). Analysis of coaching science research published from 1970–2001. *Research Quarterly for Exercise and Sport*, *75*(4), 388–389.

Harvey, S., Lyle, J., & Muir, B. (2015). Naturalistic decision making in high performance team sport coaching. *International Sport Coaching Journal*, *2*(2), 152–168.

Horn, T. S. (2008). Coaching effectiveness in the sport domain. In T. S. Horn (Ed.) *Advances in Sport Psychology*. 3rd Edition. Champaign, IL: Human Kinetics, 239–267.

Jones, R. L. (2000). Towards a sociology of coaching. In R. L. Jones & K. M. Armour (Eds) *Sociology of Sport: Theory and Practice*. London: Longman, 33–43.

Jones, R. L. (Ed.). (2006). *The Sports Coach as Educator*. London: Routledge.

Jones, R. L., & Corsby, C. (2015). A case for coach Garfinkel: Decision making and what we already know. *Quest*, *67*, 439–449.

Jones, R. L., & Wallace, M. (2005). Another bad day at the training ground: Coping with ambiguity in the coaching context. *Sport, Education and Society*, *8*(2), 213–229.

Jones, R. L., & Wallace, M. (2006). The coach as 'orchestrator': more realistically managing the complex coaching context. In R. L. Jones (Ed.) *The Sports Coach as Educator: Reconceptualising Sports Coaching*. Abingdon: Routledge, 51–64.

Jones, R. L., Armour, K. M., & Potrac, P. (2002). Understanding the coaching process: A framework for social analysis. *Quest*, *54*, 34–48.

Jones, R. L., Bailey, J., & Thompson, A. (2013). Ambiguity, noticing and orchestration: Further thoughts on managing the complex coaching context. In P. Potrac, W. D. Gilbert, & J. Denison (Eds) *Routledge Handbook of Sports Coaching*. London: Routledge, 271–283.

Jones, R. L., Bowes, I., & Kingston, K. (2010). Complex practice in coaching: Studying the chaotic nature of coach–athlete interactions. In J. Lyle & C. Cushion (Eds) *Sports Coaching: Professionalisation and Practice*. Edinburgh: Churchill Livingstone, 15–25.

Jones, R. L., Edwards, C., & Viotto Filho, I. A. T. (2016). Activity theory, complexity and sports coaching: An epistemology for a discipline. *Sport, Education and Society*, *21*(2), 200–216.

Jones, R. L., Potrac, P., Cushion, C., & Ronglan, L. T. (Eds) (2011). *The Sociology of Sports Coaching*. London: Routledge.

Jowett, S. (2007). Interdependence analysis and the 3+1Cs in the coach–athlete relationship. In S. Jowett & D. Lavallee (Eds) *Social Psychology in Sport*. Leeds: Human Kinetics, 15–27.

Lipshitz, R., Klein, G., Orasanu, J., & Salas, E. (2001). Taking stock of naturalistic decision making. *Journal of Behavioral Decision Making*, *14*(5), 331–352.

Lyle, J. (1992). Systematic coaching behaviour: An investigation into the coaching process and the implications of the findings for coach education. In T. Williams, L. Almond, & A. Sparkes (Eds) *Sport and Physical Activity: Moving Towards Excellence*. London: E & FN Spon, 463–469.

Lyle, J. (1996). A conceptual appreciation of the sports coaching process. *Research Papers in Sport, Leisure and Physical Education*, *1*(1), 15–37.

Lyle, J. (1999). The coaching process: An overview. In N. Cross & J. Lyle (Eds) *The Coaching Process: Principles and Practice for Sport*. Oxford: Butterworth Heinemann, 3–24.

Lyle, J. (2003). Stimulated recall: A report on its use in naturalistic research. *British Educational Research Journal*, *29*(6), 861–878.

Lyle, J. (2007). Modelling the complexities of the coaching process: A commentary. *International Journal of Sports Science & Coaching*, *2*(4), 407–409.

Lyle, J. (2010). Coaches' decision making: A naturalistic decision making analysis. In J. Lyle & C. Cushion (Eds) *Sports Coaching: Professionalisation and Practice*. Edinburgh: Churchill Livingstone, 27–41.

Lyle, J. (2011a). Sport development, sports coaching and domain specificity. In B. Houlihan & M. Green (Eds) *The Routledge Handbook of Sports Development*. London: Routledge, 487–500.

Lyle, J. (2011b) What is a coach and what is coaching? In I. Stafford (Ed.) *Coaching Children in Sport*. London: Routledge, 5–16.

Lyle, J., & Cushion, C. (2010). *Sports Coaching: Professionalisation and Practice*. Edinburgh: Churchill Livingstone.

Lynn, A. (2010). *Effective Sports Coaching*. Marlborough: Crowood Press.

Mallett, C. J. (2010). Becoming a high-performance coach: Pathways and communities. In J. Lyle & C. Cushion (Eds) *Sports Coaching: Professionalisation and Practice*. Edinburgh: Churchill Livingstone, 119–134.

Muir, B., Morgan, G., Abraham, A., & Morley, D. (2011). Developmentally appropriate approaches to coaching children. In I. Stafford (Ed.) *Coaching Children in Sport*. Abingdon: Routledge, 17–37.

Nash, C. (Ed.) (2015). *Practical Sports Coaching*. Abingdon: Routledge.

Nash, C., & Collins, D. (2006). Tacit knowledge in expert coaching: Science or art? *Quest*, *58*, 465–477.

Navin, A. (Ed.) (2011). *Sports Coaching: A Reference Guide*. Marlborough: Crowood Press.

Nelson, L., & Cushion, C. (2006). Reflection in coach education: The case of the national governing body coaching certificate. *The Sport Psychologist*, *20*(2), 174–183.

Norman, L. (2010). Feeling second best: Elite women coaches' experiences. *Sociology of Sport Journal*, *27*(1), 89–104.

Norman, L. (2013). The challenges facing women coaches and the contributions they can make to the profession. *International Journal of Coaching Science*, *7*(2), 3–23.

North, J. (2013). Philosophical underpinnings of coaching practice research. *Quest*, *65*(3), 278–299.

Piggott, D. (2012). Coaches' experiences of formal coach education: A critical sociological investigation. *Sport, Education and Society, 17*(4), 535–554.

Ross, K. G., Shafer, J. L., & Klein, G. (2006). Professional judgements and 'Naturalistic Decision Making'. In K. A. Ericsson, N. Charness, P. J. Feltovitch, & R. R. Hoffman (Eds) *The Cambridge Handbook of Expertise and Expert Performance.* New York: Cambridge University Press, 403–419.

Saury, J., & Durand, M. (1998). Practical knowledge in expert coaches: On-site study of coaching in sailing. *Research Quarterly for Exercise and Sport, 69*(3), 254–266.

Schempp, P. G., & McCullick, B. (2010). Coaches' expertise. In J. Lyle & C. J. Cushion (Eds) *Sports Coaching: Professionalisation and Practice.* Edinburgh: Churchill Livingstone, 221–231.

Stafford, I. (Ed.) (2011). *Coaching Children in Sport.* London: Routledge.

Taylor, W. G. & Garratt, D. (2010a). The professionalisation of sports coaching: Definitions, challenges and critique. In J. Lyle & C. Cushion (Eds) *Sports Coaching: Professionalisation and Practice.* Edinburgh: Churchill Livingstone, 99–117.

Taylor, W. G. & Garratt, D. (2010b). The professionalisation of sports coaching: Relations of power, resistance and compliance. *Sport, Education & Society, 15*(1), 121–139.

Taylor, W. G. & Garratt, D. (2013). Coaching and professionalisation. In P. Potrac, W. Gilbert, & J. Denison (Eds) *Routledge Handbook of Sports Coaching.* Routledge: London, 27–39.

Telfer, H., & Brackenridge, C. (2011). Professional responsibilities of children's coaches. In I. Stafford (Ed.) *Coaching Children in Sport.* Abingdon: Routledge, 97–108.

Vergeer, I., & Lyle, J. (2007). Mixing methods in assessing coaches' decision making. *Research Quarterly for Exercise and Sport, 78*(3), 225–235.

Vergeer, I., & Lyle, J. (2009). Coaching expertise: Examining its role in coaches' decision making. *International Journal of Sport and Exercise Psychology, 78*(3), 225–235.

20

Developments in the field

CHAPTER 2

DEVELOPING A CONCEPTUAL FRAMEWORK

CHAPTER OUTLINE

- ▩ Introduction
- ▩ Conceptual appreciation
- ▩ Contemporary sport and conceptual questions
- ▩ Building a conceptual framework
- ▩ Coaching and theory development
- ▩ Academic literature and conceptual development
- ▩ Sport as a concept
- ▩ Summary
- ▩ Projects

INTRODUCTION

Facilitating a critical appreciation of the concepts associated with sport coaching is key to the purpose of this book. This chapter identifies a set of conceptual principles about sport coaching and configures these into a framework that allows us to address more effectively basic questions such as: what is the purpose of coaching? Is there a coherent terminology and language about coaching? And can we claim that a 'theory of coaching' has been established? We will conclude that the subtlety of conceptual distinctions about sport coaching is often lost in the academic literature. Despite appearing to be a little detached from the everyday concerns of the practitioner, we stress that conceptual analysis of what is a social entity is a necessary step to a complete exploration and understanding of sport coaching.

Few individuals escape contact with sport, whether in an active or passive sense, forming as it does a significant part of our leisure, educational, entertainment and social experiences. Those who have taken part in school sport, those who watch sport on television and those who constitute the vast numbers of performers and officials in active sports participation are familiar with the public role and image of the sport coach. For many, these popular images are sufficient and there is no need to delve beyond the familiar. The breadth and diversity of coaching roles or any lack of clarity about expertise or professional development are not treated as problematic issues. To this we might add the hidden role of the coach, common stereotypes and the secondary role of the coach in our major team sports. However, the very pervasiveness and familiarity of the coach and coaching militates against precision in the depth and sophistication of knowledge and understanding required in academic study.

Conceptual precision and clarity have become more necessary. Coach education has expanded in scope and comprehensiveness, necessitating a more sophisticated appreciation of structure, purpose, application and development. For students of coaching, coaching expertise, domains, professionalisation, communities of practice and coach development have become familiar terms and the basis for academic debate. It is our contention that such legitimate questions about coaching are premised on fundamental concepts about coaching and the coaching process that are contentious and contested, but often ignored or assumed. Along with the more established professions, the coach's expertise and accountability in the public domain have come under closer scrutiny, often in the pursuit of national esteem, although perhaps in less analytical fashion than we would wish. At the same time, there has been a significant increase in the level of academic interest in all aspects of the coaching process. For each of these reasons, and also simply for the enquiring mind, the taken-for-granted assumptions about the coaching role have to be replaced by an analytical framework that will permit the level of analysis and academic enquiry necessary to sustain developments in coaching education and practice.

This book is intended as a resource text for those engaged in the study of sport coaching. The primary purpose is to provide a coherent conceptual understanding of all aspects of sport coaching, which in turn will facilitate the required analysis of practice. A consistent theme of identifying key concepts and exploring their inter-relationships is applied to all facets of coaching practice. Since the first edition of this book, there has been a significant increase in the number of specialist textbooks dealing with scientific sub-disciplines applied in the coaching context and there are emerging bodies of knowledge and principles in coach education, social milieux, interpersonal behaviour and sport-specific coaching practice. However, our central message, which is reinforced throughout and which is unchanged from the first edition, is that an explicit and comprehensive set of concepts about sport coaching is a first step, a pre-requisite, for subsequent analysis and application. Describing, understanding and improving coaching practice is a necessary stage in professionali-sation. It is important that an emphasis on athlete performance or the immediacy

 KEY CONCEPT

An explicit and comprehensive set of concepts about sport coaching is a pre-requisite for subsequent analysis and application.

of observable coach behaviour does not detract from the need to focus on these conceptual insights.

CONCEPTUAL APPRECIATION

In very simple terms, we cannot have a complete understanding of sport coaching practice until we understand what sport coaching is, what it is not, how it is experienced by athletes and coaches and how it 'works'. We can think of this as standing back from the untidiness of real practice in order to appreciate better the principles and processes that form the basis of sport coaching. Remember, however, that it is also necessary to attempt to understand the untidy, complex realities of actual practice, and to learn to cope with these in coaching research.

Conceptual appreciation deals with some or all of the following matters: meaning, relationships, principles, purpose, definitions, conditions, intentions, internal workings, processes/functions. There is a particular emphasis on definitions because this provides a set of conditions, a set of 'markers' for what is and what is not coaching. When aggregated, it is possible to form an extended vision, a structured representation of sport coaching. Remember that there are competing conceptualisations about sport coaching – but this is the reason that it is important to recognise these when interpreting coaching research and studying coaching practice. By way of illustration, we generally find it simple to distinguish between the term 'teaching' when applied in a generic way to imply helping someone to learn, and the occupations that incorporate an element of 'teaching'. In a similar way, we need to be more precise about the meaning of the term 'coaching' and the range of sport-related roles that may employ it. We argue that the absence of clear occupational boundaries and a failure to associate purpose and practice have hindered progress in education, development and professionalisation.

In each chapter we attempt a similar approach to conceptual appreciation. First, we attempt to break down for the purpose of analysis each aspect of coaching practice into its constituent parts. Second, we analyse and interpret these constituent parts. Third, we synthesise or recombine the elements with the intention that more detailed knowledge about the inter-relationships and processes will provide an increased clarity and understanding that will help us to improve sport coaching education, development and practice. Understanding how the various elements of the coaching process are reconciled and how coaches deal with this in practice is at least as important as the individual component parts, and, as we suggest later, may be central to the coach's expertise.

The term 'conceptual appreciation' suggests a set of analytical tools with which to understand better the coach and the coach's practice. This understanding will be achieved by addressing a range of questions:

- What terminology is best suited to describing unequivocally both the coaching process and coaching practice?
- What is the purpose of sport coaching and how does it differ in this respect from other sport leadership roles?

QUESTION BOX

These questions can act as a guide to conceptual analysis. Does this set of conceptual 'posers' adequately represent the full range of questions necessary for a complete analysis of coaching practice? If not, what would you add?

- Which are the constituent, pivotal and essential elements of the coaching process?
- How can the coaching process be best represented for the purposes of analysis and subsequent modelling and (potentially) prediction?
- What is the most appropriate set of concepts to describe the range and variability in coaching behaviour and practice?
- How can a balance be achieved between a focus on generic coaching concepts and the 'real-time' application of these in specific sports?
- Which criteria are most usefully applied to issues of evaluation, accountability, impact and effectiveness?
- How can sport coaching be conceptualised in order to appreciate the impact of environmental factors – organisational, ethical, social and cultural?

Providing answers to these questions has guided the structure and content of the book. The original motive for the book was a perception that these important questions had not been addressed adequately. In approaching the second edition of the book, we concluded that a much greater wealth of material was available, but that few, if any, of the questions had been resolved satisfactorily.

ILLUSTRATION

Since the first edition of the book was published there have been developments in our understanding of sport coaching, and these are exemplified in the chapters that follow. At this stage, it may be useful to point out that these advances have come about because concepts were questioned.

For example, the following advances in understanding have emerged (they are elaborated later in the book, and merely summarised at this stage for illustration):

- The cognitive element has increasingly been acknowledged as a characteristic of coaches' expertise.
- Coaching children is recognised to be in a different domain to that of performance coaching.
- Elite coaches are designated by their association with elite athletes, not necessarily by their expertise.

- The 'coaching hour' is a useful measure of the intensity of coaching practice.
- The discourse on professionalisation in sport coaching has not been matched by strong occupational identities and regulated practices.
- The impact of previously taken-for-granted social and cultural issues on coaching practice are being recognised.
- Explanations are beginning to emerge for the coach's developed capacity to manage the dynamics of coach–athlete interaction.
- The concept of 'layered' practice is emerging as a mechanism for understanding how coaches operate.

These generalisations are used to illustrate advances in insights into coaching, but the important issue is that they have emerged because researchers asked key questions about coaching concepts. For example, the growing appreciation of distinctive coaching domains has resulted from questions being asked, such as:

- What is the coach's and athlete's primary purpose?
- What is the characteristic duration and intensity of the preparation programme?
- How comprehensive is the 'scope' of the intervention programme?
- What are the key features of the coach's expertise that are being displayed?
- Are there any 'social and cultural expectations' attached to the athlete's involvement?

Once again this is not an exhaustive set of questions but they serve to illustrate that each of our advances in understanding is based on the resolution of questions about underlying concepts.

CONTEMPORARY SPORT AND CONCEPTUAL QUESTIONS

The suggestion that there are unanswered questions about sport coaching may seem a little theoretical and removed from practice. However, it is possible to illustrate the fact that *everyday practice in sports provision and delivery raises problematical conceptual issues*. Consider the following issues and associated questions:

- The accountability associated with the targeting of elite sport goals has become more specific and public (for example, in the UK the distribution of public funds in support of London 2012 Olympic Games performances and medal aspirations). The appointment of performance coaches (often from overseas) is recognition of the central place of coaching in achieving these goals. However, *to what extent can the coach be held responsible for performance outputs? Is it sufficient to be successful by association with successful performers? Can we link aspects of coaching practice with results? How much 'value added' is acceptable or desirable? How could and should it be measured? Are these questions important if the athletes are successful?!*

25

- Government policy in the UK has promoted an integrated framework of accredited learning at all levels, including vocational and work-based experience. As we write, there are efforts to incorporate coaching education qualifications into these structures. National Standards have been identified that equate sport coaching competences with expectations at each level. However, this process raises issues about the validity of a concept of a unified coaching role across a range of occupational levels. *Is it appropriate to conceive of qualification levels that embrace a concept of coaching that is differentiated by the standard of the athlete? Are there generic coaching functions that may prove useful as competence groupings? Is a competence approach compatible with professionalisation,* and, if so, *what is the threshold level for entry to the profession?*

- Changes in recent years in sport and physical education provision in schools in the UK have resulted in a broader concept of sport-related provision and an attempt to set targets for school-age participation opportunities. Initiatives by agencies such as the Youth Sport Trust and National Governing Bodies of sport have expanded provision, particularly in primary schools. This in turn has spawned a plethora of new organisations providing 'coaching' to deliver these opportunities (in addition to PE specialists and classroom teachers). *Can this activity be conceptualised as sport coaching? Which forms of sport leadership are most appropriate in these contexts? Are there any coach characteristics that might be most appropriate in these situations? Is there any distinction between sport teaching and sport coaching?*

- The continuing commercialisation of top-level sport, increases in public and private funding, and increased rewards for performers have resulted in greater levels of commitment to preparation for sport and more full-time athletes and coaches. The number of athletes on the UK Sport-facilitated World Class programmes is an example of this. This occupational development has brought with it a number of conceptual issues. *What are the recruitment mechanisms and pathways for coaches into professional and elite-level sport? Is there a clear association of an individual's expertise and role? How appropriate is coach education for the demands of elite sport? What is the role of the coach in relation to other support staff?*

- Over the years a number of high-profile cases of misconduct relating to sexual harassment, abuse of young persons and performance-enhancing drugs abuse have periodically focused attention on coaches' ethical behaviour. *Is professional development being accompanied by adequate coach education? Should individuals need to be licensed to work as coaches? To what extent are coaching behaviour and practice influenced by contextual factors? Have issues about ethical standards and expectations been adequately related to the coach's role and employment practice?*

The questions raised in this short and selective review of contemporary practice and provision form a significant agenda. The intention was to demonstrate that satisfactorily answering most, if not all, of these questions requires a precise identification of the issues, an adequate interpretation and analysis of the issues and an overarching appreciation of how they inter-relate. This is not possible in the

Developing a conceptual framework

absence of a comprehensive conceptualisation of sport coaching. Enquiry into issues about role, education, expertise, accountability and behaviour is dependent on a capacity to describe, analyse and explain coaching practice.

BUILDING A CONCEPTUAL FRAMEWORK

Earlier in the chapter a number of questions were raised, which constituted the beginnings of a conceptual schema. In other words, what would a conceptualisation of sport coaching involve? Table 2.1 incorporates these questions into a simple but helpful framework.

The value of this approach was noted earlier:

> it is a necessary part of the development of a profession to have a (conceptual) model with which to demystify practice, to provide a common vocabulary, to form a basis for research and enquiry, to create a template for education and from which ideological approaches and individual value frameworks can fashion their contextual significance. There are many empirical questions that cannot be adequately framed as a consequence of the absence of such a conceptual model.
>
> (Lyle 1996, p. 16)

There is a strong emphasis here on attempting a consensual and coherent set of principles with which to analyse and make sense of sport coaching. However, this should not imply a narrow or restrictive perspective. Individual differences are not negated by a common framework and there will be enormous variety when it comes to implementation strategies, 'styles', value frameworks and sport-specific approaches. However, we need the means to describe, compare and debate such differences. It is also important to affirm at this early stage that *an emphasis on sport coaching concepts should not be understood to understate or undervalue the human element*. There is no doubt that sport coaching is very largely an inter-personal social phenomenon and exists in social contexts. There cannot be a complete appreciation of coaching without recognition of the aspirations, qualities, motives, emotions, abilities and values of both athlete and coach, the dynamics of the interaction between them, and the contexts that frame these.

Table 2.1 Elements of a conceptual framework for sport coaching

Concept	Purpose	Typical questions
Language and terminology	Communication; education and development; professionalisation	What precisely do we mean by 'coaching practice', 'performance', the 'coaching process', 'intervention', 'decision-making' etc.? Is there a consensus in interpretation and meaning?
Purpose and nature	Defining boundaries; clarifying accountability and responsibility	What is the difference between sport coaching, teaching and instruction? To what extent can coaches be held responsible for athlete performance? What is and what is not coaching?
Essential elements	Coach education; analysis of coaching performance	Which are the most important parts of the coaching process? What is the effect of failing to implement a comprehensive intervention programme?
Modelling	Description, analysis and prediction	Can the coaching process be modelled in such a way as to facilitate analysis of practice and inform research design? Are models of coaching useful in coach development?
Specificity versus genericism	Description of individual behaviour; application	Are coaching 'styles' useful behavioural categories for analysis? How can the variety in specific sport practice be usefully comprehended?
Expertise	Coach education; professional development; identifying component knowledge and skills	In which ways do expert coaches differ from novices? Which competences distinguish coaches from others?
Role	Boundary responsibilities; professional development; inter- and intra-role conflict	How is the coaching role influenced by organisational demands? Which factors influence the role at different levels, e.g. representative group/team coaches?
Values	Understanding behaviour; recruitment and selection; professional development	Is there a relationship between context and value framework? How do personal values interact with organisational ones?
Evaluation	Professional development; accountability/effectiveness	Are there any valid measures of coaching effectiveness? Is there any distinction between effective, competent or successful coaches?

We feel that responses to the first edition of the book often failed to acknowledge that the need to balance attention to conceptual analysis with attention to social practice had been recognised.

The conceptual framework, which will be further developed as we progress through the chapters of the book, provides a bridge between coaching activity and our capacity to make sense of it and is not, therefore, a sterile exercise. The understanding derived from the framework should inform a number of practical and important issues. These can be divided into delivery issues associated with coaching practice and more general developmental issues such as coach education or research. Examples are summarised below and are elaborated in later chapters.

KEY CONCEPT

Individual differences in behaviour and practice are not negated by seeking to establish a common framework, and there will be considerable variety when it comes to delivery strategies, 'styles', value frameworks and sport-specific approaches. What is important is that the means exist to describe, analyse and compare such differences.

Coaching practice

This is a catch-all term for the totality of the coach's professional and personal activity and experience. It embraces both observable and cognitive behaviours, and acknowledges the layers of environmental context within which the coach operates. It is necessary to have a very clear distinction between direct intervention behaviour (delivery) and other coach activities because of their role-specific character and differentiated skills and knowledge requirements.

Coach education and development

Coach developers need to operate within an appropriate framework of knowledge and skills. Issues of progression, staging, role specificity, balancing of components, knowledge structures and priority skills depend on a comprehensive conceptual overview of the needs of coaches. Coach education and development guidelines and practice, whether more formal (certification) or less formal, are very much dependent on a clear concept of coaching.

Professionalisation

The development of sport coaching as a profession (in some form or other) is a ubiquitous feature of coaching discourse. The largely voluntary nature of coaching, limited certification expectations and the absence of public demand have been barriers to the professionalisation process. Further progress with this issue is dependent on a measure of agreement about role and domain boundaries, coaching expertise, and social, cultural and regulatory expectations about the coaching role.

Coaching intervention

This can be best thought of in two forms. First, there is the performance-related activity itself – an intervention programme most often comprising preparation/training components and competition. The intervention can be extensive, comprehensive and planned in detail, or more episodic, more contingent and less integrated – or any combination of these features. Second, the intervention creates and is dependent on a social milieu with myriad dynamic, complex relationships between the social actors. We might conceptualise this as instrumental structure and social structuring.

Coaching effectiveness

There are very difficult issues to be overcome in dealing with measures of effectiveness, and sport coaching is a prime example of this. Professional accountability and individual concerns over esteem, appointments, advancement and reward will maintain the spotlight on how coaches and coaching can be evaluated. There is limited consensus on measures such as achieving objectives, adding value or facilitating performance increments. A very thorough appreciation of coaching concepts is required to approach this issue with confidence.

Research

Subsequent chapters in the book will demonstrate that sport coaching research is variable in rigour, scope and impact. In particular, the variety and opportunism of sample groups and the lack of conceptual clarity on coaching domains and contexts has much reduced the validity and generalisability of findings. To some extent the absence of a consensual conceptual framework has prevented the meta-theorising necessary to generate key research questions.

Figure 2.1 summarises these relationships in a simple diagram.

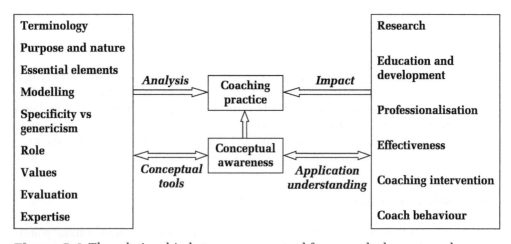

Figure 2.1 The relationship between conceptual framework elements and application issues.

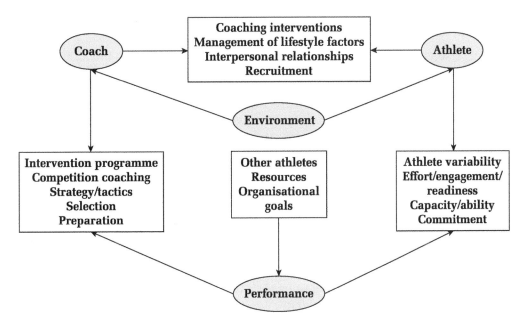

Figure 2.2 Factors arising from the complexity of interaction of athlete, coach, context and performance requirements.

The final point to be made in closing this section is that the conceptual framework and its attendant issues are made more complex by the four-way relationship between athlete, coach, performance requirements and context. This is evident in the dearth of literature and research linking the coach and performance outcomes, despite the fact that the coach's effectiveness or success is often judged by those performance outcomes. Figure 2.2 illustrates how each of these relationships generates a specific range of issues. Of course, the issues are not completely divorced from each other, but they demonstrate the number of opportunities on the conceptual map at which the integrity of the relationships can break down. They also generate questions about the factors that are under the influence of the athlete, the coach or both (or neither!). (It is worth mentioning at this stage that the coach–athlete dyad is used as a shorthand mechanism. In practice, of course, the coach(es) may be working with teams, squads or groups of individuals, and with other coaches and support personnel, with consequent implications for the complexity of practice.)

 QUESTION BOX

Do these four dimensions apply equally in all coaching domains? Would it be possible to construct a specific diagram for each coaching domain (e.g. coaching children or performance coaching) with appropriate priorities?

Developing a conceptual framework

COACHING AND THEORY DEVELOPMENT

Not surprisingly, any conceptual framework is likely to be linked to the formulation of theories about sport coaching. This is one of the aspects of the study of coaching that we hoped would have advanced since the first edition. However, broadly, this is not the case. The difficulty appears to be the notion of an overarching theory about coaching, as distinct from the theories borrowed from other disciplines to explain particular aspects of coaching or sports performance.

It would be useful, therefore, to pause for a moment and consider the characteristics of a theoretical framework. There are three levels of theory: general theory unifies theoretical development in the field and provides scaffolding for more specific theories; intermediate theory sets boundaries and identifies parameters by proposing the relationships between variables, and therefore guides model development; and specific-level theory focuses on predictions and causal relationships (after Scheiner & Willig 2008; Scheiner 2012). In general terms, theory is required to 'bring order' to the field of study. The language of theory centres on definitions, propositions, concepts, relationships and predictions. As a result we form an increasingly clearer understanding of what the field is about, its key constituents and how it works. This appreciation raises further questions, which guide the work of researchers.

Theories can be guides to policy and practice, but are most useful in identifying the crucial questions for researchers. One of the benefits of a theoretical framework is that it permits us to 'see through' the untidiness of practice, although we must acknowledge that describing and understanding this contingent element of practice is very important. Ball (2001, p. 19) emphasises both the analytical and emancipatory aspects of theory, "the purpose of theory is to defamiliarise present practices, to make them seem less self-evident and necessary, and to open up spaces for the invention of new forms of experience".

The characteristics of 'good' theories are that they integrate existing ideas and evidence, and claims and counter-claims, into a coherent set of propositions that 'make sense' and display an inherent logic and consistency. The theory should provide clear propositions that are open to disconfirmation through observation or experiment. Although simplicity is preferred, attempts to achieve generality of application may result in increased complexity.

It would be wrong to say that there has been no theoretical development in the academic study of sport coaching, but it is necessary to distinguish between attempts to provide

 KEY CONCEPT

Theory allows us to stand back from the immediacy of practice and to look beyond the familiar assumptions, which we tend to take for granted.

Developing a conceptual framework

overarching accounts of coaching practice and a 'theoretical lens' through which to understand better a particular aspect of coaching. There are many examples of the latter; for instance, leadership styles (Chelladurai & Saleh 1980), coaching efficacy (Feltz & Chase 1998), coaching as pedagogy (Armour 2004), the coach as educator (Jones 2006), humanistic coaching (Kidman 2005), interdependence theory (Jowett 2007), the coach as decision maker (Abraham & Collins 1998) and complexity theory and relational schemas (Bowes & Jones 2006; Jones *et al.* 2010). In addition, there are theoretical stances that have influenced coach education; for example, the ubiquitous reflective practitioner (Schön 1983), Bandura's (1977) social learning theory and Long Term Athlete Development (Stafford 2005). However, none of these would claim to represent a 'theory of' coaching despite being useful explanatory devices. A notable recent example has been Côté's characterisation of coaching as 5Cs (competence, confidence, connection, character, caring/compassion) (see Côté *et al.* 2010). This is an example of meta-theory in the sense that it aggregates several other theories. However, despite being underpinned by an evidential base, this is a prescription for coaches' practice rather than an explanation of the process of sport coaching.

Sport coaching aims to improve sports performance, and particular mention should be made of 'training theory'. This refers to the principles used to determine the performance intervention (planning, training workloads, types of drills and component balance). There are undoubtedly theories from the physical and cognitive sciences that will inform exercise physiology, skill acquisition, mood states and child development. Nevertheless, when these are aggregated into performance plans, training session plans and workloads for athletes in the context of particular athlete histories, competition programmes, developmental stages, multiple objectives and so on, the coaching interventions appear to become contested prescriptions, despite the identification of some generic practical principles (Bompa 1999; Gordon 2009). Performance increments and outcomes are dependent on many factors, and coaches and athletes alike acknowledge that they are often subject to factors outside their control (despite the fact that some sports are perhaps more dependent on repeatable techniques and physical capacity than others). Another way to express this is to recognise that sport coaching has no 'theory' that directly predicts the performance effect of coaching (expectancy modelling).

There are no overarching or unifying theories about sport coaching. This is not entirely surprising. The field has been conceived of as too diffuse in purpose and

 QUESTION BOX

What would you expect from a theory of coaching? Would this focus on the coaching process, the coach's behaviour or something else? Is it possible to construct a theory of coaching that might be used to predict performance outcomes?

practice to encourage this. However, in a practical sense, it would perhaps be more useful to ask whether there should be a family of theories, which, if taken together, would inform coach education and increase greatly our understanding of coaching. The focus in this book on the underpinning concepts involved in coaching practice is designed to encourage the development of coaching-related theory. To date, this has not happened, but there have been a number of steps forward:

1. The academic literature has turned its attention to the extent to which models of coaching adequately represent the coaching process. Evaluation of existing models largely reflects the debate about their underpinning assumptions, specifically the epistemological stance from which they emanate (Abraham *et al.* 2006; Cushion *et al.* 2006). We devote a subsequent chapter to a revised analysis of models of coaching.
2. As we described in Chapter 1, there is now a much clearer epistemological landscape with which to address an understanding of sport coaching.
3. When the first edition of this book was published, there were very few books that had attempted a comprehensive treatment of sport coaching. This has been remedied to some extent with a series of general and focused texts (Cassidy *et al.* 2009; Denison 2007; Gordon 2009; Jones *et al.* 2004, 2008, 2011; Jones 2006; Lyle & Cushion 2010; Potrac *et al.* 2013).

The lack of emphasis on theory development or a comprehensive conceptual framework is surprising in the context of sport coaching's emergence as a legitimate area for academic study. You may wish to consider a number of potential contributory factors.

1. It is not entirely clear to what the term *coaching theory* might apply. The verb 'to coach' is too wide-ranging and imprecise to be helpful, and in our experience is often applied solely to the business of leading practical sessions.
2. Sport coaching embraces a wide variety of domains, roles, functions, objectives and expertise, and an almost infinite range of interpersonal possibilities. Although we can argue that the purpose of 'improving sport performance' is a common feature, it may be attempting the impossible to identify an overarching theory in these circumstances.

 KEY CONCEPT

It is necessary to distinguish between overarching theories of sport coaching and theoretical lenses for addressing particular aspects of behaviour and practice. Despite greater academic interest in sport coaching, a unifying theory of sport coaching may not be possible or appropriate with so diffuse a field of study.

TEACHING VERSUS COACHING

We are reminded of the similarity between teaching and coaching in the development of theory. As with coaching, there are many theories 'for' teaching, principally about learning, but including pedagogy and child development. However, there is no overarching 'theory of teaching'. This is largely because the term *teaching* is merely a useful 'role descriptor', which subsumes many other processes – an obvious metaphor for coaching!

3. Academic writing in sport coaching has a more evident epistemological frame-work, and demands an eclectic range of disciplines. While this is welcome in bringing greater academic rigour, it might be argued that such perspectives are more suited to particular elements of coaching practice.
4. Sport coaching can legitimately be considered to be 'about' sports performance, the coach's behaviour (usually in relation to the athletes), coaching practice (a broader notion of the coaching role) and the technical sport-specific content of the interventions and competition. The term, the coaching process, may be defined in narrow behavioural terms or broader developmental terms. Given this enormous scope and the multi-layered and complex consequences, a unifying theory may well be impossible (or simply inappropriate).
5. In our coach development work, we have found that many coaches have woven an aura of mystique about coaching. A claim to esoteric knowledge, method and experience has created a protective occupational shell. This is perhaps most evident in situations in which recruitment is irregular, not based on coach education and qualifications, and may not be open to scrutiny. This is also evident in the assertion that coaching is, at least in part, an 'art' (Woodman 1993). In reality, this is likely to reflect an inability (or unwillingness) to identify and describe the skills, knowledge and processes (particularly the cognitive ones) involved.

ACADEMIC LITERATURE AND CONCEPTUAL DEVELOPMENT

Having claimed that there is an absence of sufficient attention to concepts in the study of sport coaching, it would be surprising if a review of the academic literature found to the contrary. In this brief analysis our approach is to present you with a number of statements and invite you to confirm or refute these from your own reading:

1. It is rare for authors to state their assumptions about the coaching process, or the inferences they intend the reader to draw from the sample population of coaches used in their studies. It is common to use opportunistic samples or samples based on occupational or organisational settings. This produces considerable problems for comparative studies or even for thematic analyses of the literature,

since the assumptions about the coaching process have not been made clear and therefore controlled.

2. The greatest proportion of the North American literature has a focus on institutional career coaches in high schools and in the inter-collegiate system. One of the outcomes of this is that career or occupational issues predominate. The considerable literature on opportunities for women coaches and coach 'burn-out' are examples of this. There is no doubt about the value of these studies, but they do not deal with the nature of coaching itself. An emphasis on the coach's characteristics much outweighs that available on effectiveness, planning or decision making, particularly in the context of performance outcomes.

3. Another focus within the literature has been on an 'episodic' interpretation of the coaching task. Focusing on the 'session' and on direct intervention between the coach and athletes has advantages for controlling variables, devising coaching interventions and employing methods such as systematic observation. Nevertheless, the outcome has been to highlight observable behaviour and focus attention away from the complexity and longer-term management of the process. A subsidiary effect of the episodic approach is that there has been some considerable overlap between teaching sport (particularly to children) and the direct intervention element of coaching (Lyle 1998). Much of the literature is focused on relatively simple tasks with 'beginner' athletes.

4. More recent writing on coaching has been clearer about its epistemological roots (North 2013a, 2013b), but this has not necessarily prevented authors from emphasising a partial view of the coaching process. A gross simplification of one of these conceptual axes is the balance between coaching as an interpersonal behaviour and coaching as a performance development programme. Your immediate response might be to say 'isn't it both?', but the danger is that one of these assumptions is treated as unproblematic. Read Bowes and Jones (2006), Cushion (2007) and Lyle (2007) for some insights.

5. A number of criticisms and shortcomings have been identified in research and the resultant output. These include lack of impact on coach education and coaching practice, and a failure to develop a coherent body of knowledge on coaching practice (Abraham & Collins 1998; Cushion & Lyle 2010; Gilbert & Trudel 2004). Some of these shortcomings can be attributed to the complexity of the coaching process and the interdependent athlete–coach–performance relationship. However, it has also been argued that the lack of attention to the conceptual framework supporting the research and the 'borrowing' of theory from other disciplines have reduced its usefulness and accumulative impact. Cushion and Lyle (2010, p. 9) argue that "we need to do more than uncritically accept and apply theories from other disciplines; there is an overwhelming need for our own evidence-based theories and concepts".

A useful exercise is to appraise critically any academic writing on sport coaching. The following questions may prove useful in directing such a critique:

1. Did the author define the terms *coach* or *coaching* and were assumptions stated about these terms?

EXAMPLE OF CONCEPTUAL CONFUSION

What do you understand by the construct 'effectiveness'?

Are the following terms synonymous:

- effective coaching behaviour
- effective coaching
- coaching effectiveness
- an effective coach

What is the relationship between effectiveness, success and competence?

Is your or others' perception of effectiveness value-free and/or domain-specific?

Is effectiveness about achieving objectives, adding value or successful outcomes?

We attempt to address these questions in a sequent chapter, but prepare your responses.

2. Was the role of any sample population of coaches expanded at length and the assumed tasks and functions of the coaches identified? Was there any evidence or supporting literature to complement this?
3. Was there an 'episodic' emphasis (direct intervention) or was coaching treated as a longer-term process?
4. Did the research focus on the coach's personal characteristics, an element of athlete–coach interpersonal interaction, an occupational issue or a specified intervention programme?
5. Was the research based on naturalistic (meaning undisturbed *in situ*) practice? If so, how was this recorded?
6. Was there any attempt to relate the findings to specific organisational goals or to specific athlete aspirations?
7. Was the intervention/activity related to preparation for an identified competition for which goals were specified?
8. Was there any attempt to suggest a relationship between the focus of the research and identified performance outcomes?

SPORT AS A CONCEPT

There are many contexts in which the term coaching is used – music, drama and management, for example. In each of these there is an element of supporting the individual's preparation for performance. This level of generalisation is not particularly helpful, but it raises the question of whether there is anything about the sport

The value of sport coaching research is reduced by a failure to identify the assumptions made about the coaching process. Concepts are constructs that shape our thinking about a phenomenon, such as coaching. Be careful not to make unquestioned assumptions about the coaching role or the coaching process.

context itself that might influence coaching practice. The issue is not 'what is sport?', but do the evidently different sporting milieux create distinctive requirements? We argue that participation/recreation, performance development and high performance are three forms of sport from within the same family, but requiring distinctive forms of coaching (Lyle 2008, 2011)

In the chapter that follows, we conceptualise and operationalise sport coaching as the extensive, comprehensive and multi-function process that prepares individuals and teams for participation in sports competitions. However, we are aware that the sport coaching process and role apply to a range of sporting and physical activity contexts, and may therefore involve a more limited learning or development process. Coaching's purpose and rationale are most fully expressed in sport contexts that require significant preparation, significant athlete commitment, physical conditioning, extensive planning, competition strategy and tactics, and an extrinsic reward system. This will occur most often in culturally accepted and acknowledged sport activities with an extensive infrastructure of competition and provision. A subsequent chapter will deal with the distinctions between participation, development and performance coaching. Participation coaching is understood as a truncated form of the coaching process. There is no implication that this role is of lesser 'worth' – it is simply different because the demands on the coaching process are different.

 QUESTION BOX

You will be familiar with contexts in which the term *coaching* is used to describe the teaching of sport to beginners (mostly but not exclusively young people) or when paying for lessons from the golf professional, ski instructor or tennis coach. Before reading the next chapter, examine the roles of the sports teacher, instructor and coach. Identify the common and distinguishing features.

 **SUMMARY**

This chapter should have familiarised you with the following:

- The questions that need to be answered to promote a conceptual appreciation of sport coaching.
- Examples of contemporary practice in sport that generate issues about sport coaching.
- The essential elements of a conceptual framework and how these can contribute to understanding coaching practice.
- The important issue of the four-way relationship between coach, athlete, performance and context.
- What is meant by coaching theory and what sort of theory development can be expected in sport coaching.
- A number of shortcomings in the literature on sport coaching in relation to the use of a conceptual framework or assumptions about the coaching role.
- A reminder that sport is a multifaceted practice and that sport coaching practice will adapt to the demands of the sporting context.

 PROJECTS

1. Take five research articles dealing with sport coaching. Use the questions identified in the chapter to create a critical analysis of the concept of coaching employed or assumed by the authors.
2. Choose one element of the coaching conceptual framework (for example, expertise, role or effectiveness). Explore the literature to compare the depth of understanding about this element with that in another profession. What does it tell you about academic study and research in sport coaching?
3. Identify a contemporary sport development initiative (for example, in schools' sports provision). Examine the assumptions made about the contribution of sport coaches to the initiative and highlight any significant lessons to be learned about that particular coaching process.

REFERENCES

Abraham, A., & Collins, D. (1998). Examining and extending research in coach development. *Quest*, *50*, 55–79.

Abraham, A., Collins, D., & Martindale, R. (2006). The coaching schematic: Validation through expert coach consensus. *Journal of Sports Science*, *24*, 549–564.

Armour, K. (2004). Coaching pedagogy. In R. L. Jones, K. Armour, & P. Potrac (Eds) *Sports Coaching Cultures: From Practice to Theory*. London: Routledge, 94–115.

Ball, S. J. (2001). Better read: Theorising the teacher. In J. Dillon & H. Maguire (Eds) *Becoming a Teacher: Issues in Secondary Teaching*. 2nd edition. Buckingham: Open University Press, 10–21.

Bandura, A. (1977). *Social Learning Theory*. Englewood Cliffs, NJ: Prentice Hall.

Bompa, T. O. (1999). *Periodisation: Theory and Methodology of Training*. 4th edition. Champaign, IL: Human Kinetics.

Bowes, I., & Jones, R. L. (2006). Working at the edge of chaos: Understanding coaching as a complex, interpersonal system. *The Sport Psychologist, 20*, 235–245.

Cassidy, T., Jones, R. L., & Potrac, P. (2009). *Understanding Sports Coaching: The Social, Cultural and Pedagogical Foundations of Coaching Practice*. 2nd edition. London: Routledge.

Chelladurai, P., & Saleh, S. D. (1980). Dimensions of leadership behavior in sports: Development of a leadership scale. *Journal of Sport Psychology, 2*, 34–45.

Côté, J., Bruner, M., Erickson, K., Strachan, L., & Fraser-Thomas J. (2010). Athlete development and coaching. In J. Lyle & C. Cushion (Eds) *Sports Coaching: Professionalisation and Practice*. Edinburgh: Churchill Livingstone, 63–83.

Cushion, C. J. (2007). Modelling the complexity of the coaching process. *International Journal of Sport Science & Coaching, 2*(4), 395–401.

Cushion, C. J., Armour, K. M., & Jones, R. L. (2006). Locating the coaching process in practice models: Models 'for' and 'of' coaching. *Physical Education and Sport Pedagogy, 11*, 83–99.

Cushion, C., & Lyle, J. (2010). Conceptual development in sports coaching. In J. Lyle & C. Cushion (Eds) *Sports Coaching: Professionalisation and Practice*. Edinburgh: Churchill Livingstone, 1–13.

Denison, J. (Ed.) (2007). *Coaching Knowledges: Understanding the Dynamics of Sport Performance*. London: A&C Black.

Feltz, D. L., & Chase, M. A. (1998). The measurement of self-efficacy and confidence in sport. In J. L. Duda (Ed.) *Advances in Sport and Exercise Psychology Measurement*. Morgantown, WV: Fitness Information technology, 65–80.

Gilbert, W. D., & Trudel, P. (2004). Analysis of coaching science research published from 1970–2001. *Research Quarterly for Exercise and Sport, 75*, 388–399.

Gordon, D. (2009). *Coaching Science*. Exeter: Learning Matters.

Jones, R. L. (2006). *The Sports Coach as Educator: Re-conceptualising Sports Coaching*. London: Routledge.

Jones, R. L., Armour, K., & Potrac, P. (2004). *Sports Coaching Cultures: From Practice to Theory*. London: Routledge.

Jones, R. L., Hughes, M., & Kingston, K. (Eds) (2008). *An Introduction to Sports Coaching: From Science and Theory to Practice*. London: Routledge.

Jones, R. L., Bowes, I., & Kingston, K. (2010). Complex practice in coaching: Studying the chaotic nature of coach–athlete interactions. In J. Lyle & C. Cushion (Eds) *Sports Coaching: Professionalisation and Practice*. Edinburgh: Churchill Livingstone, 15–25.

Jones, R. L., Potrac, P., Cushion, C., & Ronglan, L. T. (Eds) (2011). *The Sociology of Sports Coaching*. London: Routledge.

40

Jowett, S. (2007). Interdependence analysis and the 3+1Cs in the coach–athlete relationship. In S. Jowett & D. Lavallee (Eds) *Social Psychology in Sport*. Champaign, IL: Human Kinetics, 15–27.

Kidman, L. (2005). *Athlete-Centred Coaching: Developing Inspired and Inspiring People*. Christchurch: Innovation Print Communications.

Lyle, J. (1996). A conceptual appreciation of the sports coaching process. *Scottish Centre Research Papers in Sport, Leisure and Society*, *1*(1), 15–37.

Lyle, J. (1998). Coaching effectiveness and the teaching paradigm. In *Active Living through Quality Physical Education*. 8th European Congress of ICHPER. SD, St Mary's University College, Twickenham.

Lyle, J. (2007). Modelling the complexity of the coaching process: A commentary. *International Journal of Sports Science & Coaching*, *2*(4), 407–409.

Lyle, J. (2008). Sports development and sports coaching. In K. Hylton & P. Bramham (Eds) *Sports Development: Policy, Process and Practice*. 2nd edition. London: Routledge, 214–235.

Lyle, J., & Cushion, C. (Eds) (2010). *Sports Coaching: Professionalisation and Practice*. Edinburgh: Churchill Livingstone.

Lyle, J. (2011). Sports development, sports coaching and domain specificity. In B. Houlihan & M. Green (Eds) *Routledge Handbook of Sports Development*. London: Routledge, 487–500.

North, J. (2013a). A critical realist approach to theorising coaching practice. In P. Potrac, W. Gilbert, & J. Denison (Eds) *Routledge Handbook of Sports Coaching*. London: Routledge, 133–144.

North, J. (2013b). Philosophical underpinning of coaching practice research. *Quest*, *65*(3), 278–299.

Potrac, P., Gilbert, W., & Denison, J. (Eds) (2013). *Routledge Handbook of Sports Coaching*. London: Routledge.

Scheiner, S. M. (2012). The multiple roles of theory: A reply to Gorelick. *Issues in Ecology and Education*, *5*, 22–24.

Scheiner, S. M., & Willig, M. R. (2008). A general theory of ecology. *Theoretical Ecology*, *1*, 21–28.

Schön, D. A. (1983). *The Reflective Practitioner: How Professionals Think in Action*. New York: Basic Books.

Stafford, I. (2005). *Coaching for Long Term Athlete Development*. Leeds: Coachwise.

Woodman, L. (1993). Coaching: A science, an art, an emerging profession. *Sports Science Review*, *2*(2), 1–13.

CHAPTER 3

THE COACHING PROCESS

CHAPTER OUTLINE

- ▪ Introduction
- ▪ A definitional framework
- ▪ A definition of sport coaching
- ▪ Coaching as a process
- ▪ Boundary markers
- ▪ Process skills
- ▪ Participation and performance coaching
- ▪ Summary
- ▪ Projects

INTRODUCTION

This chapter deals with the question of what coaching is about and what makes it distinctive from other roles and processes. There has been significant inter-role and intra-role confusion about sport coaching; the ambiguity between teaching and coaching roles is a good example, as is the interpretation in some sports of the coach's sole purpose as technique and tactics specialist. The question of boundary markers is an essential part of the conceptual framework for which arguments were presented in the previous chapter. Indeed, the rationale for clarifying the precise nature of coaching is very similar to that outlined in the previous chapter.

Identifying the meaning, scope and boundaries of sport coaching is an essential task. Nevertheless, we do not intend to persuade you of the supremacy of any one definition or interpretation. Yes, we will make our position clear to you, but the more important objective is to provide you with the tools to critique any definition or understanding about coaching that might be presented to you.

Since the first edition of the book there have been a number of developments in the ways that we might conceptualise the coaching process. As identified in the opening chapter, there is an emerging clarity, although perhaps not a consensus, about the most appropriate academic disciplines, paradigms and lenses through which to understand coaching practice. This is essential but does not in itself help to define the coaching role. On the other hand, deliberations about levels of coaching qualifications (sports coach UK 2008), identification of coaching domains in the Coach Development Model (North 2009), workforce development planning (Winder & Townend 2010), and the establishment of Occupational Standards for coaching (SkillsActive 2010) have at least prompted some debate about what we mean by sport coaching. In addition, we ourselves have suggested that coaching is best treated as a 'family term', for which any generic definition may fail to do justice to the complexity and range of sport leadership roles.

The following statements point to the need to define very precisely what is meant by sport coaching:

- We might expect the research conducted by sports coach UK on the UK's coaching population (Townend & North 2007) to provide us with some guidance on the scope of the coaching process. This is a valuable account of the coaching workforce in the UK at the time of the survey; coaches were identified by a self-reported association with the definition 'undertaking coaching at least once-a-week for a minimum of a 30-minute session'. However, the term 'coaching' is treated as being unproblematically comprehended; coaching is something that is 'used' or 'received'; there is an implied emphasis on coaching 'sessions'; and much the greater proportion of coaches could be said to work with beginner children. Thus the report generates more questions about the boundaries of the coaching role than it answers.
- There is an extensive range of leadership roles in sport. The terms coaching, instructing, leading and teaching have been used somewhat indiscriminately. In practice, these roles are largely defined by the participants' intentions and, therefore, the demands of the situation, rather than the capacity and expertise of the individual leader. This distinction between the person (the coach) and the role (coaching) is one that will be explored in greater depth.
- Although there may be a generic concept termed the coaching process, common sense tells us that this process will not manifest itself in the same way in all circumstances. Therefore, a key question is, in which circumstances is it appropriate to use the term 'sport coaching'? This is not an issue of status or mere terminology. Any particular profile of expectations, accountability, skills, knowledge and planning will be dependent on the demands of the context and the coach's frame of reference.
- The matching of individuals' capabilities to the needs of the situation has a number of practical implications. Employment, recruitment and selection should be determined by the correspondence between the coach's abilities and qualities, and those required by the 'job'. The boundary markers of coaching indicate the likely demands of the job and the education, training and perhaps value system required to fulfil that role.
- The role of academic enquiry should not be overlooked here. All professions have a healthy regard for the substance and scope of their business and it is

legitimate to seek clarity of purpose and to chart developments in the field. The setting of boundary markers is part of the professionalisation of the coaching enterprise.

The following questions illustrate some of the developmental issues that the emerging profession of coaching would wish to clarify:

1. If it is accepted that there are different sport coaching roles (cf. the Coach Development Model), is there transferability between roles and is there progression from one to another? Should we be trying first to recruit coaches into the early stages of the pathway (participation coaching) or is entry into subsequent stages in coaching a more direct process?
2. Is there sufficient commonality of purpose among all who are currently termed coaches to justify one category of membership of a professional body, or should there be several categories (or several professional bodies)?
3. Professions are served by a range of products and services, including the expertise of other specialists as required. Much of this involves technical services, but would also include continuing professional development, training aids, software products, insurance services, higher levels of coaching qualifications, current awareness services and so on. These products also must be matched to the specific needs of each group of professionals.

All human endeavour is imbued with meaning: sets of values may be shared or disputed. These values are related to questions of 'should' or 'ought'. In other words, there will be many ways of operationalising the coaching process and many sets of standards by which to make judgements about them. Two separate questions arise, therefore. First, what is coaching about and how do you know that it is sport coaching? The second question is how are we to make sense of the varieties of practice? For example, are there any guidelines with which to understand how coaching practice is related to particular sets of contexts, objectives, purposes, ethical standards and personal idiosyncrasies? Overall, we should ask ourselves, how generic is the process and to what extent is this process influenced by the sport within which it is practised?

 QUESTION BOX

The search for commonality and genericism takes place in the context of a huge range of sport-specific differences and the unusual situation of coaches competing with one another. Is there sufficient commonality in the role to justify the search?

A DEFINITION FRAMEWORK

Conceptual analysis will not be well-served by reducing the complexity of the construct of sport coaching to a mere sentence. Having admitted that such a short, pithy, catch-all statement will not suffice, it is necessary to reflect on the characteristics of the more valuable 'definitional framework'. Such a framework should offer the following:

Discrimination This is the primary purpose of the definitional framework. It should delineate boundary markers in sufficient detail as to demonstrate how sport coaching differs from other roles.

Criticality The framework should identify the features that must be present in the process to fulfil the definition. Ideally, criteria will be identified to evidence these features.

Substance The detail of the definition provides some operational guidance. The vocabulary can be used as a map for the key elements of coaching practice.

Expertise The definitional framework should be obviously applicable to the practice of expert coaches, and point in the direction of the required expertise.

Applicability The usefulness of such a framework is that it can be translated into criteria that are precise and obvious in practice. On the other hand, there needs to be sufficient flexibility to permit a measure of interpretation.

This is a demanding set of requirements for any definition. However, we might begin to 'flesh out' the framework by addressing a few key questions: what is the central purpose, which are the essential features, who would it apply to and where would it be found?

Rationale

Sport coaching centres on the improvement of an individual's or team's sporting performance, both in terms of general capacity and as specific performances. The improvement is purposeful and stable, and not reflective solely of chance or maturation. The stability of the improvement and the specificity of the preparation reduce the unpredictability of performance.

Method

Performance objectives are achieved by influencing, either directly or indirectly, the factors that affect performance. These performance variables are manipulated and coordinated within an intervention programme characterised by competition and preparation (often termed 'training') units. This may also involve significant adaptation of the athlete's lifestyle.

Role

The role of the coach is to lead, direct and manage the process that leads to the achievement of identified (and normally mutually agreed) goals. This involves the integration of the performer's aspirations and abilities, the goals identified, the external environment and the required intervention programme. There may be a coaching team rather than an individual coach.

Constituent parts

These are defined by the rationale, method and role. Therefore, the substance of the coaching process is a form of contract that embraces the performer, the coach or coaching team, the form, nature and extent of the relationship between them, the intervention programme, the sporting schedule and the external context. These elements are interdependent and have many sub-elements.

Frame of reference

In the context of this conceptual analysis, sport is assumed to be essentially competitive in nature and practice, and is to be found in the organised and institutionally recognised structures and agencies that have been developed within particular sports. Improved performance becomes evident by achievement within recognised forms of competition, but the scope of coaching involves all training and preparation contexts, and is not restricted solely to the highest levels of performance. The distinctive domains into which coaching can be categorised provide their characteristic sets of meanings, assumptions and values, and thus create a 'role frame' within which the coach operates.

Terminology

There are a number of terms that need to be clarified in order to provide a consistent vocabulary and interpretation with which to analyse and understand sport coaching. The most obvious starting point is to distinguish between coaching practice and the term coach as a descriptor of an individual. This may seem rather obvious or even unnecessary, but coaching research has often treated the coach as unproblematic (expertise, frames of reference, role) and research into coaches has often failed to contextualise the sample population (the domain within which they practise).

The general position adopted here is that it is much less useful to focus on the individual than on the role characteristics adopted by that individual, because coaches can adopt different roles in different circumstances. The terminology should not concern us unduly – it is not what individuals are called but what role they fulfil that is important. The coaching role should be clearly specified. To say that someone

46

is a coach describes (a) a generic occupational practice, (b) a specific professional position (including voluntary roles), (c) a qualification status or (d) an assumed capacity/expertise. The occupational category is not helpful unless accompanied by a more specific role descriptor. (Compare this to describing someone as an engineer, a technician or a scientist – only the broadest of expectations can be attributed to the category and it does not generate the operational clarity specified earlier.) However, the 'assumed capacity' may be helpful if it describes a minimum set of attributes or skills, although this assumption can only be made if there is an agreed national accreditation and licensing system on which to rely.

Note that these initial thoughts begin to distinguish between teaching a sport, to young people or adults, unrelated to a sport competition (even if defined very broadly) and preparation for improved sport performance. Our inclination is to reserve the term sport coaching for an intervention programme associated with the latter. Nevertheless, we acknowledge the reality that the 'family term' sport coaching is very often used to refer to all sport improvement or leadership roles.

 QUESTION BOX

The idea that sport coaching can be distinguished from instructing, sports teaching, participation schemes and performance director roles will generate a 'narrower' view of coaching than is generally understood. Have you begun to form an opinion about this? Set out your arguments before moving on.

A DEFINITION OF SPORT COACHING

We define *sport coaching* (short version) as the 'purposeful improvement of an individual or team's performance in sport' and 'an extensive, comprehensive and multi-purpose process that prepares individuals and teams for participation in sports competitions'. The term *purposeful* implies a planned and specific objectives-directed intervention process. Note also the phrase 'performance in sport', in contrast to the more common 'sport performance'. This implies a purpose beyond the context-free development of sport-related skills. This is not dissimilar to the definition adduced by the European Coaching Council (2007) referred to by Duffy *et al.* (2011), which centres on 'guided improvement'. However, we stress the specificity of the competition–sport locus. It is also helpful to use the term 'the coaching process' to refer to both the intervention programmes and the principles and theories on which it might be based, and the specific engagement between an athlete/team and a coach. The use of the term 'the *coaching process*' implies both the contract/understanding which is entered into by the athlete(s) and coach, and the operationalisation of that agreement.

a The coaching process will be different and distinctive in all cases and determined by the organisational setting, the performer's aspirations and commitment and the coach's contractual obligations (formal or informal). It becomes manifest in the role responsibilities, expectations and accountabilities of both the athlete and the coach, and should be explicit in both volunteer and professional settings.

b Operationalisation consists of the purposeful, direct and indirect, formal and informal series of activities and interventions designed to improve competition performance. The most evident part of the process is normally a planned, coordinated and integrated programme of preparation and competition. This is devised by the coach and the athlete(s), although the balance of responsibilities will be determined by the nature of the agreement between them. The overall implementation of the process is the responsibility of the coach, although this may involve a group of other specialists.

c As we suggested in the first chapter, there is a distinction between the planned and managed (coordinated, systematic, instrumental) coaching process, implying a layered and interdependent set of longer-, medium- and shorter-term goals, and the reality of the implementation of the process. *The social context, interpersonal dynamics, contested and multiple goals, the difficulty of identifying and delivering precise workloads, the difficulty in assessing progress and the vagaries of an individual's effort, attention and motives can conspire to make coaching practice a challenging, dynamic and difficult-to-manage business.* However, the degree of adherence to the planned programme will differ by sport.

 KEY CONCEPT

Sport coaching is the purposeful improvement of an individual or team's performance in sport. *Purposeful* implies a planned and specific objectives-directed intervention process. *Performance in sport* implies a purpose beyond the context-free development of sport-related skills and centred on a competition–sport locus.

Using our definition above, we can say that a sport coach fulfils a leadership role within sport, which is characterised by objectives based on improved performance in sport. However, there are many coaching roles and we suggest that the term 'sport coach', although it has a popular currency, is not very helpful in describing expectations about role, expertise or practice. Using the shorthand term, the coach, is only meaningful when the role frame and boundaries of the coaching process have been identified.

Coaching practice refers to the full range of behaviours, activities, interactions, processes, individuals and organisational functions that result from the operationalisation of the coaching role and the coaching process. It is important that this is distinguished from *coaching behaviour*, which is a much narrower reference to particular actions (for example, feedback, demonstrating, directing).

These are the most important definitions. However, some clarification is required on the use of other, related terminology. These terms are less central to the definitional framework but reflect common usage.

> Coaching *(when used as a* noun*: for example, 'The basketball team needs some extra coaching and I've been asked to help').*

> Common usage of the noun would imply an isolated 'session' or 'episode' or suggest a specialist or expert input often based on previously identified technique, tactical or physical conditioning requirements. A more precise description of such an input would be helpful for identifying the appropriate expectations from such a session. Remember, of course, that the phrase '*I will be coaching at the track tonight*' merely describes the 'act of being a coach' and is too general to assist the definitional framework.

> To coach *(when used as a* verb*: for example, 'I have been asked to coach the local hockey team' or 'May I have permission to video you when you are coaching?').*

> The first of these is simply a shorthand way of describing the contract or agreement between the coach and the hockey team. However, the second is more problematical. 'To coach' is to carry out the role of a coach and not simply the delivery aspect of the role. Nevertheless, in common usage the phrase has become synonymous with the physical act of directing a training session or managing a competition episode. This is not helpful or accurate, because it has reinforced a presumption that coaching is merely a practical act and has highlighted a particular set of delivery skills. In turn, this has undervalued the less public (but perhaps more important) cognitive, planning, and interpersonal interactions that characterise the coaching process.

Having attempted to describe an appropriate terminology to assist the conceptual framework, it is now necessary to explore in more detail what is meant by the coaching process and what the boundary markers might be. Before doing so, there is a short diversion that examines the lessons to be learned from the concept of coaching as it is used in other spheres (derived from Lyle 1997).

A generic coaching construct?

It is not unusual to hear actors speaking about their 'voice coach'. Similarly, the term coach is common in drama, poetry and music (Haddon 2011). The use of a coach to prepare artistes for performances suggests the potential for a generic coaching process and, therefore, for some transfer of principles and practice. In addition, the coaching of individuals has a traditional place in industrial training and is current in management practice. In these contexts the roles of coach and mentor have become somewhat blurred.

Assisting novices or beginners to improve their craft skills has always been a feature of industrial practice. This is the basis of situated learning (Lave & Wenger 1991) or the apprenticeship process. As the practice of training in industry became rather more of a structured process and given a higher priority, so the coaching role became recognised. Torrington and Weightman (1994) differentiated between the trainer as an individual who is engaged with someone who is learning a new skill, and the coach, who is concerned to improve the performance of a worker who is already competent. These roles seem fairly narrow and restricted to manufacturing and craft-based skills. However, the development of a management ethos that was more humanistic or person-oriented began to encourage the incorporation of an element of counselling into the coaching role. This was directed towards the realisation of an individual's developmental potential and brought new purpose to the 'training' function.

Any exploration of the internet will reveal a coaching 'industry' that is apparently more developed in its professional organisation than is sport coaching, and which has spawned a vast literature and a number of academic journals (Gray 2011; Passmore & Fillery-Travis 2011). Commercial activity and consultancy appears to have coalesced around personal development, leadership, executive coaching and building workforce capacity, and there is a similar set of debates about concepts, definitions and schools of thought in this field as in sport coaching (Cameron & Ebrahimi 2014). Shortcomings have been noted which point to the preponderance of prescriptions and practitioner-derived models on which coaching interventions are based, and a failure to evidence evaluations against performance outcomes (Lyle & Cushion 2010). The search for a commonality of approach with sport coaching has perhaps been less extensive than it merits. Part of the reason may be the apparent emphasis on shorter-term interventions, a product approach to interventions and an emphasis on capacity rather than performance. Nevertheless, there may be lessons to be learned about the coaching role, a coaching/mentoring continuum and about coaching support *in situ* (e.g. Larson & Maxcy 2013).

What of mentoring? More recent attention has focused on the role of the mentor within coach education and development (e.g. Cushion 2006; Cassidy & Rossi 2006), particularly on the mechanisms through which the coach's experience can be consolidated. The mentor mediates between elements of the coach's experience and practice, and the coach's emerging expertise in order to enhance development, largely through guided reflection. It can be argued that mentoring is part of the coach's role, but also that coaching is part of the mentoring role. See Jones *et al.* (2009) for an excellent in-depth review of the mentoring concept and its application in a number of professional fields, including sport coaching.

Although there are obvious parallels in the way that coaching in the performing arts, industry, business and management is related to performance improvement, we should not try to make too much of the comparison. Whereas coaching as a management tool is generally an indirect means to an end and may be one of a number of roles exercised by a manager, sport coaching is rather more centrally concerned with the performance itself and, indeed, the coach is very often part of the

QUESTION BOX

Part of the coaching role is to be a mentor to experienced athletes. Does this partly explain the value, and perhaps limitations, of appointing recently retired performers as coaches?

execution of the performance. The roles are related in the sense that a process of development or improvement is the aim, but the assistance of these corporate coaches can be construed as external to the performance itself, often centred on a person-development agenda, and relatively modest in scale. The sport coach most often directs the performance improvement process, and is held to have a degree of accountability for achieving appropriate performance goals via an extensive preparation programme.

COACHING AS A PROCESS

The discourse associated with sport coaching has come to accept that coaching should be treated as a managed and integrated process (Lyle 1996; Abraham & Collins 2011; Cushion *et al.* 2006; Light & Robert 2010) rather than as an unsystematic aggregation of isolated training episodes. There are significant implications from treating coaching as a process: the most important is that the relative priorities of skills and function areas become process-driven. Although the emphasis has often been on the elements of the process (Abraham *et al.* 2006; Côté 2006) rather than their integration, there is no serious dispute over the serial and incremental nature of coaching. A significant emphasis on behavioural observation in research (Gilbert & Trudel 2004) has served to emphasise not only the episodic rather than extended and integrated timeline of coaching, but also the expertise required to manage its inherent complexity (Bowes & Jones 2006).

The first stage in exploring the processual properties of coaching is to match the generic aspects of a process with the characteristics of sport coaching that have previously been identified. Table 3.1 demonstrates the relationship between process characteristics and coaching practice.

The inference to be drawn from Table 3.1 is that there can be some confidence in describing sport coaching as a process. This confirms the previous assertion that the term 'the coaching process' is the most appropriate one to use when describing the purposeful engagement of the coach and the athlete for the purpose of improving performance. We should note the criticism of the first edition, that its approach is too mechanistic (Jones & Wallace 2005). It was stressed then and reiterated now that it is possible to search for conceptual clarity and at the same time acknowledge the disordered reality of some practice. The search for conceptual clarity may appear to

Table 3.1 Process characteristics and coaching practice

Process characteristic	Coaching element	Coaching practice
Multi-variable; interdependent	Sport performance	Sport performance is a complex amalgam of physical, technical, tactical, psychological and emotional elements. Performance is influenced by genetic disposition, learned behaviour and environmental factors, including opponents.
Multi-variable; interdependent	Intervention programme	The intervention programme reflects the interdependencies in performance. Technical, tactical, physical and psychological components of training impact on each other.
Multi-variable; interdependent	Athlete–coach	Sport coaching is a human endeavour with a significant element of interpersonal interaction. The vagaries of human emotional behaviour add to the multi-variable nature of the process. This is made more complex by the coach and athlete's relative social circumstances.
Incremental; progressive	Improvement profile	The limitations of the human organism and the difficulty of simultaneous and stable improvements in contributory components of performance result in incremental progress. Training principles and sub-discipline knowledge confirm that an extended serial and coordinated process is required to bring about stable performance improvements.
Principled ordering	Training schedules	Sport sciences, training theory principles and common practice demonstrate that there is a necessary ordering of preparation and competition units to achieve effective improvement. This is evident within the training unit and over an extended planning period.
Specified objectives	Competition achievement	The planning process, the specificity of goal setting, and the sport competition programme ensure that each (unique) process has targeted, albeit multifaceted (and often conflicting) objectives.
Instrumental	Competition achievement	The coaching process is not (normally) an end in itself. The coaching process is centred on performance outcomes and is a means to an end, often accountable to individual or organisational aspirations.
Planned	Planning	The interdependence of variables, the cyclical nature of the competition programme and the aggregative effect of component improvements make planning a necessity. This is compounded by the need to react contingently to the changing environment.
Regulated	Monitoring	The process nature of sport coaching emphasises planning, monitoring and regulating. Coaching practice is characterised by data gathering, testing, profiling and target setting, or by an acknowledgement that challenges in evaluating progression limit the coach's accountability.

strip the process of its human, social and emotional character. Identifying the essential elements of the coaching process is important for the development of the conceptual framework, but it should be remembered that the actual engagement of the athlete(s) and the coaches is an extended period of social activity, commitment, success and failure, emotional highs and lows, interaction within organisations, personal ambition and status, personal cost and achievement, and a mix of short-, medium- and long-term satisfaction and enjoyment. This 'human element' is recognised and explored in subsequent chapters.

 KEY CONCEPT

It is possible to search for conceptual clarity and at the same time acknowledge the disordered reality of some practice. The coaching process has a human, social and emotional character. The engagement of the athlete(s) and the coaches is an extended period of social activity, commitment, success and failure, emotional highs and lows, interaction within organisations, personal ambition and status, personal cost and achievement and a mix of short-, medium- and long-term satisfaction and enjoyment.

This acknowledgement of coaching as a process is important because it highlights two key issues: the boundaries of the process and the expertise that is particular to that process.

 QUESTION BOX

The failure to acknowledge the processual aspect of coaching raises questions about the validity of a good deal of coaching research. However, an assumption about coaching involving the aggregation and integration of an extended series of coaching interventions may be challenged by some episodic practice in team sports. Do you have a view on this?

BOUNDARY MARKERS

We have argued that not all sport coaching roles should be construed as sport coaching. The arguments presented thus far imply that an understanding of coaching practice, expectations and accountability are dependent on whether or not a set of minimum requirements for a coaching process are being fulfilled. Table 3.2 identifies a set of criteria for making such a judgement.

1. These criteria are determined by an interplay of performance improvement principles and the sporting context.
2. They have been derived from the assumptions about the coaching process already identified.
3. They presume a sufficiency of rational effort to bring about effective and efficient performance improvements.
4. To some extent, these criteria are 'setting an agenda' for research and debate.
5. They provide a basis for describing a range of coaching roles, based on variable consonance with the boundary markers.

Table 3.2 demonstrates that the criteria that set the limits to the sport coaching process will be determined by quite basic features of (any) process; for example, the extended timeline, an intervention to bring about change and identifiable inputs and outputs. However, the specificity of this process is the requirement to bring about a stable improvement in sport performance capacity, and it is this purpose that requires these particular boundary criteria.

Table 3.2 Boundary markers for the coaching process in sport

Boundary marker	Boundary criterion	Rationale
Obligation	Stability of personnel	The long-term and serial nature of the process, the intensity requirements of training principles, the establishing of interpersonal relationships and stability of goals depend on a stable group of athletes.
Obligation; commitment	Continuity of engagement	The objective of stability of performance improvements in sport requires maintenance of engagement in the process. This is exacerbated in team sports where lack of continuity would be likely to impact on social and tactical cohesion.
Scale	Extended time period	Performance goals, competition programmes and performance improvement increments are dependent on cyclical planning and preparation that is medium to long term in nature.
Scale	Frequency and duration of engagement	The improvement of performance components requires an intensity of engagement that is reflected in the total hours to which the athletes are committed. Incremental progress is linked directly to the intensity of the coaching programme.
Purpose	Commitment to a goal-oriented instrumental relationship	(Notwithstanding any immediacy of satisfactions/ enjoyment) the athletes are committed to a process in which the delayed gratification in achieving the overall goal is dependent on commitment to a continuing and pervasive set of objectives.
Purpose; nature	(Attempted) control of variables	The multi-variable nature of both performance and the intervention programme means that optimum improvement is dependent on managing/regulating all of the variables that impact on performance. This is manifest in lifestyle management and the implied commitment to the programme.

Boundary marker	Boundary criterion	Rationale
Intervention	Planned progression	The improvement objective requires progression in workloads. This is not simply a matter of scale, but implies record keeping, testing and monitoring.
Specificity	Individualisation	Performance improvements are constrained by the abilities and capacities of the individual athlete. The component parts of the coaching process will be tailored to individual needs for optimum effect. This may be more complicated in team sports.

Having set out this list of boundary markers, it is reasonable to ask whether, in implementation, this demanding list of criteria need be satisfied fully, and what the implications would be of a coaching contract that did not match these rather exacting criteria. The following series of statements expands on the implications of conforming or not conforming to the criteria.

- Building a conceptual framework can result in a rather idealised set of concepts and these boundary markers of the coaching process describe a quite specific and demanding type of engagement between athlete(s) and coach. The coaching practice of many coaches will not meet these criteria (often those related to the intensity of the process), but it would be too simplistic to judge them as 'therefore, not coaching'.
- A more realistic stance is to acknowledge the criteria as a very useful tool for analysis purposes, but to recognise that the idealised context may not always be possible or appropriate. The picture painted here is of full-time athletes operating with a full-time coach and in relatively constraint-free circumstances. It seems likely that many coaching processes will certainly be based on these markers, but the practice profile may not be an exact fit.
- The critical factor is to match output expectations from the coaching process to the degree to which it satisfies these criteria. More limited outcomes should be anticipated from a truncated coaching process. It may be worth stressing at this point that the value of this exercise is that it throws some light on the coach's practice and the way that the limitations imposed by boundary markers may impact on the preparation programme.

 KEY CONCEPT

Expectations about progression and achievement of performance goals must be matched to the extent to which the coaching process addresses the boundary markers. More limited outcomes should be anticipated from a truncated coaching process.

- There will be some common reasons for a truncated process.

    – The reward environment available to athletes in a sport may not be sufficient to justify an intensive commitment to training and preparation time. Thus, athletes who are able to train two or three times per week will make less progress relative to those who are able to commit to a more intensive programme.
    – Team sport personnel may change quite significantly during competition programmes and continuous progression in workloads may not be appropriate with league sports over an extended season.
    – Athletes who are in employment may have limited flexibility in scheduling training sessions and the demands of employment or studying will impinge on managing lifestyle factors.
    – Resource limitations may influence total training hours, access to sport science assistance and the desired competition programme.
    – We should remember that continuity of engagement will be broken by regular occurrences such as long-term illness or injury.

- Particular attention should be given to team sports (implying those involved in protracted competition schedules). The coaching process in these circumstances often appears to 'lack control'. Short- and long-term injury disruption is common, changes in personnel may also occur, performance targets are often aspirational rather than specific, maintenance rather than improvement is a common target, individualisation may be difficult and performance outputs and outcomes are not easily measured because of their relative, not absolute, values. This is discussed later in the section on systematic coaching practice, but it does point the way to differentiating between these sports and individual technique/power-output based sports.

- Most of these criteria are easily measured, but the threshold values are not a simple matter of quantification. What is an extended time period or sufficiently frequent preparation? Even more difficult is the qualitative judgement about the management of variables or commitment to a competition goal. Although sport science may be able to provide some of the answers to the thresholds for physical conditioning, many of the criteria may be relative to a particular set of circumstances and need to be understood in that context. We have difficulty in addressing the question 'what impact does coaching have on performance?', far less the relationship between the boundary features of the process and the outcomes achieved. There is a clear role for research here. There needs to be a body of knowledge that links the parameters of the coaching process to the outcomes achieved. These principles may never be translated into statistical guidelines, but analysis and understanding of coaching practice will be incomplete without an acknowledgement of the relationship between the scope and scale of the coaching process and the resultant outputs.

It is possible to create a simple typology of coaching contexts (see Table 3.3) in which the application of the boundary markers will be varied by the circumstances of the coaching contract. The most striking of the differences is that between the participation

Table 3.3 A typology of sport coaching roles and organisational contexts

Category	Participant profile	Competition profile	Deployment characteristics	Boundary Notes
Sport teacher	No long-term commitment; no permanent relationship with the coach; irregular attendance	No competition external to the programme	Sport development schemes; sports centre classes; physical education	The teacher attempts to improve skills-based performance but within short-term goals; the scope of the process is limited
Instructor	No long-term commitment; client–coach relationship; skills improvement objective	Competition not based on instructor involvement; may be recreational participation	Course of 'paid-for' lessons on a commercial basis	Skills-based objectives not normally related specifically to competition preparation; suited to individual and outdoor sports
Participation coach	Involvement irregular; formal organisation but loose membership; improvement objectives but participation emphasised over practice	Competition involvement, but unlikely to be at a high level	Leadership/ organisational roles; recreation sport context; school sport	Little formal progression in a very limited preparation programme; short-term goals, intensity low even if long-term involvement; not all performance components given attention
Performance coach	Increasing commitment; stable relationship with coach; specific competition objectives; commitment to preparation	Formal competition structures	Club/squad coaches; contractual arrangements and full-time posts more likely; administrative and other non-intervention duties increase	Full to partial implementation of the coaching process; most boundary marker thresholds reached
Representative team/group coach	High level of commitment; performance objectives are more public; less permanent relationship between coach and athletes	Formal competition, likely to be at a high standard	National team/squad coaches; area/regional coaches	Not necessarily operating at a higher level than the club coach; truncated coaching process; emphasis on some performance components, with often limited preparation programme

QUESTION BOX

Can you think of examples in a sport with which you are familiar, in which 'part-time' coaching circumstances prevent the performers from achieving their maximum potential? Which boundary features have the most impact for athletes who are able to commit themselves on a full-time basis?

sport coach and the performance sport coach. This is given much more attention later in the chapter (and in a subsequent chapter on coaching domains), but at this stage they serve to illustrate the fact that any assumption about coaching practice (for example in research samples) could be very misleading.

PROCESS SKILLS

Identifying the expertise required by the coach is a necessary feature of coach education, deployment, recruitment and personal development. It is also necessary for modelling the coaching process and analysing practice. Identifying the 'skill functions' required by the coach is highlighted at this point because an acknowledgement of coaching as a process has implications for the profile of these key skills. In a subsequent chapter we give a more detailed account of coaching expertise. On a number of occasions reference has been made to craft skills (delivery behaviours), sport-specific skills (technical competence) and process skills (largely cognitive exercises). It is now necessary to integrate these into the developing conceptual framework. The primary linkage is the existence of a process, which is the rationale for the constituent functions and their associated skills. The coaching process has been characterised as being planned, serial, progressive, multi-variable and integrated, but also delivery-centred, interpersonal and about managing complex programmes, problems and priorities. It follows from this that the skills necessary to plan, implement and sustain the process will be crucial. These are identified in Figure 3.1.

Figure 3.1 is not intended to model the coaching process itself, but merely to illustrate the coaching skills involved. The coaching process is characterised by three sets of skills functions – planning, delivery and management. The delivery element refers to the direct intervention programme between athlete and coach. Delivery can usefully be subdivided into implementation and regulation. Implementation itself is dependent on a series of craft-based skills. The craft and regulation skills are facilitated as necessary by management skills. The regulation element is important because it feeds into both the continuous planning element and the ongoing delivery. Accompanying the delivery is a management function that deals with the resources available, both human and material.

There are a number of significant issues for analysis, education and professional development that arise from this consideration of coaching process skills:

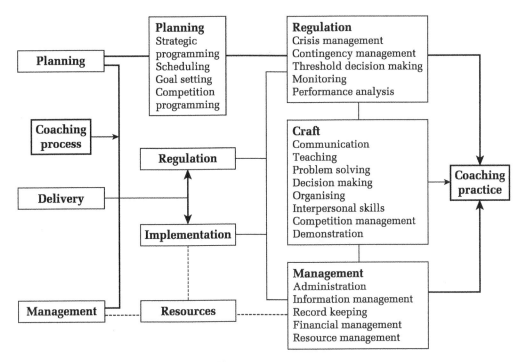

Figure 3.1 Coaching process skills.

- Delivery skills (such as communication) are only one group of essential skills, albeit very important.
- Indirect skills (those not involving the delivery of the intervention programme) are very important – planning, monitoring and regulating the process.
- We should note that the terms 'control' and 'manage' are often used to provide a shorthand way of describing the continuous series of compromises, contingencies and decisions that mediate between the coach's planned intentions and actual practice.
- Management functions are normally necessary to maintain the process – financial, personnel and resource. The scale of the management function will differ with the scale and scope of the coaching 'contract', although the detailed operations of this may not be carried out by the coach.
- Not all of the functions will be carried out by the coach. In extensive and sophisticated processes, the (head) coach's role in coordinating the contributions of assistant coaches, support personnel, sports scientists and managers will be considerable. The coordinating function is considered to be a defining feature of the coach's role.
- Sport specificity and a partially applied coaching process will influence the priorities in coaching skills. Coaches in situations in which the episodic nature of the process is emphasised will rely more on delivery and contingency planning skills. In some sports (for example, basketball and volleyball) the importance of competition management skills will be quite marked.

QUESTION BOX

The variety of skills required by the coach is considerable. This suggests that coach education should be based around (all of) these skills. Are some skills more important than others at each stage of professional development? Are there some skills that have traditionally been given less priority in coach education and development?

One of the emerging features of the conceptual framework is the comparison between the rather more idealised, conceptual representation of the coaching process and the reality of coaching practice. Differences between the two are contingent on a range of context-related factors. This is to be expected. Our focus on the nature and purpose of coaching is complemented in subsequent chapters by an emphasis on practice-driven behaviour and social context. Remember that the purpose of developing the conceptual framework is that it provides the means for an analysis that goes beyond mere description and the immediacy of the context. The capacity to base judgements about accountability and performance (including job security) on a judicious blend of individual coach contribution, application of appropriate principles and contextual factors should be the hallmark of professional behaviour and evaluations of effectiveness.

To end this section we reinforce the earlier approach, which states that the coaching process is different from other sport leadership roles and not simply a stage on a continuum of roles. In other words, one does not progress from teacher to instructor to coach. Similarly, a beginner performance coach should not be thought of as a sports teacher or participation coach. The boundary criteria are a useful device for categorising between sport leadership roles and within coaching roles. Importantly, they have implications for accountability, expectations and understanding patterns of coaching behaviour and practice. This will become clearer with an exploration of the distinctions between participation and performance coaching.

 KEY CONCEPT

The coaching process is different from other sport leadership roles and not simply a stage on a continuum of roles. In other words, one does not progress from teacher to instructor to coach. Similarly, a beginner performance coach should not be thought of as a sports teacher or participation coach.

PARTICIPATION AND PERFORMANCE COACHING

In Table 3.3 a distinction was drawn between sport leadership roles in order to demonstrate that the coaching process boundary markers are a useful device for understanding the scope of these roles. In this edition of the book we have added a chapter on 'coaching domains' to illustrate the relationship between the coach's behaviour and practice and the sport environment within which the coach operates. However, the conceptual framework of sport coaching concepts becomes very much clearer if two distinct forms of coaching are recognised – sport participation coaching and sport performance coaching. We have already expressed a preference for using the term coaching only where preparation for performance in sport is evident. Nevertheless, we acknowledge that the term 'participation coaching' has achieved a popular usage (North 2009; Duffy *et al.* 2011).

Common sense suggests that the demands of performance coaching, since they are based on the 'fullest' application of the coaching process (fulfilling the greatest number of boundary criteria to the greatest extent), will be the most complex and could be regarded as the epitome of sport coaching. Nevertheless, the conceptual framework should display comprehensiveness in addition to precision, and for that reason it is important that the framework offers an explanation for all forms of coaching behaviour and coaching roles.

The terms coach and coaching are used in a wide variety of circumstances. For example, it would not be unusual for the terms to be applied in the following circumstances:

- school-teachers working with school sports teams;
- soccer academy coaches working with players for one session per week and during school holidays;
- those leading beginner classes in local sports centres;
- instructors in ski schools;
- coaches operating with young beginner groups in gymnastics or athletics clubs;
- teaching professionals in golf clubs;
- representative team coaches in age-group rugby or soccer;
- local authority swimming programme teachers;
- those who select and organise adult teams in circumstances in which there is minimal or no specific preparation for competition;
- individuals from the commercial sector delivery programme in primary schools.

These examples have been chosen because they have several characteristics in common. Although there is an intention to improve sport performance and there is an element of sport teaching or learning, there is also a more limited intensity of involvement and often there is no specific competition preparation. It is also important to remember that, in some circumstances, only a partial application of a performance improvement process would be anticipated. For example, academy coaches in rugby may focus on developing expertise within a skills framework, and representative squad coaches may have competition management responsibilities that are separate and more restricted than the performance development programmes led by club coaches.

Despite the enormous variety of circumstances for which the term coaching has come to be used, the relationship between the criteria can be expressed in a simple diagram (see Figure 3.2) that brings together the nature of the contract, the performer's aspirations, involvement in recognised competition structures, and the performer's development stages.

1. *Participation coaching.* Largely to do with initiation into sport and with basic skills teaching. Some individuals, usually young people with greater levels of potential, will move quite quickly through this stage. Others will become more recreational or casual participants, often as they move into adulthood.
2. *Development coaching.* This is characterised by rapid skills learning and an increasing engagement with a sport-specific competition programme. This is a key stage for talent identification. This stage is almost exclusively for younger persons in age-group sport who are accelerating their way through performance standards. (Later it will be argued that 'instructors of adult sportspersons' who wish to improve but who do not satisfy the boundary criteria (golf instruction comes to mind) should be included in this category.)
3. *Performance coaching.* Performers and circumstances come together to fulfil the majority of the coaching process boundary markers. Characterised by relatively intensive preparation and involvement in competition sport. Can apply to all ages and levels of developed ability. There may be some special cases, such as representative team/group coaches.

As with all attempts to distinguish between two processes, there is a middle ground in which the characteristics of each are present. The third category, development

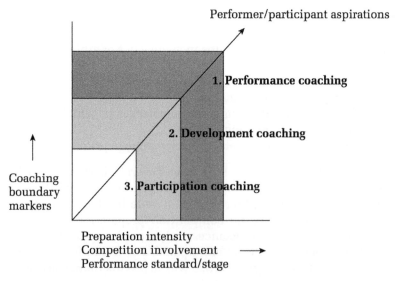

Figure 3.2 The relationship between forms of coaching and boundary criteria.

coaching, is valuable because it shows how athletes move through stages of gradual adaptation to a performance sport lifestyle. More comprehensive attention is given to stages of development in the next chapter (cf. the Participant Development Model; North 2009). Our focus here is on the utility of the boundary criteria as an analytical tool.

Sport participation coaching is distinctive because:

- competition performance and outcomes are not emphasised;
- participants are less intensively engaged with the sport;
- some sport performance components are rarely given attention (e.g. physical conditioning, psychological training);
- objectives are characterised by short-term horizons and immediate satisfaction;
- there is more focus on individual sessions (episodic) than on an integrated, progressive process;
- the coach's expertise is delivery based;
- the 'coaching contract' is often less formal; and
- in the context of these distinctive features, relatively few coaching process boundary marker thresholds are triggered.

Participation sport coaching is to be found in circumstances in which 'sports teaching' or sports team organisation would appear to be more appropriate descriptions. This implies that either the skills development is not related to specific preparation for competition, or, alternatively, that participation in competition is not supported by an extensive preparation programme. Likely contexts involve teaching basic techniques to large groups of youngsters within a club, initiating beginners who are not yet committed to a sport or organising recreational forms of activity. The most important conceptual issue is that there is almost no attempt to influence or control the full range of variables that affect performance – either because of choice (performer commitment is limited) or appropriateness (early developmental stage).

 QUESTION BOX

Participation and performance coaching are not on a coaching process continuum – they are distinctive processes. On the other hand, the performers themselves can generally be placed on a standard of performance continuum. Is level of sport performance a better conceptualisation for coaching forms?

On the other hand, *sport performance coaching* is distinctive because:

- there is a more intensive commitment to a preparation programme;
- there is a more obvious attempt to influence/control performance variables, including lifestyle;

- individual performance components are identified separately in the programme;
- objectives are both long and short term, and specific competition goals are identified;
- the intervention of the coach is integrated into a planned and progressive process;
- performers operate within recognised competition structures in their sport;
- although delivery skills are important, there is more emphasis on regulating progression and data management – analysis, recording, monitoring and planning; and
- there is more extensive interpersonal contact between coach and performer(s).

Although it is understandable that this profile would match the coaching practice of those coaches who work with elite performers, this is not exclusively the case. There will be a broad spectrum of performers who share a commitment to the sport, have a formal training programme, and who participate regularly in competition. Although the circumstances of their participation (e.g. duration or frequency) may not always suggest that the benefits of a coaching process will be fully realised, this is undoubtedly performance sport coaching. Similarly, the fact that the relative performance standards of 'age-group' performers may be modest does not prevent a performance coaching process from being appropriate with young performers. (Nevertheless, it may be appropriate to think of a 'development' stage in which the intensity of the programme is not overemphasised and control of variables is ameliorated somewhat.)

Figure 3.2 illustrates the deceptive ease with which a continuum between the forms of coaching can be portrayed. It is undoubtedly the case that, in general, the standard of performance will improve as the performers' aspirations and capacities allow them to move through competition structures and levels. It is also the case that even the best performers will have spent some (usually accelerated) time going through beginner and developmental stages. Nevertheless, the form of coaching is very different in each set of circumstances and this raises a number of issues of matching individual coaches to needs:

- An individual coach may operate within more than one form of coaching. It seems more likely that this will be feasible for the performance coach who wishes to operate in developmental or participation contexts (although this tends to raise questions about their suitability for these domains).
- Given that the coach's expertise (skills and knowledge) differs within these forms of coaching, the individual coach may not have the necessary abilities to work with performers as their performance standard improves. There is a danger that a coach may wish to be associated with a developing athlete beyond the stage for which the coach's expertise is appropriate. Deployment of coaches within a sport is, therefore, an important issue. Some coaches, particularly at the developmental stage, may be appropriately termed and deployed as 'transition coaches'.
- It can also be argued that those coaches with the skills, knowledge and experience to work with the most able performers should also work with 'developmental' performers to ensure that those athletes with potential are not always operating with 'learner performance coaches'.

64

- Many coaches will wish to have the opportunity to progress as coaches and to achieve expert status. Although this topic has received some attention (Gilbert *et al.* 2006; Erickson *et al.* 2007), further research is required on how performance coaches enter coaching roles and how they progress. One interesting feature of this is whether performance coaches have started out as participation coaches or have made a transition from recently being performers themselves. There are obvious implications for coach recruitment and education.
- The most salient ramification of a participation coaching process or a partially applied performance coaching process is that the expectations of performance improvement and competition success have to be modified to fit the scale and sophistication of the process. There are a number of examples in which there is an understandable reduction in the performance expectations from the process. For example:

  - The *sports instructor* is a commonly accepted role in many, mostly individual, sports. Golf, tennis and skiing instructors, for example, offer what might be more appropriately termed technique instruction. The use of the term 'lesson' is quite illuminating here. This is not to denigrate what may, in fact, be a very sophisticated process, but it is clear that the full range and scope of the coaching process is not the intention. Improvement may be targeted at basic skills for the beginner or at skill refinement for the more advanced (and sometimes elite) performer.
  - *Specialist* coaches may also make a contribution to the overall process. This is evident in the coaching teams of sports such as rugby in which there may be specialist coaches for the forwards and the backs. Other coaches may specialise in kicking or speed development. This is dealt with later in the 'role of the coach'.
  - *Representative* team and group coaches may deal with high-level performers, but the responsibility for the greater part of the coaching process may lie with club coaches. Given that there is a 'cooperative team approach' to this, the benefits of an integrated process will still be attainable. However, the accountability of the representative coach should be mitigated in such circumstances and the more common features of the truncated process (such as tactical and psychological preparation) recognised.

To finish this section, there are a few key statements about these coaching categories:

1. Participation coaching is generally more episodic in character.
2. Lifestyle management (reflecting an intended control of variables) is characteristic of performance coaching with 'fast-track' performers and those already pursuing excellence.
3. Not only expertise (skills and knowledge) will be specific to forms of coaching, but experience within the domain may be an important part of the coach's profile.
4. It is not the individual coach who is the discriminating factor, but the nature of the coaching process and the resultant coaching practice.

Despite what has been said, it is evident that these are broad categories and are useful for analysis (and perhaps coaching workforce management) purposes rather than precise or quantifiable definition. Figure 3.3 demonstrates how the boundary criteria might be used as a coach education and development exercise to determine the balance of criteria between participation and performance coaching, when each is rated on a simple ten-point scale.

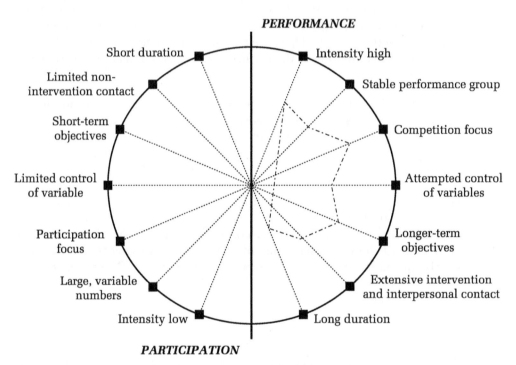

Figure 3.3 A diagrammatic representation of the balance of performance and participation coaching roles based on boundary criteria.

Note:
1. Rate yourself on each continuum using a 1–10 scale.
2. Determine your participation–performance profile based on the preponderance of responses.
3. The exemplar footprint shows a clear performance coaching profile on a scale drawn between the pairs of criteria.

 **SUMMARY**

This chapter should have familiarised you with the following:

- The reasons for establishing conceptual clarity and some key questions about the coaching process.
- The nature of a definitional framework and elaboration on the essential features of sport coaching.
- Definitions of the most important terms.
- A conceptualisation of sport coaching as a process and examples of the process elements applied to sport coaching.
- The boundary markers and criteria that delineate the sport coaching process; the likely contexts and the implications of a partially applied coaching process.
- Sport leadership roles with attendant coaching process characteristics.
- The skills necessary for the coach as a result of implementing a process – planning, delivery and management.
- The characteristics of, and differences between, participation and performance coaching, some examples of practice associated with these distinctive roles.

 PROJECTS

1. Interview two coaches who work in both participation and performance contexts. Focus on perceived differences in coaching practice and then relate these to the coaching process.
2. Devise a simple conceptual framework for coaching that conceives of the role as that of a performance mentor. What insights might this achieve?
3. Use Table 3.3 to prompt an investigation into organisational context. Interview individuals in each category and compare the details of the typology to the findings.
4. Interview six coaches to establish boundary markers. Attempt a qualitative and quantitative analysis, and add or subtract from the proposed criteria.
5. Use and adapt Figure 3.3. Is this a useful method for profiling coaches? What implications might it have for coach education and development?

REFERENCES

Abraham, A., & Collins, D. (2011). Effective skill development: How should athletes' skills be developed? In D. Collins, A. Button, & H. Richards (Eds) *Performance Psychology: A Practitioner's Guide*. Edinburgh: Elsevier, 205–229.

Abraham, A., Collins, D., & Martindale, R. (2006). The coaching schematic: Validation through expert coach consensus. *Journal of Sports Sciences*, *24*(6), 549–564.

Bowes, I., & Jones, R. L. (2006). Working at the edge of chaos: Understanding coaching as a complex, interpersonal system. *The Sport Psychologist*, *20*, 235–245.

Cameron, R., & Ebrahimi, M. (2014). Coaching in the workplace. In R. Harris & T. Short (Eds) *Workforce Development*. Singapore: Springer, 253–268.

Cassidy, T., & Rossi, T. (2006). Situating learning: (re)examining the notion of apprenticeship in coach education. *International Journal of Sports Science & Coaching*, *1*(3), 235–246.

Côté, J. (2006). The development of coaching knowledge. *International Journal of Sports Science & Coaching*, *1*(3), 217–222.

Cushion, C. J. (2006). Mentoring: Harnessing the power of experience. In R. L. Jones (Ed.) *The Sports Coach as Educator: Re-conceptualising Sports Coaching*. London: Routledge, 128–144.

Cushion, C. J., Armour, K. A., & Jones, R. L. (2006). Locating the coaching process in practice: Models 'for' and 'of' coaching. *Physical Education and Sport Pedagogy*, *11*(1), 83–99.

Duffy, P., Hartley, H., Bales, J., Crespo, M., Dick, F., Vardhan, D., Nordmann, L., & Curado, J. (2011). Sport coaching as a 'profession': Challenges and future directions. *International Journal of Coaching Science*, *5*(2), 93–123.

Erickson, K., Côté, J., & Fraser-Thomas, J. (2007). Sport experiences, milestones and educational activities associated with high-performance coaches' development. *The Sport Psychologist*, *21*, 302–316.

European Coaching Council (2007). *Review of the EU 5-level Structure for the Recognition of Coaching Competence and Qualifications*. Köln: European Network of Sports Science, Education and Employment.

Gilbert, W., & Trudel, P. (2004). Analysis of coaching science research published from 1970–2001. *Research Quarterly for Exercise and Sport*, *75*, 388–399.

Gilbert, W., Côté, J., & Mallett, C. (2006). Developmental paths and activities of successful sports coaches. *International Journal of Sports Science & Coaching*, *1*(1), 69–76.

Gray, D. E. (2011). Journeys towards the professionalisation of coaching: Dilemmas, dialogues and decisions along the global pathway. *Coaching: An International Journal of Theory, Research and Practice*, *4*(1), 4–19.

Haddon, E. (2011). Multiple teachers: Multiple gains? *British Journal of Music Education*, *28*(1), 69–85.

Jones, R. L., & Wallace, M. (2005). Another bad day at the training ground: Coping with ambiguity in the coaching context. *Sport, Education and Society*, *10*(1), 119–134.

Jones, R. L., Harris, R., & Miles, A. (2009). Mentoring in sport coaching: A review of the literature. *Physical Education and Sport Pedagogy*, *14*(3), 267–284.

Larson, D., & Maxcy, J. (2013). The industrial organisation of sport coaches: Road cycling as a distinguished case. *Journal of Sport Management*, *27*(5), 363–378.

Lave, J., & Wenger, E. (1991). *Situated Learning: Legitimate Peripheral Participation*. Cambridge: Cambridge University Press.

Light, R. L., & Robert, J. E. (2010). The impact of Game Sense pedagogy on Australian rugby coaches' practice: A question of pedagogy. *Physical Education and Sport Pedagogy*, *15*(2), 103–115.

Lyle, J. (1996). A conceptual appreciation of the sports coaching process. *Scottish Centre Research Papers in Sport, Leisure and Society*, *1*(1), 15–37.

Lyle, J. (1997). Management training and the sports coaching analogy: A content analysis of six management training products. *Fifth Congress of the European Association for Sport Management*. Glasgow: E.A.S.M.

Lyle, J., & Cushion C. (Eds) (2010). *Sports Coaching: Professionalisation and Practice*. Edinburgh: Churchill Livingstone.

North, J. (2009). *The UK Coaching Workforce*. Leeds: sports coach UK.

Passmore, J., & Fillery-Travis, A. (2011). A critical review of executive coaching research: A decade of progress and what's to come. *Coaching: An International Journal of Theory, Research and Practice*, *4*(2), 70–88.

SkillsActive (2010). *National Occupational Standards: Sports Coaching*. www.skillsactive.com/training/standards

sports coach UK (2008). *The UK Coaching Framework*. Leeds: Coachwise.

Torrington, D., & Weightman, J. (Eds) (1994) *Effective Management: People and Organisation*. 2nd edition. New York: Prentice Hall.

Townend, R., & North, J. (2007). *Sports Coaching in the UK II*. Leeds: sports coach UK.

Winder, L., & Townend, R. (2010). *The Coaching Workforce User Guide*. Leeds: National Coaching Foundation.

CHAPTER 4

COACHING DOMAINS AND THE ROLE OF THE COACH

CHAPTER OUTLINE

- Introduction
- Coaching domains
- Domain categories
- The role of the coach
- Role concepts
- Purpose and function
- Role complementarity between coaches and support personnel
- Organisational impact on the coach's role
- Summary
- Projects

INTRODUCTION

It may seem like stating the obvious to say that all coaches do not carry out the same functions or exercise the same role. However, our purpose here is to provide a conceptual basis for understanding why and how coaches behave differently. To do this, we continue with the development of a conceptual framework that illuminates the relationship between the individual (the coach), the coaching process, the athlete and the coaching environment. To do this we introduce the concept of the coaching domain to illustrate how the particular combination of sporting context and participant requirements impacts on the coach's expertise and practice. For each coach this produces a 'role frame', a perceptual filter that influences how coaches make sense of the world around them and define their professional responsibilities.

We might simply term this the 'role of the coach', a concept that can be expressed both as a matter of interpretation and as a matter of implementation. The nature of the coach's role can be divined from the basic purpose of sport coaching and from a consideration of what is necessary to put that role into practice. As this stage of the conceptual framework takes shape, an issue arises about the extent to which the role of the coach is context-specific. This is why we have introduced the concept of the coaching domain. We believe that there are distinctive sporting milieux within which the participants' needs, the organisational expectations and the prevalent practice of the sport result in quite discrete communities of coaching practice. Having identified these coaching domains, we might usefully explore the characteristic practice of the coach under the banner of the 'role of the coach'. Certainly there has been relatively little sound academic work on coaching domains or the role of the coach. Partly this is a result of an uncritical acceptance in the dominant literature of the role of the coach, but also, to return to the theme of the book, the absence of a conceptual framework within which to express such an analysis. However, relatively recent attention to participant and coach development models with attendant implications for stratified coach education (see North 2009) and some movement in the discourse attached to coaching roles has begun to create a more sophisticated approach.

COACHING DOMAINS

We have already argued that (over)using the word 'coaching' as a family term for all sport leadership roles masks the very distinctive and different forms of coaching practice in sport (Lyle 2011a). We can begin to unpick the distinguishing features of each of these roles by appreciating the characteristic context within which they are practised. 'Coaching domains' is a useful device for conceptualising the aggregation of behaviours and practice that characterise coaching in different sporting environments. This level of specificity has been acknowledged, albeit optimistically: "coaches' pre-coaching experiences, learning and development, employment and deployment and quality assurances . . . can be tailored to meet the needs of specific roles" (North 2009, p. 17).

A coaching domain can be defined as a distinctive sporting milieu in which the environmental demands lead to a more or less coherent community of coaching practice, with its attendant demands on the coach's expertise and practice. It would be accurate to infer that this leads to segmentation of the coaching workforce, with implications for workforce planning and development (Lynn & Lyle 2010). At this early stage it would perhaps be helpful to state that the coaching domain will be characterised by distinctive performer aspirations and abilities, stages of development, reward environments (in other words, motivations to engage in sport), organisational contexts, technical demands and competition formats.

 KEY CONCEPT

A coaching domain can be defined as a distinctive sporting milieu in which the environmental demands lead to a more or less coherent community of coaching practice, with its attendant demands on the coach's expertise and practice.

It must not be assumed that there are no disadvantages from a more segmented coaching workforce. For example, employment and deployment mobility will be impacted negatively if there is too firm a demarcation of expertise and experience across domains. The desire for the development of a cohesive or all-embracing 'profession' of coaching will also be impaired, although it will be argued later in the book that the loss of potential employment share may be a worthwhile price to pay to establish a more socially valued and acknowledged occupation. There are more practical issues, such as the benefit of universal coach education, and ideological issues, such as a conviction that coaching in one domain may (wrongly) be perceived as more worthy than that in another. Nevertheless, it can be argued that we already have a *de facto* segmentation. The long-term athlete development model (see Stafford 2005) divides the participants' development into a series of stages that are distinctive in their demands on coaching expertise and practice. Similarly, the sub-division into 'strands' in coach education (Duffy *et al.* 2011) demonstrates that these variable demands are already acknowledged.

The implications from recognising coaching domains are so evident that we stress their significance (Table 4.1).

To illustrate the point about the limitations that arise from not acknowledging coaching domains in coaching research, consider the researched populations in the following examples of published research studies:

- 6 coaches: volunteers, 75 per cent coached their own child, 83 per cent male, experience ranges from 3 to 20 years, maximum Level 2 certification, work with athletes 10–14 years of age (Gilbert & Trudel 2001);
- 10 coaches: employment status not confirmed, elite athletes, 80 per cent male, minimum 10 years' experience, current national team coaches (Côté & Sedgewick 2003)
- 19 coaches: 10 team sports, 9 individual sports, current or former head coaches, average 45 years, 79 per cent male, 9 sports represented (Erickson *et al.* 2007);
- 64 coaches: gymnastics clubs, 77 per cent female, average age 29 (16–57 years), coaching experience 1–35 years, 95 per cent certificated, 52 per cent at Level 2 NCCP (Vergeer & Hogg 1999);
- 24 coaches: 12 ice hockey, 12 baseball, average 40 years, 92 per cent male, at least 2 years of head coach experience (2–25), involved in recreational or developmental leagues, children coached between 9–15 years of age (Trudel *et al.* 2007).

You cannot fail to be struck by the variety and range of populations used in these studies. Ask yourself whether the findings can be aggregated in such a way that they illuminate the same or even similar coaching roles. This is not a criticism of the individual research papers, but we do make the point that research studies in sport coaching rarely explicitly stress the coaching domain within which the coaching activity takes place, nor do they highlight the implications (limitations) that the specificity of coaching domain populations produces. These populations are often described in terms of gender, age, experience and qualifications. There would be considerable merit in describing the coach's practice in much greater depth.

72

Table 4.1 Implications arising from recognising coaching domains

Accountability/ expectations	The performance outcomes from the coaching process are scrutinised more publicly in some domains than in others, and this often brings to the coach a level of accountability for these outcomes. Similarly, any increased intensity of preparation and sophistication of planning raises expectations about the control of performance and progression.
Coach education and training	The duration, depth and breadth of coach education as qualifications levels progress produce a differentiated set of expectations about the level of expertise that can be assured through such training. Increasingly, the specificity of domain preparation also impacts on the underpinning knowledge and skills required in domains such as talent development, children's coaching or high-performance coaching.
Research	The limitations in coaching research are a thread that runs throughout the book. A failure to acknowledge the implications for research design and interpretation of findings from the very varied research populations used in coaching studies is a common occurrence.
Expertise	It will be obvious that sport-specific technical demands will vary across domains. Similarly, the complexity and sophistication of application and adaptation implied by multi-year, multi-phase planning process differs significantly from more episodic programmes with shorter horizons. Many other lifestyle factors become important as the athlete's intensity of commitment increases.
Analysis	Coaching domains create a language or discourse appropriate to those domains. This forms part of a (relatively) common role frame assumed by the coach. One example of the importance of recognising this is that coach mentors and coaches should share an understanding of the role frame underpinning their conversations.
Mental models	Later in the book we will emphasise the importance of decision making in coaching expertise and practice. The operationalisation of the coach's cognitive skills depends to some extent on the use of 'mental models'. These representations are developed from knowledge and experience, and the relevance of the coaching domains from which the coach is able to draw this experience becomes obvious.
Professional development	As we will see shortly, coaching domains differ in deployment practice (level of voluntarism, for example), level of public esteem, demand for formal qualifications and reward environment (incentives or commitment, education and training). These factors impact on the professionalisation of sport coaching.
Theory development	The search for generic models and explanations for a construct termed 'sport coaching' may be bedevilled by the reality of context-specific domains.

 QUESTION BOX

Compile your own selection of research papers. Compare details (if any) of the coaches' role boundaries and practice. Should an explicit description of coaches' practice be an expectation in all empirical studies?

73

In the previous chapter we introduced a number of what we termed 'boundary markers' for the coaching process. These provide a very helpful reference point for differentiating between coaching domains. The boundary criteria identified were as follows:

- stability of personnel
- continuity of process
- extent of process
- frequency/duration of engagement
- goal orientation
- control of performance-influencing variables
- progressive intervention
- individualisation.

To illustrate domains in these terms, we might compare two examples (Figure 4.1; note that the rating system is only for illustration).

Even with a simplistic rating system, it is clear that the coaches in the example are operating in very different circumstances. We need now to examine how the very obvious differences in coaching practice, as exemplified in Figure 4.1, can be aggregated and configured in such a way that a manageable number of domains emerge; thus allowing us to be more accurate and valid when targeting research designs, coach education, CPD, coaching workforce development, evaluating effectiveness or identifying relevant expertise. We can provide a set of criteria with which the coaching domains can be identified. These are illustrated in Table 4.2.

The combination of sporting context, participant motives and aspirations, and organisational context creates a very variable and quite distinctive demand on the coach's expertise and role. Using the two simplistic exemplars illustrated in Figure 4.1, it becomes obvious that the different demands on the coach's planning skills, performance analysis, competition preparation, resource management, knowledge demands, interpersonal skills and delivery skills create an expertise package that is domain-specific. The 'coached population' provides a characteristic

Children's Coach		Boundary Criteria		Performance Coach
Introduces the	Moderate	Stability of personnel	High	
sport to primary	Low	Continuity of process	High	Head coach of a
school-age	Low	Extent of process	High	national league
children in an	Low	Frequency/duration of engagement	Moderate	adult team,
after-school	Short term	Goal orientation	Long term	training 3 times
context for 40	Low	Control of performance-influencing variables	Moderate	per week with a
minutes, once				competitive
per week for	Low	Progressive intervention	Moderate	season of
8 weeks	Low	Individualisation	Moderate	36 weeks

Figure 4.1 Example of domains using boundary criteria.

74

Table 4.2 Domain criteria

Domain criteria	Implications
Intensity of participation	This refers to the extent of the competition or recreation programme in which the participant engages. Clearly the distinction between a short-term period of instruction and a longer-term involvement in an organised competition programme will impact on the role adopted by the coach.
Intensity of preparation	The frequency and duration of the preparation or 'training' undergone by the participant will impact, not only on the commitment of the coach but also on the planning and coordination of the process. An athlete in full-time training will make demands in excess of those of a recreational participant, and the specificity of preparation will also be evident.
Complexity of preparation	Performance elements are multi-dimensional. However, participants in different domains will differ in the 'coverage' of these elements. Coaches of young children may be focused solely on skill development, whereas the high-performance coach will attend to all aspects of performance, with implications for the breadth of coaching expertise.
Participant motives	Underpinning many of the criteria are the distinctive motives of the participants within the domain. It will be obvious that motives based on immediacy of enjoyment (both children and adults) will create a coaching environment very different to one based on a desire for success based on competition results.
Recruitment	To some extent, participants in performance sport are 'recruited' via a merit or ability process. In the early stages of sport participation and in recreational and developmental sport, participation is more a matter of personal motivation. This impacts on the motivational climate and expectations within which the coach operates.
Interpersonal climate	The varied motives and forms of commitment, when allied to the intensity of the process, will impact on the interpersonal relationships between coaches and participants. The immediacy and animation required by the coach of children will differ from a relationship built up over many years and in which there is likely to be a more 'shared' responsibility.
Competition emphasis	The impact of the nature of the competition will be demonstrated in many ways, including specificity of preparation, selection and accountability. Domains with a higher level of public scrutiny may increase accountability for evident 'success'.
Value systems	Although we might agree on a consensus on appropriate values within coaching (and on the ethical behaviour that follows), we also need to acknowledge that the emphasis on some aspects of ethical behaviour is often 'tested' by the domain within which the coach operates.
Community of practice	One argument would be that domains with localised and less-intensive coaching processes are less likely to generate the networking, interaction and mutual reliance occasioned by more 'committed' coaches.
Deployment and career development	Within each domain the reward environment and consequent athlete commitment will determine a characteristic deployment pattern (part-time, voluntary, full-time, professional and so on), and potentially the demands for qualifications, education and training.

'frame of reference' for the coach in each domain. We will discuss later the extent of the commonality of expertise and role, and the dangers of operating in one domain with a frame of reference more suited to another.

Role frames

A role frame acts as a perceptual filter that influences how practitioners define their professional responsibilities. The practitioners' previous experiences, education and training, and their interpretation of the expectations of others, lead them to a particular image of the coach's role and what that entails. Individuals constantly project onto the world around them the interpretive frames that allow them to make sense of it. These filters give structure to an individual's behaviour and practice, for example, in shaping coaching problems and strategies for resolving them. The issue here is how this role frame can be purposefully developed and whether the coach's background, education and experience create a role frame that is particular to the domain(s) with which they are familiar – and the extent to which these role frames are easily amended.

It seems likely that the coach's practice and engagement in the domain community will constantly reinforce the role frame; they will be individual, but with a degree of commonality within the domain. We might speculate that there would be some benefit from a more reflective development of role over time in contrast to the continuation of a role frame based on unquestioned assumptions and experience (Gilbert & Trudel, 2004).

 QUESTION BOX

Interview coaches and compare the understandings, assumptions and expectations of a coach of young children and a coach of Olympic athletes in relation to the emphasis on results, values, response to progression issues, adherence issues, leadership style and athlete development and welfare. Can you explain any differences in their responses?

DOMAIN CATEGORIES

There have been a number of attempts to identify and categorise coaching domains (see Lyle 2011b), and there is increasing recognition that the identification of these contextual milieux are a necessary step in appreciating the role frame that it engenders for coaches in that domain (Duffy *et al.* 2011; ICCE *et al.* 2013). As we have said above, domains differ in goals, intensity, recruitment patterns, stability of personnel,

Coaching domains and the role of the coach

meanings and values, technical complexity, and the power relationships between coaches and athletes. However, there remains the question of how best to categorise domains in such a way that they are valuable discriminators without being overly fragmented.

We will see below that categories are most heavily influenced by interpretations of the needs of participant populations in sport. It is important, therefore, to have some awareness of attempts to model such participation. Two well-known models are the Participant Development Model (see North 2009) and Côté's Development Framework (see Côté *et al.* 2010). The former distinguishes between participation and performance engagement, with some emphasis on the early stages of learning and the possibility of movement between populations. The latter identifies sampling, specialising and investment phases, but distinguishes between children, adolescents and adults. These are participant-needs-led models but are prescriptions for practice rather than reflections of existing coaching domains. The following comments are for you to consider:

- The models are valuable for emphasising the distinctive needs of athletes at different stages of their development or athlete journey.
- You may consider that some of the early stages or recreational categories do not merit the term 'coaching', but perhaps some more general form of sport leadership.
- The populations need to be made sport- and age-specific.
- The relative scale of these 'groups' is markedly different (see Lyle 2011b), but is useful information for policy makers.
- Much less attention has been paid to entry and exit pathways and these may underplay the meritocratic/selective/sifting nature of the athlete journey in sport.
- Despite their obvious merit, personal experience tells us that sports bodies have a tendency to categorise their sporting populations by the level of competition in which they are engaged.

Given the orientation of the book, the reader would not be surprised if we pointed out that the choice of coaching domains depends on underlying conceptual understandings about the social world of the coach. Table 4.3 offers a brief overview of a number of alternative categorisations; we stress yet again that these are provided to stimulate your thinking about domains and for you to challenge and amend. You may wish to take the following questions into account when you respond to these alternatives or construct your own.

There is a very real tension between very discrete reflections of coaching practice in multiple domains and a small number of workable domains that adequately capture domain communities with sufficient commonality of coaching practices. This refers to the balance between simplified, generic domains and more numerous reflections of practice. The former may be of more practical assistance to policy makers. Perhaps the most important matter is that the concept of coaching domains is acknowledged and this begins to permeate research designs and coaching workforce development in the same way as it has begun to influence coach education qualification structures.

Table 4.3 Alternative domain categorisations

Model	International Sport Coaching Framework
Reference	ICCE *et al* 2013
Categories	*Participation*: coaching adults, coaching adolescents, coaching children *Performance*: coaching high-performance athletes, coaching performance athletes, coaching emerging athletes
Comment	This is based on an acknowledgement of a clear distinction between participation and performance meta-domains. However, the participation domains are based on child/adult status and the performance domains on level of performance. There are variable boundaries and pathways. This is not unlike our original participation/development/performance structure, but adds an age dimension to the participation strand.
Model	Coach Development Model (sports coach UK)
Reference	North 2009
Categories	Children's coaching, participation coaching, performance development coaching, high-performance coaching
Comment	This has an attractive neatness about it but this belies the mixture of characteristics – age, nature of motive, development stage and standard of performance. It also presents a problem of 'placing' performance coaching that is not classified as 'high performance'. The domains are further subdivided by a continuum from novice to master coach, and acknowledged as a 'pre-coaching' stage.
Model	Trudel and Gilbert Model
Ref:	Trudel & Gilbert 2006
Categories	Recreational coaching, development coaching, elite coaching
Comment	This is a less developed framework but raises some interesting issues. Recreation in this instance is intended to imply coach-dependent participation, but there is no sense of either age or development stage basis for the categories. These domains fail to acknowledge coaching of highly committed performance athletes who would not be classed as elite.
Model	Lyle's Participation–Development–Performance Model
Ref:	Lyle 2002
Categories	Participation coaching, development coaching, performance coaching
Comment	This is a categorisation that has influenced many other 'groupings' of coaches and the participation/performance distinction has been widely adopted. The domains are based on the nature of the athlete's engagement with the coaching process and the extent to which this satisfies the coaching process 'boundary markers'. This was intended to be a starting point for debate and we acknowledge that there is a need to distinguish between participation coaching for children and adults, and a need to acknowledge a further (much lesser scale) subdivision for truly high-performance athletes.

Nevertheless, you might consider that the conceptual underpinnings in terms of role, function and boundaries/scope have not been satisfactorily resolved. There is certainly much more work to be done to populate the domains with characteristic coaching behaviour and practice.

78

A rule of thumb has been that there is some relationship between categories and competition structures in each sport. Would this be true for your categories?

How does your structure of domains relate to stages of athlete development?

Is the number of domains a manageable reference point for research designs and coach education structures?

Is there a relationship between the domains that suggests that some form of coach mobility is likely?

Are you able to state that the domains have a common defining criterion – e.g. social context, athlete development, standard of performer, competition structure?

How does your categorisation deal with the issues of relative standards of performance across sports and age-group performers?

Does your choice of an appropriate framework assume all 'levels' of sport leadership and thereby a broad definition of coaching, or have you established a threshold level?

 QUESTION BOX

The coaching domains should be able to be represented diagrammatically in such a way as to illustrate the relationships between them. Are you able to do that for the conceptualisation of coaching domains that you favour?

THE ROLE OF THE COACH

'Role' will be conceptualised as the typical and expected range of behaviours and practice that follow from the coach's interpretation of the part to be played by the coach in a particular set of circumstances in order to achieve the improved or sustained performance that is the purpose of sport coaching. This allows for an individual interpretation of role, but raises the question of whether there is a generic role or whether each role is context specific. Therefore, to take a simple starting point, role needs to be considered in the context of: (a) any 'essential' element; (b) the organisational or contextual dimension; and (c) the contributions of other relevant individuals. It is immediately obvious that the discussions of the previous chapter are very important. Boundary markers may play a considerable part in defining or delimiting the role, and domain expectations are likely to impact on role behaviours.

KEY CONCEPT

'Role' will be conceptualised as the typical and expected range of behaviours and practice that follow from the coach's interpretation of the part to be played by the coach in a particular set of circumstances in order to achieve the improved or sustained performance that is the purpose of sport coaching.

From this consideration of the issues involved, a number of questions can be identified that give shape to the remainder of the chapter:

1. In what way might the role of the coach be most usefully portrayed, so as to inform an analysis of practice?
2. What degree of freedom is available in the individual's interpretation and implementation of the role?
3. Which conceptual and practical issues arise from the relationship between the coaching role and that of others involved in contributing to the coaching process?
4. Is there a correlation between organisational structure and purpose and the role of the coach?

The argument to be developed in the remainder of the chapter is that the primary role of the coach is the direction and control of the coaching process and all that this implies: to coordinate and integrate all of the inputs to the coaching process. The club coach, even in performance sport, may well find it necessary to perform most of the duties and responsibilities necessary. With more elite sport and larger-scale support teams, the coach may have a more specialised set of 'delivery responsibilities' (perhaps technique and tactical development, in addition to overall strategy). Nevertheless, the role of the coach is to provide the direction (perhaps the term 'management' would be appropriate) necessary for the strategic overview of the design and implementation of the coaching process.

 KEY CONCEPT

The primary role of the coach is to coordinate and integrate all of the inputs to the coaching process and to deliver that part of the intervention programme required by the role.

To define the role of the coach in this way has implications for the role of the performer and the performer's contribution to the operationalisation of the coach's role. We see no ambiguity in acknowledging the coach's direction of the coaching process and anticipating that athletes could be very centrally involved in determining a good deal

80

of the detail of the process. It is also obvious that it raises questions about relationships with performance directors, managers, sport scientists and others.

ROLE CONCEPTS

There is a set of commonly used concepts and terminology that is employed as a framework for most discussions about role. It would be valuable to review these before moving on to their application to sport coaching.

Expectations accompany the execution of a particular role – expectations that are independent of the individual performing the role. This is the basis of a definition of role as *a pattern of behaviours or tasks an individual is expected to perform because of a particular position he or she holds*. The coach inhabits an occupational role (even if conducted in a voluntary capacity), but one that is often not constrained by a very rigid set of expectations.

An *assigned or ascribed role* generally refers to the pattern of behaviours associated with a set of relationships or hierarchical position within a formal organisation. The expectations of the assigned role are the *core expectations* circumscribed by the contract or shared assumptions attached to the role. In practice, a lack of consensus about the coaching role and the marked variation in working practices and organisational requirements across sports have prevented a common set of assigned role expectations.

The *achieved role* refers to the element of embellishment or additionality that the individual can bring to a role, beyond that of the core expectations. This will be a personal interpretation of the role, but within the limits of the assigned role. In sport coaching the achieved role will be dependent on a mix of personal qualities and situational factors.

A role exists only in relation to other roles and helps to define the other roles. A *role-set* describes the family of roles that act together in a particular context or organisation. *Complementarity of roles* is achieved if there is a shared set of expectations within the role-set. The key 'other' is the athlete and the nature of this relationship is one that deserves detailed attention. Role conflict will be prevented if there is an agreement about the complementarity of the roles of athlete, manager, coach, parent, doctor, sport scientist, agent and so on.

Role conflict takes a number of forms: (a) lack of complementarity in the role-set; (b) inter-role conflict resulting from an individual fulfilling two or more roles that have competing expectations; and (c) intra-role conflict in which the demands within the role are incompatible. A potential lack of complementarity has already been identified in the athlete's support team. Inter-role conflict may arise if a coach attempts to fulfil club coach and national team coach responsibilities. The broad range of responsibilities within the coaching role means that intra-role conflict is common. Compare, for example, the incompatibility of acting as a counsellor and a selector, or of fulfilling an expectation to win with a demand to develop younger players.

81

Role ambiguity is the result of individuals not being aware of the demands or expectations of the role. One important issue here is how new professionals learn about (become socialised into) their roles. It would be wrong to overplay the 'uncertainty' element of the coaching role. Despite an apparent lack of commonality, individual coaches appear to have a firm grasp of anticipated patterns of behaviour within their sports. Perhaps the more important question is how they learned this. What part in their learning was played by coach education, by mentors, by copying traditional practice or by their own experience as performers?

 QUESTION BOX

This role-related terminology can be applied to all complex occupational activities. Nevertheless, the role of the coach appears problematical. Is it a matter of piecemeal historical development, lack of development as a profession, domain differences or simply the vast array of situations within which athletes wish to improve their performances that causes the confusion?

These concepts will now be woven into a more detailed examination of the coaching role, although in this edition we have attempted a much more concise presentation. We examine the lessons to be learned about the coach's role from an examination of the purpose and function of sport coaching, the role of the coach in relation to other support team roles and the impact of organisational constraints.

PURPOSE AND FUNCTION

One common approach is to provide short, pithy statements reflecting an individual's views on what is important in coaching. This is more relevant to the additionality of the achieved role than identifying something fundamental about the assigned role. Nevertheless, each statement will imply that one interpretation of what coaches are trying to achieve is the most important. For example:

- *The role of the coach is to become redundant* – implying a developing sense of self-reliance and self-direction in the athlete and suggesting an emphasis on a combination of coaching styles, leadership and inter-personal relationships.
- *The coach's role is to mediate between the performer's goals and their achievement* – emphasising an 'objectives model' of planning, but also stressing the centrality of the athlete and the importance of goal setting.
- *The role of the coach is to reduce the unpredictability of performance* – suggesting well-structured and detailed preparation, careful management of variables and comprehensive competition preparation.

The important point is not whether there is any consensus about such statements (this is unlikely), but whether or not these 'role statements' are a valuable part of our

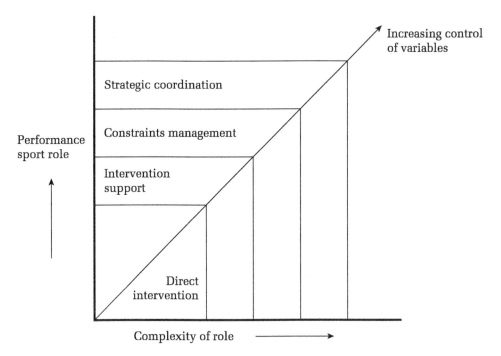

Figure 4.2 The functional roles of the coach.

developing conceptual framework. They do not convey enough about the coach's practice, and it is necessary to provide a more function-related representation of the coaching role in order to construct a useful analytical tool.

For this, we sub-divide the coach's role in relation to the implementation of the process, for which it is necessary to construct a conceptual diagram of the coach's functions. The general statement that the coach is responsible for the direction and coordination of the coaching process will be better understood if the role is divided into a number of subsidiary roles: direct intervention, intervention support, constraints management, and strategic coordination. This is illustrated in Figure 4.2.

Direct intervention connotes the purposeful delivery activities that are focused on the athlete/team's performance enhancement. The athlete is always engaged in this and the coach will normally be present or involved. This activity is recognised as training sessions (including recovery), competitions, schedules, remedial activity

---

 KEY CONCEPT

Role is divided into a number of subsidiary parts: direct intervention, intervention support, constraints management and strategic coordination.

and so on. The coach's behaviours will match the delivery aspect of the sub-role: technical instruction, feedback, demonstration, rallying, observation, organisation and recording. (There is a recent tendency to refer to this as coaching pedagogy.)

Intervention support refers to those coaching activities that support or prepare for the direct intervention. These are mostly carried out by the coach, although the athlete will be involved to an extent determined by their working arrangements. The most common activities are planning, administration, data management and counselling.

Constraints management is the coach's attempt to manage the situational factors to the best advantage. First, the coach will micro-manage the situational factors within the intervention programme (e.g. training access, support services, competition schedules, funding and availability of personnel and equipment). Second, the coach will attempt to influence positively the contextual features of the sport organisation and system that impact on the coaching process. This may involve recruitment issues, athlete support services, governing body policies, development plans, financial support, sponsorship matters and so on. The influence of the individual coach may be limited in some of these matters.

Strategic coordination ensures a continuous overview of the progress of the coaching process in relation to the stated objectives. This involves a degree of strategic planning based on a process of monitoring and regulation, and judge-ments about inputs, progress and likely outcomes. In acknowledging the complexity of the coaching process, the knock-on effect is that prediction of performance outcomes is imprecise.

 QUESTION BOX

The balance of responsibilities will differ by role and sport. Consider the roles of head coach, performance director and assistant coach. What is the likely balance of functional roles for these posts?

Sub-dividing the coach's role function in this way provides an additional and very powerful analysis tool for understanding coaching practice. The relationship between the functions can also further an understanding of coaching practice and the role(s) of the coach.

Using functional roles as an analytical tool

The scale of the intervention increases as the more strategic roles are exercised. The participation coach will largely implement only the direct intervention role and this reflects the more limited attempt of the participation coach to control variables

Coaching domains and the role of the coach

outside the contact activity. However, it is necessary to return to the role of the performer in the process. Depending on the nature of the formal or informal contract between coach and athlete, the athlete's contribution to the coaching process may be quite extensive or fairly minimal. One extreme version of this would be the athlete who is 'self-coached'. This implies that the athlete performs many, if not all, of the functions that would be exercised by the coach. The strategic and management roles can be fulfilled by knowledgeable, experienced and mature athletes, and the prevalence of 'self-coached' athletes is likely to be greater in those sports in which the direct intervention role is not complex (individual power/repetition-technique sports). Elite athletes will also have the assistance of their governing body support systems.

The relative balance of emphasis between the functional roles is a potentially very useful tool for cataloguing and analysing coaches' behaviour. It also gives a potential for comparative studies. With such a tool, it would be possible to address untapped (but seemingly obvious) research questions:

- Is there a greater or lesser emphasis on intervention support with elite athletes?
- Is the balance of functional roles different for team and individual sports?
- What is the balance of functional roles between club coaches and international squad/team coaches?
- Does the extent and balance of responsibilities and functions vary with the intensity and scale of the coaching process?

The link between participation coaching and a preponderance of direct intervention behaviours (albeit of a reduced intensity and complexity) has already been noted. Performance coaching skills and knowledge will be centred on the planning and regulation function of intervention support and the management and coordination functions that give direction to the intervention programme. The participation coach has much less need for strategic and coordinating skills since the thresholds of the requisite boundary markers of the coaching process are not reached. The strategic function will be made more complicated, both intellectually and practically, if there is a large team of support personnel and other parties involved in the process.

Common sense will point to the fact that few coaches will operate in completely constraint-free circumstances. It is also evident that coaching is a contested activity and coaches will operate with different resources, but at the same time try to optimise their access to such resources. Resources are exemplified by the most able performers, the best equipment, access to the best facilities, optimum financial support, personal development opportunities, etc. The constraints management function is therefore particularly important to those coaches who are held accountable for competition success or whose agreed goals with performers match these aspirations. Given that not all coaches can operate in the most optimum conditions, their options are as follows:

- Simply to incorporate the prevailing conditions into the planning of the process.
- To adjust organisational, performer and personal goals to match the available inputs.

85

- To take action, where possible and feasible, to improve or ameliorate the resource position (including using the efforts of other officials, managers, etc.).
- To contribute to attempts to ensure that the resources generally available to deliver performance sport are optimised.

It is possible for strategic coordination to be exercised (perhaps along with constraints management), but with the direct intervention and much of the intervention support implemented by others. This 'chief coach' role is best illustrated in the American football 'head coach' role in which a team of specialist assistant coaches deals with much of the direct intervention. Another parallel is the British soccer 'manager', who exercises the strategic coordination and constraints-management roles of the coach but is often assisted by one or more individuals who are given the designation 'coaches'.

It is also possible that in some circumstances the strategic coordination and constraints management roles are shared, or even dominated, by other individuals. This helps to explain the role of the 'performance director' in relation to the coach. Increased funding and a more system-oriented approach to Olympic sports have produced a role in which the incumbent exercises an overview of objectives and programmes to ensure that they are commensurate with organisational policies and plans, in addition to assisting with administration and management of resources. The performance director may also be the coach's line manager. The interaction between these roles – coach, head coach, manager and performance director – increases substantially the potential for role confusion and conflict.

ROLE COMPLEMENTARITY BETWEEN COACHES AND SUPPORT PERSONNEL

For the purpose of this section, it is assumed that a 'team' approach to implementing the coaching process has been adopted. This is common in performance sport and is epitomised by top club or national squad support teams. In addition to the coach there could be an extensive range of personnel – physiotherapist, assistant coach, doctor, masseur, team manager, trainer, sport psychologist, video analyst, notational analyst, performance director, team captain and so on. In developing a conceptual framework, there is a need to understand the interactions within this role-set. A number of potential issues can be identified, but perhaps these are best encapsulated in the following questions:

1. Does the presence of a large team of support personnel diminish or increase the 'directing' role of the coach?
2. It is assumed that support personnel are composed of discipline specialists (medicine, science), generalists (managers, notational analysts, conditioning coaches) and sport-specific persons (assistant coaches, performance directors). How is decision making affected by such a wide range of specialist inputs?
3. Which role functions within the coaching process are most appropriately complemented by the support team?

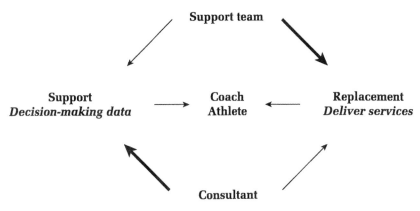

Support team

Support
Decision-making data

Coach
Athlete

Replacement
Deliver services

Consultant

Figure 4.3 The support and replacement roles of the coaching role-set.

To bring clarity to these inter-related roles, it is necessary to appreciate the distinction between a *support role* and a *replacement role* (Figure 4.3). In the former, the activities of the support team improve the coach's decision-making capacity by providing information (and recommendations). In the latter, the support team member provides a direct service, which replaces a delivery function that would otherwise be carried out by the coach (or conceivably not carried out at all). This is also made more complicated because these services can be provided by personnel who are 'attached' to the team/squad/club, or by 'consultants' who provide specialist services to clients from many organisations.

It is understandable that the 'consultant' is more likely to provide a specialist service in a support capacity. Such a specialist is unlikely to have a sufficiently detailed insight into that particular coaching process and may not be sport-specific. Advice and recommendations based on data collected have to be weighed against many other interdependent factors. The replacement role may be more appropriately implemented by personnel attached to the club or squad. In the context of role complementarity, it is easy to understand how the consultant roles may become somewhat detached from the other roles. The replacement role may be found at all levels from direct intervention to constraint management, but not at strategic coordination. The support role is more likely to impact at intervention support.

 KEY CONCEPT

Support personnel exercise either a *support* or *replacement* role. In the former they improve the coach's decision-making capacity by providing information and recommendations. In the latter they provide a direct service that would otherwise be carried out by the coach, or nor carried out at all.

87

A number of potential conflicts arise within the coaching process role-set:

- The performance director will have responsibility for the direction of the performance system, perhaps including: identifying targets, selection of athletes, recruitment of coaches and other personnel and resource management. A number of these functions will contribute to the coaching process but do not replace the strategic coordination of the athlete's intervention programme. Nevertheless, the potential for role ambiguity is evident.
- In some sports, the coach's competition/game management role brings with it a potential time pressure and the problem of making information available in a timely fashion to support decisions. This emphasises the central but often ignored role of the competition coach.
- The availability of specialist assistance for elements of the delivery of the coaching process does not diminish the coach's role. Indeed, it serves to emphasise the key process skills identified earlier – planning, monitoring, decision making, crisis management, contingency management and regulation.
- The contributions of sport scientists (and other specialists) can be less effective when not integrated into the coaching process. This can happen when the sports science programme is 'imposed' by a governing body and/or when the coach is unwilling or unable to utilise the information provided. Stable teams of specialists within a coaching team are preferred and direct intervention functions should not be replaced by personnel from outside this team, if at all possible.
- The advice of the support member can conflict with the goals of the team/coach. One example would be the advice on the implication of injury given by a doctor or physiotherapist during a competition. Although there will be clear cases of severe injury in which there is no question but that the specialist's advice must be taken, there will be many 'grey areas' in which there are a number of options. This can lead to an issue of 'who makes the final decision?'.
- Where the coach is perceived as just one of a number of technical specialists to be 'brought in' to assist the athlete, there is potential for a lack of direction and role clarity (indeed, this suggests an ignorance of the coaching process). Such a situation may be more likely with individual sport athletes, but seems less likely with team sports.
- Issues of status and hierarchical decision-making chains should not be underestimated. Highly trained discipline specialists may not feel comfortable, or that their professional interests are best served, by being part of a process that is integrated, managed and directed by a coach. This, of course, devalues the cognitive skills required for strategic coordination, in addition to the craft skills of the coach.

The fewer individuals involved in the coaching process, the less likelihood of conflict and loss of focus. However, this has to be set against the contribution of specialists and the number of performers involved. It is difficult to imagine that in team sports or with medium to large squads of performance-level athletes, a sophisticated coaching process can be devised and delivered without a team of support personnel. It is obvious that no one individual can provide the range of sophisticated, in-depth, focused and specialist performance analyses and enhancement required. For reasons of ethical values (athlete welfare), individualisation, practicality (the complexity of team training drills) and, most importantly, to access specialist expertise, it is necessary to take a team approach to the optimal execution of the coaching process in performance sport. A good deal of energy is expended on prescriptions for better communication between the coach and sport scientist. Further progress would be achieved by recognition of their respective roles in relation to the coaching process.

ORGANISATIONAL IMPACT ON THE COACH'S ROLE

Role is normally defined in an organisational setting and refers to the expectations of an individual who holds a particular position within that organisation. Therefore, it is important to put organisational constraints into the conceptual framework. There is interdependency between organisational demands and expectations, the boundary marker measures and the coaching role. This needs to be understood to appreciate fully the coach's resultant practice.

The interdependence of these factors can be illustrated in a number of simple examples:

- *The university team coach*: a number of the resource requirements and support mechanisms may be in place, but the team personnel changes regularly and there may be a seasonal effect because of vacation and examination periods. There may be conflict between university competition commitments and representative and club commitments. Organisational goals may be quite explicit, but governance of the organisation may be problematic.
- *The professional club coach*: reward systems are in place and the recruitment process is established. Players are full-time and resources are generally available. Player movements are unpredictable, however, and organisational goals are not set by the players or coach. A support team is likely to be available.
- *The player coach*: incorporating the coach's preparation requirements into the team's training schedule can be problematic. Unless supported by a number of assistants, the direct intervention functions can be restricted. This includes competition management. The coach's personal performance provides potential issues for selection, emotional response and interpersonal relationships.
- *Representative team coaches*: the total hours for the coaching process may not be extensive if the coach meets with the team on a regular but infrequent basis. The coaching process is focused on tactical and immediate psychological preparation, although the coach tries to influence technique development over time. Selection and developmental pathways are very important.

These are merely creative examples. They use a team sport context to illustrate how boundary markers such as intensity, frequency and duration can be affected. The comprehensiveness of the coaching process (reflected in performance expectations) may be limited by organisational factors such as resources, the emphasis on performance outcomes (success), the availability of training hours and the stability of personnel.

89

There may also be role conflict between the coach's value system and the expectations of the organisation. This is more likely in some organisations than others, and is likely to be related to the reward system and perceived pressures from outcome accountability.

To reiterate: the role of the sport performance coach is the direction and control of the coaching process and this can be exercised at a number of functional levels from direct intervention to strategic coordination, and by a range of personnel structures from the individual coach to the extended support team. The role is determined by the nature of the coaching process, which, in turn, is determined by a range of contextual and environmental factors. The outcome is a range of potential coaching roles to accompany the similar range of coaching processes. The role of the coach, particularly in the relative balance of functional roles, and relationships within the role-set, is significantly under-researched.

Intra-role categories

The term 'assistant coach' is one determined by an organisational context and is not necessarily an indication of novice status. It is true that many assistant coaches will be relatively inexperienced. However, an assistant coach in performance sport, and with a large-scale organisation, should not necessarily be thought of as a 'beginner' in status or capacity. Interestingly, there is some research evidence that assistant coaches exhibit different role behaviour (Solomon *et al.* 1996). The use of the term is indicative of the question of intra-coaching roles.

This question has recently been addressed by the International Council for Coaching Excellence (ICCE) (ICCE *et al.* 2013). This refers to the use of terms such as coach, senior coach or master coach, and this raises a number of interesting conceptual issues because of the attempt to link to coaching qualifications and (potentially) licensing of coaches. It has generally been assumed that coach education award structures are linked to intra-role categories and capacity or expertise to fulfil tasks on a continuum from novice to master. There have been many iterations of such frameworks, but limited cross-sport and cross-cultural consensus. The United Kingdom Coaching Certificate framework (sports coach UK 2008) was an attempt to harmonise levels of award with capacity to fulfil increasingly complex and more responsible tasks. The ICCE framework builds on this goal, although it is stressed that it remains a 'work in progress'.

Four principal role descriptors are identified: coaching assistant, coach, advanced/senior coach, and master/head coach, and core functions are associated with each role.

This is a difficult task and the mixture of delivery functions, assumed expertise, development responsibilities and management functions illustrates this. However, in relation to the conceptual position established to this point, and while we appreciate that this is a work in progress, we are unconvinced by the unnecessary attempt to synthesise these various aspects of the coaching role. Proposals such as

Coaching domains and the role of the coach

Coaching assistant: assists with the intervention programme at a basic level.

Coach: operates independently, and plans and delivers over a full season.

Advanced/senior coach: takes a leading role, and helps to develop other coaches.

Master/head coach: has an overseeing role in larger scale contexts, and evidences advanced expertise.

(ICCE *et al.* 2013, p. 26)

these are inevitably prescriptive. Nevertheless, we suggest that the confusion would be reduced by separating the role descriptors and relating these to the needs that they satisfy, and we offer the following comments for you to challenge:

- The central question is 'what is a coach?' A coaching assistant is not a coach, and the functions exercised by the coach depend on the nature of the coaching process (more or less complex, extensive or sophisticated). As a general descriptor, there is no need for any descriptor other than 'coach'.
- We feel that there should be an expertise-based threshold (perhaps largely evidenced via education and training) for 'coach' status, with recognition of advanced or expert status by use of the term 'master' coach.
- Qualifications can be responsive to the needs of the extended family of sport leadership roles but should be 'badged' appropriately. There should be a clear statement about the minimum qualifications or demonstration of expertise necessary for the right to use the term 'qualified coach'. Having an 'advanced award' should not confer the title 'advanced coach'.
- Coach development functions should not be related to coach status (but should be part of the coach's role).
- Organisational titles – squad coach, head coach, defence coach, under-16s coach – should be specific to the organisation conferring the title and need not imply a status to be recognised elsewhere. They should not be conflated with expertise and qualifications, but should have clear role descriptors.

The four functional roles are a very important conceptual and analytical tool. Indeed, strategic coordination is the distinguishing feature of the coach's role, although expertise in the other functional roles is required. Strategic coordination will always be the role of the performance coach, although some aspects of the direct intervention, intervention support and constraints management may be undertaken by others – assistants, sport scientists or team managers.

The strategic coordination and management role reinforces an emerging theme throughout the book. Performance coaching requires higher-order cognitive functions in addition to craft-based intervention delivery. This also reinforces the centrality of decision making as the key skill for performance sport coaches. Much of the cognitive functioning is tacit and not easily verbalised: it is rarely part of coach education and has depended on situated learning and experience. Nevertheless, it is important to correct the perception of the role of the coach as tracksuited intervention. Although very, very important, it is one part of a complex coaching role.

 SUMMARY

This chapter will have familiarised you with the following

- The importance of domains in understanding sport coaching practice.
- Useful criteria for distinguishing between coaching domains.
- Examples of potential sport coaching domain categories.
- The importance of role in understanding fully the coach's practice.
- A set of commonly used concepts and terminology with which to analyse role.
- The four functional roles in coaching – direct intervention, intervention support, constraints management and strategic coordination.
- Issues arising from an extensive role-set surrounding the performance athlete – in particular, the distinction between a support role and a replacement role.
- The effect of organisational factors on the coach's role.

 PROJECTS

1. Identify five empirical research papers dealing with similar issues. Analyse each for (a) evidence of the researched population's coaching practice, and (b) comparability of personal and professional characteristics. Draw conclusions about their potential for generalising across these populations.
2. Interview five practitioners with distinctive roles in the same sport. Use the domain criteria in Table 4.2 to compare their practice, and form a view on potential domain categories.
3. Devise a questionnaire based on the four functional roles. Investigate the proportion of time spent by coaches on each of the roles. Design the investigation by seniority of coach within each sport, or comparable responsibilities across sports.
4. Identify a performance sport case study within extended role-set working within the same organisation. Carry out an in-depth qualitative analysis of the support and replacement role functions, and identify any potential issues and role conflicts.

REFERENCES

Côté, J., & Sedgwick, W. (2003). Effective behaviours of expert rowing coaches: A qualitative investigation of Canadian athletes and coaches. *International Sports Journal, 7,* 62–78.

Côté, J., Bruner, M., Erickson, K., Strachan, L., & Fraser-Thomas, J. (2010). Athlete development and coaching. In J. Lyle & C. Cushion (Eds) *Sports Coaching: Professionalisation and Practice.* Edinburgh: Churchill Livingstone, 63–84.

Duffy, P., Hartley, H., Bales, J., Crespo, M., Dick, F., Vardhan, D., Nordmann, L., & Curado, J. (2011). Sport coaching as a 'profession': Challenges and future directions. *International Journal of Coaching Science, 5*(2), 93–123.

Erickson, K., Côté, J., & Fraser-Thomas, J. (2007). Sport experiences, milestones, and educational experiences with high performance coaches' development. *The Sport Psychologist, 21,* 302–316.

Gilbert, W. D., & Trudel, P. (2001). Learning to coach through experience: Reflection in model youth sport coaches. *Journal of Coaching Education, 21*(1), 16–34.

Gilbert, W. D., & Trudel, P. (2004). Analysis of coaching science research published from 1970–2001. *Research Quarterly for Exercise and Sport, 75,* 388–399.

ICCE, ASOIF, & Leeds Met (2013). *International Sport Coaching Framework*: Version 1.2. Champaign, IL: Human Kinetics.

Lyle, J. (2002). *Sports Coaching Concepts: A Framework for Coaches' Behaviour.* London: Routledge.

Lyle, J. (2011a). What is a coach and what is coaching? In I. Stafford (Ed.) *Coaching Children in Sport.* London: Routledge, 5–16.

Lyle, J. (2011b). Sports development, sports coaching, and domain specificity. In B. Houlihan & M. Green (Eds) *Routledge Handbook of Sports Development.* London: Routledge, 487–500.

Lynn, A., & Lyle, J. (2010). Coaching workforce development. In J. Lyle & C. Cushion (Eds) *Sports Coaching: Professionalisation and Practice.* Edinburgh: Churchill Livingstone, 193–208.

North, J. (2009). *The Coaching Workforce 2009–2016.* Leeds: The National Coaching Foundation.

Solomon, G. B., Striegel, D. A., Eliot, J. F., Heon, S. N., Maas, J. L., & Wadya, V. K. (1996). The self-fulfilling prophecy in College basketball: Implications for effective coaching, *Journal of Applied Sport Psychology, 8,* 44–59.

sports coach UK (2008). *The UK Coaching Framework.* Leeds: Coachwise

Stafford, I. (2005). *Coaching for Long-term Athlete Development.* Leeds: National Coaching Foundation.

Trudel, P., & Gilbert, W. D. (2006). Coaching and coach education. In D. Kirk, M. O'Sullivan, & D. McDonald (Eds) *Handbook of Research in Physical Education.* London: Sage, 516–539.

Trudel, P., Lemyre, F., Werthner, P., & Camiré, M. (2007). Character development in youth sport. *International Journal of Coaching Science, 1*(2), 21–35.

Vergeer, I., & Hogg, J. M. (1999). Coaches' decision policies about the participation of injured athletes in competition. *The Sport Psychologist, 13,* 42–56.

CHAPTER 5

EXPERTISE IN SPORT COACHING

CHAPTER OUTLINE

- Introduction
- Describing expertise
- High-performance coaching expertise
- An interpretation of coaching expertise
- Discussion points
- Summary
- Projects

INTRODUCTION

This chapter adopts a slightly different approach to how we have approached the process of updating. We felt that coaching expertise had become a current topic in the sport coaching literature (Collins *et al.* 2015; Nash *et al.* 2012; Gilbert & Côté 2013), and John Lyle had recently compiled a paper for UK Sport[1] that examined the concept of expertise as it applied to performance coaching, and as a precursor to identifying coach development programme principles. This discussion paper was compiled by distilling the views of a group of experienced coach developers,[2] bringing a degree of experienced interpretation and order to this corpus of opinion, and informing the process by evaluating the contribution of the academic literature to date. Each of the interviews was based on a literature-informed agenda of expertise-related questions, but more resembled a one- to three-hour conversation. The composition of the group and the organising agency orient the starting point to 'high-performance sport', although we will inevitably deal with the issue of whether the expertise identified applies to all coaching domains. We first examine the developers' views and then present an interpretive summary, followed by a series of questions and issues for discussion. You should note that the purpose of the paper was to stimulate debate about important concepts in coaching; it is therefore deliberatively polemic in nature.

The meaning, scope, associations and usages of the term *coaching expertise* are socially constructed to represent a social phenomenon and professional distinctiveness, and the purpose of this chapter is to understand expertise, rather than merely define it, and to provide some conceptual clarity. There are a number of uses of the term that are quite distinct.

- First, expertise can be a generic term to represent the totality of the specialist knowledge and skills that are required to carry out an occupational role (raising an immediate issue about which coaching role we are talking about). When used in this way, expertise applies to all sport coaches, perhaps above an entry-point threshold, and not only to the behaviour of experts. Thus our coaching expertise is what distinguishes us from other occupations or non-specialists.
- Second, expertise (or the behaviour of experts) may be thought of as the culmination of the development of capacities that differentiate how we perform as sport coaches. It would be presumed that different levels of expertise could be classified/categorised according to some profile of capacities that 'improve' as coaches acquire or develop greater expertise. Each of these 'levels' would have identifiable knowledge and skills. This perspective leads to the development of models of expertise that identify stages of development.
- A third conceptualisation of expertise emphasises how individuals do the job (usually referring to high-status jobs). The implication is that doing the job in a certain way makes effectiveness or success more likely. This interpretation may focus on personal qualities, priorities, role or occupational ideologies, or essential skills or capacities. Expertise might be described in terms of particular knowledge and skills that are argued to lead to effective coaching in a particular role or context. What is it that coaches do that makes them effective? This is represented in the aphorism, *what works for who and in which context and why?* This approach describes expertise as 'getting it right' and might apply to all coaches, not just experts. Is it possible to model this expertise in ways that are sufficiently detailed to describe practice, rather than merely represent component parts?
- A fourth, and common, approach interprets expertise as the behaviours or characteristics of experts, with its accompanying challenge of agreeing on a set of criteria or definition of 'expert'. In practice, the term 'expert' is normally ascribed to individuals according to a measure of performance that emphasises sustained achievement (usually by association with successful athletes/teams) across time or varied contexts. In more 'skills based' activities, expertise may be conferred according to performance on consensual reproducible tasks. This would not apply in more complex tasks such as sport coaching. There may be some indication that this expert behaviour will not necessarily be 'good practice' (at least in terms of values), and may rely on some 'stand out' features, rather than a complete profile.

These approaches to expertise are not mutually exclusive, but illustrate that it is possible to approach an understanding of the construct in different ways. We might conceptualise coaching expertise as the epitome of sport coaching practice, an aspirational level of specialist capacity or performance that characterises our best coaches. A reasonable question to ask, therefore, is whether there is some '*sine qua non*' that expert coaches demonstrate – a core of expertise that runs through any interpretation – and whether this has been established by research. Is there something/

anything about sport coaching that makes the interpretation of 'expertise' particularly problematical? These arguments are developed throughout the book: (1) measures of effectiveness are contested and underdeveloped; (2) the contribution of the coach to performance success is largely assumed (from myriad exemplars) but difficult to pin down; (3) coaches often work as part of a team of specialists; and (4) it is not uncommon for the coaching role to be partial (e.g. head coaches, specialist positional team coaches, representative squad/team coaches, 'assistant' coaches and so on).

Common usage has created a specific challenge – we may be attempting to work with a term that does not have any useful meaning! The use of the term 'coaching' is unhelpful because all coaches operate in domain-specific, context-specific and role-specific circumstances. Academics have searched for a generic model to represent the occupational manifestation of coaching and perhaps not surprisingly have had very limited success. In other professions we would be likely to find extensive underpinning knowledge, selection criteria, professional training and identifiable professional standards. These would combine to confer 'expertise' (and a starting point), but it would be acknowledged to be at an 'entrant' professional level with subsequent specialisation. In sport coaching we have some difficulty in identifying this 'entrant level'.

In so far as we need a definition, a simple adaptation of Ericsson's (2006, p. 3) definition will suffice; thus we might define expertise as *the characteristics, skills and knowledge that distinguish experts from novices and less experienced people*. Ericsson notes that not all domains have 'representative tasks' that can be used to demonstrate superior, reproducible performance, but there is an inextricable link between 'expert' and 'expertise', and recognition that a 'pre-expert' phase exists. We might, therefore, adopt a working definition that expertise is represented by *the capacity to be highly effective in the high-performance coaching domain*. We intend expertise to be understood in two apparently contradictory ways: first, it is the culmination of expert practice (aspirational and perhaps idealised for many, and descriptive of their practice for a much smaller number), but useful for describing the required characteristics, knowledge and skills; *and* second, a more generic term that is descriptive of the coach's capacity in the pre-expert stage – but only in a particular domain. This acknowledges two things: first, the practical use of the term to refer to the abilities of coaches who may never become 'experts', but who are recognised to have a highly developed capacity that distinguishes them from novices; and second, an apparently unresolved (or unresolvable) issue of identifying 'when expertise starts' in coaching. The common sense approach would be some 'threshold measure' of expertise (core capacity of an advanced nature), an approach that we have not yet conquered.

DESCRIBING EXPERTISE

In the next section of the chapter, we summarise the views of experienced coach developers and present a series of diagrams that are derived from the feedback of those interviewed. Note that this is not intended to be a 'model' of coaching.

KEY CONCEPT

As a working definition, expertise is represented by *the capacity to be highly effective in the (high-performance) coaching domain*. It is both a culmination of expert practice and a description of the coach's capacity at the pre-expert stage.

The purpose is to use the diagrams to create a synthesis of the views expressed and to provide a simple reference point for further discussion (see Figures 5.1–5.5). The basic premise in the diagrams is that there are a number of elements of expertise that are required to enable the coach to act effectively in performance sport. These 'pillars' will be subject to further discussion and confirmation, but they embrace functional skills, sport-specific technical knowledge, personal qualities, experience, philosophy/ approach and disciplinary knowledge. These 'building blocks' are able to be called upon as the situation demands. We might argue that these pillars form a 'core capability', with a clear implication that this can be learned, developed and enhanced, and that individual coaches will be likely to have distinctive capability profiles. Common sense tells us that there are likely to be sport-specific differences in coaches' capability profiles and that the particular balance of elements that is necessary to be effective is still unclear (or that many different combinations of elements might be effective).

The role of the coach can be described in terms of the nature and level of responsibility, athlete status, standard of performance, status within the sport's performance hierarchy/pathway, deployment/employment conditions and relationship to other professionals/practitioners, and the role determines what capability will be required and, therefore, which building blocks will be required. This helps us to understand how the different roles within performance sport (for example: assistant coach, head coach) will require different capabilities. However, there is a further characteristic of expertise that mediates between the core capacity of the coach and (evident) effective coaching performance – in some ways perhaps, the most demanding, most likely to distinguish coaches from other professionals, and least well understood. These core capabilities have to be deployed 'to order', that is, in response to the particular demands of the coaching context. The coaching context is often depicted in the academic literature as complex, contradictory, messy, emotive and dynamic. The expertise required is couched in terms of coordination or 'orchestration'. At least initially, it might be more useful to use simpler terms. The coach's capabilities and consequent action decisions have to be applied, matched and aligned to the needs of the (often 'unfolding' or emerging) situation. When we take into account that it is inappropriate to create a coaching template that can be superimposed on a particular set of circumstances, it is easier to understand why this feature of coaching expertise is vitally important but least explored, and understood, and difficult to exemplify.

The coaching context is the environment in which the coach deploys a 'second level' of expertise, in which the coaching intervention (which implies formal, informal, planned and emergent activities and relationships) needs to be aligned to the needs of the athletes and the different layers of goals within which coaches and athletes are working. The context element of the diagram is intended to imply that the coaching context is (in practical terms) unique, although it seems likely that coaches will seek for and use 'regularities' in their practice to help them cope with the dynamics of their practice. Therefore, evaluation (of coaching impact) is very difficult. There is a need to understand the particular combinations of practice and context that create effectiveness; and identifying and evaluating levels of expertise is very challenging because we cannot apply 'templates' to individual coaching contexts, although we might be able to measure/assess some of the 'pillars' more effectively. We might speculate that there are some coaching practices that could be expected to 'work' in a wide range of contexts (in a number of domains!), and that coaches use these to make their practice more 'doable' and efficient. This can be exaggerated by critics as 'formulaic' and less athlete-centred, but it does seem likely that some coaches may take a least-resistance approach to this second layer of expertise, and use their 'expertise' to make it relevant on a day-to-day basis. This would be a useful focus for research.

 QUESTION BOX

Using your expertise to adapt and apply your coaching strategies to the needs of your athletes and the context is at the core of professional practice. How can this be best developed in coach education?

The academic literature seems to be in no doubt that there are stages in the development of expertise (e.g. Berliner 2004). This can be in terms of occupational status (assumed capacity to do the job) – from novitiate to master, or recognition that the capabilities 'grow' in stages and the expertise becomes (a) capable of dealing with more demanding and complex tasks, and (b) deploys increasingly more sophisticated cognitive skills – for example, novice, competent, proficient, expert (note that the former is a role descriptor, the latter is a level of expertise). These are useful devices for building a development strategy, but are not completely straightforward in sport coaching because of our practice of attempting to speak of coaching in a generic all-embracing way. Thus, we are left with a dilemma: do the 'stages' apply to coaching in terms of roles, levels of certification, domains or standard of athlete performance? Note the position of Duffy *et al.* (2011), who acknowledge earlier attempts to establish 'core concepts' including 'apprentice coach, coach, senior coach and master coach', and propose a dissociation between certification and role. It is certainly very tempting to adopt the principle of defining levels of expertise within the domain, providing that domain can be 'isolated' satisfactorily. It is important to appreciate that the role played by the coach (including the contextual siting) is significant because it

98

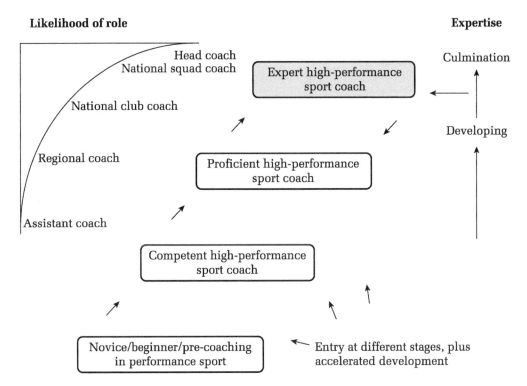

Expertise

Head coach
National squad coach

Expert high-performance
sport coach

Culmination

National club coach

Regional coach

Proficient high-performance
sport coach

Developing

Assistant coach

Competent high-performance
sport coach

Novice/beginner/pre-coaching
in performance sport

Entry at different stages, plus
accelerated development

Figure 5.1 Stages in the development of expertise.

determines the substance of the necessary expertise. However, it is also tempting to make the assumption that a capacity to be effective in a high-status role such as head coach implies that the individual would be similarly effective in 'less demanding' roles. We also need to note that there is a distinction between an aspiration, for example, that all head coaches should be 'expert' and highly certificated, and perhaps even regulated within the sport as such, but it is presumably also possible to be a not-yet-expert head coach.

Figure 5.1 attempts to show this in simple form.

There is an assumption of 'deliberate practice' as the coach moves through these stages of development, and an accumulation of learning/development in the core 'pillars' that build the coach's capability. Experience suggests that many practitioners operate 'within expert's clothes' without the core pillars being evidently developed. This is another of the factors that may limit our development as a profession.

HIGH-PERFORMANCE COACHING EXPERTISE

What follows is a selective digest of the opinions of those interviewed; the substance of the feedback from the coach developers has informed the creation of the resultant diagrams. Clearly the views of those interviewed are neither self-evidently entirely appropriate nor inappropriate; they represent their personal opinions on the concept of expertise in coaching, but reflect, cumulatively, many years of development and coaching experience. These have been incorporated into a relatively cohesive account, with some interpretation from the author.

Before looking at the different features of expertise, there are two conceptual issues to discuss. First, a key issue is the relative weight to be given to each element of expertise. Interviewees found it difficult to identify the 'core' elements, and the academic literature provides little help. There are 'list-like' accounts of the various knowledges and skills that are required (Lyle 2002), and many 'prescriptions' (for example, Abraham *et al.* 2006; Abraham & Collins 2011). However, there is no evidence on the hierarchy, relative priorities, prior requirements or preferred 'balance' of the various elements, when put in the context of effectiveness or impact. We might adopt the view that a 'different profile' of strengths and weaknesses is to be expected in coaches, and perhaps across sports. While this is a pragmatic approach, and is a useful device for 'accommodating' different individuals in post, it might be argued that it 'masks' our lack of knowledge about the relative contributions of the various elements. Second, there is some value in the idea of 'necessary' and 'desirable' features of expertise. This might be best explored in the context of the 'personal qualities' identified by interviewees as characteristic of our best coaches. A considerable number of qualities were identified (everything from non-judgemental, passionate, likeable and single-minded, to motivated and well-organised). However, which of these can we put into the 'necessary' box, and are any of them more impactful than the others?

Understanding of 'expertise'

Our tentative definition that 'being highly effective' characterises expertise tended to be expressed by developers as 'impacting on performance', evidenced by:[3] *ability to influence a group of people*; *move the athlete forward*; *don't make mistakes very often*; *high quality of output*; and *better judgements more often*. How expertise could be recognised was a common theme. This was commented on in relation to time (*applied your expertise over a reasonable period of time*), context (*demonstrably applied in the most challenging contexts*) and function (*can see load management; has a technical model, can advance athletes over time, has an interpersonal management style that works*). There were conflicting views on 'results' – *the expert coach is associated with results* and *not measured by athlete outcomes*. In summary, most descriptors tended to be qualitative criteria and there are potential dilemmas about being associated with athlete outcomes.

Domain specificity

As a general rule, those interviewed recognised domain, role and sport-specificity: *domain specific; don't use it in the other domains; keep it for the highest levels of performance*; *would differentiate between high level and others*. Although the high-performance domain was the frame of reference for the discussions, it was also clear that expertise could be recognised in other domains: *yes, but different*. The high-performance domain was acknowledged to have particular challenges: *aggregation of marginal gains*; priorities – *performance on the day, margins are different, gains smaller*. There was certainly a view that there were commonalities across domains: *the 'how' is common across the domains*; *commonality across domains*; *expertise in the development coach has the same skills, but different balance, less nurturing in high-performance context, 'slower' process with talent/adolescents*. Nevertheless, this was accompanied by a general presumption (and many examples) that expertise would be sport-specific and related to specific roles: *individual and team coaches different*; *coaches don't operate by themselves*; *expertise being sport-specific, role-specific expertise*; *role is important*; (head coach) *good grasp of skills, but can use support team*. It was difficult for individual interviewees to identify common elements across sports, roles and domains, but there did seem to be an underlying understanding that similar skills would be involved.

Experience

The extent of any necessary experience as a high-performance athlete was raised with each developer. The summary position was that high-level performing experience was desirable, although its absence was not a barrier in some sports: *experience is important but not sufficient by itself*; *most coaches have experienced the 'game', not necessarily at the highest level*; *don't have to have it but it helps if you had*; *being an ex-performer helps, assumption of knowledge – empathy for the 'frame of reference'*; *25 per cent of* [our] *coaches have been high-performance* [competitors].

Personal qualities

It is worthy of note that over one-fifth of the attributes identified by interviewees related to personal qualities. However, these generally observable qualities, while characteristic of the best coaches, may not be the capacity that actually confers expertise. It is unlikely that the qualities identified would be exclusive to sport coaches, and many non-experts would also exhibit these qualities. The underlying presumption appeared to be that highly effective coaching practice was more likely if these qualities were present, although, perhaps not surprisingly, the great majority were related to the coach's inter-personal relationship with the athlete(s). It may also be helpful to refer to the distinction between necessary and desirable qualities. The responses from the developers fell into two categories: first, qualities that more directly enable the coaching function to be carried out, and, second, more general characteristics. The former are exemplified by: *expert coach has a 'sponge analogy'*; *exceedingly well-organised*; *continually challenging*; *willing to change* (having learned from things going wrong); *motivation*; *non-judgemental*; *attention to detail*; *reflective*; *organisation*; *very responsive*; *trust*; *likeability*; *evident expertise*; *not frightened to make decisions*; *adaptive* (innovative); *robust under pressure*; *open to new ideas*. The latter (general qualities) are exemplified by: *humility*; *extremely tenacious*; *hardness*; *single-mindedness*; *go the extra mile*; *growth mind set*; *motivated*; *drive and passion*; *good listeners*; *fascination with coaching*; *passion for sport and people*; *fast track learning*; *understand what they don't know*; *confidence in ability*; *aware of limitations*; *self-awareness*; *don't have ego*.

Approach/philosophy

Many of the comments were associated with 'how' the coach conducts business, and it was difficult to distinguish between personal qualities and 'approaches' or philosophies. Some of these were more general 'ways of working' and others were linked to specific functions. The former were exemplified by: having a *consistent philosophy*; *reflect-in-action*; *aware of expectations*; *acknowledge what's going well or badly*; *accept can't get perfection in an imperfect world*; *management of expectations*; *consistency of approach*; *continually evaluate what they're doing*; *constant questioning of self*; *self-correcting*. There were a number of themes in the latter set of comments: having a clear vision and direction (*have a bigger picture*; *sense of direction, strategy*; *vision, road map*), planning (*plan well in advance*; *clarity in coaching model for success*; *focus on process goals not outcomes*); relationships (*recognise who they're working with as players, as people*; *courageous enough to let the athlete self-develop*; *element of rapport required*; *stretch behaviour of self and others*). There was an evident emphasis on openness and a commitment to learning (*commitment to continuous learning*; *open to continual learning*; *a relentless inquisitiveness*).

Functional skills

It might have been expected that greater emphasis would be placed on skills associated with the role. This may partly have been a result of poor direction by the interviewer or a general assumption that the skills were important. There was no intent at the time to explore these in greater detail, but it was clear that a capacity to analyse performance and manage interaction with athletes were significant. These 'functional skills' were grouped into: general (*breadth and depth of knowledge and skills, very, very proficient*), performance planning (*planning*; *can break performance down into key elements*; *performance modelling, shape and share with athletes*; *deliberative planning*; *good at performance planning*; *analytical skills*; *load management*; *decision making*), managing the learning environment (*set appropriate learning activity at a high level*; *create learning environment*; *mostly good at delivery skills*; *efficient routines*; *organisation*), and managing relationships (*communication skills*; *perceptive about people*; *can lead, manage, cajole*; *communication*; *communication and rapport*; *leadership*; *managing the 'face'*; *they 'manage' the relationship*; *leadership style*; *of the best coaches, 100 per cent have good relationship with athletes*).

102

Sport-specific knowledge

This feature of expertise may also have been rather taken-for-granted, but the comments received certainly placed a great deal of emphasis on the coaches' immersion in the technicalities of the sport: *experts have the highest levels of technical knowledge*; *mental models, technical models*; *massive technical/tactical knowledge*; *basic technical models* (need to be better) *understood*. The capacity to predict future directions in performance standards was also highlighted: *if they don't understand where the performance is going to go*; *predict the direction the event will go, technical model.*

Intellect

There was no doubt that intellect played a part in coaches' expertise, although there appeared to be something of a sub-text that acknowledged this as an issue. Nevertheless, the comments received were very 'strong': *experts have higher order intellectual skills*; *there are no dumb expert coaches, well-read, reflective, but exceptions*; *they have an intellectual capacity, not academic qualifications*; *intellectual capacity, Level 4 shows that it is needed*; *intelligence, EQ*; *intellectual capacity, no doubt there is a threshold level*; *experts described as smart*; *coaches can work with the extended abstract.*

Knowledge

There was limited evidence of this 'pillar' and it had originally been subsumed under 'knowledge and skills'. It may be the case that the *explicit* use of such knowledge (rather than being incorporated into such skills as planning, motor-skill development or psychological strategies) is sport-specific. In the examples given, there was a physiological bias: *physiologically driven sport*; *understanding of conditioning is essential*; *essential profile is understanding the technical model, understanding the physiology and integrating with medical practitioners*; *element of cross-disciplinary with medical*; *good underpinning knowledge*; *underpinning scientific knowledge is not obtained in a tacit way*; *need to deal with knowledge of sports science, how much?*

Synthesis and pertinence (alignment)

This feedback very strongly influenced the final proposals. Coaching expertise is recognised in the need to adapt the coach's capabilities to the needs of the particular context in which they are operating. This suggests a particular set of skills (and some further underlying capabilities that enable this to take place). The feedback given by developers was in great detail and reinforced the primacy of this element of coaching expertise. The interview comments constitute a very valuable account of how this process (align, match, orchestrate, make decisions) takes place, particularly as this feature of expertise is least well understood in the academic literature.

The key to this part of the expertise profile is that the coach's actions (activities, decisions, intervention) match the needs of the athlete and the situation (including short-, medium- and longer-term perspectives): *the particular combination of 'expert performance' is not transferable to another athlete, therefore expertise is in deciding on the appropriate action; function of context; thorough understanding of the context; manage and orchestrate.* This involves 'shaping' the intervention: *better coaches able to identify the performance model required and align goals to it; expertise is taking the technical framework and applying it in specific situations; expert coaches know how to cope with crises* [although they] *may not always be resolved; what works for who and in which context and why; shaping the environment and giving high-quality feedback.* There is a very full range of necessary skills: *work with 'routines' but can adapt as required; adaptive expertise; can fit behaviour to the need; expert has good solutions available; best coaches are not just copying; reason logically and reason heuristically; they don't guess; don't do the same things all of the time; need to be able to adapt by reading the individual; can adjust during the session; adapt the programme as required; the best coaches are consistently trying to 'work through' athlete problems; observation.* The resultant practice looks 'appropriate': *synergy, between coach and athlete/team members, is usually evident, but difficult to explain what has caused this; decision-rich; there is a synergy that creates something greater than its parts.*

It seems evident that the synergy that is achieved has an element of structure to it: *coaches are intention driven, there is a performance goal in mind; modelling important, practice needs to match the needs of the game; key is layered-ness, a process shaped by physical environment and stakeholder expectations; more attention to purpose, then can prioritise, able to align on day-by-day basis; has a context for the adaptation and short-term response, some of which looks like intuitive decision making;* although this is a complex and dynamic context (*the intention, goals, plans, models, expectations are messy in delivery/actuality for a number of reasons*); and *even experts will have blind spots, deficiencies.*

 KEY CONCEPT

The coach's actions (strategies, behaviours) are aligned, adapted and applied to the needs of the coaching context. This is the essence of coaching expertise.

AN INTERPRETATION OF COACHING EXPERTISE

It is necessary for us to synthesise the evidence presented and to provide a working model of coaching expertise. The following set of diagrams is an attempt to illustrate how the literature and the views of the coach developers have been incorporated into a sequential illustration of coaching expertise. The key messages are:

1. The coaching role determines the likely balance of expertise components.
2. The development of underpinning knowledge and skills of delivery and application (for example, planning) create a *capacity* for effective performance

104

(the building blocks also embrace the coach's intellectual capacities, experience and personal qualities).

3. A process of selection, application, alignment, accommodation and adaptation of this capacity to specific context-dependent coaching tasks leads to effective *performance*.
4. Knowledge, skills and application develop in a staged way that is both particular to each component and cumulative in its effect.
5. Figure 5.4 shows the relationship to the UKCC Level 4 guidelines (Bailey *et al.* 2011) and how the beginnings of an assessment framework might be devised.

 KEY CONCEPT

The adaptation, accommodation, alignment and application of the coach's capacities to a particular context is the key element of sport coaching expertise.

 QUESTION BOX

Expertise is context-dependent. To what extent is coaching expertise sport specific and domain specific? Consider the notion that alignment/adaptation in high-performance sport requires extensive technical knowledge and prior experience of training and competition processes.

DISCUSSION POINTS

In the spirit of a book about coaching concepts, and to stimulate debate, we have identified a series of statements, questions and discussion points to which you might give your attention.

1. Coaching expertise is conceptualised as the culmination of coaches' capabilities and reflective of the performance of our expert coaches *and* the stages in the development of that expertise (beyond a minimum level that it is difficult to specify). Individual coaches may have well-developed expertise but not have reached the final stage in which highly effective high-performance coaching is exhibited.
2. Expertise consists of a capacity for coaching, made up of a range of capabilities, which the coach then deploys in the particular circumstances of her/his role and occupational deployment. This 'second level' is an alignment and application of the necessary coach-led actions and activities to the needs of the athlete/team and context. The capabilities may be thought of as aggregative and the alignment as integrative ('an aggregative capacity leading to an integrated performance').

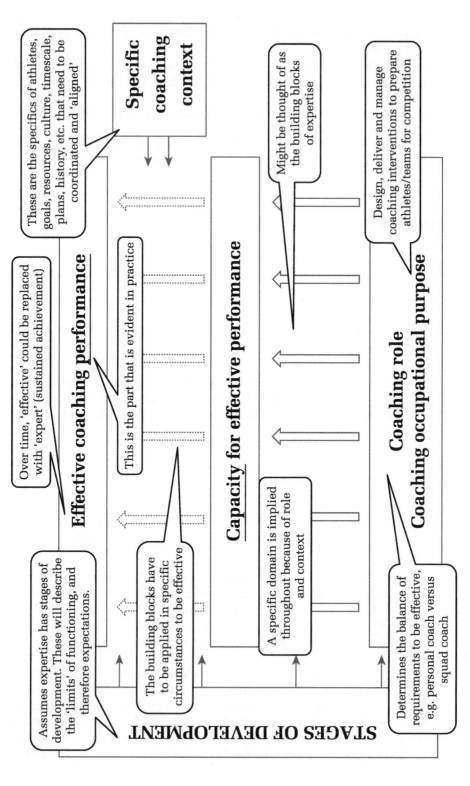

Figure 5.2 Explanation of the component parts of the conceptual framework.

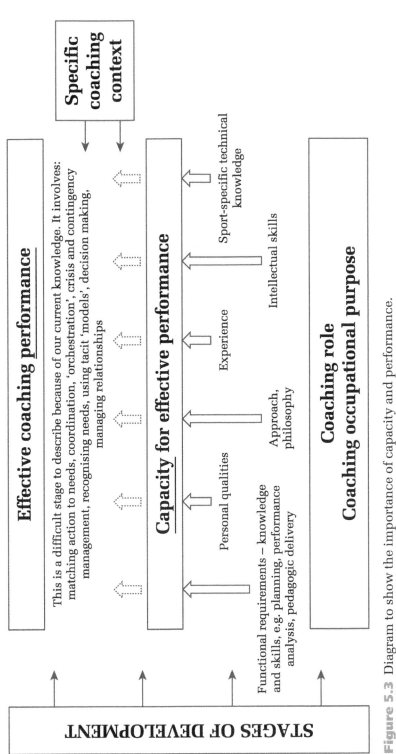

Figure 5.3 Diagram to show the importance of capacity and performance.

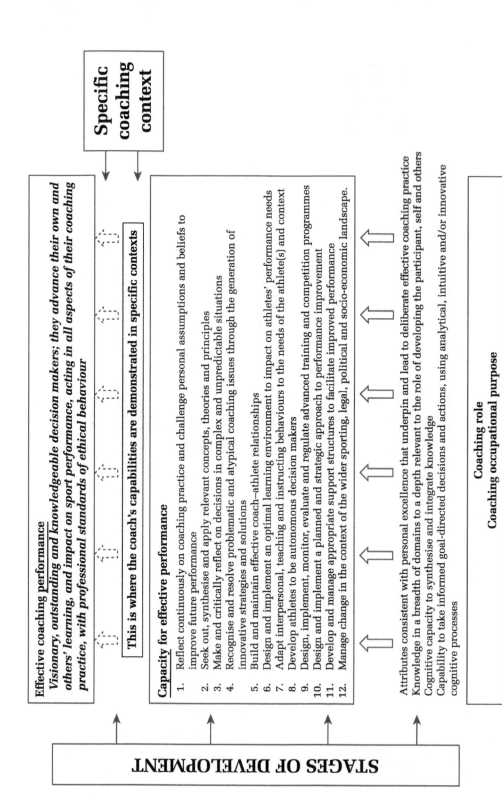

Effective coaching performance
Visionary, outstanding and knowledgeable decision makers; they advance their own and others' learning, and impact on sport performance, acting in all aspects of their coaching practice, with professional standards of ethical behaviour

This is where the coach's capabilities are demonstrated in specific contexts

Specific coaching context

Capacity for effective performance

1. Reflect continuously on coaching practice and challenge personal assumptions and beliefs to improve future performance
2. Seek out, synthesise and apply relevant concepts, theories and principles
3. Make and critically reflect on decisions in complex and unpredictable situations
4. Recognise and resolve problematic and atypical coaching issues through the generation of innovative strategies and solutions
5. Build and maintain effective coach–athlete relationships
6. Design and implement an optimal learning environment to impact on athletes' performance needs
7. Adapt interpersonal, teaching and instructing behaviours to the needs of the athlete(s) and context
8. Develop athletes to be autonomous decision makers
9. Design, implement, monitor, evaluate and regulate advanced training and competition programmes
10. Design and implement a planned and strategic approach to performance improvement
11. Develop and manage appropriate support structures to facilitate improved performance
12. Manage change in the context of the wider sporting, legal, political and socio-economic landscape.

Attributes consistent with personal excellence that underpin and lead to deliberate effective coaching practice
Knowledge in a breadth of domains to a depth relevant to the role of developing the participant, self and others
Cognitive capacity to synthesise and integrate knowledge
Capability to take informed goal-directed decisions and actions, using analytical, intuitive and/or innovative cognitive processes

Coaching role
Coaching occupational purpose

STAGES OF DEVELOPMENT

Figure 5.4 Incorporation of UKCC Level 4 competences into the conceptual framework.

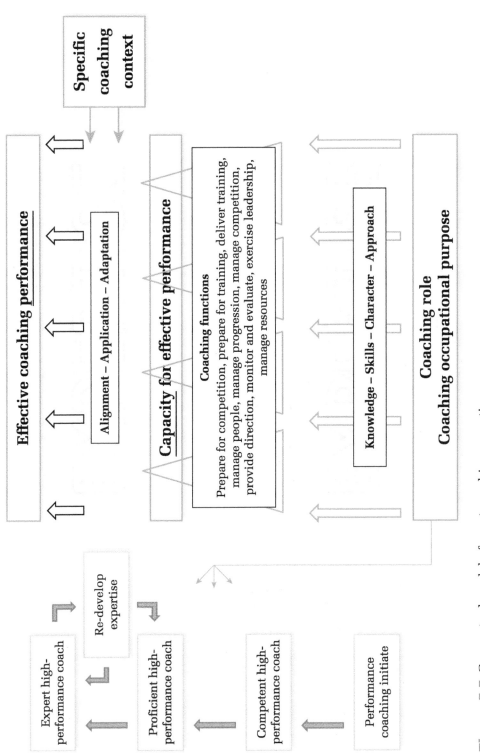

Figure 5.5 Conceptual model of sport coaching expertise.

3. Expertise is domain-specific (and the particular balance of capabilities is role and sport-specific). The domain, role and context provide a 'frame of reference' that defines both the likely expertise needed and a means of evaluating whether these have been adequately exercised (although our capacity for doing this is limited).
4. There are a number of issues that are not susceptible to being easily resolved:
   a. Are there any particular profiles or 'balance of capabilities' that are particularly effective?
   b. Do we accept lesser coaching performance because we accept that 'coaches cannot be good at everything'?
   c. Is our acceptance of particular (limited) profiles of capabilities a pragmatic response to poor coach education, absence of professional requirements and/or primacy of experience and technical knowledge?
   d. Anecdotally we are aware of coaches who have limited planning skills, capacity to manage interventions or poor relationship skills. Is it possible to 'appear' to have passable alignment skills without the supporting capabilities?
   e. It may be possible that coaches in high-status roles require a more limited range of both alignment and basic capabilities expertise (although subject to greater scrutiny).
5. The alignment skills are based on using coaching expertise capabilities to match the coach's behaviour and intervention to the needs of the athletes, goals and context. This is relatively easy to conceptualise but also difficult to assess. Do we have the capacity to evaluate this level of coaching expertise? Is it only visible when there appears to be an evident mismatch?
6. Coaching policy makers have attempted to take 'standard of athlete performance' out of the debate about expertise. However, this is another way of identifying athlete needs, and from this one can infer intensity of preparation, sophistication of performance development, social and psychological 'pressures', lifestyle implications and the complexity of the coaching 'team'. These factors determine the alignment parameters. Is it time to acknowledge that being highly effective in the high-performance domain requires the most developed quality of expertise?
7. A tremendous range of personal qualities was identified. It is necessary to distinguish the necessary from the desirable. The necessary qualities are those that make highly effective coaching practice more likely. This raises the question of whether these qualities are capable of being developed in individuals, pre-dispose some individuals to want to be coaches or are criteria for recruitment and selection.
8. The capability elements of expertise we might assume have developed from the deliberate acquisition of knowledge and skills, leading ultimately to a capacity to operate within any combination of circumstances. The development of the alignment skills is a challenge that coach education has not yet dealt with. Are we to assume that this might consist of (in addition to basic capabilities) developing the underlying contributory skills (decision making, problem solving), an experiential element and structured intervention (feedback).
9. Note that in most professions the knowledge required for a minimum level of capacity, and subsequently professional expertise, is assumed to be needed. The majority of professionals, therefore, go through extended degree courses and probationary training *before* practice. In relation to coaching expertise: (a) is it

110

different in some way, or are we accepting a lesser 'expression' of expertise? And (b) do we place the emphasis on the second level of expertise (the alignment) because this can be 'faked' more easily? (It is interesting that 'confidence' is identified as a characteristic of experts – perhaps because of an ability to cope with the unexpected or challenging situations, but note that 'confidence' is recognised as a substitute for expertise in the literature.)

10. Role is very important because it delimits the necessary expertise. Head coaches may rely on other professionals and may 'need' a limited range of capabilities (for example, relationship management, selection, tactical awareness). We may need to 'map' expertise across roles in each of our sports.

11. The literature distinguishes between routine and adaptive expertise (Hatano & Inagaki 1986). The 'adaptive' would appear to be a fairly apt description of our alignment element of expertise, which deals with the emergent, contingent conditions. It seems likely that coaches will employ a significant amount of 'relatively routine' practice (well-tried interventions) in order to make the day-to-day business of coaching 'less-effortful'. Identifying this routine expertise and the thresholds and catalysts for change may be a useful area for exploration.

    Although it may not be possible to identify a 'template' that can be applied to all contexts, coaches appear to use routines/templates with a reasonably 'wide' coverage. It may be that research will identify that coaches with the most developed expertise are able to 'tweak' their routines/templates in the most effective way to suit the athletes/context.

12. Within the alignment/application expertise, it will be possible to separate the deliberative (time to consider) alignment (planning, intervention content) from the less-deliberative (contingency because of injury, inter-personal disharmony, weather, recent results, missed performance targets, match coaching, micro-management of interventions, or crisis).

13. The word 'craft' is often used. This refers to the skills elements of expertise (output-related activity) and may be subject to our concept of capability and performance. Thus coaches may have a capacity for planning or delivering (pedagogy), but in practice this can be subject to the alignment criterion – is it appropriate for the circumstances?

14. The alignment element of expertise is not evident to the public (and other stake-holders), nor easily researched. Capabilities can be compared to non-experts, but the alignment skills and practice are difficult to simulate and replicate for research purposes. It is difficult to demonstrate that coach A is better/worse than coach B.

15. A different language for coach education and coach development may be required. One interviewee used the term *sensitive to variables within the training and competition environments* – apt, but not easily recognised. Problem solving, tailoring and adapting activity, reading the environment (situational analysis, pattern recognition), contingency planning, intuitive decision making and using mental models may become part of the development language.

16. One of the criticisms of stage models is that they describe a 'linear' development of expertise that is not evident in practice. In other words, the capabilities in the 'pillars' do not develop at the same rate. It is clearly possible for a coach to be more advanced in some capabilities than others. We do not have a practical answer to this; it is easy to say that stages should be interpreted flexibly and that

'domain shift' may allow the same profile of capabilities to be interpreted as being at different stages in the model.

17. One of the capabilities that are needed in some sports is the management of the competition itself (coaching from the sidelines – but including the pre- and post-routines that are part of the episode). This is a particular form of intervention and the anecdotal observation that some coaches are better than others suggests that it is worthy of investigation as part of expertise. It has been singled out as it is often neglected in accounts of coaching skills.

18. It has been suggested that there may be a link between stage of development (assuming it to mean advanced skills in the 'later' stages) and athlete outcomes. For example, it should be more evident as the coach moves from competent to expert (in the Berliner model) that better performances would follow. This is not completely convincing, although the nicety of correspondence between the two, expertise and athlete outcomes, can be appreciated. In practice, as coaches gain more experience and are associated with successful athletes, they are appointed to work with better athletes (or are approached by the athletes, or recruit more successfully). Thus there is a constant and circular association between experience, 'coaching track record' and athlete outcomes. However, there are a number of unresolved issues: how long does an association between coach and athlete have to have been established before the coach could be said to 'take credit' for the athlete's performance? Can the coach be just as expert with a slightly lesser athlete? However, we might reasonably suggest that the higher levels of expertise should mean that the coach is more likely to optimise progress for athletes – and doubly so for the elite athlete as the decisions about appropriate interventions will be more subtle. It may be difficult to substantiate this!

19. To reiterate, coaching expertise is a latent capacity *and* a performance element that becomes evident when the coach draws upon the capacity reservoir to produce a coaching intervention that best suits the needs of the athlete and situation. There is little doubt that the synthesis and pertinence (alignment, adaptation, alignment) element of expertise constitutes the essence of coaching expertise and it is this (in its domain context) that distinguishes sport coaches from other professionals.

 SUMMARY

This chapter should have familiarised you with the following:

- Common descriptors and definitions of expertise.
- The distinction between coaches' capacity and performance.
- Components of expertise as identified by a panel of expert coach developers.
- The importance of accommodation to context in the coach's expertise.
- A number of diagrams that synthesise the findings into a conceptual model of expertise.
- A series of discussion point and questions to stimulate your studies.

PROJECTS

1. Discuss with three expert coaches how they have dealt with similar situations. Try to identify how they have adapted their approach to solving the problems that arose.
2. Observe and interview three coaches in different coaching domains. Ask them to identify their priorities and which aspects of their expertise they rely on most. Consider the likelihood that coaching expertise applies across all domains.
3. Interview coaches of athletes in three distinctive sports (performance, game, race). Compare the profiles of their expertise components. Can you identify the key aspect of the sport-specific environment that impact most on their expertise?
4. Discuss and debate with your colleagues. How can the adaptive/alignment element of coaching expertise be fostered through coach development?

NOTES

1 We are grateful to UK Sport, who originally funded the project, for permission to use the report as a basis for the chapter.
2 Kevin Bowring, Rugby Football Union; Andy Bradshaw, sport coach UK; Sarah Craven, UK Sport; Bryan Jones, University of Central Lancashire; Gordon Lord, English Cricket Board; Alan Lynn, University of Stirling; Rosie Mayglothling, British Rowing; David Mellor, Royal Yachting Association; Bob Muir, Leeds Metropolitan University; Alan Olive, UK Sport; Jayne Powell, English Hockey; Richard Wheater, English Athletics.
3 Direct quotations from the coach developers are presented in italics.

FURTHER READING

Austin, N. C., Sparrow, W. A., & Sherman, C. A. (2007). Skills of expert basketball coaches: An investigative study. *Applied Research in Coaching & Athletics Annual, 22,* 149–173.

Chi, M. T. H. (2006). Two approaches to the study of experts' characteristics. In K. A. Ericsson, N. Charness, P. J. Feltovitch, & R. R. Hoffman (Eds) *The Cambridge Handbook of Expertise and Expert Performance.* New York: Cambridge University Press, 21–30.

Côté, J., & Gilbert, W. (2009). An integrative definition of coaching effectiveness and expertise. *International Journal of Sports Science & Coaching, 4*(3), 307–323.

Côté, J., Young, B., North, J., & Duffy, P. (2007). Towards a definition of excellence in sport coaching. *International Journal of Coaching Science, 1,* 3–18.

Ericsson, K. A., Charness, N., Feltovitch, P. J., & Hoffman, R. R. (Eds) (2006). *The Cambridge Handbook of Expertise and Expert Performance*. New York: Cambridge University Press.

Jones, R. L., Bowes, I., & Kingston, K. (2010). Complex practice in coaching: Studying the chaotic nature of coach–athlete interactions. In J. Lyle & C. Cushion (Eds) *Sports Coaching: Professionalisation and Practice*. Edinburgh: Churchill Livingstone, 15–25.

Jones, R. L., & Wallace, M. (2006). The coach as 'orchestrator': More realistically managing the complex coaching context. In R. L. Jones (Ed.) *The Sports Coach as Educator: Re-conceptualising Sports Coaching*. London: Routledge, 51–64.

Kahneman, D. (2011). *Thinking, Fast and Slow*. London: Allen Lane.

Turner, D., Nelson, L., & Potrac, P. (2012). The journey is the destination: Reconsidering the expert sports coach. *Quest, 64*, 313–325.

REFERENCES

Abraham, A., & Collins, D. (2011). Effective skill development: How should athletes' skills be developed? In D. Collins, A. Button, & H. Richards (Eds) *Performance Psychology: A Practitioner's Guide*. Edinburgh: Churchill Livingstone, 207–230.

Abraham, A., Collins, D., & Martindale, R. (2006). The coaching schematic: Validation through expert coach consensus. *Journal of Sports Sciences, 24*(6), 549–564.

Bailey, R., Stafford, I., & Navin, A. (2011). *The UKCC Level 4 Support Guide*. Leeds: sports coach UK.

Berliner, D. C. (2004). Describing the behaviour and documenting the accomplishments of expert teachers. *Bulletin of Science, Technology and Society, 24*(1), 200–212.

Collins, D., Burke, V., Martindale, A., & Cruickshank, A. (2015). The illusion of competency versus the desirability of expertise: Seeking a common standard for support professions in sport. *Sports Medicine, 45*, 1–7.

Duffy, P., Hartley, H., Bales, J., Crespo, M., Dick, F., Vardhan, D., Nordmann, L., & Curado, J. (2011). Sport coaching as a 'profession': Challenges and future directions. *International Journal of Coaching Science, 5*(2), 93–123.

Ericsson, K. A. (2006). An introduction to *The Cambridge Handbook of Expertise and Expert Performance*: Its development, organisation and content. In K. A. Ericsson, N. Charness, P. J. Feltovitch, & R. R. Hoffman (Eds) *The Cambridge Handbook of Expertise and Expert Performance*. New York: Cambridge University Press, 3–19.

Gilbert, W. D., & Côté, J. (2013). Defining coaching effectiveness: Focus on coaches' knowledge. In P. Potrac, W. Gilbert, & J. Denison (Eds) *Routledge Handbook of Sports Coaching*. London: Routledge, 147–159.

Hatano, G., & Inagaki, K. (1986). Two courses of expertise. In H. Stevenson, H. Azuma, & K. Hakuta (Eds) *Child Development and Education in Japan*. New York: Freeman, 263–272.

Lyle, J. (2002). *Sports Coaching Concepts*. London: Routledge.

Nash, C. S., Martindale, R., Collins, D., & Martindale, A. (2012). Parameterising expertise in coaching: Past, present and future. *Journal of Sports Sciences, 30*(210), 985–995.

Expertise in sport coaching

CHAPTER 6

MODELLING THE COACHING PROCESS

CHAPTER OUTLINE

- Introduction
- What is meant by a model?
- Problems in model building
- An evaluation of existing models
- Models: application, constraints, implementation
- Summary
- Projects

INTRODUCTION

This chapter focuses on the extent to which sport coaching can be modelled. By that we mean the coaching process can be appropriately represented in such a way that it symbolises practice, is adequate for analysis, development and research, and adheres to a conceptual understanding of the coaching process. We will show that this task is far from easy, and is made more difficult by the 'processual' and multi-variable nature of sport coaching, and that no consensual model of the coaching process has emerged in recent years. The problems of model building are emphasised and the attempts of model builders to date are described and evaluated against a set of principles.

It is important that we set out our position on model building. We have already emphasised our belief that (a) sport coaching is a family term for a multitude of related leadership roles, and (b) the practice of sport coaching is so context- and situation-dependent that it can only be understood at the level of the particular. This is a problem for the model builder as it calls into question the capacity of any model to represent adequately such complexity.

We begin with a clarification of what is meant by a model and identify some of the difficulties in model construction. A number of models of sport coaching from the literature are briefly evaluated. The chapter closes with an examination of how models can be used for analysis, dealing with the vexed issue of application and reality constraints. In summary, the following statements represent the current 'state of play':

- There are no all-embracing models of the coaching process that have received consensual agreement (Abraham & Collins 2011a; Cushion 2007; Lyle & Cushion 2010).
- Models of practice have mistakenly been criticised for 'not being put into practice by coaches or coach developers'. This is a serious misunderstanding of the role and purpose of models. Coaches should not be 'adopting' any particular model; the model is a guide to analysts, developers and researchers.
- The 'coaching episode' is easier to model than the extended process and this has influenced the literature.
- The balance between the advantages of the generic model (albeit difficult to achieve and possibly to defend) and the advantages of sport-specific models has not been resolved.
- There are many prescriptive proposals for sport coaching practice but very few models 'of' coaching practice that have been derived from rigorous research. Côté et al. (1995) is an exception, and their model is discussed later in this chapter. On the other hand, the elaboration of the model (Côté et al. 2010) is a set of prescriptive proposals for coaching practice.
- The shortcomings in the literature identified earlier in the book – absence of stated assumptions and lack of conceptual vocabulary – are evident in model building.
- There are a number of sources that have discussed the use of models in sport coaching. In general, these accounts point to the shortcomings of existing attempts without producing alternative models (Cushion et al. 2006).
- The 'coaching schematic' (Abraham et al. 2006; Abraham & Collins 2011b) is a form of 'eclectic' model that attempts to bridge the divide between models 'for' and models 'of' coaching (with an emphasis on coaches' decision making).

A number of earlier attempts at modelling are reviewed in the latter part of the chapter. Each of these models has something useful to offer but each exemplifies the difficulties and shortcomings of model building in sport coaching. There are also many examples of 'part-models' – detailed accounts of sub-processes within the coaching process (for example, see Saury and Durand (1998) for an excellent example of this) – but these do not amount to models. Therefore, it would be reasonable to ask why so much time is being devoted to models of coaching when it is clear from the outset that this is such a challenging enterprise. The capacity to devise appropriate and perhaps diverse models is one measure of the health of the conceptual development of the field. It is important, therefore, to evaluate the state of play and to contribute to the development of this feature of academic development in sport coaching. The intention of this chapter, therefore, is not simply to review existing attempts but to contribute to future developments.

WHAT IS MEANT BY A MODEL?

The outcomes of the sport coaching process are observable in athlete performances and athlete and coach behaviours. However, the coaching process itself is a construct, an abstraction. The purpose of this abstraction (the conceptual framework) is to provide a mechanism for better understanding the observable practice. A model can be used to describe the components of the phenomenon (for example, the coaching process) and the relationship between the components.

 KEY CONCEPT

A model is a representation of the relational aspects of (usually) complex phenomena by using symbols or simplified descriptions that help to conceptualise the phenomenon itself.

Most individuals would be familiar with the notion of a replica model – that is, a smaller representation of a physical object, often capable of being 'taken to pieces' to demonstrate 'how it works'. On the other hand, models of the coaching process are symbolic representations. These may appear to have a different function, but really they are designed for much the same purpose. Models are valuable for:

- description and scoping;
- explaining relationships between components;
- analysing practice by 'comparative' methods;
- focusing attention on more discrete features of the process;
- providing guidelines for research and education; and
- (potentially) predicting outcomes.

The potential for predicting outcomes (for example, how much performance will improve with a given process) by replacing default values in a model with real measures is an appealing prospect. The more the inter-relationships in a model can be specified and the components quantified, the more likely is prediction. However, it will not come as a surprise to learn that the great majority of sport coaching components cannot easily be quantified. The common practice of representing relationships by lines or arrows, or by juxtaposition, has an apparent simplicity. However, these connections imply *causal*, *sequential* and *conditional* qualities, the dimensions of which may not yet be justified by research. It may be possible to predict performance 'gains' in some individual (usually power-repetitive technique) sports, although the environmental effects are difficult to measure and control. On the other hand, there have been few attempts to predict the outcome of a coaching process. This seems likely to be a result of the difficulty in controlling the enormous range of variables that influence performance. Subsequent evaluation will demonstrate that the models available have been more concerned to describe, rather than predict.

Modelling the sport coaching process should underpin any analysis of coaching behaviour and performance, and is central to evaluating effectiveness. A key feature of modelling is that it normally embraces a set of assumptions about performance, performance enhancement, social interactions and the coaching role. These assumptions have a conceptual basis that is rarely specified. As a result, there are few models of the sport coaching process and certainly none that have achieved consensual agreement or application. One of the objectives for this chapter is to develop in the reader a capacity to examine in a critical fashion any attempts to model the sport coaching process.

It has been acknowledged that models are representations of phenomena, the complexity of which is difficult to represent solely in words. A visual/spatial/relational representation allows an enhanced appreciation of the phenomenon and its qualities. It is important at this point to acknowledge that the term 'model' has tended to be used for a range of representations ranging from simple diagrams to mathematical and complex modelling that allows some degree of prediction. There are also many limitations in building and displaying models. Among other problems, it is not easy to represent complex interactions, the impact of context, continuity of process, variation in scale and variations in practice. The most commonly used two-dimensional representations have inherent limitations.

 KEY CONCEPT

Models are generalised representations and are not causal at the level of the individual.

In order to critique the literature more easily, it would be helpful to categorise the various types of models and the purposes for which they might most appropriately be used. Table 6.1 describes the common types of models.

Extreme care must be taken with the casual use of the term 'model' when authors are intent merely to give a visual reinforcement of their ideas. This is evident in 'lists' or diagrams of sub-categories of phenomena, which have no explanatory powers and no sense of relationship between components.

Models 'of' the coaching process are derived from a description and analysis of coaching practice. Of course, the variety in practice, the domain specificity and a unique aggregation of contextual features would pose problems for generating an all-embracing model, but this process has the advantage of a strong relationship between principles and practice. We have already suggested that an all-embracing generic conceptualisation of sport coaching is not appropriate. The model 'of' approach is very like the 'case-building' approach in the social sciences. On the other hand, the model 'for' the coaching process begins from a set of assumptions about sport coaching and builds a more idealistic or conceptual model for practice.

Table 6.1 Common types of models

Type	Feature	Purposes
Diagram	Visual representation; reinforcement; modest relational qualities; usually simplistic abstraction from practice	[Understanding]
Model	Represents structure and process; indicates the relationship of the parts	Understanding [Analysis]
Operational model	Represents a function or process; shows 'how it works'. Model 'of', usually derived from practice or research	Understanding Analysis Prediction
Ideal model	Idealised representation; shows 'how it *should* be'. Model 'for', but should be able to say what the assumptions for the model are.	Understanding Analysis Prediction Planning
Planning model	Represents intentions; somewhere between operational model and ideal model. Real-life parameters built in.	Understanding Analysis Prediction Planning
Normative model	Identifies elements in a process but with less emphasis on specific relationship of parts; used for development and education purposes	Understanding Analysis Education
Schematic	Often called a schematic diagram; represents a process through symbols and concepts; not intended to be realistic; the emphasis is on a visual representation of elements and relationships	Understanding Analysis Education
Also:		
Conceptual model	Helps to reflect/represent relationships between concepts and/or ideas. Useful for setting up research. Doesn't describe the particularity of practice	Understanding Analysis

The model builder may not expect the model to be found in practice in exactly its idealised form, but it provides a useful analytical tool for identifying the issues that are worthy of further attention.

Models are used for a variety of purposes. They may model intentions at the planning stage or be used to evaluate practice. They may also be used to help understand the implications of particular practice. For this reason it is important that we should be able to make judgements about the worthiness or appropriateness of a model. The following questions would be a valuable beginning in determining the usefulness of a coaching process model:

- How comprehensive is it? Does it attempt an all-embracing description of the process?
- Is it easy to understand? Are the key features easily discernible?
- Is it accurate/representative? Does it have an immediate sense of being valid?
- How does it describe variations in practice? (This, of course, would be an ambitious task.)

- Does it build towards an outcome? Is it predictive? (Operational and planning models.)
- Is it sufficiently detailed to be discriminating and, therefore, useful for analysis?
- Does it apply to all domains? How have contextual features been built into the model?
- Is it clear how the process described represents practical/concrete manifestations of sport coaching behaviour?
- How well is progression/continuity represented?
- Can it be quantified (mathematical models only)?
- Is the nature of the relationship between component parts (if A then B) established? Have the linkages been described in terms of direction, strength and causal condition?

Given this demanding list of questions, it would be reasonable to wonder whether there are any good/useful models. Clearly this is not an easy business! At this stage in the evolution of sport coaching as a social phenomenon, a concept and a profession, there would appear to be no acceptable models with universal application. We have already noted that domain specificity and the context-dependency of the coaching process means that coaching practice can only be understood at the level of the particular. This suggests that models that are sufficiently practice-like would be almost impossibly detailed and models that have more extended application may be so 'reduced' as to be almost meaningless.

 QUESTION BOX

Models are representations of reality. They are not 'used' by coaches but are available for education and analysis purposes. Nevertheless, this raises the question of whether the principles embedded in the model are (a) used in coach education design, and (b) sufficiently understood by coach developers to be used for these purposes.

PROBLEMS IN MODEL BUILDING

There are some general problems that model builders will have to overcome in modelling the coaching process:

- The coaching process is not an inert system. The human behaviour element invokes issues of volition, emotion and cognitive organisation and decision making, which are difficult to represent and replicate.
- The scope of the coaching process involves direct intervention in training and competition, intervention support, constraints management and a meta-cognitive adaptation, integration and coordination that is largely a mental exercise. Although

the coaching process may be individualised, it often applies to large groups of performers.

■ Many of the variables that influence performance and performance enhancement are inter-dependent. However, this is a complex pattern of inter-dependency with variables co-acting, interacting and sequence dependent. In addition, the process is mediated by a similarly complex set of short-, medium- and longer-term goals and objectives.

■ Despite the best attempts of the sport scientists, performance enhancement is not a linear process, nor is the output/improvement related to inputs (training) in a constant fashion. While simple measures of performance components such as strength or power may be more predictable and manageable, complex game skills with opponent interference are much more difficult to track.

■ The model builder must choose between modelling a generic core process that is manageable and attempting to create a sufficiently all-embracing and sophisticated model that resonates with practice. Core process models may be useful analogies, but may not be sufficiently detailed or 'applied' to be helpful in analysing practice.

■ The picture that is emerging is that of a coaching process that is largely a cognitive exercise both in planning and in expert execution. Illustrating this cognitive activity and integrating it with more observable activity is a significant challenge for the model builder.

■ One further challenge is the paucity of systematic data collection (particularly given the potential quantity of data available) with which researchers can establish insights into the relationships between process components.

It is also important to pay attention to one further problem. Performance sport coaching is a process and the serial and dynamic nature of a process is difficult to capture in a model. In addition to the questions identified above, it will be necessary to incorporate the essential features of a process, which can then be used as an evaluation tool. Table 6.2 identifies the components of a process and the consequent coaching issues to be integrated into a model of practice.

Table 6.2 Process components and coaching issues

Process component	Evaluation	Sample coaching issue
Initiation	What is the catalyst for beginning the process? How is this related to performance development systems?	Is this stage dependent on the talent identification process? What are the criteria for establishing the contract?
Development	What is the essential nature of the process? How can this be demonstrated in the model?	Adaptation of the athlete is the goal of the coaching process. To what extent is this compatible with other objectives?

(continued)

121

Table 6.2 Process components and coaching issues *(continued)*

Process component	Evaluation	Sample coaching issue
Operation	How can the different forms of delivery be illustrated and integrated?	Can the model overcome the tendency to focus on the direct intervention stage?
Progression	Process implies a cyclical aspect to the model. How can this be displayed? Is there a feedback mechanism for controlling progression?	Has there been sufficient research on the threshold criteria applied by coaches to regulate progress?
Monitoring	Are monitoring stages built into the model? How responsive is the model to changes in status?	Is coaching practice sufficiently systematic to generate monitoring data and to be able to incorporate this into practice?
Contingency	Is the model able to incorporate unplanned variance in performance and changes to the environment?	How stable is the environment in particular sports? Does this influence the degree of forward planning possible?
Evaluation	Does the model work towards an outcome? How is this 'goal direction' incorporated into the model?	Evaluation of the coaching process is central to measuring the effectiveness of the coach.
Termination	Is a 're-consideration of the "contract"' stage built into the model?	Which criteria are used to decide on the appropriateness of continuation?

The difficulties of model building have become clear and, although the principles through which existing examples might be evaluated have been established, the demands are very challenging. The chapter continues by presenting and evaluating a number of attempts to model the process. The examples have been chosen because they illustrate some of the difficulties involved and because they are cited most often in the literature.

AN EVALUATION OF EXISTING MODELS

In the first edition of this book a number of early models of the coaching process were evaluated (Franks *et al.* 1986; Fairs 1987; Côté *et al.* 1995; Sherman *et al.* 1997). Collectively these were rather limited attempts to represent the coaching process, although the emphasis on coaching as a process was encouraging. The conclusions, when evaluated against the model-building criteria, were that each 'model' had something to offer but that none of them were comprehensive or dealt with the situational or complexity features of the process that we have identified earlier. The Franks and colleagues model identified an episodic sequence that resonated with team sport processes, and usefully demonstrated the importance of regulation/ goal setting and the contingency impact of regular matches. The Fairs model was a simple objectives model with no real application to sport coaching. The model of Sherman and colleagues was narrowly focused on a skills instruction. With each of the models, the conceptual framework was a useful analytical tool, but the models themselves made no contribution to developing the framework.

The 'mental model' of Côté *et al.* (1995) is deserving of some attention. It continues to be widely cited (Gordon 2009) and was identified as an influential paper in coaching science (Rangeon *et al.* 2012). This model is different in that it is a model 'of' coaching, being derived from the experiences, opinions and insights of expert gymnastics coaches, although notably not from an analysis of coaching practices. There are a number of distinguishing features of what the authors term a 'conceptual model'. There is a prioritising of coaching process components and an acknowledgement that there are significant limitations in the extent to which teaching paradigm conceptualisations of coaching adequately represent its complexity. The distinction between core and peripheral process elements is similar to the distinction between direct intervention/intervention support and constraints management. However, the most interesting contribution is the centrality of the coaches' 'mental model' of athlete potential, moving beyond the observable behaviour of the coach and reinforcing the cognitive nature of sport coaching.

It is not immediately obvious that this is a process model. The authors use the phrase 'constantly monitored and adjusted', but the dynamics of the process are explored in insufficient detail. As a conceptual model (perhaps simply a diagram), it is not immediately representative of practice, and its various elements are identified rather than the potential relationships between them exemplified.

The richness of the empirical data has not been fully represented in this particular conceptualisation of the coaching process. The emphasis may have been on the coaches' knowledge structures, and this has limited the process elements of progression and regulation. Nevertheless, the mental-model construct points usefully to the mechanism for operationalising the coaches' expertise. The limitations of conceptual diagrams/models for analysis purposes are illustrated in this example. The advantages of simplicity and reduction to core constructs have to be set against the absence of sufficient process detail to adequately represent the complexity and scope of performance coaching practice.

A more recent model that deserves attention is the 'coaching schematic' (Abraham *et al.* 2006; Abraham & Collins 2011b). The authors' stated objective was to "accurately reflect the coaching process in its entirety" (Abraham *et al.* 2006, p. 550), and is a mixture of normative (what it should be like) and empirical validation (being compared to coaches' descriptions of their practice). It would be accurate to say that it is a very useful identification of the varied elements of the coaching process, with some value for education and training. The emphasis on coaches' decision making is particularly useful.

However, as with other models, there are some significant limitations. The authors state that the schematic should be applied irrespective of situation or context. Given our emphasis on the context-dependency of the coaching process and the need for adaptation and application, this is not convincing. There is no sense in the schematic of the dynamic flow of the processes involved, or their iterative nature. The text accompanying the schematic provides some valuable detail of the coaches' reported behaviour and practice.

The schematic has been further developed by Abraham and colleagues and has formed the basis of a model of the coach's decision-making process (see Muir *et al.* 2011; Abraham *et al.* 2015). The model identifies three main considerations – an understanding of the athlete, the sport and teaching and learning – and emphasises the wider social environment with which practice takes place. This model of the key elements of coaches' expertise illustrates the limitations of such diagrams. The essential features of the (decision-making) process are identified, but there is no dynamic to the process and the nature of the inter-relationships are not specified. Such models perform the function of normative models: they have an element of prescription and identify development-related aspects that are very valuable for analysing practice.

MODELS: APPLICATION, CONSTRAINTS, IMPLEMENTATION

The next chapter describes a proposed model for the coaching process. However, before that some consideration is given to the further development and application of models. The clear message thus far is that the importance of modelling the coaching process has been established, but that attempts to date have fallen short of what is required. It is worth stressing that, notwithstanding the inherent complexity of the coaching process, models can never reproduce the subtlety and nuances of real life and there is a danger of expecting too much. The model should be fit for its purpose. A second point is that model building and use should be a dynamic affair. Broadly, the process could look like this:

1. begin with theories, collected wisdom and assumptions;
2. decide on the type of model required;
3. develop the model;
4. test the aptness of the model by comparing to practice;
5. modify initial assumptions;
6. re-design the model; and
7. retest.

This then becomes an iterative process with the model being constantly refined either through comparisons with practice or being informed by more specific research output.

We take the opportunity to emphasise the fact that models represent elements of practice. Although they may be helpful to coach educators, it is never intended that coaches should use such models directly to amend their practice. There are three principal uses for models, and these are re-emphasised here:

1. *Education and training:* an accepted model and interpretation of the coaching process should be the basis for coaching education and training. However, it is

not evident that detailed models or the output of research on performance coaching have yet become the basis of coach education in the UK (Abraham & Collins 1998). Recent conceptualisations of coaching have emphasised decision-making skills and the development of adaptive expertise (Abraham & Collins 2011b). Our experience of coach education suggests that coach education is not yet configured to emphasise these features.

2. *Research*: we expand upon this in a subsequent chapter. For the moment it is enough to say that the model can help to identify the questions to which the researchers should turn their attentions, and researchers should attempt to 'populate' these models. For example, which decision-making heuristics are used by coaches of team sports during matches (cf. Debanne & Chauvin 2014)? Which criteria are employed by coaches to evaluate satisfactory progression towards training targets? Parts of a model might be assessed against the practice of expert coaches in a range of sports to test the applicability of the model.

3. *Analysis and understanding*: analysis of practice is often carried out in order that the lessons learned can be incorporated into future practice. This may be part of personal development or an accountability exercise to evaluate the coach's performance. Data on coaching practice and contextual resource features can be compared to the model with the intention of understanding how goals have or have not been achieved. This can (perhaps more easily and sensibly) be done on sub-processes within coaching practice, for the purpose of understanding and developing expertise.

Analysis of the issues that arise from research into performance coaching practice and the discontinuities between these and current models would help to generate an understanding of performance coaching practice. The lack of consensus in conceptualising coaching practice points to the paucity of appropriate research, the failure to communicate widely and the absence of a useful model.

In the context of the above, it is reasonable to ask what further developments might be expected in model building. Table 6.3 incorporates some speculation of the future of model building. However, this table is largely reproduced from the first edition, and we invite the reader to judge how much progress has been made.

Two comments that are sometimes heard when discussing models are that (a) they cannot be put into practice; and (b) they are pointless without understanding the context of practice – in particular the infinite variety of idiosyncratic responses to situational demands. This raises a number of issues:

- Models are intended to be used in the ways described in this chapter. They are not designed to be adopted by individuals, although the models can help with analysis and subsequent development of practice.
- All coaching practice is idiosyncratic and unique. We have already emphasised that it can only be fully understood at the level of the particular – aggregation may have limited value. It is the complexity and uniqueness that brings challenge to its study. Nevertheless, there are regularities and patterns of behaviour that can be identified. Two matters are relevant:

Table 6.3 The future of model building in sport coaching

Models 'of'	Models 'for'
Greater attention to *in situ* research into coaching practice should lead to more modelling based on empirical investigations of practice.	Models 'for' coaching will continue to be the 'bridge' between academic disciplines and coaching, e.g. psychology, decision making and coaching behaviour.
It is unlikely that detailed and all-embracing models 'of' the coaching process will be the focus. Rather, research and subsequent models will be targeted at sub-processes.	Models 'for' will continue to be used as templates for research and to reflect theory development. These will become increasingly refined as research paradigms are more precisely delineated and applied.
More sophisticated models of novice and expert practice will become important features of education and professional development.	Models 'for' will be used to analyse practice. However, attention may well turn from components and structure to 'what works for whom and in what circumstances'.
Comparative model building will be encouraged. This may be domain-specific, cross-cultural or merely across sports.	Simplified models may be used to understand the influence of different sets of constraints on the performance coaching process.

1. Models 'of' usually involve some aggregation and 'averaging' of practice in order to generalise. Case studies may help to overcome this, as will an emphasis on effective practice in context.
2. Highlighting the dissonance between individual practice and the models is a very valuable mechanism for identifying the elements of practice worthy of investigation.

- The issue of sport specificity is likely to be solved in the future by the creation of a 'family of models'. Individual/team/elite/performance/representative models will follow from increased domain specificity and appreciation of role.
- The charge that constraints must be taken into account is a powerful one. This is partly what is meant by suggesting that future research will be focused on relationships between components. In other words, we know what the decision is that needs to be taken, but what do coaches do in a variety of situations? How does restricted competition access, athlete injury or underachievement of training targets affect decision making in various situations? The answer is not to create a huge number of variations of models, but to focus on contingency planning, the criteria used by coaches to make decisions and the coaches' access to an effective repertoire of solutions. This will increase our understanding of how the context influences coaching practice.

The way forward is not to argue about the component parts of the coaching process. There will be a fair measure of agreement over these, although some models may be more detailed than others. Attention must be focused on the coaches' practice represented in the implementation of the model. This is why the examples of

Modelling the coaching process

decision criteria, thresholds for progression and contingency factors are constantly emphasised. Inevitably this reinforces the central theme of the conceptual framework thus far that coaching is essentially a cognitive exercise with elements of craft delivery.

 SUMMARY

This chapter should have familiarised you with the following:

- The current status of modelling the coaching process.
- A definition of a model and common presentation of models.
- The distinction between models 'of' and models 'for' coaching.
- Questions with which to judge the usefulness of models.
- The problems inherent in model construction.
- The elements of any process that need to be incorporated into a coaching model.
- Issues of implementation and application.
- Likely developments in model construction.

 PROJECTS

We would not expect you to create a 'model'; become familiar with the process and limitations.

1. Engage in the creative process. Devise a possible model of one function within coaching (match coaching, managing a training session) and invite six coaches to contribute contextual features that will bring it to life.
2. Assumptions are important in model building. Review four research articles and catalogue their assumptions about the coaching process. Consider whether these assumptions would be useful in model building and demonstrate why.
3. Choose two components of the coaching process and consider in depth the relationship between them and how this might be represented in a model.
4. Select one process characteristic (e.g. contingency, progression). Consider how that characteristic could be incorporated into a coaching process model.
5. Use the readings and 'usefulness' questions to devise your own table of strengths and weaknesses.
6. Consider your experience of coach education. Was a 'model' of coaching practice made evident? Discuss this with a tutor.

REFERENCES

Abraham, A., & Collins, D. (1998). Examining and extending research in coach development. *Quest, 50*, 55–79.

Abraham, A., & Collins, D. (2011a). Taking the next step: Ways forward for coaching science. *Quest, 63*(4), 366–384.

Abraham, A., & Collins, D. (2011b). Effective skill development: How should athletes' skills be developed? In D. Collins, Button, A., & Richards, H. (Eds) *Performance Psychology: A Practitioner's Guide*. Edinburgh: Churchill Livingstone, 207–230.

Abraham, A., Collins, D., & Martindale, R. (2006). The coaching schematic: Validation through expert coach consensus. *Journal of Sports Sciences, 24*(6), 549–564.

Abraham, A., Saiz, S., McKeown, S., Morgan, G., Muir, B., North, J., & Till, K. (2015). Planning your coaching: A focus on youth participation development. In C. Nash (Ed.) *Practical Sports Coaching*. Abingdon: Routledge, 16–53.

Côté, J., Bruner, M., Erickson, K., Strachan, L., & Fraser-Thomas, J. (2010). Athlete development and coaching. In J. Lyle & C. Cushion (Eds) *Sports Coaching: Professionalisation and Practice*. Edinburgh: Churchill Livingstone, 64–83.

Côté, J., Salmela, J. H., Trudel, P., Baria, A., & Russell, S. (1995). The coaching model: A grounded assessment of expert gymnastic coaches' knowledge. *Journal of Sport and Exercise Psychology, 17*(1), 1–17.

Cushion, C. J. (2007). Modelling the complexities of the coaching process. *International Journal of Sports Science & Coaching, 2*(4), 395–401.

Cushion, C. J., Armour, K. M., & Jones, R. L. (2006). Locating the coaching process in practice models: Models 'for' and 'of' coaching. *Physical Education and Sport Pedagogy, 11*, 83–99.

Debanne, T., & Chauvin, C. (2014). Modes of cognitive control in official game handball coaching. *Journal of Cognitive Engineering and Decision Making, 8*(3), 283–298.

Fairs, J. (1987). The coaching process: The essence of coaching. *Sports Coach, 11*(1), 17–20.

Franks, I., Sinclair, G. D., Thomson, W., & Goodman, D. (1986). Analysis of the coaching process. *Science Periodical on Research and Technology in Sport*, January.

Gordon, D. (2009). *Coaching Science*. Exeter: Learning Matters.

Lyle, J., & Cushion, C. (2010). Narrowing the field: Some key questions about sports coaching. In J. Lyle & C. Cushion (Eds) *Sports Coaching: Professionalisation and Practice*. Edinburgh: Churchill Livingstone, 243–252.

Muir, B., Morgan, G., Abraham, A., & Morley, D. (2011). Developmentally appropriate approaches to coaching children. In I. Stafford (Ed.) *Coaching Children in Sport*. Abingdon: Routledge, 17–37.

Rangeon, S., Gilbert, W., & Bruner, M. (2012). Mapping the world of coaching science: A Citation Network Analysis. *Journal of Coaching Education, 5*(1), 83–108.

Saury, J., & Durand, M. (1998). Practical knowledge in expert coaches: On-site study of coaching in sailing. *Research Quarterly for Exercise and Sport, 69*(3), 254–266.

Sherman, C., Crassini, B., Maschette, W., & Sands, R. (1997). Instructional sport psychology: A reconceptualisation of sports coaching as sport instruction. *International Journal of Sport Psychology, 28*(2), 103–125.

Modelling the coaching process

CHAPTER 7

A PROPOSED MODEL FOR COACHING

CHAPTER OUTLINE

- Introduction
- Prior assumptions for the proposed model
- Identifying the building blocks
- The model
- Adapting the model
- Summary
- Projects

INTRODUCTION

In the previous chapter the issues in model building were explored and an overview of several early examples of models 'of' and 'for' the coaching process illustrated their inherent limitations. This chapter consists of an updated version of a proposed model for sport coaching, which is intended to act as a catalyst to further exploration of model building in this academic field of study. The proposed model both builds on the conceptual framework elaborated thus far, and is also a key part of the complete framework. The context and intentions are important. It is necessary to emphasise strongly that, as a model 'for' coaching, it is a template to be used to compare to practice and to stimulate research, and thereby to contribute to a gradual refining of our understanding of sport coaching. We acknowledge that the model has many of the weaknesses of model building already described. Nevertheless, by proposing a more detailed account of how coaches operationalise their coaching, it is intended to be more comprehensive and detailed than previous attempts.

Having acknowledged these limitations, it is necessary to describe the steps taken to obviate these as much as possible. Our purpose in the first part of this chapter is to present an ideal model of the coaching process. The use of the ideal model is a feature of the work of seminal sociologist Max Weber (Albrow 1990). It can be argued that practice models developed from aggregating the behaviour of many examples of that practice will provide a cumulative overview of the phenomenon but will have limited value for describing, or perhaps understanding, the practice of the range of individuals who make up that population. Such a model describes the behaviour and practice of an 'average' coach – one who does not actually exist. Better therefore to work with case histories or to construct an ideal model against which empirical descriptions of practice can be compared, based on the action that would be taken in the rational and informed pursuit of appropriate objectives in constraint-free conditions. It is very important to stress that the model is not intended as a coach development tool – that is, as a template for practice. It is a catalyst for researchers and should be continually refined as research evidence gradually increases our understanding of the process.

■ The ideal model is based on the question 'What would the rational coach do if there were no contextual limitations?'. The researcher may then demonstrate how the reality of practice requires the coach to adapt the process (and perhaps expectations) in certain sets of circumstances.

■ Previous criticism of the model stresses its emphasis on a systematic linear approach, being too structured, and, since it cannot hope to account for all contextual eventualities, failing to account for the dynamics and untidiness of real practice. This fails to understand the nature of the model; it is a starting point against which the uncertainty and complexity of practice can be compared.

■ The issue is one of operationalisation. 'Ideal' models are not 'put into practice' – this is not their purpose. It is the operationalisation of practice that the researcher is invited to establish. You will recall that we have stated many times that coaching can only be understood in the particular – there is limited value in generalising across contexts. This model is intended to provide a common language and set of descriptors against which the implications of the particular can be evaluated.

■ It is necessary to identify a further and very important aspect of operationalisation. How does the coach actually carry out the coaching process? For the moment we might loosely term this the coach's expertise. The knowledge, skills and other features of expertise are brought to bear by the coach in order to bring the process to life. How the coach does this is part of the model and can be used as a framework against which an emerging appreciation of the coach's expertise can be compared. We devoted an earlier chapter to a conceptualisation of the coach's expertise.

■ We must also acknowledge that we have made much of the domain-specific nature of the coaching process. This model assumes a sufficiency of time and frequency of interaction, along with a stable relationship and the primacy of improved competition performance, and might therefore be thought of as performance coaching.

There is no doubt that the complexity, dynamic flow and context-dependent nature of the coaching process has been attested to by sport coaching academics. We can only agree that there is great difficulty in describing, conceptualising and portraying the actuality of practice. However, we hold to the view that too many writers have used this conceptualisation of coaching to stress the difficulties of both practice and

A proposed model for coaching

KEY CONCEPT

'Ideal' models are not 'put into practice' and are not coach development tools. They are intended to stimulate research and to provide a conceptual starting point against which the reality and particularity of coaching practice and the essence of coaching expertise can be compared.

description, without identifying the solutions. As in a previous paper (Lyle 2007), we emphasise our experience of coaching:

- Coaches have strategies for coping with complexity and uncertainty.
- Much of the process can be routinised, and coping strategies employed when a threshold of problem severity is breached.
- Coaches are able to maintain a focus on the instrumentality of the coaching process. This is goal/outcome driven and its stability is maintained by the planning process.
- Performance coaching has an interpersonal dimension that exists within, and is given meaning by, the specifics of the athlete/team goals and the social/organisational context.
- Although illustrated well in the dynamic interaction of team sports, there are many sports in which the coaching process can be characterised (for the most part) by a more measured and controlled environment.

As stated above, it is entirely accepted that it is not possible to construct (partly because of the problem of illustration) a model that represents all of coaching practice: 'a singular all-encompassing model may not be possible' (Cushion 2007, p. 395). The issues of domain specificity, particularity, context dependency and continuity act as barriers for the model builder and illustrator. This is in addition to the practical problems of illustrating in two dimensions, representing cyclical processes and having the capacity to represent the dimensions of effect and causality in the relationships between the different parts of the model. The model builder rarely addresses this last challenge; what would be the impact of varying levels/degrees of application by any one factor? This can be interpreted as the 'what-if' question: 'What will happen to the coaching intervention if it is changed/delivered in this way?'. (There is a research corollary to this: What works best in given circumstances and goals?)

It is not the coaching process that is problematic; that is, the intentions and the principles/concepts/constructs behind it. It is the reality of application. We must point out, however, that academics who attempt to describe the former are not unaware of the latter! The conceptual or ideal model is a baseline statement that may be used as a reference point for the variability of actual practice. We also pointed out earlier that we discern two misrepresentations of the coaching process:

1. First, it has to be remembered that academic writers tend to deal in extremes; for example, diligent implementation versus inventive practitioners. However, our experience tells us that the novelty and inventiveness is much less in extent and practice than the expert routine, and that new solutions are generally based on existing principles of good practice. There is a danger of 'tilting at windmills' that don't exist. No-one, for example, has ever suggested that coaching is 'merely delivered'; although we accept that it can be treated unproblematically. The athlete's activity takes place within a multi-layered interconnection of social and cultural practices, in addition to the subtlety of performance management and intervention strategies.

2. An over-reliance on Saury and Durand (1998) leads to the primacy of 'improvised practice' – what has been termed "opportunist improvisation and extensive management of uncertainty and contradictions" (1998, p. 268). However, this is merely a restatement of the very essence of coaching expertise – the adaptation, alignment and application of the expert's capacities within a very particular set of (evolving) circumstances. The coach's practice is rarely novel in the sense that it represents untried and untested solutions, but the description used by Hagger and McIntyre (2006) is very enlightening:

   > interactive (coaching) is necessarily framed by decisions made in their planning; . . . there is a very high degree of similarity and continuity between (pre-active and interactive) thinking . . . thinking in the pre-active phase – continuity with previous decisions, informality, creativity, orchestration of many kinds of knowledge, flexibility and responsiveness to context – also characterise (coaches') thinking during the interactive phase.
   >
   > (p. 30)

   The statement that "hence, coaching expertise has limited roots in either planning or reason" (Cushion 2007, p. 396) is plainly absurd.

3. We favour a more common-sense approach – which we term realistic complexity – in which we acknowledge the particularity of context, and the inherent complexity and disconnected continuity of intervention. However, coaches deal with this (as do many other professionals in similar occupations) by seeking regularities, routinising and adopting actions/solutions with wide application.

We do emphasise that the pictorial representation is only one part of the model. The reader has to take into account how the model designer intended it to be interpreted and used. We also accept that the model can only be taken so far. Thereafter, it needs to be re-created many times over and populated by empirical findings. In constructing the model, the model-builder would not expect it to correspond exactly to reality, but it should have an obvious and testable validity for those in that field. The ideal model also provides a vehicle for the aggregation of existing studies on coaching practice. Following the principles of model building and the requirements of the ideal model, the proposed model will have four parts:

132

1. assumptions about the sport coaching process, on which the model is based;
2. identification of the sub-processes and 'building blocks' from which the model has been constructed;
3. a representation of the components parts of the model and the inter-relationships between them; and
4. the dynamics of the model and how the process is operationalised.

PRIOR ASSUMPTIONS FOR THE PROPOSED MODEL

This is an important set of statements. Not only do they represent the basis for constructing our model, but they also provide a means of critically evaluating the model and the emerging conceptual framework. It is also important because we would rightly be critical of authors who do not make explicit the assumptions on which their research is founded.

1. Sport coaching is a culturally acknowledged practice of leadership in sport that is intended to enable individuals/teams to achieve improved performance in sport competition.
2. Sport coaching is a process, the effect of which is dependent on the integration and aggregation of a significant number of component parts. Partial implementation reduces its impact on performance outcomes.
3. The performers' involvement is normally sport-specific and recognised by membership of and association with that sport's agencies, organisations and competition framework.
4. Sport coaches manage a process based on the rational and instrumental pursuit of identified performance objectives, although the process may have other concomitant and socially valued developmental and personal objectives.
5. The essence and scope of the coaching process is circumscribed by a number of factors: duration, frequency, continuity, stability, progression, long-term planning, goal orientation, competition objectives and control of variables.
6. The preparation/training phase of performance improvement is effected by strategic improvements in the component elements of sport performance. Over time this will create a potential (and more or less predictable) improvement in competition performance.
7. The direct intervention element of the coaching process will incorporate principles of teaching and learning behaviour and practice that facilitate improved sport performance. However, coaching practice circumstances rarely permit a completely systematic approach.
8. Although rooted in planning and instrumental practice, the reality of the coaching process in many instances is less controllable, more uncertain in prospect and less predictable than an ideal model would suggest.
9. Implementing the coaching process in a systematic fashion will facilitate optimum improvement and performance.
10. Performers are committed to the process and engage voluntarily (or within a desirable reward environment) in pursuing agreed and/or beneficial goals.

11. The limitations in performance capacity and the extent of the improvement in sport performance are constrained by the performer's genetic capacities and early environmental experiences, including physique and intellect.
12. Improvements in sport performance are difficult to predict because of the range of factors influencing performance, including the number of and complexity of inter-relationships between variables and the non-mechanistic response by performers to training stimuli.
13. The assessment of coaching effectiveness is made more challenging by the balance of relative and absolute measurement of outcomes.
14. The implementation of the coaching process is constrained by the resources available, such as funding, equipment, facility access and appropriate competition. This also includes human resources such as the skills and knowledge of the coaching team.
15. The intensity of the interaction characteristic of the coaching process is most often, but not exclusively, marked by empathy between coach and performer, which is likely to enhance the process.
16. The core elements and assumptions of the coaching process are not negated by the very wide range of behavioural styles, ideological approaches or value frameworks adopted by performers and coaches.
17. Although core processes remain constant, the balance of performance component priorities and the coach's role in competition management are determined by sport specificity.
18. The range of skills and knowledges required to implement fully the coaching process implies that the process can be most appropriately facilitated by a team of coaches and other specialists.
19. The sport coaching process is best conceptualised and modelled as having four levels or stages: direct intervention, intervention support, management of constraints and strategic coordination and integration.
20. The defining feature of performance sport coaching leadership is the strategic integration and coordination of the process. This defines sport coaching as a cognitive process.
21. The fullest expression of the sport coaching process is to be found in circumstances in which the intensity of performance preparation and the accompanying committed engagement and resourcing are appropriate to the optimum achievement of performance objectives.
22. The competition programme and scheduling, the need for rehearsal and repetition in training, the principles of planning, training theory and session design conspire to produce a process that is cyclical.

IDENTIFYING THE BUILDING BLOCKS

These 'building blocks', or component parts, are a further set of assumptions (Figure 7.1). In contrast to the previous set of assumptions, which characterised the coaching process, these starter concepts identify those constituent parts of the model of the coaching process that are necessary to 'bring it to life'. They may be thought of as implementation assumptions. These features of the model will not necessarily

The information platform
Coaching expertise
Performer capabilities
Analysis of performance
Operationalisation
Systematic development
Planning
Goal-setting
Regulation procedures
Monitoring procedures
Preparation and training programme
Competition programme
Individualisation
Personal and social meaning

Figure 7.1 The building blocks of the coaching process.

QUESTION BOX

These assumptions can be divided into those that are socio-cultural, about performance, about the nature of the process and about effective practice. Are these assumptions sufficient and internally consistent? Do they reflect performance coaching only? What would you add?

be obvious in any diagrammatic representation of the process, but they are necessary for it to be both constructed and implemented. These may be present to a greater or lesser extent in each manifestation of the model.

The multiple variations in and between the building blocks go some way to explaining how the model can accommodate differentiation and contextualisation without losing the core pattern evident in the model. It may be helpful to think of the coaching process as a 'wall constructed of building blocks'. The same building blocks are used in each wall, but they are of different sizes and quality, and constructed differently by each coach. Each of the components is described in some depth.

KEY CONCEPT

The same elements of the coaching process are present in each manifestation of the model, but they are present to different degrees and constructed differently by each coach.

The information platform

Information is the fuel required to feed the implementation of the process. Planning, decision making, regulating, monitoring and evaluating in a systematic, informed and rational fashion depend on the availability of the necessary and appropriate information. An enormous amount of detailed information can be generated about the athlete's or team's performance and this is used in the planning of training schedules. However, there is a wealth of other 'intelligence' that has to be available: opposition characteristics and form, developments in technical and tactical knowledge, competition programme and venues, and, of course, information about the performers themselves – social, educational, historical performance record and so on.

Coaches may differ in the extent of their analyses of performance and this may also be sport-specific. It is likely that coaches will often operate without full access to all the information they would wish to have, and this will impact on their decision-making styles.

 QUESTION BOX

Is evidence of the generation, storage and use of information/data a valuable way of determining the extent to which the coach operates in a systematic fashion?

Coaching expertise

The knowledge and skills of the coach will be a key feature of the implementation of the coaching process and the form and nature of the process is likely to be shaped by these capabilities and the coach's personal characteristics and values. Each of the four functional roles of the process, from direct intervention to strategic integration and coordination, requires a distinctive set of skills and knowledge. The matrix of cognitive and professional craft skills will be exercised in communication, management, leadership and decision-making contexts, sometimes requiring speedy action and at other times with considered reflection. Coaches may also require sport-specific skills and expertise, although this is very sport specific and may also depend on role.

Knowledge can be usefully sub-divided into three categories: sport-specific knowledge (technique, tactics, equipment, performance developments, etc.); established principles of practice (training theory, coping strategies, planning, injury prevention, learning and teaching strategies, etc.); and sub-discipline knowledge (sport psychology, exercise physiology, sport biomechanics, etc.).

In the accompanying chapter on expertise we identify a hierarchy of expertise components but stress that the coaches' capacity to align and adapt the necessary decisions about the training and competition programme to the needs of the athlete or team in a particular context and towards a particular set of goals is a defining feature of expertise.

As a building block for the coaching process, it is assumed that the necessary skills and knowledge are present within the coaching team and the specialists available, and not only as exercised by the individual coach. In practice, however, the performance coach is required to exercise or appreciate the full range of expertise in order to exercise the strategic coordination role. The delivery of the coach's expertise involves a complex series of professional shortcuts and decision making, dependent on tacit knowledge and routines, but open to crisis management or more considered reflection as required.

Performer capabilities

In practice, the coaching process is meaningless without individual performers or teams and they are, therefore, a crucial and indispensable building block. The performers' current and potential capabilities determine both performance goals and achievement, although this is not an easy judgement to make. The complex interaction between genetic endowment, environmental influences and learning, technology and the vagaries of specific performances make prediction of achievement very difficult. This is evident in talent identification and recruitment procedures, which remain somewhat subjective exercises. Nevertheless, while hereditary factors may set the limits of performance, the quality of the coaching process will determine how close to those limits the performer will reach.

A degree of individualisation is implied in the delivery of the coaching process; in other words, maximising individual capabilities. This is made much more challenging for coaches who are working in team sports.

 KEY CONCEPT

Hereditary factors may set the limits of performance: the quality of the coaching process will determine how close to those limits the performer will reach.

Analysis of performance

Improvement of sport performance is the central purpose of the coaching process and a detailed knowledge and understanding of performance is essential for almost all stages in the process – from target setting, prediction and monitoring progression to training programme design, and planning strategy and tactics. One of the assumptions on which the coaching process is based is that systematic and coordinated improvements in individual components of performance, and, of course, rehearsal and repetition of the partial and total performance under appropriate conditions, will lead to improved competition performance.

Although sport performance can be expressed in terms of result, time, score, position, etc. (and this is useful for recording progress and measuring outcomes), it can only usefully be understood and accounted for in terms of the component parts of the performance. Sport performance has a number of component parts, which are always present: primary components (technique, physical, tactical, strategic, event-related psychological, attitudinal) and secondary components (equipment, general psychological disposition, medical condition, social interaction). The balance between primary and secondary components (for example, on the dependence on equipment or medical status) will differ between sports.

Coaches will attempt to ensure that explanations for performance are couched in terms of stable, controllable factors (tactics, physical condition) rather than unstable factors (opposition tactics, weather and effort). The preparation programme will be designed to influence directly the stable factors and to prepare performers to cope with less predictable factors. Coaches will often distinguish between the outcomes of performance (comparative result) and the outputs of performance (achievement in components, or absolute measures).

 KEY CONCEPT

Systematic and coordinated improvements in individual components of performance and rehearsal and repetition of the partial and total performance under appropriate conditions will lead to improved competition performance.

 QUESTION BOX

Are coaches in some sports more likely to adopt a systematic approach to the coaching process? Why might this be the case?

Operationalisation

The coaching process becomes evident in coaching practice. This involves the behaviour and practice of performer and coach, and the translation of planning and intentions into preparation and competition. The detailed operationalisation of the process is individualised and contextualised, but it can be recognised in three management functions: practice management (planning and directing training sessions and other forms of preparation); competition management (preparation, selection and direction); and programme management (administration, organisation, finance, liaison, etc.). Our view is that competition management (game coaching) is rarely accorded significant attention in coach education and development programmes.

The balance of practice and competition management duties will be very much influenced by the sport and the availability and contribution of support personnel. The extent of programme management responsibilities is dependent on the organisational context within which the coach operates.

Systematic development

The assumption of a rational approach and the purposeful integration of the contributing performance variables towards an identified goal imply the use of systematic progression processes towards those goals. Improvement in performance is intended to be stable, predictable and, of course, manageable. In addition, there is a scientific foundation (or principled practice approach) to performance enhancement. It is not intended that this improvement should (or could) result from chance or unplanned activity. Taken together, this approach points to progression being based on attempts to control the variables influencing performance and to implementation decisions being based on evidence, principle and accuracy.

Nevertheless, there may be some sport-specific parameters (team sports may offer some examples) that challenge the capacity to act in a systematic fashion when implementing the coaching process. When discussing coaching practice, it will become evident that this is one of the building blocks that is used with great variation by each coach. It is worth recalling that we are adopting assumptions from an ideal model. In practice, coaching may not reflect a systematic approach because of the difficulties of reconciling multiple goals, the absence of the necessary information, the dynamics of the athlete's response to training stimuli, the coach's approach to planning or the impact on the variability in performance skills of contested activity.

Planning

As a result of the adoption of a rational and systematic approach to improving performance and the assumption that coaching involves an intention to reduce the unpredictability of performance, planning is an essential and a central element of the coaching process. Planning involves a predetermination of practice, which is intended to capture the sequencing, level and nature of activity necessary to achieve goals. Planning has its own principles of good practice and these incorporate principles from other sub-disciplines involved in improving and sustaining performance. The output from planning also provides a regulation and evaluation mechanism.

Planning follows a recognised set of procedures: status review, goal-setting, structuring of targets and objectives, implications for performance components identified, pre-planning model devised (extent of the programme) and preparation (including performance components) and competition cycles identified. This template is then used to devise workloads and activities for shorter cycles and individual sessions. (See Lyle 2010 for a more detailed account.) Planning models are quite distinctive for league sport activity and for target sports (long periods of preparation). Contingency planning may be an important feature of planning in many sports.

 KEY CONCEPT

Planning involves a predetermination of practice, which is intended to capture the sequencing, level and nature of activity (also termed the intervention programme) necessary to achieve performance goals.

Goal-setting

Goal-setting is a planning exercise and is necessary to give direction and purpose to the coaching process. The targets set are also an important part of the management of progression, achievement, success and failure by the athlete. Acknowledgement of the goals set will also impact on the purposeful engagement of the athlete in the learning process. Goal-setting provides an integrative element that links the athletes' potential and aspirations, environmental and organisational resources and aspirations, and the operationalisation of the process. The goals and the preparation and performance needed to reach these goals drive the planning exercise.

There will be distinctions drawn between outcome goals (related to results and public measures of success) and output goals, which are best described in terms of performance components and, if possible, absolute measures of performance or performance improvement. Goals can also be described in process (e.g. attitudes and adherence to training) and product terms. It may be necessary to reach an accommodation between individual, team and organisation goals, and this is very evident in team sports.

Regulation procedures

The process nature of coaching brings with it a requirement for regulating the process. It can be assumed that variation and change are inevitable: achievement against

140

targets will be variable, the environment is changeable and ensuring the benefits of systematic application of training principles requires constant adjustment of workloads. Regulation implies a continuous process of achieving a best fit between planning and goal-setting, the current and projected status of the athlete and evolving circumstances. Regulation is the action that follows from and builds on monitoring to ensure that the objectives are likely to be achieved.

There are some general sub-processes that should ensure appropriate regulation – planning, goal-setting and monitoring, for example. However, perhaps more challenging is to identify and quantify the thresholds, catalysts and decision filters that constitute the decision-making criteria by which the coach exerts control over the process. This might best be conceptualised as a 'goal model'. The coach uses the goals that have been set as a set of 'markers' against which to evaluate progress. One set of questions that the coach may use is: are the goals still attainable? Are we making suitable progress? Is what I'm doing likely to contribute to or hinder the achievement of the goals?

Monitoring procedures

Many of the features of the coaching process – rational approach, planning, performance analysis and progression – are based on the premise that sufficient and suitable data are available on which to make judgements. The operationalisation of the coaching process therefore assumes that there is a continuous process of monitoring, not just in competition but also in training and preparation. The range of monitoring mechanisms will include video recording, athlete responses, telemetry, notation, field procedures (heart-rate, timing) and laboratory measurement when appropriate. A further implication is that the data gathered will be stored in an organised and retrievable fashion.

We ought to recognise that there will be approaches to coaching in which the monitoring by the coach is not dependent on quantifiable, recorded or retrievable measures. The coach may rely on judgements based on 'feel', or what is mistakenly termed 'intuition'. Elsewhere we discuss this in greater detail. Such a process of tacit, experiential decision making contributes to the challenge of determining coaches' expertise.

Preparation and training programme

The improvement or maintenance of performance implicit in the coaching process cannot be achieved in the longer term by participation in competition alone. The need to isolate performance components, to provide opportunity for rehearsal and practice and to control workload intensity is achieved by a series of preparation (or training) sessions. The adaptation of the performer in performance components (physical capacity, technique, decision-making, patterns of play, emotional resilience, etc.) and the stability and integration of those component changes are achieved through a planned series of activities. It is partly this emphasis on extended preparation that distinguishes the performance sportsperson from the less committed participation sportsperson. Preparation involves a very full range of activities, including recovery activities, strategy discussions, individual psychological preparation, rehearsal competitions, and so on, in addition to the more obvious 'training session'.

Competition programme

Involvement in sport competition is assumed in the characteristics of the coaching process, although clearly this involvement can vary significantly in level, scale and intensity. Competition scheduling and the relationship between competitions and goals set have a very significant influence on planning and periodising the yearly (and beyond) programme. Competition results are also used to measure progress and success. The very nature of sport competition means that the intended goals in one coaching process are actively contested by the athletes and coaches associated with another coaching process.

The selection and scheduling of competitions will be important in some sports and implies a degree of flexibility and choice. For other sports (notably team league sports), the competition framework may be pre-determined, but to some extent (success in cup competitions leading to a prolonged competition programme, for example) also difficult to predict.

Individualisation

One of the basic principles in the operationalisation of the coaching process is that it will be individualised to the needs of the performer, and the coach's expertise involves accommodating those specific needs. The extent of this individualisation will depend on factors such as the size of squads and team groups, sport specialisms (events, distances and positions), the extent to which the individual's needs have been identified, and the degree of systematic interpretation and implementation of the process. Although the use of training principles and other principles of practice may result in 'recipe' type planning and delivery, it is assumed that the coaching process will operate most effectively when individualised to the performer.

All coaching processes will be unique, and we have already stressed that coaching can only be fully understood at the level of the particular. Not only do individual performers and groups of performers differ in their aspirations and potential, but the resource context of the process (including other performers) will differ.

Personal and social meaning

Dealing with processes and sub-processes based on rationality and systematic application, and the instrumental nature of performance preparation, can tend to mask the fact that the coaching process is essentially an inter-personal activity.

A proposed model for coaching

The coaching process takes place in a constructed personal and social space and its operationalisation both is determined by and impacts on the individuals concerned and the social world around them. The added dimension that this brings to any conceptualisation of the coaching process highlights the potential for different lenses and emphases to be adopted.

The values, idiosyncrasies and personal qualities of individuals (coaches and performers) are reflected in their inter-personal behaviour and are exacerbated by perceptions of success and failure. The performers' psychological state (and that of the coach) forms part of their performance readiness and it is hardly surprising that this is linked to emotional responses. In addition, the individual's engagement in the process has a personal meaning in terms of commitment, self-identity and potential satisfaction. Once again these are challenged by perceptions of success and failure and by social interaction throughout the process. The coaching process also occupies a social space and this brings with it elements of social recognition, status, legal and ethical behaviour, and its operationalisation cannot be divorced from these social meanings.

 QUESTION BOX

Can you think of additional features of sport coaching that should be considered building blocks in devising an ideal model? Of those already identified, are they equally weighted or are some more essential than others?

THE MODEL

The third part of the model is a visual representation of the component parts of the coaching process and the relationships and sequencing between components. Figure 7.2 illustrates the model in a two-dimensional diagram. At this point it is worth reiterating that the model may be more detailed than the others available, but it also demonstrates a number of the weaknesses of the model 'for'. The chief of these is that the component parts and sub-processes are identified but the relationships between them (including the means by which these relationships are effected) cannot easily be illustrated in such diagrams. This is a limitation of model description, but also reflects our current dearth of knowledge about what strategies and behaviour work most effectively for which athletes and in which circumstances.

Nevertheless, there has been an attempt to emphasise the feedback circles and decision points within the process. The mechanisms for executing this decision making will be dealt with in the next chapter. It will have become obvious that the coaching process has an element of layering, also termed nested, embedded or consequential. Actions taken are informed both by more strategic concerns and by

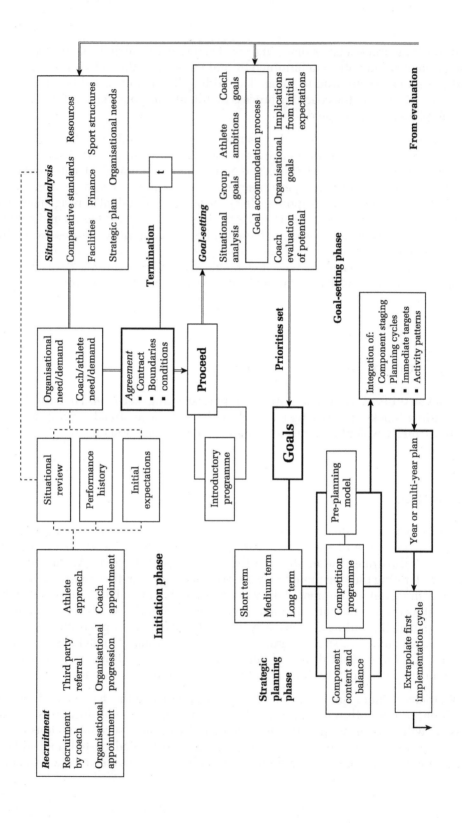

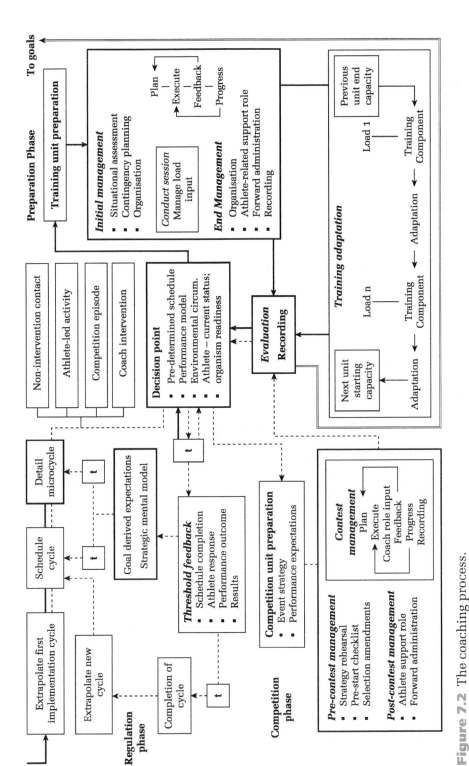

Figure 7.2 The coaching process.

immediate precursors. These actions then impact on the actions that follow. The result is that the process has a constant quality of cyclicality and reference; the constant regulation and recreation of the process is a feature of sport coaching. We have thus far failed to devise appropriate means of illustrating this quality in diagrams and models.

 KEY CONCEPT

Sport coaching is characterised by operating within the constant influence of more-strategic, intermediate and more-immediate goals. This results in a property of cyclicality and continuous cross-referencing that impacts on day-to-day practice and coaching expertise but is difficult to describe and illustrate.

The model of the coaching process can be summarised in the following way (and treated as a key concept):

 KEY CONCEPT

The sport coaching process is a cyclical series of activities centred on a dynamic set of performance goals. The process is serial and continuous. A variable pattern of coach interventions, athlete performance and organisational activity is devised, coordinated and regulated to respond to a set of external constraints and personal and performance goals, which are time dependent. A flexible model of expectations, based on current status and identified performance targets, is generated and used to regulate the process. Constant feedback loops and a series of threshold decision points (indicated as 't' in diagrams) regulate the implementation of the model.

EXTENDING THE MODEL

We have stressed repeatedly that this is an ideal model and not one that coaches will attempt to adopt or implement. It is designed to guide research, inform education and training, and may be valuable for analysing and reflecting on practice. The practice of coaching is much more complex than can be easily conveyed in models of this kind. Coaching intervention and interpersonal behaviour will be much more context- and response-dependent, and there is a need to explain how the coach copes with not only the complexity and contingency, but also the more routine management of a coaching process that is often described as apparently tacit and intuitive.

A proposed model for coaching

It is our intention to offer a tentative conceptualisation of how the coach operationalises the coaching process, which we will do in the succeeding chapter. This should be seen as part of the model, and once again we offer this as a stimulus to research. In the meantime, we have identified three specific examples of how the model is likely to be adapted by coaches. We examine the issues of sport specificity, systematic coaching practice and building research into the model. The chapter concludes with an acknowledgement of the model's limitations.

Sport specificity

In the previous edition, the research used to identify potential thresholds for coaching intervention also highlighted differences between sports. However, an idealised conceptual model is designed to apply to all coaches and coaching processes. Of course, when the reality of practice is mapped onto the model, the resultant pattern will be different for all coaches and most sports. It is partly this diversity that necessitated the ideal model approach. We cannot hope to describe all of the variation in practice. Nevertheless, we can look for some regularities in the way that the model might be adapted for different sports.

If the model is not appropriate for describing a particular coaching practice, this should be evident in the assumptions or building blocks. Remember also that the process was described in some detail and it has already been acknowledged that a partial application of the model is possible (an example is the club coach versus the more episodic representative squad coach). Research is likely to show that the key phases are emphasised and balanced differently across sports. Figure 7.3 lists the key stages in the model. Sport-specific differences will lead to differential emphases on these stages of process components. Given the process characteristics of the coaching process, these stages are interdependent and cyclical. They form a useful reference point for identification of the component elements of coaching expertise and for research and education.

Developing the conceptual framework has inevitably emphasised the common, generic elements of the coaching process. Nevertheless, one of the recurring themes within the text is the variability in the operationalisation of the coaching process, and much of this stems from the nature of the sport itself. The conceptual framework must therefore be able to account for variability in practice in relation to sport

| Initiation |
| Goal-setting |
| Strategic planning |
| Regulation |
| Preparation |
| Competition |

Figure 7.3 Principal model phases.

Table 7.1 Planning issues related to competition cycle

Competition category	Characteristics	Planning issues
Target sports (e.g. rowing, swimming, athletics, gymnastics)	Tendency to have on- and off-season; major competitions can be distinguished from more minor ones; extended periods of preparation; most often individual sports	Few constraints to cyclical planning; detailed planning framework with periodised cycles; action plans for 4–6 weeks; coach's intention is to adhere to plan; maintenance period depends on competition schedules
League sports (e.g. hockey, soccer, rugby, netball)	Extended and regular competition programme; results are aggregated for success; often team sports; normally performance composed of multiple components	Longer-term planning is more difficult; priorities influenced by the result and imminence of competition; contingency and crisis planning common; detailed planning is unlikely beyond short cycles
Circuit sports (e.g. skiing, tennis, golf)	Extended competition programme but results are normally not aggregated; major and minor competitions, with some interdependence; multiple performance components	Maintenance of 'form' with peaks for identified targets; planning for overall progress; comparative performance; longer-term planning shell with short-term competition preparation; contingency planning likely

specificity. Consider the distinctiveness of performance-routine sports such as gymnastics and ice dance, with their technical rehearsal demands and quality judgements of performance in comparison to the repetitive, uncontested, volume training of long-distance athletes, cyclists and rowers. These can be contrasted with the technical and tactical drills/skills-led interactive practices and game routines of team sports such as basketball and hockey. Each of these sports brings its delivery challenges and different coaching practices. Table 7.1 indicates differences in sports by the nature of their competition demands, and illustrates the impact on the planning aspect of sport coaching.

In which elements of the coaching process will there be differences? Table 7.2 provides more detailed examples of differences in coaching practice. However, these can be summarised as follows:

■ Differences are most likely to occur in the direct intervention roles. Differences in managing the external environment are more likely to be dependent on organisational structures and level/intensity of engagement. It is possible that the strategic coordination role will be more demanding in team sports with large coaching teams and support personnel, and with organisational goals to be satisfied.

148

- Three elements of coaching practice – planning, involvement in exercises/drills and competition role – are central to sport specificity. Many of the differences between sports impact on one or more of these functions.
- Workload management is a key concept. Earlier sections have highlighted the continuum between carrying out training and competition planning intentions with some degree of predictability and the variability in delivery and performance expected in interactive and contested sports. Sports with high levels of tactical decision making and degrees of freedom in technical execution require more workload management and feedback.
- The phrase 'coach dominated' is often used for those sports in which the competition role of the coach involves decision making that has a significant impact on the patterns of play and the outcomes of the game/sport. (This is most likely in sports in which tactical management, use of substitutions, and opportunities to conduct time-outs or other breaks in continuity are evident.) Conversely, there are sports in which the observation and interpretation of the external environment is less significant and can be accomplished, in many cases, by the performer. It is not unusual in a number of sports, and for athletes of some experience, for the coach's role to be 'reduced' to adviser or occasional consultant.

Table 7.2 Sport-specific factors in coaching practice

Sport characteristic	Sport example (compare)	Impact on coaching practice
Role in competition	Basketball *with* athletics	Expertise required in contest management; high level of intervention; presence required; coach dependency in decision making; level of independence fostered in performers; active engagement in competition with attendant emotional demands
Performance profile (race, game, performance)	Swimming *with* hockey *with* rhythmic gymnastics	Control of performance outputs, target setting; interactive tactics; psychological preparation for uncertainty; focus on opposition performance; coach's competition role; specificity of preparation/ rehearsal
Team/individual	Netball *with* archery	Complexity of processes; control of variables; level of individualisation; amount of data; methods of communication; control of interactive workloads; specificity of goal-setting; selection
Competition pattern (league, target, circuit)	Ice hockey *with* athletics *with* golf	Periodisation of year; goal-setting; impact of illness/injury; variability in threshold values; monitoring horizons
Equipment dependence	Rugby union *with* motor racing	Need for technical expertise; control of variables; psychological preparation

(continued)

A proposed model for coaching

Table 7.2 Sport-specific factors in coaching practice *(continued)*

Sport characteristic	Sport example (compare)	Impact on coaching practice
Environmental conditions	Sailing *with* badminton	Stability of planning intentions; ease of communication; delivery style; control of environment; ease of monitoring
Balance of performance components	Cricket *with* rowing	Priority given to major components – tactical capacity, physical conditioning, technical development, etc.; complexity of process – planning, monitoring; incremental versus systematic progression
Interactive role in training	Volleyball *with* skiing	Constancy of feedback; management of workloads; skill required for feeding/control; communication control; use of support team; monitoring and evaluation
Characteristics of performers (age, gender, disability)	Gymnastics (elite age) *with* soccer (elite age)	Leadership style; physical and psychological maturity into planning; lifestyle support issues; interpersonal relationship issues; communication; independence
Development profile	Soccer *with* handball	Performer reward environment; availability of funding; support personnel; sport science support; recruitment; education opportunities

Systematic coaching behaviours

When the ideal model of the coaching process was proposed, it presumed a rational, logical and constraint-free approach: in other words, a systematic approach to the business of coaching. However, a more pragmatic and common-sense perspective might begin with the view that this would be a very difficult practice to fulfil, and that some coaching processes are likely to be more systematic than others. Figure 7.4 illustrates this in a simple diagram.

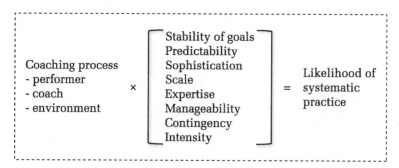

Figure 7.4 Factors influencing the likelihood of systematic practice.

A proposed model for coaching

The purpose of this section of the chapter is to examine the nature of more and less systematic practice as an overarching feature that will provide a reference point for more specific behaviours. In passing, it should also be noted that this may be a useful comparative evaluation tool for coaching practice. The questions to address are: what is meant by systematic practice, and to what extent is the systematic operationalisation of the model to be expected?

The characteristics of systematic coaching practice are that:

- the process will be comprehensive in its coverage and attention to detail;
- actions will be instrumental, that is, planned, regulated and goal-directed;
- there will be a marked degree of management or 'control' of the process, particularly through regulating performance preparations; and
- decision making is based on established principles of good practice.

In an earlier passage, sport coaching was described as an attempt to reduce the unpredictability of performance within specified boundaries of time, place and resource. The word 'attempt' is important. When dealing with human behaviour, it is not unreasonable to preface the use of the term systematic with the caveats 'as possible' or 'within reason'. The description of systematic practice follows logically from that earlier statement. The argument has been presented in this way:

> In order to reduce unpredictability (which assumes tailoring to suit individual needs), the coach will attempt to control as many as possible of the variables affecting performance and their preparation. The systematic regulation of the process will involve planning, recording, monitoring, problem solving and calculated decision-making. In constraint-free circumstances, we might expect the coach to adopt a rigorous detailed approach to practice. This implies monitoring progress, compiling player profiles, measuring performance capacities and operating from predetermined plans and schedules. The coach's strategic goals are constantly evaluated through the monitoring and recording of the individualised workloads from each training session. Strategic and tactical decisions in competition and based on objective analyses of the performances of the performers and their opponents.
> (Lyle 1998, p. 69)

One of the key features of systematic practice is the attempt at quality control by the coaching team. The extent to which the quality of the process and its sub-processes are assured may also be a useful measure of accountability and efficiency. Note also that it is the quality of the output and not the outcome that is assured. Control, in this sense, implies 'management to best advantage' and should not imply negative connotations. There is no suggestion that 'control of the performer' is a feature of systematic coaching practice. Indeed, quality management is a useful maxim for coaching effectiveness studies.

In looking back to the model, you will notice that there are many feedback loops and evaluation stages. Quality control occurs at a number of different stages. Figure 7.5 identifies these control stages using a simple input–treatment–output model. There

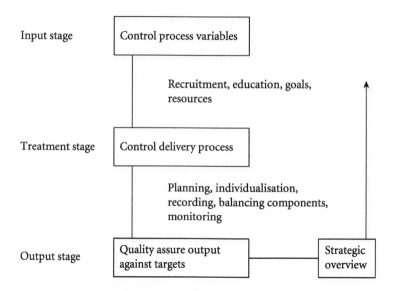

Input stage | Control process variables

Recruitment, education, goals, resources

Treatment stage | Control delivery process

Planning, individualisation, recording, balancing components, monitoring

Output stage | Quality assure output against targets | Strategic overview

Figure 7.5 Quality control stages.

 QUESTION BOX

The use of the words 'control' or 'manipulation' are intended to be directed to the range of performance variables, but is often interpreted as a negative feature of interpersonal behaviour, and some academics infer a loss of independence by the performer. How could this confusion be better explained?

will also be a number of predictable features of the process (Table 7.3) that will provide an indication of the likelihood of more or less systematic practice.

Identifying these potential barriers suggests that the likely operationalisation of the model in a systematic fashion is a demanding exercise and will need to be evaluated in the light of what is feasible and realistic in the circumstances in which the coach and the athletes are engaged. However, there are further considerations. It is reasonable to expect that coaches will adopt a professional practice that is the most efficient and effective. 'Systematic' should not imply that unnecessary procedures are employed or that coaches are constrained not to prioritise their time and effort. In describing and evaluating coaching behaviours, a number of common features should appear if the coach is to act efficiently in managing the process:

- routinise regular practice where possible;
- adopt option-reducing strategies for decision making;
- prioritise record keeping;
- focus attention through thresholds and key catalyst indicators to prevent over-monitoring;

152

Table 7.3 Potential barriers to systematic practice

	Process feature	Potential barrier to systematic behaviour
Role	Part-time athlete or coach	Less impact of training theory principles Time pressures
	Number of assistants	Specificity of expertise available in full range of process
Complexity	Number of contributory performance components	Potentially enormous number of measurements and recording possibilities Specificity of goals, targets
Implementation	Individualisation	Problem of squad size, facility availability, positional specialisation
	Workload management	Difficulty of measuring psychological, technical workloads Managing game drills in complex sports Injury, illness, emotional response
	Monitoring	Maintaining an intelligence system Variable response to training loadings Interdependence of performance components Volume of data accumulated
	Human response	Emotion and effort as integral features of performance Reaction of performer to purely rational decision making
The sport	Pattern of engagement	Competition scheduling Competition role of coach Relative immutability of training cycles
Education	Coach expertise	Sufficiency of experience to assess and incorporate evidence-based decision making Evidence of good practice
Environment	Resources, finance, facilities	Impact of resourcing on option choices Impact of external agency goals and priorities

- avoid over-planning, maintain a contingency approach; and
- retain flexibility and the human response approach.

However, these potential features of coaching practice are also tools for analysing evidence of coaches' practice. It is necessary to establish the extent to which coaches actually operate systematically, and it is this type of research that we hope to encourage. It is important to point out that the term 'systematic' may have different connotations for the participation coach. In so far as participation coaches are more episodic in their outlook and are less involved in longer-term planning, resource or competition management, it is possible for them to deliver sessions, and series of sessions, which are well-organised and adhere to good principles of session structuring and management. It can also be assumed that the management of the programme is well organised. However, the absence of control of variables, the absence of instrumental preparation towards longer-term goals and the lack of comprehensiveness in the programme signal that the term 'systematic' would be inappropriate.

QUESTION BOX

Systematic behaviour is perceived not to be a feature of all coaching practice – even successful practice! Does this imply that describing and interpreting coaching practice is difficult or that successful athletes are not necessarily the product of effective coaches?

How would the systematic approach be recognised? There are many possible criteria relating to the regulation of the programme. The following are examples of such criteria:

- the degree of adherence to pre-determined plans;
- the quality and scale of record keeping;
- the individualisation of athletes' training programmes;
- precision in implementing training drills and exercises;
- the extent of workload monitoring and progress across performance components; and
- the degree of incorporation of rigorously obtained evidence into programmes.

The chapter continues by examining two pieces of evidence on coaches' practice. In the first, Lyle (1992) investigated the self-reported coaching behaviours of 30 coaches of international performers, ten in each of athletics, volleyball and swimming. Table 7.4 indicates the percentage of coaches who reported that they fulfilled the criteria described.

The evidence suggests that a number of criteria of systematic practice were clearly not fulfilled. The two tasks that stand out are the failure to monitor training programmes carried out when the coach is not present and the low incidence of individualisation of programmes. Although it is evident that planning is a central concern for these coaches, there are significant differences between sports and in recording and monitoring progress. Perhaps not surprisingly, competition performance is obviously a key factor for monitoring progress.

It should be noted, however, that this evidence can only be illustrative of coaching practice. There is no doubt that the coaches were 'performance oriented', but the coaches were almost all part-time, as were the great majority of the performers. The study needs to be repeated to assess the coaches' practice in less constrained circumstances. Nevertheless, it is valuable for highlighting areas in which more systematic behaviour might not be endemic.

In a similar investigation into the behaviour of hockey and swimming coaches, Cross (1995a, 1995b) found that there were a number of significant constraints to the implementation of the coaching process and that hockey coaches in particular exhibited a high degree of apparently less systematic practice.

A proposed model for coaching

Table 7.4 Coaches' responses to systematic coaching criteria

Criteria	Swimming	Volleyball	Athletics
Planning elements			
Written record of goals	20	10	0
Short-term goals identified	90	80	70
Long-term goals identified	90	30	90
Outline periodisation of the year	100	60	100
Plan for 4–5 weeks	100	70	90
Plan for one week	50	70	70
Use of pre-planning model	50	10	40
Total hours identified	40	38	40
Training targets identified	44	60	50
Competition targets identified	50	33	29
Monitoring elements			
Written plan for session	70	80	50
Written record of session	80	50	70
Workloads identified	90	40	80
Drills/exercises based on testing	90	0	0
Programmes individualised	40	20	80
Recording in systematic form	90	40	40
Close monitoring of personal training	50	30	20
Performance potential estimated:			
constantly	10	50	30
each session	30	50	30
at competition	90	80	90
by objective testing	90	20	20
Sufficient data for goal-setting	20	70	60

The data collected in these studies were supplemented by in-depth interviews. These examples point to a conclusion that coaching practice is not best described as systematic in the sense that a rational, detailed application of principles to all components of performance in conditions of evidence-based decision making takes place, competition and training targets are always established and individualised training programmes are constantly delivered, monitored and recorded. On the other hand, coaching practice can be described as systematic in the sense that there is attention to planning, the approach is methodical, practice is based on principles of good practice and there is a set of procedures for efficient and prioritised monitoring, recording and decision-making behaviour. The findings can be described in a way that raises interesting suggestions about coaching practice. The following became clear:

- There is a fairly detailed planning umbrella within which coaching action is determined.
- Delivery activity is more likely to be applied contingently.

- Monitoring of progress and the decision making related to delivery is subject to a professional expertise that is largely cognitive.
- The apparently intuitive practice of the performance coach (even within the rigorously applied schedules of some coaches) masks a complex set of cognitive processes which is the hallmark of the expert coach.
- Experiential decision making is supplemented by a series of objective data and testing, and by competition outcomes.

 KEY CONCEPT

Coaching practice can be described as systematic in the sense that there is attention to planning, the approach is methodical, practice is based on principles of good practice and there is a set of procedures for efficient and prioritised monitoring, recording and decision-making behaviour.

We are also aware that the use of the term systematic can be criticised on ideological grounds. Writers who are classified as humanist or who use the term 'athlete-centred' would be likely to oppose such an approach on the grounds that it dehumanises the process and implies a mechanistic approach. We reject this criticism. The systematic approach is focused on the performance itself, and on data-led judgements. This need not render it anything other than athlete-centred, or prevent innovation, creativity and the need for experience-led professional judgements. Indeed, improvement in performance is the defining purpose of sport coaching and anything other than a systematic approach to its enhancement could hardly be argued to be in the interests of the athlete. The coach's role in achieving a balance of emphasis between interpersonal communication and care, sport specificity and context, and performance management marks the coaching process as one requiring an advanced, higher-order occupational expertise.

ADAPTING THE MODEL

One of the intentions of working with the conceptual framework is that the model should be adapted continuously, as evidence of practice becomes available. This example shows how the generalised conceptualisation in the model of part of the competition phase can be made more detailed when evidence of coaches' behaviour is incorporated. Figure 7.6 reproduces the section of the model dealing with the competition phase. On the basis of our experience as coaches and incorporating further evidence (Lyle 1999), this might be reconceptualised more usefully (and accurately) as represented in Figure 7.7.

156

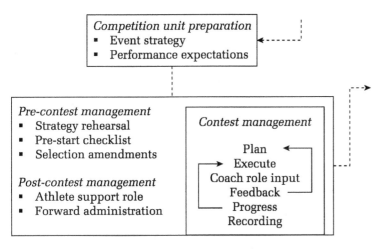

Figure 7.6 Generalised competition phase.

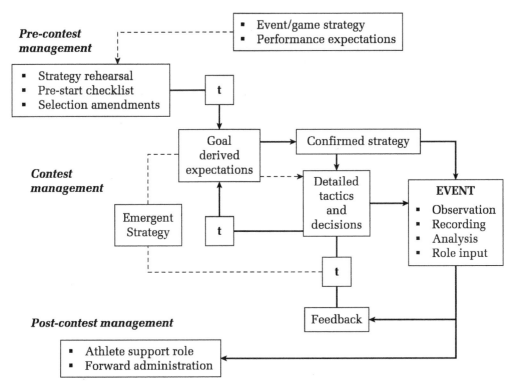

Figure 7.7 Upgraded model of the competition phase.

The more detailed model identifies threshold decision points and, perhaps more interestingly, the distinction between a confirmed competition strategy and an emergent strategy. The competition role input is, of course, very dependent on the sport and the coach's role in competition. It is this gradual refinement of the model that will lead to a better analytical tool, a more accurate model and, ultimately, a better understanding of coaching practice.

Limitations

The model exhibits many of the strengths and weaknesses of modelling described in the previous chapter. We reiterate that a comprehensive model 'of' coaching is neither appropriate nor currently feasible. It is possible to have prescriptions for better practice and/or for value-led practice, but to capture and represent the entirety of the coaching process is not possible (and we have already argued that it is inappropriate). This chapter identifies an ideal model approach. The strengths are that the assumptions on which the model is based are identified, as are the key building blocks. It may also be said to be comprehensive and to emphasise both the process nature of coaching and the strong element of layering as evidenced in the feedback loops and independencies.

However, the model has some very obvious limitations. Inevitably, it is stronger in structure than function. The context-free and constraint-free nature of an ideal model makes it appear too detached from operationalisation, with a tendency to forget that it is intended to stimulate research. A weakness that the model shares with others is

---

 SUMMARY

This chapter should have familiarised you with the following:

- A model for the sport coaching process based on the concept of an 'ideal model'.
- The prior assumptions on which the model is predicated. These can be used to critique the model.
- The building blocks of the model – the information platform, coaching expertise, performer capabilities, analysis of performance, operationalisation, systematic development, planning, goal-setting, regulation procedures, monitoring procedures, preparation and training programme, competition programme, individualisation, personal and social meaning.
- A graphical representation of the model.
- Extending the model: sport specificity, systematic coaching behaviours, adapting the model.

A proposed model for coaching

PROJECTS

1. Select a component part of the model. Devise an investigation to test its aptness for describing coaching practice. Redesign the model in line with your findings.
2. Review the 'prior assumptions'. Select three or four and consider their impact on the model. What would be the impact of a change in these assumptions?
3. Design an investigation into the comparability of two sports in the way that coaches from those sports demonstrate different priorities in their application of the building blocks.
4. Select two component parts of the model. Attempt to identify the nature of the relationship between the components. This might require an investigation into coaching practice in a variety of circumstances, or coaches with different levels of expertise.

that the consequential nature and extent of the linkages between elements are not specified. As a final point, we reiterate that the 'model' consists of the whole chapter, and the one to follow, and should not be interpreted as merely a diagram.

REFERENCES

Albrow, M. (1990). *Max Weber's Construction of Social Theory*. London: St Martin's Press.

Cross, N. (1995a). Coaching effectiveness in hockey. *Scottish Journal of Physical Education*, *23*(1), 27–39.

Cross, N. (1995b). Coaching effectiveness and the coaching process. *Swimming Times*, *72*(3), 23–25.

Cushion, C. J. (2007). Modelling the complexities of the coaching process. *International Journal of Sports Science & Coaching*, *2*(4), 395–401.

Hagger, H., & McIntyre, D. (2006). *Learning Teaching from Teachers: Realising the Potential of School-based Teacher Education*. Maidenhead: Open University Press.

Lyle, J. (1992). Systematic coaching behaviour: An investigation into the coaching process and the implications of the findings for coaching education. In T. Williams, L. Almond, & A. Sparkes (Eds) *Sport and Physical Activity*. London: E&FN Spon, 463–469.

Lyle, J. (1998). *The Coaching Process*. Leeds: National Coaching Foundation.

Lyle, J. (1999). Managing the game: A coach derived model of tactical decision-making. In G. Costa *et al.* (Eds) *Sport Management in the Next Millennium*.

Proceedings of the 7th Congress of the European Association for Sport Management, Thessaloniki, Greece, September, 1999, 200–205.

Lyle, J. (2007). Modelling the complexity of the coaching process: A commentary. *International Journal of Sports Science & Coaching, 2*(4), 407–409.

Lyle, J. (2010). Planning for team sports. In J. Lyle & C. Cushion (Eds) *Sports Coaching: Professionalisation and Practice*. Edinburgh: Churchill Livingstone, 85–97.

Saury, J., & Durand, M. (1998). Practical knowledge in expert coaches: On-site study of coaching in sailing. *Research Quarterly for Exercise and Sport, 69*(3), 254–266.

A proposed model for coaching

CHAPTER 8

OPERATIONALISING THE MODEL; OR, WHAT COACHES REALLY DO!

CHAPTER OUTLINE

- ▦ Introduction
- ▦ The coaching process
- ▦ A summary description of coaching practice
- ▦ The control box
- ▦ Decision making: the foundation of coaching practice
- ▦ Pedagogy
- ▦ Miscellaneous
- ▦ Summary
- ▦ Projects

INTRODUCTION

An ideal model was described in the previous chapter, the intention of which was to provide a template for coach development and research. It was acknowledged that this was 'removed from the actuality of practice' and represented a model *for* coaching. Features of coaching practice such as its tacit – apparently intuitive – nature, layers of socio-cultural complexity and dynamic goal environment were the basis for a number of questions:

- ▦ How do coaches operationalise their practice?
- ▦ How do coaches decide what should constitute performer activity, and when and how they should intervene in its delivery?
- ▦ It is difficult to be prepared for all eventualities. How do coaches cope with this complexity and ever-changing circumstances?

In addition to the problems of model building and representation, we now emphasise the challenges of representing 'expertise in practice', when much of that expertise can be said to be cognitive and tacit. In other words, sport coaching has an observable, practical dimension; the coach's behaviour, utterances and actions are evident to a great extent, as are those of the athlete. Coaching can be said to be a 'practical activity' in so far as the outcome is an intervention process in which the coach and athlete (and others) interact and engage in activities designed to improve performance or prepare for competition. It is practical in the sense that it is planned, delivered, experienced, monitored and reflected upon, and, of course, sport performance itself is 'physical' in nature. However, the coach's role in directing the intervention process is dependent upon a cognitive process that is mostly tacit (subconscious) and is reliant on a complex interplay of knowledge (of various types), deliberative planning and decision making, and semi-deliberative coping strategies, reactive decision making and problem solving. How this core aspect of expertise is manifested in day-to-day practice is a current preoccupation of many academic writers and coach developers.

We might expect that the operationalisation of the coaching process would be challenging. It is an occupational task/role in which the 'treatment' is applied through human action and interaction, and determined by the influence of dynamic circumstances. It is therefore susceptible to rational and logical action only to a limited extent. The simplest way to think about sport coaching is that it is a task with fairly obvious goals, with the coach's expertise used to identify and enact the most effective means of achieving those goals – but the goals are not straightforward, there is no agreement on the best way to achieve a given goal, the athletes are an active part of the process and effective practice is very contextual. Therefore, it is not a straightforward exercise to specify how coaches operationalise the coaching process.

Decision making has been identified as the most important part of sport coaching (Abraham & Collins 2011). There has been some criticism of this statement, but, if anything, we feel that the point is understated. Decision making is not just the most important part of coaching intervention – it *is* coaching intervention, and, in our view, should be the essential element of coaching education. The coach's intervention programme is based on a continuous series of action decisions: training programmes, conduct of drills and exercises, feedback, organisation, selection and so on. The 'micro-management of the flow of intervention' is a key aspect of the coach's expertise.

THE COACHING PROCESS

We have dealt earlier in the book with many of the conceptual issues that underpin the coaching process. In order to provide a context for operationalising the model, that is, how coaches operate on a day-by-day, moment-by-moment basis, we need to reprise some of the influencing factors:

- Sport coaching is a family term for a number of domain-specific roles. The 'boundary markers', such as frequency, duration and intensity, associated with domain roles will impact the extent and intricacy of operationalisation.
- The coaching process is complex, has conflicting or aspirational goals, is characterised by multiple approaches to achieving goals and solving issues

KEY CONCEPT

Decision making is not just the most important part of coaching intervention – it *is* coaching intervention, and, in our view, should be the essential element of coaching education.

We accept that coaching practice is a dynamic interplay of many actors, most importantly, including the players/athletes, and sport- and domain-specific circumstances that have enormous variation and emergent energy. In practice, in the vast majority of circumstances, the conduct of the 'session' is dependent on the coach's direction or management of the intervention programme.

Any debate about the extent of the 'direction', whether it reflects a traditional and limiting style of coaching, or whether it has the potential to demonstrate an abuse of power, is worthwhile. It seems likely that, in many instances, individual coaches will be replicating unquestioned, taken-for-granted assumptions about coaching. There are undoubtedly implications for coach development in these circumstances. However, there is a 'bottom line' reality – the preparation and competition programmes that are the essence of sport coaching depend on the coach's direction and management of the process, and on a myriad aggregation of action decisions at both strategic and micro-management levels. We need to understand how the coach operationalises this role.

(often idiosyncratic or based on personal theories), operates with incomplete information, takes place (for performance coaching) over an extended duration and is a contested endeavour.

- Coaches rely (to varying degrees) on plans, performance analysis and data, and principles of development for physical conditioning, skill development and competition preparation, and construct a linked series of training and competition episodes characterised by routines, rehearsals, iterative drills and exercises, and manipulation of performance variables and intensities, designed to improve performance.
- Performance-enhancement goals are central to the coaching process, but because these are brought to life by human beings and communicated to and by human beings, there is a layer of interpersonal activity that is both synonymous with and contemporaneous with the sport-related activity itself.

Sport coaching, therefore, has multi-dimensionality (social phenomenon, competition, stakeholder network, multiple practitioners and athletes), simultaneity (layered, multiple goals), immediacy ('hands-on' process experienced physically, emotionally and so on), unpredictability (dynamic context, contested environment, human response), publicness (visible outcomes, accountability, observable behaviour), and historicity (extended duration, multiple meanings and serial nature creates personal, performance and organisational histories).

A SUMMARY DESCRIPTION OF COACHING PRACTICE

To a large extent, we have been influenced by the work of Hagger and McIntyre (2006) in their description of teachers' expertise and practice. We find there to be a very valuable correspondence between the teaching and coaching 'intervention' and a great deal of similarity in the practitioner's response to coping with a fluid set of circumstances. Our description and analysis of the micro-management of the coaching intervention owes much to their work, and their description of practice is in accord with our own experience of coaching.

> [Coaching] expertise is so subtle, so complex, so individual and so context-related that it can only adequately be understood in relation to particular practice, not in general. The core of expert practice is the [capacity] to make subtle judgements.
>
> (Hagger & McIntyre 2006, p. 33)

- Coaches weave together seemingly effortless sessions which are made up of many smaller session segments. These segments, in turn, depend on small, socially scripted parcels of behaviour called routines that coaches deliver, participate in and utilise extensively.
- Coaches have a rich repertoire of instructional scripts (in other words, delivery strategies) that are updated and revised through their personal history of coaching. The key elements of these interventions are stored and retrieved as 'mental notes'.
- Complex coaching judgements are made more or less instantaneously; they are made tacitly (in other words, without conscious recall of the cues and prompts that led to action decisions); they are made by each coach according to a distinctive 'personal theory or vision' of how coaching 'should be'.
- Coaching practice is situationally specific. The choice of intervention and the conscious micro-management of the intervention rests on both pre-planned session structures (that the coach has determined in the light of a considered response to performance development and competition needs at the time) and the more immediate and contingent adaptation to the circumstances and athlete responses as they arise. Coaches are precise, flexible and parsimonious planners (they plan what they need but not what they already 'know').
- Sport coaching practice is so context-dependent and decision variations so subtle that it cannot be understood in terms of general responses to the 'coaching moment'. It must be appreciated and understood at the 'level of the particular'.
- Subtlety (and variation) will be evident in (1) the manipulation of training drills, exercises and loadings; (2) the management of feedback and progression; and (3) the myriad interactions between athletes and coaches.

164

QUESTION BOX

Coaching has its basis in systematic, controlled practice because performance is strongly influenced by training theory principles.

- Some coaching appears to have less emphasis on pre-planned activity and more on broad-goal-driven activity.
- The role of the coach is influenced by the nature of the competition.
- Smaller increments of improvement and regulation are dependent on the assistance of science rather than more general prescriptions.
- Delivery is craft-based and subject to interpretation, personal bias and perception of demand.
- All aspects of coaching are open to innovation, but it is not a constant condition; routine is more common.
- The absence of systematic, regulated training and principled decision making does not justify calling coaching practice an art. (Our inability to describe 'professional craft knowledge-in-action' does not make it esoteric or art – just poorly understood and researched practice.)
- Coaching involves 'context-specific' and 'contract-specific' role factors.

Do these descriptors reflect your experience of coaching or being coached?

This is one conceptualisation of coaching practice; there will, of course, be many others. Rather than debate the aptness of the description of practice, it raises questions about how the coach is able to manage this process and, perhaps more importantly, what the implications are for coach education and development. This raises a number of issues that need to be resolved:

- apparently intuitive decision making of the coach;
- coping with changes in the environment;
- coping with fluctuations in performance;
- maintaining focus on goals;
- managing the interdependence of consequences;
- balancing stability and innovation; and
- maintaining an overview of the short- and longer-term implications of action.

Therefore, the remainder of the chapter identifies a catalogue of helpful metaphors for conceptualising the way in which coaches deal with the actualisation of their roles. How do coaches cope with this demanding role on a day-to-day basis? We might characterise this as: 'The expertise of coaches depends on effective and efficient decision making in order to create, direct and manage the strategic process that leads to the development of performance and the series of coaching episodes and moments of which it is constituted.'

THE CONTROL BOX

We conceptualise the coach's operationalisation of their practice as involving the regulation of the process; for this reason, the regulating function was built into the model in the previous chapter – we call this the 'control box'. Part of the model is reproduced here to focus attention on the regulation process (see Figure 8.1). An accumulation of ideas (about integration, coordination, mental models, decision making and the coach's overview of the process) has been incorporated into the model. This section is intended to represent the control box that regulates the process. We speculate that an essential feature of moving from a novice to expert coach is the gradual development in the capacity of the control box.

Key to the cognitive organisation of the control box is a series of threshold points that help the coach to control the myriad potential decisions to be taken and to integrate

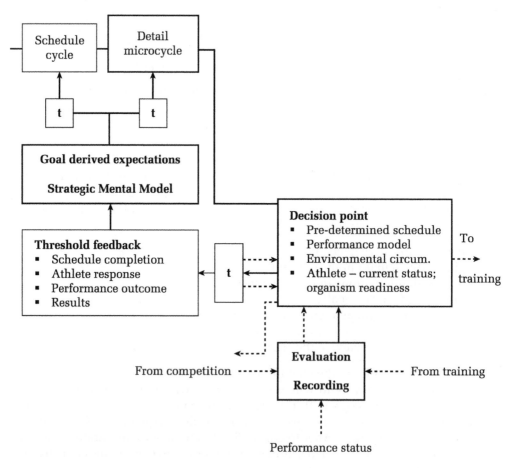

Figure 8.1 The control box of the coaching process.

the great range of data that is constantly available. Feedback loops from training and competition (and from interaction with the athlete) come to the control box where the feedback both informs current status evaluations and is evaluated against the performance model, existing planning intentions and any external environmental circumstances that may have influenced performance. In most cases, the cognitive computations that take place in the immediacy of the coaching moment will fall well within acceptable limits (degrees of freedom that might be expected in performance-related activity) and the coaching process interventions continue as planned. In some cases, there will be too great a difference between the anticipated and actual achievement. If this persists, a threshold is breached and the coach will effect changes to the programme of interventions (or possibly alter the level of expectations).

The system of thresholds allows the coach to use efficient and effective professional shortcuts in decision making. There is a hierarchy of threshold decisions, some of which are capable of being effected within modest contingency planning and some of which require more substantive re-planning. The hierarchy moves from sessional interventions that require adjustment to the training loadings, to the next stage in which accumulative breaches lead to deliberative re-scheduling of preparation cycles, and finally to the point at which goals may need to be adjusted. The breaches of the thresholds can be in training, in competition and in process elements of adherence/resourcing, etc.

Thresholds

One of the weaknesses acknowledged in the model, and in any similar model, is the absence of detailed relationships between component elements or stages of the model – partly about threshold values, but also the effect of changes in one element on others (the influence of organisational goals on individual goal-setting, or the impact of coaching behaviour on competition performance). It is one of the purposes of the coaching process model that it should be used to generate research on such questions. Tables 8.1 and 8.2 exemplify the findings that can be used to illuminate coaching practice. Two examples are given, each of them from some earlier work by one of the authors (Lyle 1991, 1992). The tables are composed of responses to questions posed to experienced coaches about how they would deal with 'threshold issues'. The responses were not quantified and are provided merely to illustrate that it is possible to particularise these decision stages.

Table 8.1 details the responses of coaches to the following question: 'For how long would the non-achievement of training targets be allowed to continue before taking steps to alter the situation?'. Although used merely for illustration, these data were given by practising, experienced coaches. For the most part, coaches were concerned to take fairly immediate or short-term action, although the range of responses is extensive and there is a sense of 'not wanting to react too immediately'.

In the second example, coaches were asked the following question, which was couched in terms of a reference to mental models of performance: 'How significantly

Table 8.1 Threshold responses by coaches in three sports

Coach	Athletics	Volleyball	Swimming
1	One week	Wait as long as possible	1 session
2	One week	If major – two games	Quickly
3	Immediate action	As short a time as possible	Less than one cycle
4	Immediate action	Two weeks	Four weeks
5	Less than four weeks	If critical, constant attention	2–3 days
6	2–4 weeks	Three training sessions	One week
7	Four weeks	Half a season	3–4 weeks
8	Eight weeks	Three-quarters of a season	Investigate immediately
9	Two weeks	Immediate action	2–3 sessions
10			Two weeks

Source: Lyle 1991, 1992.

would the likely performance differ from the predicted before there would be a change of expectations?'. This question probes the threshold values required to change goal-derived expectations. The responses were collated in textual form and again display a wide range of values (see Table 8.2).

There are some clear sport-specific differences and also some significant differences between coaches. It would seem that coaches are reluctant to change – perhaps recognition that fluctuation is normal, or perhaps that too much change is unsettling

Table 8.2 Coaches' responses to performance deficit

Coach	Athletics	Volleyball	Swimming
1	Not change if possible	Try to hold on	Would need to be significant
2	Threshold (not specified)	If two games don't match image – change	Leave as long as possible
3	Leave as long as possible	Try to leave	Intuitive action when not achieving
4	Leave as long as possible	Would have to be very significant	Very small
5	Leave as long as possible	Pretty far off course	Significantly
6	I have faith in planning	Until manifestly obvious	Not much
7	When obvious to the athlete	One session	Keep going if possible
8	Leave to right itself	If critical or bad (unexpected) result	Quite a lot
9			Significantly

Source: Lyle 1991, 1992.

for the performer. What is reinforced from these data is that coaches operate idio-syncratic practices and that a good deal of further research is required with successful, expert coaches in order to identify these coping mechanisms.

DECISION MAKING: THE FOUNDATION OF COACHING PRACTICE

The first edition of *Sports Coaching Concepts* devoted considerable attention to decision making; partly by being diffused throughout the book, but also as a specific section of chapter 7 (p. 132). Since that time, there have been additional publications (Lyle 2010a; Lyle & Vergeer 2012) and decision making as a mainstay of a cognitive lens on coaching practice has received further attention (Abraham & Collins 2011). In the absence of a significant body of research evidence, this remains in a relatively emergent state of development and understanding. There are unanswered questions about the development of propositional knowledge and how the coach's experiential decision making can be educated and further developed. We have taken a decision therefore not to include a chapter specifically about decision making, but to incorporate it in this chapter on operationalising the coaching process.

The thesis, which has emerged over time, is that Naturalistic Decision Making (NDM) (Klein 1998; Lipshitz *et al.* 2001; Ross *et al.* 2006), with its emphasis on experiential decision making, relying on recognition and memory to make sense of what is happening and subsequently moving (relatively rapidly) to a single option response, is an appropriate vehicle for understanding how coaches make their apparently intuitive action decisions. The NDM paradigm is generally applied to single episode events, and the application of NDM in the context of coaching's serial and aggregative nature requires further investigation.

 KEY CONCEPT

Naturalistic Decision Making (NDM), with its emphasis on experiential decision making, relying on recognition and memory to make sense of what is happening and subsequently moving (relatively rapidly) to a single option response, is an appropriate vehicle for understanding how coaches make their apparently intuitive action decisions.

Experiential decision making is contrasted with other forms of decision making – rational (in which the coach has sufficient time and information to make a rational choice between considered alternatives) and intuitive (which relies on 'gut feeling'). When the concept of deliberative/non-deliberative cognition is taken into account, the application of decision making to coaching interventions may be illustrated in the following way:

- Slower deliberative decision making: planning, regulating programmes, selection
- Semi-deliberative decision making: drills/scrimmage control, inter-personal interaction
- Speedy non-deliberative decision making: drills/scrimmage control, match coaching, crisis management

We continue with a description of the conceptual framework of coaches' decision making that was originally described by Harvey *et al.* (2015). This made use of the NDM paradigm, although one of the aims of the research was to evaluate whether or not the paradigm could usefully be applied to a serial process such as sport coaching. The framework also acknowledged the characteristics of the coaching process that have already been identified: goal-directed but multiple, contest goals; non-linear response to training stimuli; uncertain environments with limited information available; a complex, multi-layered process directed and responded to by human beings, with the emotional, partial, variable and idiosyncratic behaviour that this entails. It was envisioned that decisions could be categorised as crisis events (major injury, complete disruption to the programme), goals threatened (lack of progress, 'losing' position in a game), personal status or image of the coach threatened (coach's knowledge challenged, undisciplined behaviour, loss of control) or planned activity not achieved (activity not successful, lack of momentum, outcomes not achieved).

The decision-making process is conceived in three stages – situational assessment, triggering and management of the decision taking. Active and passive scanning of the environment (for example, a training session) allows the coach to recognise patterns. Experience and training has primed the coach to attend to 'key attractors' that can be general (unforeseen events, lack of quality and lack of focus) or specific (drills not working, loss of momentum, unforced errors, lack of progress). A cognitive process is simultaneously taking place: features of the environment are matched against stored memory and interpreted. The coach is subconsciously putting the 'events' in a historical context and evaluating their typicality. The story that the coach internally digests leads to a judgement about whether or not a problem is evident.

Clearly, not all coaching moments require the coach to take action (remember that this can be merely a word to an athlete, an element of feedback, an amendment to a drill or a tactical change during a competition). The 'triggering' stage involves evaluation of the threat to the intentions and expectations, and the degree of risk to be tolerated. Coaches will have priorities to which they attend, and there will be threshold values that apply. If these threshold values are breached, the coach will be likely to take action of some kind. Part of the evaluation is a forward reflection about the likely outcome of any action taken (this may be retrieved from previous events).

The final stage is the management of the decision taking. Depending on the time and information available, there will be a mix of deliberative and semi-deliberative or experiential decision making. The decision outcomes are modelled and provide the input to an iterative process of evaluation, scanning and interpretation. The decisions

Operationalising the model

themselves are subject to decision policies (perhaps not of the coach's making) and 'heuristics'. These are preferred ways of acting that the coach has become comfortable with over a period of time. Examples of heuristics might be:

- attending to the most recent events;
- taking decisions with minimal risk attached;
- intervening only reluctantly;
- taking decisions that 'satisfice' (have acceptable outcomes but are acknowledged not necessarily to be optimal because sufficient information is not available); and
- preferring to communicate 'privately'.

 QUESTION BOX

Think about your own coaching. Are you aware of any 'rules of thumb' that influence your priorities in decision making?

We are well aware that this description, or any diagram that might accompany it, appears to support a linear model of practice. This is a limitation of presentation (although useful for identifying component parts) and does not portray adequately the interdependence of the sub-process, the simultaneity of these, the immediacy of experiential decision making, and its iterative nature. The usefulness of breaking down the component parts is that this is necessary for education and training. We highlight two features:

1. The time available to the coach will determine the deliberative, semi-deliberative or non-deliberative characteristic of the decision making. We suggest that much of the majority of the decisions taken by the coach in training and competition situations will be semi-deliberative. There will be sufficient time for some consideration of options, but crisis events or time-pressured game circumstances may require more rapid decisions that mirror the NDM paradigm.
2. The knowledge and prior experience necessary to provide the coach with the substance of the decision-making process, and to create the 'memories' against which observations can be matched are stored in various forms of mental models and cognitive structures. These are less well understood or researched than we would wish for sport coaching. It is generally assumed that there are knowledge frames or schemata that store declarative and propositional knowledge ('what happens if') in complex, integrated, sophisticated but retrievable structures. Catalysts can trigger particular combinations of cause and effect, problems and solutions, and previous outcomes that are matched against the coaching moment being observed. Memories are also stored as 'scripts'. These are stories or scenarios that have previously been experienced. These provide the basis for judgements of 'what has been tried before' or 'what might happen if I try this'.

It will be obvious that not all possible scenarios can be 'stored'. The essence of the NDM paradigm is that experts have more sophisticated knowledge and memory structures and can therefore 'recreate' or 'fill in the gaps' in a more effective and efficient way.

Mental models

'Mental models' is a generic term for the internal representations that help individuals to interpret and predict events in the world around them (Johnson-Laird 1983). There are many types of mental model, and the knowledge structures (that we called schemata) and unfolding scenarios (that we termed scripts) are versions of these models. Models are domain-specific, although some will also contain condition-action rules that might be more generally applied. It has been argued that everyday reasoning depends on the simulation of events as mental models, and that such models are part of the expertise on which NDM depends (Ross *et al.* 2006).

Mental models can be accessed in conscious and subconscious ways. We have used the terms 'deliberative' and 'semi-deliberative' to describe two types of thinking: the former implies time for considered, effortful, rule-based and knowledge-rich computation; the latter has recourse to associative memory that we have illustrated in an NDM context. This is analogous to System 1 (associative memory) and System 2 (deliberate process) thinking (see Kahneman 2011). The important point here is that the 'thinking' – that is, the decision making – is trainable. The message goes something like this:

1. Kahneman concurs with the view that intuition (which is said to characterise coaching practice) is a subconscious recognition process.
2. Klein's (1998) Recognition Primed Decision model of decision making, a mainstay of NDM, is a formalisation of this process but involves a phase in which the initial judgement of appropriate action is checked (simulated) to see if it is likely to work. This is a 'speedy association' in time-pressured situations.
3. The mental representations we hold need to be organised and structured to make them readily accessible to this use.
4. Judgements made in this way are more believable if (as Kahneman says) (a) they take place in an environment that is sufficiently regular to be predictable; and (b) the regularities have been learned through practice.

The important point for education and development is that mental models can be built up through learning and experience.

There may be some debate about the extent to which the sport coaching practice arena has sufficient regularity to be susceptible of this kind of decision making.

In the sport coaching context, we conceptualise the coach's decision making as being filtered through a series of mental models (Figure 8.2). These assist the coach to interpret the coaching environment, to make sense of it, to relate it to their longer-term and more immediate purposes, to predict likely outcomes, to internalise and store experience and to provide a mechanism for personalising novel experiences.

Although there are sport-specific differences, we conceive of sport coaching as having a goal-directed process based on performance-enhancement principles and theories, and with a regularity of organisation and structure that enables athletes and coaches to take part in the process with relatively high levels of predictability. This is not directly at odds with the conception of sport coaching as complex – we believe it to be a matter of degree (Lyle 2007). Sport coaching is certainly complex, multi-variable, contested, emotional, unsteady in progress and has an element of uncertainty of both responses and outcomes. However, coaches do work towards goals, make decisions based on sound training theory and pedagogical practice, and deal with problem situations and interpersonal relationships, and there is an element of control or order about this practice.

In other words, coaches cope (albeit not all of them and presumably not all equally effectively) with the demands of the day-to-day operationalisation of the coaching process. It seems clear, across many sports, that coaches' expertise enables them to fulfil their roles in a way that may be challenging but 'doable'. The management of the intervention (and its uncertain and unpredictable nature) is characterised by the coach's use of

- learned shortcuts (associative thinking, thresholds, and heuristics);
- accepting 'degrees of freedom'; and
- routine practices.

How much of the coach's behaviour is routinised and how much is improvised? We acknowledge a particular lens on coaching that emphasises its social construction and shared meanings that are continually created and recreated. This is perhaps the rationale for saying that sport coaching practice is characterised by 'structured improvisation' (Cushion 2007). However, we know that coaches are not improvising in any meaningful sense of the word (largely because it implies an element of being 'unforeseen' or to which there are no effective answers). We conceive of a climate of 'constant accommodation' to context, some of which is conscious and some subconscious. Coaches appear to rely on routine behaviour and practice, within which there is considerable variation in practice. Their acceptance of thresholds and 'degrees of freedom' in performance and interaction is a coping mechanism. Progress is not linear, nor solutions based on mathematics. The human, emotional responses of coaches and athletes, and the inherent difficulty of skilled performance in contested circumstances, means that flexibility and variation in progression, momentum, athlete behaviour and performance quality and outcomes have to be accepted, and do not provoke immediate or rule-based responses. Coaches rely on various mental models and stored solutions to problems that allow them to amend their actions in subtle and nuanced ways. Thus the micro-management of the flow of interaction may be said to involve 're-creation', but not improvisation.

There will be many mental images or representations, but we identify three mental models as targets for development: a goal model, performance model and simulation model.

Goal model: this is the basis of the coach's constant set of judgements about the scale and appropriateness of progression over time. There is a continuous process of comparison against longer-term, medium-term and more immediate goals (the basis of 'layered' or 'nested' goals). These alter as the season progresses and the likelihood of achieving goals is assessed. Goals are a mixture of process and outcome goals and are also used to identify intermediate targets and progression points. The result is a dynamic, flexible reference point for decision making. It is difficult to overstate their importance; despite often being unwritten, assumed and contested, the goal model provides a framework for all coaching-related activity. Evidence from coaches' plans (Lyle 2010b) demonstrated that coaches often used the goal model as a 'shell', within which less-detailed planning was evident. However, the goal model was used as an evaluative reference point for variations in the intervention programme.

Performance model: this is also a reference point for planning and monitoring progress. The performance model is a (usually detailed) indication of what is required to achieve the goals set. It also helps to set these goals. The model takes into account athlete profiles, monitoring data and observations, analysis of opponents, previous achievements and current status. These are set against what the coach knows about performance levels and requirements for athletes at varying stages of development. This will be a 'technical' model, with technique, tactical, physical conditioning and other performance components, although it is very sport-specific. In some sports (perhaps best described as 'engine' sports, largely dependent on physical capacity) the model may be very systematic and based on data derived from detailed analyses of performance. The model becomes an amalgam of requirements, current status and expectations. The coach uses the performance model to evaluate performance and progress, and to plan. As with other features of the coaching process, it is a 'live' model and is constantly updated as the coach's technical knowledge is increased, awareness of current trends and projections becomes available and the athletes' performance develops.

Simulation model: this can be conceived of as the coach's day-to-day management tool. It provides a set of expectations about how an episode or event can be expected to unfold – based on previous experience and with current contextual information factored in. It therefore becomes a reference point against which practice can be monitored. Once again, priority features of the environment and thresholds will be used to judge whether any action is required. Training sessions, athlete interactions, specific drills and exercises and game/competition will all be simulated.

174

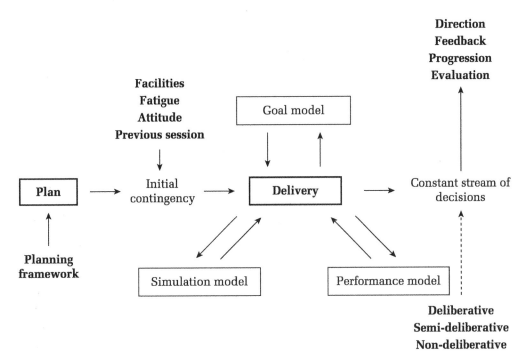

Figure 8.2 Overview of implementation.

Novices will have a wide range of expectations, whereas experts are capable of narrowing the range of expectations. A specific type of simulation occurs when coaches decide on a course of action but use 'anticipatory reflection' to evaluate the likely effectiveness of their actions. For all of the reasons already noted (contested, uncertainty, partial information, emotional response, inherent variability) the simulation model will inevitably be imperfect.

PEDAGOGY

Although there has been an emphasis on decision making in our conceptualisation of the coaching process, it is important to acknowledge that there is an element of 'craft' in the delivery of the intervention. Coaches may plan well and have a sound cognitive structure that facilitates their personal- and performance-related interaction with athletes and other practitioners. However, the practicalities of the intervention itself need to be operationalised. In simple terms, coaches will organise and manage athletes or groups of athletes in a physical space, communicate, feedback, demonstrate, observe, record and many other tasks and competences that together comprise coaching practice. At this point we will make only a few comments, as the substance of the coach's intervention behaviour is covered in the chapter on pedagogy and, to some extent, in the chapter on expertise.

1. There is, as you would expect, interplay between intervention strategy (also termed coaching style), type of planning employed (see Lyle 2010b), balance of attention to detailed workloads and more interactive team activity, and so on. Sport coaching intervention practice becomes the culmination of philosophy, expertise, craft, decision making and planning. The ongoing rhetoric about re-creation of the coaching moment, flexibility and systematic practice, complexity and routine, control and collaboration is a necessary part of the drive to understand how coaches operate, but it is important to acknowledge the immediacy of direction, organisation and feedback in the 'coaching moment'.

2. Prescriptive accounts of craft skills can be found in textbooks, and they form a significant part of coach education and training. (You should note that the assumptions about what constitutes a craft skill will differ, and there is a tendency to aggregate these into 'skill sets'.) For example, Navin (2011) identifies the following 'how to' skills: safety, building rapport, fun, organisation, explanation, demonstration, observation, analysis and feedback. Lynn (2010) uses the term 'expert coaching actions': building relationships, creating a learning environment, effective communication, organisation and control, coaching pedagogy, goal-setting, planning and preparation, observation and analysis and reflective practice. Stafford (2011) uses a figure from the first edition of this book, which identifies craft skills as a sub-set of process skills (Lyle 2002, p. 50). Stafford's list identifies planning, organising, building rapport and relationships, providing instruction and explanation, questioning, observing and analysing, providing feedback and evaluating and reflecting. These might be considered 'higher-order' terms, and Stafford adapts the work of Downey (2003) to demonstrate that there are more specific elements. For example, the intervention behaviour might include: giving feedback, making suggestions, giving advice, challenging, evoking creativity and innovation and giving instruction (p. 78). It will be immediately obvious that there is a good deal of agreement about how coaches go about their business.

3. We have emphasised the experiential decision making that we believe to be central to the coach's operationalisation of the coaching intervention. This brings with it a new set of competences that perhaps have not yet formed a significant part of coach education, but we suggest should be introduced. These have been incorporated into Figure 8.3. Although these may be identified in isolation for conceptual and developmental purposes, it is clear that they are interdependent, and provide a significant challenge for coach education and analysis of practice.

MISCELLANEOUS

Focus on breakdowns

When investigating how coaches operationalise their practice, it is an obvious ploy to attend to the skill sets or underlying cognitive processes that characterise their adaptation to the demands of the athletes and the environment. However, an alternative approach is to attend to those features of practice that are likely to break

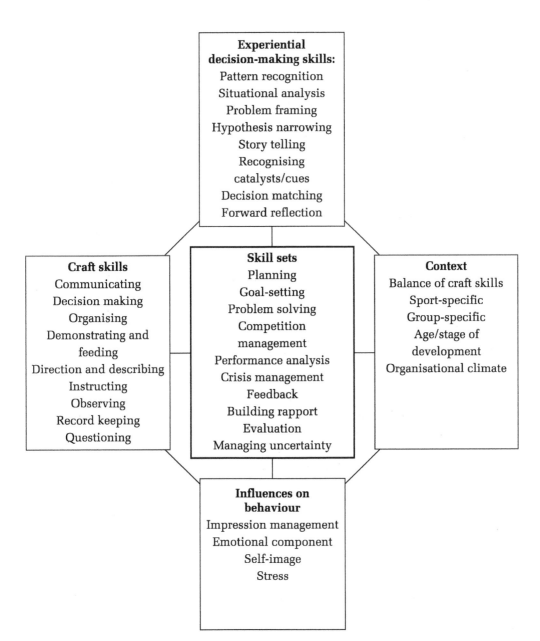

Figure 8.3 Craft skills in context

down or cause additional disruption. These pressure points provide a potential focus for research.

Examples of these might include introducing a new technique or tactic, a change in role, negative feedback from athletes or peers, stagnation in progression, critical incidents, failure to achieve goals or athlete dissatisfaction. These 'difficult' aspects of practice may provide an appropriate vehicle for an investigation into the 'coping strategies' that we have emphasised.

What constitutes 'good' operationalisation?

Coaches use a speedy form of experiential decision making to make sense of the complexity around them and act on it, and mechanisms such as thresholds and routines to reduce that complexity. We conceptualise intervention practice as a constant series of action decisions that accommodate to the environment, within a set of goals and planned intentions. This implies that there are many action decisions taken without complete availability of information and the complexity and variability of the task means that there is uncertainty in the appropriateness of the coach's response. Coaches may act differently when presented with similar circumstances.

If we accept this variability in perception, interpretation and response, operationalisation is never 'correct' – merely appropriate. A good action decision will address the task or problem, but can rarely be subject to a yes/no evaluation. This is partly because the serial and iterative nature of coaching practice means that any action is rarely a final one. Good decisions will be 'close to what is required', may adopt 'broad coverage' (to embrace change and uncertainty) and will be subject to amendment. Good decisions might be evaluated as those that require fewer amendments as situations unfold.

 QUESTION BOX

Does this mean that it is difficult to tell if a coach is effective or 'doing a good job'? Is it a partial explanation for a reliance on athlete performance as an evaluation of coaching effectiveness?

'Normal desirable state of activity'

We return to Hagger and McIntyre (2006) for another mechanism used to reduce complexity. Their characterisation of teaching as not susceptible to scientifically established models of good practice is entirely in accord with our own interpretation of sport coaching. They emphasise not only the complex variation in tasks and circumstances, and cultural contexts, but also the 'thinking, creative and imaginative beings' with whom they work. They refer to 'normal desirable states of . . . activity' (Brown & McIntyre 1993). The term refers to a kind of 'steady state' in which there is recognition of activity levels, behaviour and quality as appropriate to the task in hand. In other words, there is a form of threshold that acknowledges activity as 'within acceptable boundaries of expectations'. The implication is that variation and complexity in the day-to-day business of coaching can be reduced by recognising

178

acceptable limits of variation; these then do not excite immediate action, and perhaps permit the coach a more instrumental or goal-directed focus.

Accommodation and reflecting-in-action

In the chapter on expertise there is considerable emphasis on what is termed alignment, adaptation or application. This is that component of expertise in which coaches use their capacities (knowledge and decision-making skills) to accommodate the particular contexts in which they are operating. We conceptualise this higher-order expertise as characteristic of sport coaching and an explanation for the apparently intuitive and tacit decision taking that is a common descriptor of coaches' behaviour. It is mentioned here because it is a means of operationalising practice and complements Schön's (1983) metaphor of 'reflection-in-action'.

There is a distinction between reflection-in-action (conscious engagement in a self-referenced reflective conversation during competition or practice), reflection-on-action (the same process but after the 'direct action present') and retrospective reflection-on-action (conversation after the event). In operationalising coaching practice, it may be that Schön's reflecting-in-action is adequately accounted for by the adaptation and accommodation element of expertise. There will be moments during the 'coaching moment' when a more deliberative interpretation of circumstances is possible, but there is a greater reliance, for the most part, on the recognition/memory process that we have described.

Training and development

We deal elsewhere with education and development of coaches, but spend a little time here to offer a few insights that are generated by the challenges of operationalising coaching practice. Much is made of formal/informal and incidental modes of learning, and mechanisms such as reflection, mentoring and so on. However, we should note the particular challenges of helping coaches to develop the 'accommodation' expertise. We have 'painted a picture' of coaches coping with complexity through sound planning in the pre-active phase, and the judicial application of routines, experiential decision making and their (extensive) repertoire of intervention scripts and solutions. Our experience in coach education and development leaves us with the view that this 'higher-order' expertise has, thus far, been largely left to time and experience.

We offer one approach here as an exemplar of what might be possible. This is to break the sport-specific coaching moment into (problematic) functions, to construct model themes, devise a series of highly complex and unpredictable (tactical) situations or vignettes (typical and challenging), and to use these to develop 'thought habits with complex structures' – particularly by attending to the 'triggers' for action (Shadrick & Lussier 2009). In this approach, thinking skills are treated in a similar way to physical skills. A training programme would exhibit repetition, conscious focus, focused feedback, immediacy of performance, emphasis on difficult aspects and focus on areas of individuals' weakness. Coaches' performance during scenarios is halted for discussion of the implications of decisions taken and decisions are defended. The time taken is gradually reduced until coaches attend to the decisions subconsciously. This can be assisted by identifying a set of model themes or questions that the coach uses to direct attention. A typical set of questions for a volleyball coach during competition might look like this:

- Why did the opposition coach do that?
- Why are the opponents playing like that?
- Are my players performing as expected?
- Is my (action) helping to achieve my goal?
- What is the balance of strengths and weaknesses on each side?
- Are we still on course for achieving our goal/targets?
- What is the current balance of momentum?
- What is the big strategic picture?

 SUMMARY

This chapter will have familiarised you with the following:

- The need to understand how coaches operationalise coaching practice.
- The characteristics of the coaching process that shape the operationalisation.
- A summary interpretation of coaching practice.
- The 'control box' as a metaphor for regulating the coaching process.
- The importance of thresholds as a coping mechanism.
- The centrality of decision making in operationalising practice.
- Mental representations as a means of effective and efficient thinking.
- A number of aspects of pedagogy that assist in understanding how coaches operationalise practice.

REFERENCES

Abraham, A., & Collins, D. (2011). Effective skill development: How should athletes' skills be developed? In D. Collins, A. Button, & H. Richards (Eds) *Performance Psychology: A Practitioner's Guide*. Edinburgh: Churchill Livingstone, 207–230.

Brown, S., & McIntyre, D. (1993). *Making Sense of Teaching*. Buckingham: Open University Press.

Cushion, C. (2007). Modelling the complexities of the coaching process. *International Journal of Sports Science & Coaching*, 2(4), 395–401.

Downey, M. (2003). *Effective Coaching*. 3rd edition. New York: Texere Pub.

Hagger, H., & McIntyre, D. (2006). *Learning Teaching from Teachers: Realising the Potential of School-Based Teacher Education*. Maidenhead: Open University Press.

PROJECTS

The following projects will assist you to engage with the content of the chapter.

1. Read Hagger and McIntyre (2006). (a) Evaluate the description of teaching practice as an analogy for coaching practice; (b) consider how their recommendations for teaching practice might be introduced into coaching education.
2. Identify a technical theme from your sport. Interview an experienced and less experienced coach and create a 'model' of their knowledge on that subject. Evaluate the sophistication of mental models.
3. Discuss a pre-active plan for a training session with an experienced coach. Observe the session (perhaps video). Record the activity and question the coach about her management of the session. Discuss amendments made to the plan and identify reasons for the changes.
4. With some colleagues, observe coaches in four different sports. Create a simple observational analysis tool and record the craft skills displayed by the coaches. Discuss the sport-specific aspects of what you find.

Harvey, S., Lyle, J., & Muir, B. (2015). Naturalistic Decision Making in high performance team sport coaching. *International Sports Coaching Journal, 2*(2), 152–168.

Johnson-Laird, P. N. (1983). *Mental Models*. Cambridge: Cambridge University Press.

Kahneman, D. (2011). *Thinking, Fast and Slow*. London: Penguin.

Klein, G. A. (1998). *Sources of Power: How People Make Decisions*. Cambridge, MA: MIT Press.

Lipshitz, R., Klein, G., Orasanu, J., & Salas, E. (2001). Focus article: Taking stock of naturalistic decision making. *Journal of Behavioral Decision Making, 14*, 331–352.

Lyle, J. (1991). The development of an ideal-type model of the coaching process and an exploratory investigation into the appropriateness of the model for coaches in three sports. Unpublished MSc thesis, University of Stirling.

Lyle, J. (1992). Systematic coaching behaviour: An investigation into the coaching process and the implications of the findings for coach education. In T. Williams, L. Almond, & A. Sparkes (Eds) *Sport and Physical Activity: Moving Towards Excellence*. London: E&FN Spon, 463–469.

Lyle, J. (2002). *Sports Coaching Concepts*. London: Routledge.

Lyle, J. (2007). Modelling the complexity of the coaching process: A commentary. *International Journal of Sports Science & Coaching, 2*(4), 407–409.

Lyle, J. (2010a). Coaches' decision making: A Naturalistic Decision Making analysis. In J. Lyle & C. Cushion (Eds) *Sports Coaching: Professionalisation and Practice*. Edinburgh: Churchill Livingstone, 27–41.

Lyle, J. (2010b). Planning for team sports. In J. Lyle & C. Cushion (Eds) *Sports Coaching: Professionalisation and Practice*. Edinburgh: Churchill Livingstone, 85–98.

Lyle, J., & Vergeer, I. (2012). Recommendations on the methods used to investigate coaches' decision making. In W. D. Gilbert, P. Potrac, & J. Denison (Eds) *The Handbook of Sports Coaching*. Abingdon: Routledge, 121–132.

Lynn, A. (2010). *Effective Sports Coaching: A Practical Guide*. Marlborough: Crowood Press.

Navin, A. (Ed.) (2011). *Sports Coaching: A Reference Guide for Students, Coaches and Competitors*. Marlborough: Crowood Press.

Ross, K. G., Shafer, J. L., & Klein, G. (2006). Professional judgements and 'Naturalistic Decision Making'. In K. A. Ericsson, N. Charness, P. J. Feltovitch, & R. R. Hoffman (Eds) *The Cambridge Handbook of Expertise and Expert Performance*. New York: Cambridge University Press, 403–419.

Schön, D. A. (1983). *The Reflective Practitioner: How Professionals Think in Action*. New York: Basic Books.

Shadrick, S. B., & Lussier, J. W. (2009). Training complex cognitive skills: A theme-based approach to the development of battlefield skills. In K. A. Ericsson (Ed.) *Development of Professional Expertise: Towards Measurement of Expert Performance and Design of Optimal Learning Environments*. New York: Cambridge University Press, 286–311.

Stafford, I. (2011). The essential skills of a coach. In I. Stafford (Ed.) *Coaching Children in Sport*. Abingdon: Routledge, 70–83.

CHAPTER 9

APPROACHES TO COACHING PRACTICE

LINKING THEORY AND PRACTICE

CHAPTER OUTLINE

- Introduction
- Coaching practice theory and paradigms
- Understanding different approaches to coaching
- Summary
- Projects
- Reading

INTRODUCTION

Despite a growth in research, coaching resources and materials, an in-depth understanding of coaching and a conceptual underpinning with which to inform coaches' practice remains elusive – to address this and to develop the conceptual framework we need to do more than consider coaching practice in an overly systematic and unproblematic way. Currently, the nature of coaching practice is often taken for granted and assumed, but in reality *is* ill-defined and under-theorised. Hence, we need to take both a critical and a reflexive stance towards coaching practice; in undertaking this task theory provides the necessary and useful 'thinking tools'. Coaching practice, in the sense of the operationalisation of the coaching process through the micro-management of the coaching intervention, i.e. 'what the coach is doing' is considered in detail in Chapter 7. Instead, the purpose of this chapter is to examine theory–practice relations more closely to develop a more sophisticated (and intellectual) understanding of coaching practice – the chapter still considers practice from the perspective of coach intervention, but goes beyond the obvious and descriptive through unpacking the assumptions and beliefs that inform 'what the coach is doing'.

Coaching practice is always 'infected' by the values and beliefs of its community – coaching practice is not objective and it is therefore neither benign nor neutral. Thus, when setting out to investigate and understand coaching practice it has to be recognised that coaching situations and approaches are already permeated by the interpretations, beliefs and intentions of coaching practitioners – coaches' subjective experience and knowledge has already been shaped by historical and cultural circumstances, as well as prevailing coaching ideology. Therefore, coaching practice should be understood not as some kind of thoughtless behaviour that exists separately from theory and to which theory can be 'applied'. Instead, coaching practice is viewed as having theory embedded in it and being conducted for distinctive purposes by means of specific procedures and skills informed by particular values and beliefs. In other words, coaching practice has an underlying paradigm, or 'philosophy', a theoretical framework that guides the activities of coaches engaged in coaching. Hence, conceptual development and understanding needs to be grounded in coaching practice if it is to inform coach education and importantly be recognised as legitimate by coaches. However, this chapter does not focus on the local or micro (and management) issues of particular *coaches' practice*, but looks beyond the obvious across and into *coaching practice* more broadly and deeply. The assumption here is that coaching is the complex interaction of the coach, athlete and context. It is the relationship between these factors that is of utmost importance, with the complex concerns and invested activity binding together in various ways, and from this practice arises, is shaped and is in turn judged. In this sense, coaching practice is not taken to be the simple application of an instructional model where the coach is the principle actor and the athletes are passive receivers (Cushion 2013).

Typically, and unsurprisingly, coaching research has more often than not focused on the coach as the unit of analysis rather than coaching practice. Therefore, there has been limited exploration of coaching practice as the articulation between coaches' experiences, conceptual understanding, pedagogical practices and the wider cultural and political realities of coaching. As a result, we have weak and impoverished notions of coaching practice that are insufficiently developed to inform coach education and coaching's conceptual development in a sophisticated fashion.

In terms of coaching practice there has been an emergence of a range of coaching approaches and advocates arising from varying theoretical and paradigmatic perspectives. Theoretical perspectives such as behaviourism, cognitivism, constructivism and situated learning are commonly presented as, and more often implicit in, underpinning coaching practice. These describe approaches to understanding athlete and coach learning, as well as offering frameworks to guide coaching interventions and designing coaching practice (see, for example, Cushion *et al.* 2010; Cassidy *et al.* 2016). Such theoretical perspectives have their roots in philosophy concerning the nature of knowledge and the nature of reality and will differ according to their underlying assumptions – hence coaching practice should differ according to the approach taken and also should supposedly be consistent with a given theoretical approach.

However, the reality of coaching practice suggests that a positivistic and behavioural approach remains the dominant element in coaching where such perspectives form a subtle but coherent set of rationalities and techniques that underpin coaching practices and coach education (Piggott 2013). Interpretive or constructivist approaches are often considered 'alternative' or 'innovative' and the rhetoric of such

184

approaches has done little to change coaching practice or challenge positivist domination of coaching thought. Taken together these micro or individual and macro or contextual factors mean that coaching practice and approaches to coaching are grounded in the complexities of coaches' practical reality. Therefore, far from being benign activities, coaching practice (and coach education), always contains and advances values and agendas – and supports certain approaches to coaching practice. Hence, uncovering theoretical layers alongside theoretical debate remains important and necessary in coaching to act as a springboard for discussion and to prompt coaches to question the relationships among philosophical assumptions, coaching perspectives, learning and instructional theory and coaching practice.

 KEY CONCEPT

Uncovering theoretical layers alongside theoretical debate remains important and necessary in coaching to act as a springboard for discussion and to prompt coaches to question the relationships among philosophical assumptions, coaching perspectives, learning and instructional theory and coaching practice.

Coaching practice is informed by assumptions about learning and knowing, and theoretical perspectives will be implicit in coaches' practice. When coaches (and researchers) describe coaching practice and approaches to coaching practice, a number of issues become apparent:

1. The philosophical roots and assumptions of practice are not always clear.
2. The theoretical perspective underlying practice is not always clear.
3. Often the same coaching practice is described in different ways, depending on the answer to points 1 and 2.
4. The same coaching practice can be distinguished from one theory or another differently.

The result is a confusion that limits the development of the conceptual framework and the growth (and acceptance) of different approaches to coaching practice. To provide a theoretical grounding or foundation to coaching practice it is important to have what Schuh and Barab (2007) have suggested as sharper boundaries between theoretical categories to help inform designers of coach education and coaching practice.

To address these issues a number we will take a number of steps. First, we consider the nature of coaching theory and paradigms and examine the assumptions of different philosophical approaches (i.e. epistemology and ontology). These are then placed within a historical context and considered alongside the wider development (or lack thereof) of the coaching field. We then look at broad categories of theories of coaching that underpin coaching practice. While the categories we suggest are open to discussion, and we would encourage debate and discussion about these, we have made our own theoretical commitment here and would want practitioners to do the same. The chapter therefore presents four theoretical perspectives that are most salient to explore coaching practice:

1. behaviourism
2. cognitivism
3. cognitive constructivism
4. social constructionism.

Each of these will be considered in terms of their epistemology, ontology and their main areas of focus related to coaching practice, and we then go on to suggest what coaching practice would look like informed by each perspective. The chapter will go on to differentiate between common paradigmatic perspectives and suggest alignments between assumptions associated with the various perspectives, coaching practice and athlete learning. Knowledge of the assumptions and characteristics that underpin different approaches is important as it not only informs the development of the conceptual framework, but also provides a vocabulary for interpreting coaching practice. In practical terms, it also allows coaches and coach educators to link to perhaps previously unconsidered theoretical approaches informing different ways to reflect on and develop coaching practice (cf. Cassidy *et al.* 2016).

COACHING PRACTICE THEORY AND PARADIGMS

Paradigms are worldviews that define the nature of the world, the individual's place in it, and the possible relationships to that world and its parts (Schuh & Barab 2007). A paradigm embodies the particular conceptual framework through which a community operates and in terms of which a particular reality is generated – it incorporates models of practice, standards, rules and a set of techniques and methods consistent with the view of reality the paradigm supports (Carr & Kemiss 1986). Paradigms are informed by a complex set of beliefs, values and assumptions where these are seldom made explicit in the 'theories' and practice produced, but nevertheless structure perceptions, and in coaching shape subsequent coaching practice.

 KEY CONCEPT

Paradigms are informed by a complex set of beliefs, values and assumptions where these are seldom made explicit in the 'theories' and practice produced, but nevertheless structure perceptions, and in coaching shape subsequent coaching practice.

These perspectives are important as they form the foundation for all coaching practice, and allow the recognition of the association with a particular discipline or approach. Therefore, all coaching practice and approaches to coaching activities are informed by – or inform – theory at one level or another, and it is paradigms that are the foundation for such theories. Hence, paradigms become visible through decisions in coaching. For example:

- What constitutes a coaching problem?
- What knowledge is appropriate to provide a solution to the problem?
- How is such knowledge acquired?
- What activities are the most appropriate?

Therefore, coaching practice cannot be analysed without reference to the shared values and beliefs of those engaged with it. Hence, the notion of paradigm is very much applicable to coaching – it is only against the backdrop of coaching paradigms that coaching practice can be made intelligible to researchers and practitioners – and therefore contributes to a sophisticated conceptual framework and informs coach education. Importantly, as Carr and Kemiss (1986) argue, "the assumptions that all 'theory' is non-practical and all 'practice' is non-theoretical are entirely misguided" (p. 113). An understanding of coaching practice and different approaches to coaching, therefore, is an enterprise requiring a critical appraisal of the adequacy of concepts, beliefs, assumptions and values incorporated in prevailing *coaching theories* and *theories of coaching*.

Theories of coaching are descriptive, describing how coaching occurs within a particular instance. For example, operant conditioning is a theory within the behavioural perspective (discussed below) that describes how coaching practice occurs through developing a relationship between stimulus and response. *Theories of coaching* tend to be general theoretical frameworks (typically imported from outside coaching) and knowledge in this case is associated with that which has been 'verified' through some research process or scientific enquiry. In contrast, *coaching theories* are prescriptive and provide guidance on the design and structure of coaching practice to facilitate athlete learning. They are theories that arise out of coaches' practical reality and activity, where knowledge tends to be grounded in practical experience and the theory is a process of codifying existing coaching ideas and practice.

 KEY CONCEPT

Coaching theories are prescriptive and relate to practice-based 'lay' or 'folk' ideas or concepts, while *theories of coaching* are descriptive and based on abstract scientific or academic ideas or concepts.

Therefore, a *coaching theory* identifies coaching methods to be used and, more importantly, identifies situations in which these methods should or should not be used – for example, the appropriate time to give feedback or in what order an element of technique or skill should be practised. Often coaches operate with a *coaching theory* or practice theory acquired in a subconscious manner rather than being 'taught theoretical practice' or a taught *theory of coaching*. Importantly, both theoretical approaches are prescribed ways of thinking (Carr & Kemiss 1986) and an apparent theory–practice gap is instead illustrative of a lack of critical reflection about the inter-relationship between theory and practice. That is, theories are not bodies of knowledge appearing from a practical vacuum, while coaching practice is not a mechanical performance that does not reflect underlying theory.

A *coaching theory* is probabilistic rather than deterministic and is employed by coaches with a belief in increasing the chances of achieving athlete learning goals – i.e. 'it works' – but no *coaching theory* guarantees goal achievement. The methods identified within a *coaching theory* provide for coaches specific ways to support and facilitate coaching practice. *Coaching theories* and their associated methods are often based on or linked to *theories of coaching*, providing an important linkage between how coaching practice occurs and how to facilitate that process. When we discuss different approaches to coaching practice later in the chapter, we describe some different *theories of coaching* and link these to what coaches do and what coaching practice looks like.

Coaching theories and *theories of coaching* will reflect assumptions about coaching – a wider paradigm that considers the nature of knowledge in coaching, how coaches and athletes think, as well as the nature of the coaching world and how one comes to know about each of these. An important point here is that given the practitioner-driven nature of *coaching theories*, the linkages between approach to coaching practice (what the coach perceives they do), *theories of coaching* (the theoretical foundation) and *coaching theory* (the coach's assumptions and beliefs about what works) alongside their associated coaching methods (what the coach actually does) are not necessarily simple and direct. In practice, *coaching theories* may not be confined to a single perspective and in the real world coaches will be more pragmatic and draw on a number of approaches to inform their coaching practice.

 KEY CONCEPT

In practice, *coaching theories* may not be confined to a single perspective, and in the real world coaches will be more pragmatic and draw on a number of approaches to inform their coaching practice.

Therefore, it is not always straightforward to categorise a particular approach to coaching practice with a particular paradigmatic or philosophical perspective.

Moreover, as Schuh and Barab (2007) remind us, it is important to acknowledge that paradigms with respect to epistemological and ontological assumptions are not coaching practice methods and that coaching practice methods are not paradigms. However, coaching practice strategies and methods are influenced by underlying paradigmatic assumptions, thus theories of knowing and learning are implicit in coaching practice and its design (Barab & Duffy 2000; Cushion 2013). Therefore, it is important for coaches designing coaching practice to engage in discussions about the differences between paradigms, *coaching theories* and *theories of coaching* – that is, individuals examine their ontological and epistemological commitments (discussed in the next section). In particular, the underlying assumptions that provide the theoretical basis for coaching practice that have implications for designing a particular approach to coaching practice. In other words, we would argue that it is important to have conceptual clarity in approaches to coaching practice. This is particularly the case when coaching practice and knowledge remains developed overwhelmingly by informal sources, particularly observation and experience. The aim here, then, is to move coaches' practice from being habitual or customary action towards practice that is informed, committed action – hence, we need to theorise practice in the sense of setting it in a critical framework of action that makes it rational, prudent and appropriate, and can be considered under critical control. Coaching practice then becomes action that is considered and consciously theorised to inform and transform.

 QUESTION BOX

Could conceptual clarity about the theoretical approach underpinning coaching practice be considered an element of coaching effectiveness? That is, an effective coach can explicate the theory underlying their practice.

Ontology and epistemology

As the chapter has begun to illustrate, there are significantly different ways of understanding coaching – and therefore viewing and delivering coaching practice. And to reiterate, any understanding relates to assumptions about how the person is perceived, the nature of reality and the nature of knowledge. Such assumptions are inherited and transmitted in coaching through a process of socialisation and initiation and provide important linkages "between how learning occurs and how the learning process is facilitated" (Schuh & Barab 2007, p. 76). Epistemology and ontology are foundational elements of philosophy (see Chapter 11 on coaching philosophy) which mutually support one another, and are useful concepts to explore different paradigms or approaches to coaching practice (Lombardo 1987; Reber 1995). As Schuh and Barab (2007) argue, paradigmatic or philosophical perspectives reflect certain assumptions with respect to the nature of the world and how we come to know about it; however, these are sets of beliefs and are not open to proof in the positivist sense of the word: "There is no way to elevate one over another on the basis of ultimate, foundational criteria" (Guba & Lincoln 1983, p. 108).

 KEY CONCEPT

Paradigms have underlying assumptions informing practice and can be explored through ontology and epistemology. Ontology raises questions that are concerned with the nature of reality. Epistemology raises questions concerning the nature of knowledge.

Epistemology

Epistemology is the systematic consideration of knowing, what is knowledge, when knowledge is valid and what counts as truth; it addresses the "origins, nature, methods, and limits of human knowledge" (Reber 1995, p. 256). Coaching and coaching practice can be said to have an epistemological purpose (i.e. supporting coaches or athletes in coming to know) regardless of the practice perspective with which they are aligned. Understanding how a coach or athlete comes to know and how that process can be facilitated forms a basis for understanding coaching practice. Questions of epistemology can be found in, for example:

- assumptions about a 'single' technical model in a sport versus multiple models;
- assumptions of knowledge about a sport being objective, 'out there' and acquired versus knowledge being subjective and experienced;
- coaches' practice that transfers objective knowledge to athletes versus helping athletes 'construct' their own subjective knowledge.

It is clear that epistemology – the theory of knowledge – plays a key role in how we think of coaching practice, and consequently affects how we coach and how athletes learn.

Ontology

Ontology is a branch of philosophy (within metaphysics) that is concerned with the consideration of being and reality (Schuh & Barab 2007; Reber 1995) – what exists and what it means 'to be'. Ontology defines what is real in the world, whether physical or abstract structures (Schuh & Barab 2007). Those engaged in coaching and coaching practice indicate their ontological position through identifying what are considered truths about being, the self and the world. Ontology can be found in assumptions such as:

190

- coaching practice is universal versus coaching practice is contextually variable;
- coaching contexts are objective versus contexts are socially constructed and subjective.

Ontology and epistemology: consequences for practice

Why are these distinctions and categories important? Many conceptions and models of coaching practice are often vague in terms of philosophical roots. This lack of transparency in our philosophy of coaching practice therefore creates inconsistency when we translate our beliefs into practices. Paradigmatic assumptions will frame theories, theoretical models and coaches' subsequent practice. Coaching and coaching practice are developed and linked to a particular set of assumptions and are influenced by these assumptions; therefore, theories of knowing, learning and being are implicit in coaching practice. When situational variables require some decision on the part of the coach, their underlying set of assumptions (whether they be tacit or explicit) will drive the decision (Barab & Duffy 2000; Cushion & Partington 2014) (see also Chapter 11, discussing coaching philosophy). All coaches design and advocate a particular approach to coaching practice with at least a tacit theory about who their athletes are (ontology), and how their athletes think and learn (epistemology). Coaches' assumptions will not only inform their coaching practice, but also the degree to which they understand and apply a particular approach. Importantly, coaching practice is not a value-free activity and therefore cannot be divorced from the wider world of ideology and belief. Thus, because of different outlooks, either explicit or implicit, coaching can be viewed, understood and practised with different aspects addressed – the goal of the coaching intervention may be the same, but the means to go about achieving it can be hugely variable. Coaching practice therefore should be based on a defensible theoretical framework. Such frameworks help us identify assumptions that are consistent with our beliefs and methods of coaching practice design. We run the risk of presenting conflicting and incoherent views when we attempt to merge theories with little regard for the philosophical underpinnings supporting such approaches.

 KEY CONCEPT

All coaches design and advocate a particular approach to coaching with at least a tacit theory about who their athletes are (ontology) and how their athletes think and learn (epistemology).

Do we really need to have these discussions, as it could be argued they have no real practical consequences? We would argue they are essential particularly when we consider that coaches generally do not realise the influence of their personal experience nor appreciate the ways in which powerful assumptions inform and guide their coaching practice. Everyday coaching practice judgements are made in an uncritical and non-reflective way, with 'what works' and a way of coaching that coaches perceive 'gets results' becoming regarded as self-evident. Hence, theoretical preconceptions – *coaching theories* – are the product of habit, precedent and tradition, having rarely been formulated as a result of clearly articulated thought processes. Typically, these are based on an established 'traditional' behaviourist approach (discussed in detail below) characterised by being coach-led and coach-centred – that is, highly directive, autocratic and prescriptive.

The implications for coaching practice are clear, coaches need to examine and question their ontological and epistemological assumptions and whether or not their coaching practice is consistent with those assumptions – that is, assumptions that are for example 'constructivist', but practices that are behavioural. Incongruence between assumptions and coaching practice provide moments to develop coaching and expose and eliminate inadequacies in values and beliefs, where coaches can question why such inconsistency exists and what steps are required to resolve these. This does not mean abandoning practical ways of thinking and becoming 'theoretical', but adopting a more critical and reflective attitude and developing the skills and resources to enable reflection where such reflection supports greater self-awareness, as well as enabling a critical examination of the merits of different conceptions of practice.

UNDERSTANDING DIFFERENT APPROACHES TO COACHING

Framing coaching and coaching practice in terms of paradigms requires some commentary on its 'cultural grounding' – that is, the historical and intellectual frameworks that influence thinking and practices in the coaching field. Approaches to coaching are historically situated in the changing conditions within wider academic and practical cultures such as education, physical education and psychology. Coaching, as a 'hybrid discipline', will reflect its own theoretical and practical struggles as well as being a proxy for wider debate over 'turf' and what constitutes legitimacy in practice and research. Such debates have their roots in different conceptions of the province of different disciplines in shaping, for example, coach behaviour, thinking processes, social interaction and patterns of culture.

Ideas related to nineteenth-century positivism have proliferated in coaching in a range of forms, including logical positivism and behaviourism (discussed in further detail later in the chapter). Positivism is a broad notion and lacking in clear-cut boundaries, but it:

- incorporates a cluster of doctrines based on meaning as being verifiable empirically through direct observation;
- is based upon the logic of scientific methodology; and
- has an interest in explanation, prediction and technical control.

Linking theory and practice

Positivism has been particularly manifest in coaching through behaviourism and has had a pervasive influence and legacy on coaching practice and shaping coach education – evidenced with, for example, coaching as behaviour modification and competency-based with standardised curriculum packages and pre-packaged information and skills (for athletes and coaches in coach education).

Criticised as reductive, and mirroring developments in other discipline fields (e.g. education and psychology), behaviourism in particular has been in part replaced by, and in part merged with, a cognitive paradigm (discussed in more detail later in the chapter). Still operating with positivistic assumptions, this paradigm assumes that we have universal cognitive structures that shape our experience of reality. The human individual is 'cogito', an epistemic person unchanged by the construction of knowledge – hence, coaching identity is unchanged by new knowledge. Coaching practice, research and thought is saturated by cognitive assumptions and language. In addition, coaching is also chiefly considered in terms of epistemology – that is, changing knowing/knowledge 'structures' with explanations that view coaching as a process by which the coach or athlete internalises foundational or objective knowledge, whether discovered, transmitted from others or experienced in interaction with others (Cushion 2016; Lave & Wenger 1991).

 KEY CONCEPT

Coaching is chiefly considered in terms of epistemology, that is changing knowing/knowledge 'structures' with explanations that view coaching as a process by which the coach or athlete internalises foundational or objective knowledge, whether discovered, transmitted from others or experienced in interaction with others.

The term 'instrumental rationality' is often used in coaching literature to conceptualise and critique cognitive and behavioural approaches to coaching practice, and derives from Habermas' 'paradigms of interest' as 'technical interest'. Technical interest reflects a need to control and manipulate the external environment. This remains a dominant view in coaching, where practice is said to be driven by 'instrumental rationality' – that is:

- the manipulation and control of the environment;
- prediction about observable events;
- coaching reality based on empirical knowledge; and
- coaching governed by technical rules.

Coaching practice activities, in this sense, are goal-directed and feedback-controlled in a presumed objective world. Coaching is assumed as a means to a given end and coaching practice is an element in a controllable system. The logical extension of this form of rationality is to view coaching practice as a skilled craft based on technical 'expertise'. Here, coaching can be viewed in terms of abstract, universal categories, such as motivation, decision making and feedback. Coaching from this perspective is made up of causal relationships between the different variables, a 'framework' of relevant categories. Patterns in the interactions between these variables are identifiable, and can be controlled to maximise effectiveness and therefore performance. Coaching in this sense is viewed as complex but open to analysis; the complexity is penetrable and regarded as susceptible to control. Theory, from this perspective, is something that is applied to practice, and coaching is cast as an applied science – 'coaching science'. Traditionally, coaching, viewed as instrumental rationality, has been informed through the discipline of psychology, and in particular behavioural psychology, which remains highly influential in informing coaching practice, coaching curricula design and coach education and it could be argued is a pervasive ideology.

Despite the dominance of cognitive and behavioural thought running through coaching, there are a number of alternative worldviews and critiques of positivist approaches and instrumental rationality. These have been described as, for example, hermeneutic or interpretive, and include critical theory, poststructural and postmodern approaches. Such approaches would be critical of the focus on the person as a primarily unitary, autonomous and cognitive entity. Coaching viewed from this perspective means that persons acting and the social world of activity cannot be separated (Lave 2009), and coaches and coaching do not exist in isolation; they are part of a broader system of relations in which they have meaning (Lave & Wenger 1996). From such a perspective, coaching is understood as social, historical and embodied (practical, physical, emotional as well as cognitive); and from a relational perspective of persons within a socially and culturally constructed world, understanding and experiences are in constant interaction (Buysse *et al.* 2003).

 KEY CONCEPT

Despite the dominance of cognitive and behavioural thought running through coaching, there are a number of alternative worldviews and critiques of positivist approaches and instrumental rationality.

Having set out a broad overview of the different approaches to coaching practice, the key theoretical standpoints will each be considered in detail, with examples of coaching practice and practice activities presented for each.

Behaviourism

Behaviourism was the predominant psychological school of thought during the first half of the twentieth century, and its ontological roots are objectivist (Schuh & Barab

2007; Greeno *et al.* 1996). That is, the coaching world is real and is objective, as is knowledge, existing outside of the individual coach. To come to know something within a behaviourist framework is to come to engage in specific behaviours in the context of particular stimuli, and from this perspective "knowledge is unchanged and transitive" (Brown & Duguid 1996, p. 49); once grasped, knowledge is easily transported from a particular learning situation to different contexts in which that knowledge can be put to work (Brown *et al.* 1989). According to Schuh and Barab (2007), three types of learning (coaching) practice can occur:

1. respondent learning (e.g. use of classical conditioning where involuntary actions are elicited);
2. operant conditioning (development of a relationship between a stimulus and response); and
3. observational learning (change of behaviour brought about by experience of observing others – see, for example, Bandura) (Schuh & Barab, 2007; Burton *et al.* 1996).

From a behavioural standpoint, coaching practice will facilitate learning by utilising reinforcement, punishment and feedback to illicit the correct response. Practice should be progressed step-by-step, building on previously learned material. The role of the coach is to deliver or transmit coaching through small, simple tasks – for example, breaking down a skill into its constituent parts. These tasks are practised repeatedly and feedback on performance reinforces the desired behaviour and stimulates motivation for the athlete to continue. As Schunk (2009) suggests, 'learning' will require establishing responses to stimuli. Because of its objectivist roots (knowledge is external to the individual), coaching practice will typically define the learning to occur and instruction has specific observable outcomes that progress in small steps and deliver re-enforcement – so 'session plans' are pre-planned and likely to contain 'coaching points' to be achieved. Because knowledge is objective, instructional content can also be pre-planned, organised and programmed, with specific outcomes defined. Behaviourism assumes that all learning can be measured; therefore, in terms of what an athlete 'can do', i.e. a behaviour is a learning outcome, this session's outcome will be to coach the top-spin serve. Often in coaching technological vehicles are used to facilitate the reinforcement process (for example, see the growth and proliferation of performance analysis technologies to provide feedback and reinforcement of desired coach and athlete behaviour). Coaches' practice, therefore, will be focused on the behaviour of the athlete and that of providing correct responses. With this type of coaching practice, cognitive processes are not necessary to explain the acquisition, maintenance and generalisation of behaviour (Schunk 2009).

As Cassidy *et al.* (2016) point out, a behaviourist view of learning still prevails in coaching and is indicative of much coaching practice, being considered a 'natural' way of coaching. Hence, a behaviourist approach to coaching practice has established itself as a 'traditional' approach in many sporting contexts where it has become 'what is expected' within the coaching role by coaches, athletes, parents and clubs (cf. Potrac *et al.* 2007). Indeed, findings of contemporary research mirrors

195

KEY CONCEPT

From a behavioural standpoint, coaching practice will facilitate learning by utilising reinforcement, punishment and feedback to illicit the correct response.

work conducted over the last 35 years, consistently reporting an extraordinary sameness in coaching practice that features actions aligning with a behavioural approach, including:

- high levels of coach-led instruction;
- feedback and re-enforcement;
- a predominance of 'drill' type activities that are broken into tasks progressing from simple to complex; and
- coaches talk most of the time and athletes listen while engaging in repetitive activities.

 QUESTION BOX

What 'type' of coaching practice is viewed as 'traditional'? How might this vary by sport? What role does coach education have in challenging or reproducing 'traditional' coaching practice?

Cognitivism

In examining different approaches to coaching it is not uncommon for behavioural and cognitive approaches to coaching to be joined together as positivist 'cognitive/ behavioural' approaches. However, it is important to stress that these are distinct theories and approaches, and as Bruner (1990, p. 1) suggests, cognitivism "was intended to bring the 'mind' back into the human sciences after a long cold winter of objectivism . . . not out to 'reform' behaviourism, but to replace it" (1990, p. 3). However, cognitivism, like behaviourism, has its roots in objectivism as an ontological base (coaching reality exists outside the individual) and grew in psychology, where the mind is viewed as an information-processing system considering the organisation, encoding and retrieval of knowledge (Schuh & Barab 2007). Hence, both behaviourist and cognitivist perspectives of coaching view knowledge as objective, where the coaching world is real and external to the coach and athlete – that is, that much of the information-processing view in cognitive psychology is based on an objectivist epistemology, with an "independent existence of information and the acquisition of

196

that information" (Duffy & Jonassen 1992, p. 3). The acquisition of knowledge structures does underlie the cognitive perspective and Schuh and Barab (2007) argue that a rationalist epistemological base, where each coach or athlete has an a-priori knowledge base before experience, provides the distinction required to define a meaningful boundary between behaviourism and cognitivism (Ertmer & Newby 1993).

Because cognitivism retains an objectivist ontological outlook, it has some of the same design goals as behaviourism (Schuh & Barab 2007; Schunk 2009), resulting in the following:

- Coaching practice, material, information and drills would be analysed and sequenced, in a simple to complex or hierarchical type of organisation (Gagné *et al.* 1992).
- The coach would be concerned in their practice with the development of athletes' knowledge or cognitive structures (as opposed to their overt behaviours) – presenting knowledge so it relates to existing knowledge and its use is understood (Schunk 2009).
- With a focus on rationalist knowledge building (reason rather than experience is the source of knowledge), it is possible to detach the learner from the environment – that is, practice does not have to be 'in context' or the drills themselves can be de-contextualised.
- The coach would focus on the organisation of the to-be-learned information to facilitate its acquisition by the athlete.
- As with a behaviourist approach, the resulting session objectives or outcomes can be made explicit and objective.

Coaching practice is, therefore, designed to align with the components and stages central to an information-processing type of approach. From this perspective, encoding and retrieval strategies align to explicitly define skills and knowledge that the athlete will learn and subsequently produce (Schuh & Barab 2007). Although the learning outcome may be an identifiable behaviour, the coach remains interested in the athlete's knowledge structures – and the development of knowledge structures, schema, conceptual frameworks and so on is to talk in cognitive terms about knowledge and practice. In coaching, this presents a non-personal and objective view of knowledge, skills, tasks, activities and learning (Lave & Wenger 1996). Subsequent coaching practice will result in coach 'instruction' driven by knowledge while being governed by mechanisms to be understood in terms of acquisition and assimilation of said knowledge (Lave & Wenger 1996).

 KEY CONCEPT

The development of knowledge structures, schema, conceptual frameworks and so on is to talk in cognitive terms about knowledge and coaching practice.

Cognitive constructivism

In understanding coaching, a number of models of practice are routinely conceptualised as 'constructivist' in their assumptions – typically these are 'game based' or 'game centred' approaches (e.g. 'TGfU', 'Game Sense'). However, there is typically a lack of conceptual clarity that can create difficulty in understanding what 'constructivism' means. Cognitive constructivism is generally aligned with the work of Piaget (Cassidy *et al.* 2016; Schuh & Barab 2007). This link to Piaget synthesised the various names that had been applied to this perspective:

- radical constructivism (Derry 1996; von Glasersfeld 1995);
- cognitive constructivism (Cobb 1994; Duffy & Cunningham 1996);
- psychological constructivism (Prawat 1995);
- constructivism (Bednar *et al.* 1995).

Cognitive constructivism has emerged as a theoretical entity separate from cognitivism and social constructionism. Chiefly, the differences lie in the emphasis on individual cognitive processes or the social co-construction of knowledge, and this also marks differing ontologies and epistemologies, resulting in differences in coaching practice. (Cognitive) constructivism argues that individuals construct the world of experience through cognitive processes with a dualist epistemology and ontology (Young & Collin 2004). These processes are internal to the individual, involving the integration of knowledge (or meaning) in pre-existing schemes, or changing the schemes to fit the environment (assimilation and accommodation, respectively) (Piaget & Inhelder 1969).

From the cognitive constructivist perspective, there is a real coaching world that we experience (Schuh & Barab 2007; Duffy & Jonassen 1992), thus appearing to find an ontological base in objectivism; however, this world cannot be directly known but has to be experienced (Derry 1992; von Glasersfeld 1995), which broadens the nature of the ontology to realism (coaching reality is separate to the mind, but to know it requires a connection between them). Therefore, there is an objective coaching reality; however, from this perspective what we know of the coaching world is only an interpretation based on our experiences (von Glasersfeld, 1995) – our knowledge of it is constructed. As such, cognitive constructivism is subjective and relativist (meaning is found in the relationship between things), providing no absolute in what is right or wrong (Bednar *et al.* 1995).

Cognitive constructivism also finds its epistemological basis largely in rationalism (Greeno *et al.* 1996) and the emphasis in knowing is in the cognitive activity of an individual as they make sense of and experience the coaching world (Schuh & Barab 2007; Cobb 1994). The cognitive constructivist perspective still foregrounds the individual as in cognitivism, but focuses on the conceptual reorganisation of the coach's or athlete's knowledge rather than on the extant structure of that individual's knowledge (Schuh & Barab 2007). Looking at the cognitive self-organisation of the individual, Cobb stated that, "constructivists are typically concerned with the quality of individual interpretive activity" (1994, p. 15). The mind is placed in the head of the individual coach or athlete (Cobb 1994), but the coaching culture and coaching context play a role in the meaning making of each individual (Schuh & Barab 2007). Therefore, the individual mind, although influenced by social context, is not one with the social context (Bereiter 1994) – mind is separate from environment (Schuh & Barab 2007; Prawat & Floden 1994). Therefore, while often considered a 'social' approach to coaching practice, the social character of learning in many 'constructivist' approaches mostly consists in a small 'aura' of socialness that provides input for the process of internalisation, but coaching practice and learning is still viewed as a process of individualistic acquisition of the cultural given (Cushion 2016).

 KEY CONCEPT

'Constructivist' approaches mostly consist of a small 'aura' of socialness that provides input for the process of internalisation, but coaching practice and learning is still viewed as a process of individualistic acquisition.

Hence, cognitive constructivism supports that the world exists, with coaching practice proceeding from an individual's uniquely and individually constructed interpretation of that world. As with the cognitivists, the rationalist epistemology provides for the importance of the development of cognitive structures; however, in contrast to the cognitive view, information is not pre-structured and presumed-to-be mapped into an individual's mind (Schuh & Barab 2007). Coaching practice from this perspective would:

- provide sense-making opportunities for athletes to experience and thus construct new understandings through the design of drills and activities;
- means coaches would take a more interactive but less directive role in the instructional process (Greeno and the Middle School Mathematics Through Applications Project Group 1998), which would involve more questioning and problem setting;
- provide a means for athletes to construct their world; and
- ensure that activity allows experience to fit into an existing conceptual structure.

Within coaching practice should the experience and mental scheme not fit together well, something described as perturbation develops (von Glasersfeld 1995), and the new experience will not be assimilated into the existing cognitive structure (Schuh & Barab 2007). Accommodation then occurs, and a new scheme is developed – both assimilation and accommodation are based on subjective experiences where the individual athlete is constructing a personal interpretation of the world (von Glasersfeld 1995; Schunk 2009).

Typically, these types of coaching practice interventions have been described as 'discovery' coaching. Discovery or 'guided discovery' provides a coaching practice structure where the task is designed for the athlete to re-arrange information and to integrate it into his or her own existing cognitive structure (i.e. discover it) (Schuh &

Barab 2007; Schunk 2009). Bruner (1961) described discovery methods as not just "finding out something that was unknown to mankind, but . . . [to] include all forms of obtaining knowledge for one-self by the use of one's own mind" (p. 22). His view was that learning was an "active process of imposing organization or order on experience" (Goetz *et al.* 1992, p. 313). From this, coaching practice using discovery methods is intended to support experience that allows athletes to explore new concepts and develop new skills. The realist ontology argues that what is discovered or made sense of exists, with a correspondence developed between the world and the mind (Schuh & Barab 2007). Therefore, coaching practice and the way it is structured will impact the development of athlete cognitive structures, and the order imposed upon the experience will support the restructuring of cognitive structures, i.e. learning through assimilation and accommodation.

 KEY CONCEPT

Coaching practice and the way it is structured will impact the development of athlete cognitive structures, and the order imposed upon the experience will support the restructuring of cognitive structures, i.e. learning through assimilation and accommodation.

Social constructionism

The final perspective we discuss sees coaching as a relational and socio-historical entity that can only be understood in context and as reflexive. That is, coaching changes as knowledge changes, only as both products and producers of social states and interactions. Coach and athlete perspectives are paramount and practice is structured through language and strategic action. Social constructionism or socio-culturalism is distinguished from cognitive constructivism (Cobb 1994; Duffy & Cunningham 1996; Phillips 1995; Wood 1995), and is often described as interpretivist, which takes the view that knowledge has both individual and social components, and is sustained by social processes linked to knowledge (Cobb 1994; Young & Collin 2004). Knowing is distributed in the world, among objects and individuals. Knowledge creation is a shared rather than an individual experience (Prawat & Floden 1994) and evolves through social negotiation (Savery & Duffy 1995). Thus, in constructionism, understanding and experience are in constant interaction and, through participation, persons, action and the world are connected in knowing and learning (Lave & Wenger 1996).

As a result, constructionism rejects a dualist ontology and epistemology, with multiple constructed realities and relations produced and emergent in relational processes (Hosking 2002). Coaching knowledge is historically and culturally specific; language constitutes rather than reflects reality and is a pre-condition for thought and a form of social action with a focus on learning in interaction processes and

200

social practice (Young & Collin 2004). Phillips (1995) described this emphasis on socio-political processes as a tendency towards relativism, where meaning was only incurred with respect to relationships, thus providing an epistemological distinction among constructivist theoretical perspectives. Thus, ontologically, as with the cognitive constructivists, reality exists through interpretations; however, from a constructionist or socio-cultural perspective, society and an individual's relationship to society have a primary role in the shaping of that reality (Schuh & Barab, 2007; Prawat & Floden 1994). Constructionists are distinctive in their insistence that knowledge creation is a shared rather than an individual experience (Prawat & Floden 1994). Importantly, as Young and Collin (2004) suggest, constructionism is more than 'constructing' knowledge, but positioned within the historical and cultural location of that construction.

Therefore, a constructionist focus on coaching practice shifts attention away from individual coaches or athletes to their interaction with the location in which coaching and learning takes place. It is this process, rather than the mental structures of the individual or the environment, that are the focus for the coach (Strauss 1993); thus, the mind is placed in society, and the individual's cognitive structures as a unit of analysis are essentially meaningless (Schuh & Barab 2007).

 KEY CONCEPT

A constructionist focus on coaching practice shifts attention away from individual coaches or athletes to their interaction with the location in which coaching and learning takes place. It is this process, rather than the mental structures of the individual or the environment, that is the focus for the coach.

Evolving from social constructionism are notions of situated learning or situativity – and this approach has been discussed in relation to coach and athlete learning and practice. Roots to situativity theory can be found in the work of various anthropologists such as Lave and Wenger (1991), describing learning and cognition in the everyday world (Cushion 2016; Kirshner & Whitson 1997). From this perspective, the coaching environment is not distinct from the individual coach or athlete; the individual is merely a part of a highly interconnected system of relationships (Barab & Roth 2006). Within this environment, we perceive and act based upon the affordances and constraints of the environment and the situations that arise within it (Schuh & Barab 2007). A fundamental notion for the situativity theorist is that "cognition must be viewed as an integral part of the physical, social, and cultural contexts to which it belongs" (Barab & Plucker 2002; Derry 1996, p. 416). From this perspective, knowing, identity and context stand in dialectic, not dualistic, relations and are all constituted in coaching practice (Barab & Duffy 2000; Lave 1996). Therefore, coaching practice "is not merely situated – as if it were some independently reifiable process that just happened to be located somewhere"; coaching practice "is an integral part of generative social practice in the lived-in world" (Lave & Wenger 1991, p. 35). Understanding is developed through continued, situated coaching practice involving complex social negotiations in activity, context and culture. Hence, coaching practice and therefore learning takes place within the practices of a community; thus the "socio-cultural setting in which the activities are embedded" (Kirshner & Whitson 1997, p. 5) is paramount. Although other perspectives also support interaction and peer collaboration as ways of constructing or acquiring knowledge, constructionism *requires* that this process occur; thus, the knowledge developed is not with the individual but in the interactions among individuals.

 KEY CONCEPT

Although other perspectives also support interaction and peer collaboration as ways of constructing or acquiring knowledge, constructionism *requires* that this process occur; thus, the knowledge developed is not with the individual but in the interactions among individuals.

For coaching practice this means a shift to more interactive, complex and unpredictable coaching environments (Darling-Hammond 1996; Light 2004; Light & Wallian 2008). Within this approach, coaches are repositioned in practice to stand back and observe more, and act as a facilitator. Facilitation requires more than providing 'hints' to unambiguous right answers; instead, in order to develop autonomous learning, the coach maybe required to:

- model;
- scaffold;
- question;
- guide;
- advise;
- de-brief;
- converse;
- offer heuristics or conceptual structures.

The idea is that coaching practice supports the athlete to develop increasing competence while supported in a 'community', and this support can be removed over time (Schunk 2009). This support should allow the tasks to remain complex and motivating, yet still within the athlete's reach. In coaching, game-centred approaches to practice have attempted to position themselves as providing a vehicle for constructionist learning. The coach designs activities as information-rich, modified sporting environments (i.e. games). Within the environment, learners are presented with complex, realistic problems that they solve using information that is embedded within the context, while supported by the coach. That is, the learning opportunities emerge as a result of the learner's problem-solving role within the activity. Thus, the coach's practice focus rests not just with the athlete, but with the athlete and their

202

inter-relationship with, and as part of, the context in which the problem-solving activity takes place.

Despite the philosophical differences described above, constructionist approaches would have four characteristics as central to coaching practice:

1. Athletes are in a practice environment that allows the construction of their own learning and knowledge.
2. New learning depends on athletes' existing knowledge.
3. Social interaction plays a critical role in coaching practice.
4. Coaching practice will provide authentic tasks and activities.

Developing coaching practice and contributing to the development of the conceptual framework means that understanding different conceptions of coaching practice, their underlying theories and the assumptions that underpin these is essential (see Table 9.1). Moreover, implementing any approach to coaching practice requires a

Table 9.1 Theoretical approaches, implications for coaching practice

Theoretical approach	Implications for practice
Behavioural/ conditioning	Complexity reduced into smaller progressive parts, reinforcing desired behaviour. Clear measurable objectives, proceed in small steps, deliver reinforcement
Cognitivism/cognitive constructivism/social cognitivism	Relate new information to known information, understanding the uses of new knowledge. Give strategies that allow the practice of concept learning, problem solving and self-regulation. Learn by doing, and observing, modelling. Learners set goals.
Constructionism	Interact with others, using meditational tools. Structure learning environment to construct understanding, provide support (scaffolding) for learning. Engage in social practice

Source: adapted from Schunk (2009) and Cushion *et al.* (2010).

 SUMMARY

This chapter will have familiarised you with the following:

▪ The relevance of undertaking a closer examination of theory–practice relations.
▪ The importance of examining the assumptions underlying coaching practice.
▪ Different paradigms relating to coaching practice and different ideas concerning coaching practice theories and theories of practice.
▪ Four different theoretical approaches to examining coaching practice and what coaching practice looks like informed by each.

PROJECTS

1. Interview six coaches from different sports and ask them to describe what they consider as 'traditional' coaching practice in their sport.
2. Observe 2–3 coaches working in different domains (performance, development and participation) and align their practice to a theoretical framework(s) – is there a dominant mode of practice?
3. Conduct a content analysis of a governing body coaching award – does it advocate a particular approach to coaching practice? Does the language used align with a paradigm?

sound knowledge of its principles – a foundation upon which to build. Understanding assumptions about coaching practice, and challenging them with alternatives, allows a deeper understanding of coaching to be developed, and the growth of a more sophisticated conceptualisation of coaching based on a clear understanding of underlying theory.

READING

For a summary of different theories applied to coaching, see Cushion *et al.*'s (2010) review of coach development. Schunk (2009) provides a detailed overview of varying theoretical perspectives, including looking at 'practice' guided by these theories. Nelson *et al.*'s (2016) recent book reviews learning theory applied to coaching, while Cassidy *et al.* (2016) take an athlete learning perspective in considering coaching practice and different theoretical approaches.

REFERENCES

Barab, S. A. and Duffy, T. (2000). From practice fields to communities of practice. In D. Jonassen and S. M. Land (Eds), *Theoretical Foundations of Learning Environments*, pp. 25–56. Mahwah, NJ: Lawrence Erlbaum Associates.

Barab, S. A., & Plucker, J. A. (2002). Smart people or smart contexts? Cognition, ability, and talent development in an age of situated approaches to knowing and learning. *Educational Psychology*, *37*(3), 165–182.

Barab, S. A., & Roth, W. M. (2006). Intentionally bound systems and curricular-based ecosystems: An ecological perspective on knowing. *Educational Researcher*, *35*(5), 3–1.

Bednar, A. K., Cunningham, D. J., Duffy, T. M., & Perry, J. D. (1995). Theory into practice: How do we link? In G. J. Anglin (Ed.) *Instructional Technology: Past, Present, and Future*. Englewood, CO: Libraries Unlimited, Inc., 100–112.

Bereiter, C. (1994). Implications of postmodernism for science, or, science as progressive discourse. *Educational Psychology*, *29*, 3–12.

Brown, J., & Duguid, P. (1996). Stolen knowledge. In H. McLellen (Ed.) *Situated Learning Perspectives*. Englewood Cliffs, NJ: Educational Technology Publications.

Brown, J., Collins, A., & Duguid, P. (1989). Situated cognition and the culture of learning. *Educational Researcher*, 18(1), 32–42.

Bruner, J. S. (1961). The act of discovery. *Harvard Educational Review*, 31(1), 21–32.

Bruner, J. S. (1990). *Acts of Meaning*. Cambridge, MA: Harvard University Press.

Burton, J. K., Moore, D. M., and Magliaro, S. G. (1996). Behaviorism and instructional technology. In D. H. Jonassen (Ed.), *Handbook of Research for Educational Communications and Technology*, 46–73. New York: Macmillan.

Buysse, V., Sparkman, K. L., & Wesley, P. W. (2003). Communities of practice: Connecting what we know with what we do. *Exceptional Children*, 69(3): 263–278.

Carr, W., & Kemmis, S. (1986). *Becoming Critical*. Basingstoke: Taylor & Francis.

Cassidy, T., Jones, R.L., & Potrac, P. (2016). *Understanding Sports Coaching* (3rd Edition). London; Routledge.

Cushion, C. J. (2013). Applying game centred approaches to coaching: A critical analysis of the 'dilemmas' of practice impacting change. *Sports Coaching Review*, 2(1), 61–76.

Cushion, C. J. (2016). Jean Lave: Learning in coaching as social praxis. In L. Nelson, R. Groom, & P. Potrac (Eds) *Learning in Sports Coaching*. London: Routledge, 189–201. Cushion, C. J., & Partington, M. (2014). A critical analysis of the conceptualisation of 'coaching philosophy'. *Sport, Education and Society*, 1–17, doi:10.1080/13573322.2014.958817

Cushion, C. J., Nelson, L., Armour, K., Lyle, J., Jones R. L., Sandford, R., & O'Callaghan, C. (2010). *Coach Learning and Development: A Review of Literature*. Leeds: sports coach UK.

Cobb, P. (1994). Where is the mind? Constructivist and socio-cultural perspectives on mathematical development. *Educational Researcher*, 23, 13–20.

Darling-Hammond, L. (1996). The right to learn and the advancement of teaching: Research policy and practice for democratic education. *Educational Researcher*, 25(6), 5–17.

Derry, S. J. (1992). Beyond symbolic processing: Expanding horizons for educational psychology. *Journal of Educational Psychology*, 84, 413–418.

Derry, S. J. (1996). Cognitive schema theory in the constructivist debate. *Educational Psychology*, 31(3/4), 163–174.

Duffy, T. M., & Cunningham, D. J. (1996). Constructivism: Implications for the design and delivery of instruction. In D. H. Jonassen (Ed.) *Handbook of Research for Educational Communications and Technology*. New York: Macmillan, 170–198.

Duffy, T. M., & Jonassen, D. H. (1992). Constructivism: New implications for instructional technology. In T. Duffy & D. Jonassen (Eds) *Constructivism and the Technology of Instruction*. Hillsdale, NJ: Lawrence Erlbaum Associates, 1–16.

Ertmer, P. A., & Newby, T. J. (1993). Behaviourism, cognitivism, constructivism: Comparing critical features from an instructional design perspective. *Performance Improvement Quarterly*, 6(4), 50–72.

Gagné, R. M., Briggs, L. J., & Wager, W. W. (1992). *Principles of Instructional Design*. 4th edition. Fort Worth, TX: Harcourt Brace Jovanovich College Publishers.

Goetz, E. T., Alexander, P. A., & Ash, M. J. (1992). *Education Psychology: A Classroom Perspective*. New York: Macmillan.

Greeno, J. G. and the Middle School Mathematics Through Applications Project Group. (1998). The situativity of knowing, learning, and research. *American Psychologist*, 53(1), 5–26.

Greeno, J. G., Collins, A. M., & Resnick, L. B. (1996). Cognition and learning. In D. C. Berliner & R. C. Calfee (Eds) *Handbook of Educational Psychology*. New York: Macmillan, 15–46.

Guba, E. G. and Lincoln, Y. S. (1983). Epistemological and methodological bases of naturalistic inquiry. In G. F. Madaus, M. S. Scriven, & D. L. Stufflebeam (Eds) *Evaluation Models: Viewpoints on Educational and Human Services Evaluation*. Boston, MA: Kluwer- Nijhoff, 311–334.

Hosking, D. M. (2002). Constructing change: A social constructionist approach to change at work (and beetles and witches). Katholieke Universiteit Brabant. www. geocites.com/dian_ma-rie_hosking/oratie.html.

Kirshner, D. & Whitson, J. A. (1997). Editors' introduction to situated cognition: Social, semiotic, and psychological perspectives. In D. Kirshner and J. A. Whitson (Eds) *Situated Cognition: Social, Semiotic, and Psychological Perspectives*. Mahwah, NJ: Lawrence Erlbaum Associates, 1–16.

Lave, J. (2009). The practice of learning. In K. Illeris (Ed.) *Contemporary Theories of Learning*. London: Routledge, 200–208.

Light, R. (2004). Coaches' experiences of Game Sense: Opportunities and challenges. *Physical Education and Sport Pedagogy*, 9(2), 115–131.

Light, R. L., & Wallian, N. (2008). Constructivist-informed approach to teaching swimming. *Quest*, 60, 387–404.

Lave, J. (1996). Teaching, as learning, in practice. *Mind, Culture and Activity*, 3(3), 149–164.

Lave, J., & Wenger, E. (1991). *Situated Learning: Legitimate Peripheral Participation*. New York: Cambridge University Press.

Lave, J. & Wenger, E. (1996). Practice, person, social world. In: H. Daniels (Ed.) *An Introduction to Vygotsky*. London: Routledge, 143–150.

Lombardo, T. J. (1987). *The Reciprocity of Perceive and Environment: The Evolution of James J. Gibson's Ecological Psychology*. Hillsdale, NJ: Lawrence Erlbaum Associates.

Nelson, L., Groom, R., & Potrac, P. (Eds) (2016). *Learning in Sports Coaching*. London: Routledge.

Phillips, D. C. (1995). The good, the bad, and the ugly: The many faces of constructivism. *Educational Researcher*, 24(7), 5–12.

Piaget, J., & Inhelder, B. (1969). *The Psychology of the Child*. London: Routledge.

Piggott, D. (2013). The Open Society and coach education: A philosophical agenda for policy reform and future sociological research. *Physical Education and Sport Pedagogy*. DOI: 10.1080/17408383.2013.837435.

Potrac, P., Jones, R. L., & Cushion, C. J. (2007). Understanding power and the coach's role in professional English soccer: A preliminary investigation of coach behaviour. *Soccer and Society*, *8*(1), 33–49.

Prawat, R. S. (1995). Misreading Dewey: Reform projects and the language game. *Educational Researcher*, *24*(7), 13–22.

Prawat, R. S. & Floden, R. E. (1994). Philosophical perspectives on constructivist views of learning. *Educational Psychologist*, *29*(1), 37–48.

Reber, A. S. (1995). *The Penguin Dictionary of Psychology*. New York: Penguin Books.

Savery, J. R., & Duffy, T. M. (1995). Problem based learning: An instructional model and its constructivist framework. In B. G. Wilson (Ed.) *Constructivist Learning Environments*. Englewood Cliffs, NJ: Educational Technology Publications, 135–148.

Schuh, K. L., & Barab, S. A. (2007). Philosophical perspectives. In J. M. Spector, M. D. Merrill, J. van Merrienboer, & M. P. Driscoll (Eds) *Handbook of Research on Educational Communications and Technology*. New York: Lawrence Erlbaum Associates, 69–82.

Schunk, D. H. (2009). *Learning Theories: An Educational Perspective. International edition*, 5th edition. Upper Saddle River, NJ: Pearson Prentice Hall.

Strauss, A. L. (1993). Theories of learning and development of academics and educators. *Educational Psychology*, 28(3), 191–203.

von Glasersfeld, E. (1995). *Radical Constructivism: A Way of Knowing and Learning*. London: Falmer Press.

Wood, D. (1995). Theory, training, and technology, part 1. *Educational Training*, *37*(1), 12–16.

Young, R. A., & Collin, A. (2004). Introduction: Constructivism and social constructionism in the career field. *Journal of Vocational Behavior*, *64*, 373–388.

CHAPTER 10

COACHING AND SOCIAL CONTEXT

CHAPTER OUTLINE

- Introduction
- Coaching: as a social process and applying sociological thinking
- Sport coaching and social theory
- Social issues
- Commentary
- Summary
- Projects
- Reading

INTRODUCTION

In considering the conceptual framework, we are minded that any given coaching context can be made up of, for example, the club, the coaches, the athletes, the sport's governing body and the league, all of whom have an influence on the coaching process and coaching practice. The coaching process will, then, be a social process involving the interactions, interdependence and interests of these stakeholders. Indeed, conceptualised in this way the coaching process and coaches' practice will refract wider social forces from a range of interested parties, in addition to the obvious coach and athlete, including producers of knowledge, the wider economy and society. Thus, a number of issues fall out of such a perspective, which this chapter will address:

- coaching as a 'social process';
- coaching's relationship in constructing and being constructed by its context and wider social forces;
- the value of sociology theory to conceptualising and analysing coaching; and
- how different theoretical lenses from sociology provide layers that develop more nuanced understanding and can inform conceptual development.

Because coaching is a social construction, operating in, and part of, wider society it will reflect wider social issues. These include macro concerns – such as race, gender and social class – and micro concerns – such as power, the body, politics and social interaction. So, in addition to the points described above, this chapter will also consider two of these issues: first, the macro issue of inequality and inclusion through looking at the under-representation of women in coaching; and second, the micro issue of the role of power in coaching.

COACHING: AS A SOCIAL PROCESS AND APPLYING SOCIOLOGICAL THINKING

Coaching is increasingly understood as a social practice, not narrow, instrumental or neutral, operating in social and political vacuums, but arising in, with and from the socially and culturally structured world (Cushion & Jones 2014). Despite this understanding, there remains a need to provide a critical appreciation of sport coaching in its social context – coaches and coaching practice are always situated in a larger context that has to be understood as more than the 'container' into which coaches are dropped (Cushion 2011a). Hence, coaching needs to recognise that coaching practices, discourses, subjectivities, coach–athlete relationships and so on can only be understood by the way they are articulated into a particular set of complex economic, political and technological relationships that comprise the social context (Bush *et al.* 2013). The notion of social context is broad and comprises the coaches' and athletes':

* histories;
* cultures;
* races;
* genders;
* physical abilities;
* roles and responsibilities; and
* prior knowledge and experiences,

as well as:

* the coaching programme design;
* the curriculum and learning activities; and
* the history, culture and structure of the sport.

The interaction of these micro and macro factors influences the meaning that coaches and athletes make of the coaching process. Such factors can impact the coaching process in overt and covert ways, and can be powerful in terms of a 'hidden curriculum' forming a tacitly understood framework of norms, expectations and values – a coaching culture (Cushion & Jones 2014). Therefore, just as with any social phenomenon, sports coaching practice will have been shaped by social structures, power relationships and social trends and will, in turn, have contributed to those emerging social patterns. Specifically, sport and coaching are part of, but at the same time cannot be immune to, the social space that they occupy.

ASKHAM BRYAN
COLLEGE
LEARNING RESOURCES

209

Coaching and social context

Just as with any social phenomenon, sport coaching practice will have been shaped by social structures, power relationships and social trends and will, in turn, have contributed to those emerging social patterns. Specifically, sport and coaching are part of, but at the same time cannot be immune to, the social space that they occupy.

C. Wright Mills (1959) famously described the 'sociological imagination'– that is, the capacity of individuals to recognise the influence of larger structural forces on their lives and concerns. The ability to link the micro of day-to-day behaviour to the macro of structural factors is something that sociology offers sport coaching (Jones 2011). Sociology is also the development of systematic knowledge about social life, the way it is organised, how it changes, its creation in social action and its disruption and renewal in social conflict – it provides answers but also helps pose better questions (Calhoun *et al.* 2012). Therefore, sociology in relation to coaching as Jones (2011) suggests is 'doable', a process for coaches to question and challenge the 'traditional' and dominant rationalistic view of coaching. Sociological research and theory, therefore, has much to contribute to the understanding of coaching, coach education, and coach and athlete learning. This potential has, to date, been largely ignored, as current trends in coaching, research and practice have been towards 'what works', seemingly content to fulfil instrumental ends (Cushion & Lyle 2010).

A sociological perspective can address this gap as it considers both issues and explanations (Moore 2004). It also ensures that there is a place for critical theory in the wider practices of coaching and coach education; that is, "those sets of ideas which endeavour to explain the nature of relationships in the social world . . . and which in so doing, generate opportunities not just for further reflective action but also social amelioration and change" (Evans & Davies 2002, p. 18). For example, using social theory to deconstruct coaching compels us to problematise conventional, taken-for-granted, or common sense ways of thinking about coaching – for example:

■ hierarchies of content in coach education (e.g. 'appropriate' for Level 1);
■ taken-for-granted notions such as 'skills', 'competences' and 'good coaching'; and
■ disciplinary discourses (e.g. sport science and performance) that are routinely employed to organise and constrain coaching's social reality.

Indeed, one of the most interesting, but under-researched, lines of enquiry in coaching is the extent to which coaching practice contributes significantly to the maintenance of the status quo, or can act as a 'transformative praxis' (Bush *et al.* 2013) with an emancipatory interest in issues such as sporting ethics, racial inequality, perceptions of the sporting body or gender imbalance.

210

Sport coaching, then, is recognisable in social life as an occupational grouping, as an accumulation of social structures and processes within sport, and as a series of symbols and social values associated with the coaching construct. More particularly, it can be interpreted as a form of social interaction and inter-personal relationship. The mere fact that coaching is a social, relational, historical and interactive human phenomenon means that the social weight of coaching practice will be worthy of study.

 KEY CONCEPT

Sport coaching is recognisable in social life as an occupational grouping, as an accumulation of social structures and processes within sport and as a series of symbols and social values associated with the coaching construct.

Over a decade ago, Jones (2000) made a strong case for a sociological investigation of coaching as a counterweight to the previous conceptualisation of coaching along 'bio-scientific fragmentary lines'. The case was made for sociology's relevance to coaching with the argument that social thought was an unappreciated but essential 'invisible ingredient' in coaches' knowledge (Jones 2011). This line of argument provides an excellent account of the need to educate coaches to be aware of the social matrix within which they operate – socially informed decision-making based on the social environment, social relations, practical realities and the individual 'habitus' of accumulated 'social capital' (previous experiences, education, upbringing, social expectations, etc.). Jones also points to the social construction of knowledge and 'received wisdom' within coaching, but suggests that coaches can forge their individual perspectives through awareness of competing perspectives, informed action and critical reflection.

More recently, as coaching has come to be acknowledged as a social activity and more work has been forthcoming, the argument has been further refined through empirical and theoretical work (e.g. Jones 2011; Jones *et al.* 2002, 2004). This has also seen an increase in the use of sociological theorists applied to coaching – for example:

- Michel Foucault (e.g. Cushion 2016; Denison 2011, 2015);
- Pierre Bourdieu (e.g. Cushion & Jones 2014);
- Erving Goffman (e.g. Jones *et al.* 2004);
- Anthony Giddens (e.g. Purdy *et al.* 2009); and
- Harold Garfinkel (e.g. Jones & Corsby 2015).

To reinforce the case further, Jones *et al.* (2011) published the first collection of work demonstrating the utility of 'social thinkers' as appropriate to inform coaching – *The Sociology of Sport Coaching*. However, despite a growing body of work it is only

Bush *et al.* (2013) who treat coaching as a problematic concept using critical theory to challenge the conceptual base of current understandings – and re-imagine sports coaching using a Physical Cultural Studies (PCS) approach.

It is important to note that this chapter cannot hope to do justice to such a broad field of enquiry and to the issues involved. It would be very ambitious to address completely a social analysis of coaching. The objective for the remainder of the chapter, therefore, is to provide an overview by addressing the following areas:

- Balance the attention given to the 'scientific model' of the coaching process through introducing differing social theoretical approaches to coaching.
- Delineate the issues involved, and overview two current issues in coaching – namely 'power' and 'inequality' by way of example and outline a potential social agenda.
- Demonstrate that a full understanding of the social context requires the insights that can only be provided by an appreciation of the conceptual framework within which the coaching process and the social context find meaning.

SPORT COACHING AND SOCIAL THEORY

> Theories are nets cast to catch what we call 'the world': to rationalize, to explain, and to master it. We endeavour to make the mesh ever finer and finer.
>
> (Popper 1992, p. 59)

As we have already discussed elsewhere in the book, ideas about coaching and coaching practice are often underpinned by recourse to foundational disciplines (see Chapter 9). Coaching has been embedded in a variety of theoretical discourses – predominantly rooted in a dominant psychologism, but also some elements of social theory. Broadly speaking, social theories are analytical frameworks or paradigms (see Chapter 9) used to examine and understand social phenomena. The term 'social theory' encompasses ideas about "how societies change and develop, about methods of explaining social behaviour, about power and social structure, gender and ethnicity, modernity and civilisation, revolutions and utopias" (Harrington 2005, p. 1). In contemporary social theory certain core themes take precedence over others, such as the nature of social life, the relationship between self and society, the structure of social institutions, the role and possibility of social transformation, as well as themes such as gender, race and class (Murphy 2013; Elliot 2008). Contemporary social theorists also tend to be interdisciplinary, drawing on a range of disciplines including sociology but also, for example, philosophy, anthropology, psychoanalysis and cultural studies, and it is perhaps this level of complexity that explains why the contemporary work seems more influential in coaching (e.g. Bourdieu, Foucault, Goffman) rather than more 'classical' sociological theory such as Marx, Weber, Durkheim and so on (though this also reflects wider shifts in theoretical approach in the wider sport and sociology literature), although the influence of classical sociology, particularly Marx, is evident in much contemporary social theory (Murphy 2013).

The application of social theory to coaching intellectualises the problems and issues of the day. It also provides spaces for coaches and researchers to adopt an intellectual stance to the subject with some level of legitimation and credibility – and provides an antidote to the 'anti-intellectual' stance of some practitioners who reject theory as irrelevant to coaches' everyday actions (Jones 2011). It is also clear that in existing coaching-related work, theories are delivered with normative intent – that is, they examine specific problems (e.g. under-representation of women coaches) and also attempt to problematise everyday taken-for-granted actions (e.g. the 'hidden curriculum').

There are a number of competing social theoretical paradigms that offer distinctive perspectives on the social world. Each of these operates from a set of assumptions and priorities about 'how the world works' and the role of individual 'agency' in creating that world. This balance of structure and agency is very often at the heart of the contrasting interpretations of the social world. Indeed, what Giulianotti (2005) describes as the sociological dichotomy exists – concerning structured power relations and elements of cultural agency – and theoretical approaches tend to gravitate towards one or the other of these. The relationship between structure and agency can be seen as a key theme running through different theoretical approaches and in the examination and understanding of coaching.

 KEY CONCEPT

The relationship between structure and agency can be seen as a key theme running through different theoretical approaches and in the examination and understanding of coaching.

Not surprisingly, these different theoretical positions adopt distinctive modes of enquiry and issue agendas. The dichotomy between structure and agency can provide a plausible basis for examining contributions to the field, but this chapter adopts a more conventional course and examines five discrete perspectives or paradigms and relates these to coaching:

- functionalism
- interpretive sociology
- conflict theory
- postmodernism/poststructuralism
- feminism.

Functionalism

Functionalism is perhaps the closest to a dominant paradigm in sociology and in its approach as 'science'. The sport sociology of the 1960s and 1970s (particularly in North America) was dominated by functionalist and structural-functionalist perspectives that emphasised order and cohesion in society, and focused on the structures and processes that were perceived to bring stability to society – education, the family, religion, politics and the workplace (see Ball & Loy 1975; Loy *et al.* 1978). In an interesting social analysis of coaching (from a functionalist perspective), Lombardo (1999) compares coaching behaviour and the 'powerful socialising agencies' of the time and finds congruence in their authoritarian principles. Coaches are socialised into values and norms necessary for the effective performance of their role in society. Coaching is tacitly an unproblematic and worthwhile endeavour acting as a complex system functioning to service other parts of the sub-system for the needs of wider society. The coach from this perspective appears as little more than an amalgam of the expectations, values and attitudes handed down to them by one of a variety of socialising agencies. However, as Giulianotti (2005) suggests, problems or 'failure' to succeed from this perspective are too easily explained as an individual, group or sectional pathology rather than an issue with coaching itself or wider social issues – a view of coaching that still pervades the thinking of some coaches and researchers in the field. Ritzer (2003) contends that functionalism not only neglects history, conflict and social change, but is deeply oriented to show how systems are perpetuated and defines actors as passive 'dupes' of social structures. Hence, functionalist theories highlight the importance of social consensus and social order and play down conflict, and as such have lost much of their disciplinary influence in part to more critical and conflict-based theories (Giulianotti 2005).

More micro-sociological work draws in part on the functionalist sociology of Durkheim to examine the social order underpinning everyday interaction (Giulianotti 2005). While often positioned within symbolic interactionism (described below), Goffman draws on and elucidates Durkheim with respect to the significance of rituals to societies (Joas & Knobl 2009). Goffman uses notions such as 'face', 'impression management' and a dramaturgical metaphor to explain social life, but at the individual level. Arguably, the extensive use of Goffman by Jones and colleagues (see Jones *et al.* 2011 for an overview), applying these concepts to coaching, is a founding for a contemporary 'sociology of coaching' – and as a social theorist has the largest body of empirical work related to coaching.

Interpretive sociology

While functionalism has been associated with the elucidation of structure, interpretive sociology has been linked more with agency. Originating in the thoughts of Weber, its aim is to accomplish an interpretive understanding of subjectively meaningful human action that exposes the coach's motives and causes of action to open view. Interpretive sociology contains many conceptual branches (Giulianotti 2005; Joas & Knobl 2009), such as:

- Weberian sociology;
- social phenomenology (Husserl, Merleau-Ponty);
- ethnomethodology (Garfinkel); and
- symbolic interactionism (Mead, Blumer).

It is beyond the scope of this chapter to do justice to an interpretive paradigm identified as broadly and comprehensively as this. However, it is possible to say that this theoretical approach explores the inter-relations of social action to status through:

- subjectivity;
- meaning;
- motives;
- symbols;
- context;
- the self;
- roles;
- identity processes; and
- social change.

Interpretivist approaches posit that individuals develop meaningful understandings of subjective motives, of the actions of others and of their social contexts (Giulianotti 2005; Joas & Knobl 2009). Under the auspices of symbolic interactionism, Goffman has been used to examine coaching practice. While informative, this has not been extensive across different sporting settings or coaching domains. Other aspects of interpretive sociology are the subject of one-off (e.g. Purdy *et al.* 2009 – power in rowing coaching) or position papers (e.g. Jones & Corsby 2015 – a social approach to understanding decision making) advocating the application of a theorist to help understand coaching. With their basis in *in situ* or ethnographic qualitative methods, an interpretive approach has potential to help understand the construction of subjectivities within coaching contexts. However, a focus on solely interactions does not, for example, consider the influence of power in shaping practice, and interpretivist approaches have therefore been criticised for playing down the structural and historical elements in the construction of social contexts in coaching and social (coaching) practice.

 KEY CONCEPT

A focus solely on interactions does not, for example, consider the influence of power in shaping practice, and interpretivist approaches have therefore been criticised for playing down the structural and historical elements in the construction of social contexts in coaching and social (coaching) practice.

Conflict theory

Falling under the auspices of conflict theory, another trend in sociology includes Marxian and neo-Marxist analysis. Marxist sociology encourages an examination of the cultural and aesthetic principles in sport (and coaching therein) according to the logic of capitalism (Giulianotti 2005). For example, the commodification of sport and sports people where under capitalism sport is bourgeois and suffused with alienation and ruling class ideology. Little contemporary sport research utilises Marxist sociology and none that directly analyses coaching – yet echoes of ideological critique and understanding athletes as 'imprisoned, indoctrinated, regimented and repressed' (Brohm 1978) can be found in more contemporary coaching research that draws on critical and postmodern theory (e.g. Denison 2011; Cushion 2016).

A neo-Marxist perspective is recognised as the 'Frankfurt School' of critical theory. Critical theory was never a fully articulated philosophy that was shared unproblematically, but had a core premise of being an emancipatory endeavour. Theorists associated with this line of thinking include Adorno, Horkheimer, Marcuse and latterly Habermas. In this tradition, Kincheloe (2000) argues that critical thinking is "the ability of individuals to disengage themselves from the tacit assumptions of discursive practices and power relations in order to exert more conscious control over their everyday lives" (p. 24). The Frankfurt School would characterise this as ideology critique, which acts to describe the ways in which people learn to recognise how uncritically accepted (and unjust) ideologies are embedded in everyday situations. Key to this is hegemony – Gramsci's notion whereby people are convinced to embrace dominant ideologies as being 'natural' and in their best interest, and these can include values, ideas and practices. Key to the critical theory project is, as Brookfield (2009) argues, to:

- challenge ideology;
- contest hegemony;
- unmask power; and
- overcome alienation.

Critical theory is linked to coaching through critiques of coaching ideologies and the hegemony of positivism. This, in turn, links to coaching being viewed as rationalistic and technical in nature with coaching practice and research reduced to solving technical problems and producing given outcomes, so-called 'technocratic rationality' (see Chapter 9). This critique of coaching as 'technocratic rationality', and an indirect use of ideas derived from critical theory, has been the foundation of many of the arguments for a more sociological approach to coaching.

Postmodernism/poststructuralism

It is difficult to define or characterise poststructuralism and postmodernism – though both are associated with the displacement of 'grand' or 'totalising' narratives by more fragmented, relativised 'micro' narratives. Rail (2002) suggests these are "an amalgam of often purposively ambiguous and fluid ideas" (p.180). Structuralist or objectivist

216

arguments posit that all societies (and hence coaching will) have an underlying logical structure that exists beyond the consciousness of their members. Subjectivist or interpretivist arguments suggest that the social world is founded on subjective understanding and explanation. Taking and stretching both structuralist and interpretivist ideas, as well as adding in new theoretical ideas, sees certain theorists described as 'poststructuralist' and often 'postmodern'. Both Bourdieu and Foucault – used to explore different aspects of the coaching process – examine how structures are constituted and re-constituted through the use of conceptual devices, but importantly in and through day-to-day practices. For Bourdieu, a practical comprehension of the world is embedded in subjectivity and social reality is intrinsically relational, created from relations between groups (see Cushion 2011b for a review of this work applied to coaching). For Foucault, subjective experience and knowledge have already been shaped by historical and cultural circumstances, meaning coach subjectivity is not determined but elicited, fostered and shaped (Cushion 2016); thus coaching becomes a central discursive concept shaping coaches as active subjects through practice discourses (see Denison 2011 for a review of this work). Giulanotti (2005) argues that such approaches represent an important strain of postmodernist theorising – providing more critical theories of rationality and power and exposing the interdependencies between power and knowledge in practice domains such as coaching.

Feminism

Sport remains a reflection of wider social and societal issues and is a cultural domain for constructing and reproducing gendered identities. Feminist perspectives give rise to a number of feminist social theories – with a theoretical landscape that is multifarious, drawing on a range of theoretical building blocks and often having different goals and projects (Joas & Knobl 2009). However, feminist theories have in common a normative or political goal – that is to critique relations of power and domination that discriminate against or repress women, and thus to liberate women from these relations (Joas & Knobl 2011). Thus, coaching has the potential to reinforce such relations and provides a clear demonstration of inequality of attainment and regressive gender hierarchies, although it can also provide a location for resistance and challenge to that position. The issue of 'women coaches' and gender inequality in coaching is discussed in more detail in the next section of the chapter.

This section has offered an overview of general schools or social theory perspectives and each offers potential for increasing understanding of coaching and coaching practice in context. What is important to highlight is that there is a high degree of variability in the extent that these have been applied to an analysis of sport coaching in any rigorous fashion. Analysis of coaching using Foucault, Bourdieu and Goffman remain as the only examples where there are the beginnings of a body of work that has been linked to empirical research. What this work does do, as Jones *et al.* (2011) argue, is confirm that coaching is rich, complex and diverse – and the varied insights provided by this work shows that what is to be known about coaching "cannot be contained in sound bites and 'chat-show' logic" (p. 179) – thus advocating a greater critical understanding of coaching that challenges instrumental reasoning and "enthusiastic 'song-and-dance' pedagogy" (p. 181). However, it should be said that the work to-date as yet fails to problematise coaching with debate and argument about the logic of the means (how and what) of coaching rather than considering more fundamental questions about the nature and aims of coaching (why and what for) (Cushion 2011b; Fernandez-Balboa & Muros 2006). These issues are further compounded by a lack of nuanced and fine-grained analysis about coaches in performance, development and participation contexts, and by a lack of consideration of cross-cultural differences in sporting systems related to those particular contexts between North America, Europe and Asia.

For example, there remain significant differences between professional spectator sports and other forms of top-level sport in terms of the social structures that operate and that allow coaches to be and to do. Social forces at work in these contexts are often constraining if not determining coaches' behaviour, and often in opposition to popular cultural portrayals of the coaches as "free floating heroes or villains" (Stones 1998, p. 3). Moreover, an assumed, unquestioned and perhaps naive transatlantic validity exists between discussions of 'youth coaches' or 'elite coaches' and their respective research findings from North America.

It is worth pointing out again that this is a very superficial account of theoretical approaches into the social context of sport coaching. It is also the case that analyses of social contexts, as demonstrated by the range of theoretical thinking, are contested in terms of perception of reality, interpretation and explanation. However, sport coaching is growing as a mature area of study that can provide the evidence necessary to carry out comparative sociological interpretations of practice. This, of course, is not the focus of the text in this case, and it is more important to point to the extent to which a greater understanding of sport coaching concepts would enlighten these analyses.

 KEY CONCEPT

Sport coaching is growing as an area of study that can provide the evidence necessary to carry out comparative sociological interpretations of practice.

SOCIAL ISSUES

A number of social issues impinge on coaching practice. Social issues can be considered in terms of broader social issues (macro) that find expression in sport coaching and those that through day-to-day practice become local or are particular to sport coaching contexts (micro). It is important to acknowledge that such issues do exist more widely and that practice in sport coaching cannot be divorced

Coaching and social context

from social practice in other fields. In fact, understanding and explanations from other social contexts may shed light on issues such as racial inequality, gender bias, moral standards or power and authority in coaching.

Power

Social theory relates a special status to the concept of power, and sociological analysis of power remains one of the principle concerns of the discipline, with power an omnipresent feature of social life; indeed, all interactions in coaching are "tinged by issues of power and difference" (Snyder & Kiviniemi 2001, p. 133; Potrac & Jones 2011). Therefore, in coaching there is an evident interest and attraction between the coaching process and the various mechanisms used to generate and distribute power. Following Foucault, power is omnipresent in coaching, and power and knowledge have a bond that is not easily broken (Denison *et al.* 2015; Cushion 2016). The working of power should never be underestimated or taken lightly, given that coaching and its institutions, as well as their assorted practices, provide what Murphy (2013) describes as the ideal environments for the interplay of multiple forms of power – cultural, social and structural – that in turn are not irreducible to the others.

It is important to accept the fallibility of a single 'theory of power' when faced with the complex and highly differentiated institutionalised arrangements of varying coaching domains. Power can, of course, be viewed from a range of lenses and, like the wider field, these lenses have been reflected in work concerned with coaching. In the first instance, power can be viewed as a 'zero sum game' (Parsons 1969) – that is, power is a finite resource where one or other parties has power and the other does not (see, for example, Jones *et al.* 2004). A second view of power that has been applied in coaching research is that where it is inherently linked to manipulation and strategy (see Potrac & Jones 2009) and acts as a capacity. This view gives primacy to the processes of power and the ways in which "alliances are formed and the processes of legitimation are secured" (Westwood 2002, p. 135; Potrac & Jones 2011). Lastly, power can be viewed not as a thing to be "grasped, seized or shared, or something that one holds on to or allows to slip away" (Foucault 1979, p. 94) but is instead relational – that is, it is everywhere and always present in our day-to-day interactions. As Potrac and Jones (2011) suggest, and is already alluded to in this section, power is intersectional and different types and meanings of power interact and overlap to create and shape the social context of coaching.

 KEY CONCEPT

Power is intersectional and different types and meanings of power interact and overlap to create and shape the social context of coaching.

Jones *et al.* (2004), Cassidy *et al.* (2009) and Groom *et al.* (2012) have used a framework of power developed by French and Raven (1959), where sources of power (legitimate, expert, informational, reward, coercive, referential) are used by coaches to influence the coaching process through granting them legitimacy within it – power acts as a capacity. This work has led Potrac and colleagues to consider coaching from a micro-political perspective where coaches manage, negotiate and orchestrate coaching contexts against a backdrop of individual struggle, ideological diversity and conflict between members.

In contrast, Foucauldian notions of power have been applied to coaching in a number of ways (see Denison and colleagues, for examples). Foucault (1972) defines discourse as rule-governed, socio-historically situated language "practices that systematically form the objects of which they speak" (p. 49) and that "position subjectivities" (p.182). Power produces discourses and knowledges – the couplet power–knowledge indicates that "power produces knowledge" and that "power and knowledge directly imply one another" (Foucault 1972, p.27). Therefore, power in coaching is exercised through coaching practice and the complex web of discourses and social practices that characterise it. Work utilising this approach argues that discourses of, for example, 'expertise' can create cultures of conformity and compliance, with athletes and coaches considered to be passive, 'docile' and conforming (Cushion 2016; Denison 2011). Such discourses become 'normalising' where coaches and athletes conform and are subject to 'surveillance' and coaching becomes a disciplining technique (e.g. Dension 2011; Cushion 2016; Johns & Johns 2000). Hence, power circulates in coaching rather than being manifest through direct authority, and power and knowledge have an interdependent relationship.

Work by Cushion and colleagues has explored power in coaching and coach education using the concepts of Bourdieu. This work positions coaches and athletes in a struggle for 'capital' within the coaching field. Capital is described by Bourdieu as being the capacity to exercise control over one's future and the future of others, and exists in a variety of forms:

- social (position in the hierarchy);
- cultural (renown, prestige);
- symbolic (achievements); and
- physical (playing or coaching ability).

The distribution of capital (power) structures the context, and for coaches gives them 'legitimate' power. Evidence from research undertaken from this perspective suggests this leads coaches to an overly authoritarian approach, where the given cultural norm (for example, the importance of 'hard work', 'respecting authority' or winning) is imposed on athletes through coaching practice. That is, the power inherent in the context is manifest through dominant ideologies and practices and a common-sense acceptance of 'how things should be done'. Coaching norms thus provide an overriding, powerful and historical view of what coaches *should* do and what coaching *should* look like. These may be deeply held pre-existing coaching norms with unquestioned ends that directly impact coaching and its methods. For example, Cushion and Jones (2014) highlighted within coaching discourse the transformation of the athlete as subject to object (a resource for the next level of the sport). Coaching moves from developing athletes, an end in itself, to supplying athletes to the broader sporting field, a means towards other ends (Cushion & Jones 2014). This objectification of players arises from, and is controlled through, coaching practice. Coaching has a curriculum designed to deliver such ends directly or indirectly. These messages are passed through the daily (re)production of practice, to the extent that they become accepted as legitimate. Thus, beliefs and behaviours come to be unquestioned as the 'way things are' (Cushion & Jones 2014).

This brief overview provides some insight into what Potrac and Jones (2011) describe as the multifaceted, dynamic and fluid nature of power within coaching. A grasping of the work of power has much to offer to an understanding of the workings of the coaching process and the complex interplay between the coach, the athlete and the coaching context.

 QUESTION BOX

How might power manifest itself in different coaching domains; performance, participation and development? Do power relations leak from one coaching domain to another?

Inequality and inclusion

Sport has long been a site for the naturalisation of oppressive ideologies related to gender, race, sexual orientation, class and able-bodiedness, where we have come to naturalise discriminatory social constructions of different individuals' and groups' sporting skills and abilities (Norman 2015; Messner 2011). The way that coaching is mediated by and impacts on issues such as disability, class, race and gender have had some traction in the coaching field. Indeed, social theory has been applied to explore issues of power and privilege particularly in relation to gender and the notion of a dearth of 'women coaches'. Sport is a gendered hegemonically masculine institution – that is, meanings, identities, organisational practices and processes of control and action are distinguished between and for men and women, in favour of and dominated by men (Acker 1990; Norman 2015). There is a substantial literature on gender aspects of coaching, but much of this predominantly based on North American interscholastic and intercollegiate coaching and the emphasis on institutional and employment issues limits its relevance. However, the empirical work on gender aspects of coaching and coach education in the UK is evolving (see, for example, authors such as: Fielding-Lloyd, Graham and colleagues and Norman and colleagues).

The evidence demonstrates that there is a dearth of women coaches in performance sport and women coaches are under-represented more generally in coaching (Fasting

& Pfister 2000; Norman 2014, 2015). According to data from sports coach UK (2011), 69 per cent of coaches are men, 92 per cent are able-bodied and 97 per cent are white; 82 per cent of qualified coaches are men. Norman (2015) reports that of the 52 national team sports in the UK, only nine had a woman head coach. These data trends are mirrored in the US, with Acosta and Carpenter (2012) reporting that in 1972 90 per cent of women's collegiate teams were coached by women, but by 2010 this figure had dropped to 42.9 per cent, while in men's sport the number of women head coaches is consistent at just 3 per cent, the same as it was in 1972. Therefore, the institution of sport and its many sub-cultures can clearly be described as male dominated, and this has received considerable attention in the academic literature. Despite recent increases in participation by women in active recreation, opportunity and access are denied to women through a combination of overt, structural, and hegemonic discrimination. In particular, elite sport and the demands and values associated with it are perceived to constitute a masculine arena in which women coaches do not play a significant role. Indeed, Hargreaves (1994) suggested that "coaching remains one of the most prestigious areas of sport which embodies grossly unequal gender relations" (p. 185). The issue of under-representation is important for a number of reasons:

- Any factor that reduces the number of coaches available to work in sport is a concern. This can also be argued to reduce choice and, therefore, the quality of coaching.
- From a promotional point of view, the dearth of women coaches, particularly in senior positions, leads to fewer role models with whom to encourage recruitment into sport and into coaching.
- If there is evidence of manifest discrimination, this is an ethical issue that should be tackled and policy action implemented to redress the situation. Of course, institutional or structural discrimination requires similar policy action.

Norman (2014) utilises Dewar's (1991) framework to identify two dominant and ideological positions in considering this under-representation of women in coaching. One is the empirical investigation and quantification of sex differences in relation to ability and behaviour, known as 'categorical' research (Dewar 1991, p. 18) – such research highlights 'differences' between men and women in terms of, for example, low confidence, low motivation and less intent. Women in coaching do report feelings of low self-confidence and a reluctance to advance or put themselves forward in the field. However, women are not naturally less confident or motivated but are faced with a masculine coaching culture that is isolating and results in a continuing struggle and an erosion of confidence and motivation (see Norman 2015).

The second position is 'distributive research' (Dewar 1991, p.18). Research from this approach looks at 'technical' issues and barriers such as opportunity, but assumes the sporting system and coaching systems are meritocratic (Norman 2014). However, women and men have different coaching experiences and to treat coaches as a homogeneous group in a male-privileged culture is to alienate women. Moreover, Shaw and Slack (2002) argue that sporting organisations need to address their gendered language, policies and practices to address unequal gender relations. This involves a move away from acting solely as barriers and facilitators to a recruitment of more diverse coaching populations.

In essence, both of these approaches position the power and the 'problem' with the individual, and reproduce women as responsible for their under-representation. Ely and Meyersen (2000) and Norman (2015) identify a number of 'remedies' arising from this position, including the following:

- 'Fix the women' – fix espoused issues to allow women to compete with men.
- 'Value the feminine' – celebrate and champion women's 'differences' and 'unique skills'.
- Create 'equal opportunities' – remove barriers to access for minority groups.

These approaches are problematic on two important levels. First, there is little understanding of how social practices are historically produced and culturally and socially defined to create and maintain hegemonic ideas of dominant social groups (Norman 2014). Second, such analysis accepts coaching and the coaching process as unproblematic or 'neutral', thus leaving sports cultures and coaching untouched by critique or held responsible for women's marginal status – therefore legitimate gendered inequality remains unproblematised (Norman 2015). Moreover, Norman (2015) argues that coach education informed by equal opportunities ideological frameworks set up 'them and us' thinking with consideration of coaches' identities only in a separate, abstract and detached manner.

While identified 25 years ago, Hall *et al.*'s (1991) summary of explanations for women being under-represented in sport sadly still provides a valuable template for understanding women's participation and organisational progress more widely. They identify the following reasons:

- stereotypical notions about women's competence despite their qualifications and expertise;
- questions about background, motivation and commitment;
- an emphasis on achieved rather than ascribed status (having to prove themselves);
- the prevalence of male symbols and values;
- a presumption about family responsibilities;
- the maintenance of a male 'status quo' through the exercise of power by existing elites and a formal and informal social and professional network;
- the absence of affirmative action to address the needs of women in sport.

These social factors are produced and reproduced in the early experiences of young females through sporting, coaching and educational socialisation. While commentators would suggest that this process may be less pronounced than was previously the case, the evidence would suggest otherwise. Indeed, researchers such as Fasting and Pfister (2000) and Norman (2015) suggest that male dominance in coaching has to be understood in the culture of sport and the gendered power structure in both sport and society. This will influence the coaches themselves, but also the perceptions of the athletes about the coaching role. This work summarises some more specific explanations:

- Men use sport to reinforce their male hegemony (perhaps because it is reducing in other spheres).
- Women are marginalised in areas in which they do not occupy the principal leadership roles (and that this becomes self-perpetuating).
- The 'system' is reproduced in the image of the dominant group.
- 'Female deficit' is not an explanation for the disparity. In other words, the explanations do not lie in the characteristics of women coaches themselves (although they acknowledge that lack of confidence may be a factor).

The way that coaching practice and the coaching process are mediated by and impact issues of inequality is a growing concern for sociological analysis of sport coaching. Social theory is concerned with the exploration of questions of power and privilege and the coaching process, systems and outcomes are intimately connected to these questions. However, notions of power, culture and practice are challenging and this challenge is compounded when aligned with coaching concepts and outcomes. Hence, there comes a set of issues that require addressing in coaching's practical setting. The following topics, while not an exhaustive or substantive list of issues, is a representation of significant issues:

- inequality and inclusion, including the relative absence of women coaches in high level sport;
- the coaching self and subjectivities;
- coaching practice (including issues such as pedagogy, performativity, the reinforcement of dominant social values and topic areas such as humour, emotion and trust);
- power and power relationships;
- socialisation into sport coaching domains: social learning and formal education;
- the congruence between the ethics of sub-cultural social practice and social values;
- the language and symbolism of sport coaching;
- governance and management; and
- coaching as an arena for alternative practice and resistance to dominant values.

Investigation of such issues can provide original and innovative forms of knowledge that can help coaching progress through stale and moribund arguments and paradigms and would be a welcome addition to the field. A potential route into these issues is to move from macro to micro, providing layered and interconnected levels of social knowledge and awareness – for example:

- taken-for-granted assumptions about the social world;
- current trends in performance sport practice;
- features of the social environment in sport coaching;
- awareness of specific organisational cultures and social group relationships; and
- social awareness of self, self-identity, previous experiences and 'social capital'.

However, there remains a need to be cognisant that such issues are embedded in forms of coaching practice that also require differentiation between participation and performance coaching, adding a further layer of complexity. Thus, sports

224

coaching domains can be considered as a particular set of distinctive sub-cultures. The key features of sub-culture analysis is the extent to which members create and defend boundary markers, diffuse values and recruit new members (Donnelly 2000). It is clear, however, that the clarity of the conceptual framework is necessary to provide a conceptual terminology within which to understand such boundary markers – therefore the journey from practice to theory is necessary but challenging.

 QUESTION BOX

The sub-cultural features of performance sport may be very important both as determinants of social cohesion and as markers for 'acceptable' coaching behaviours. Do coaches build walls around their areas of expertise and security?

A further area for study, which has perhaps been under-researched, is the influence of organisational structures and culture on behaviour. There is a considerable body of evidence on the relationship between organisational variables and many aspects of individual behaviour. However, this has focused on administrators – professional and volunteers – rather than coaches. It has already been acknowledged that coaches can operate for national governing bodies, large sports clubs, within self-contained coaching groups and, of course, within one-to-one relationships. This is exacerbated by the performance system within which the coach and athlete operate and the dynamics operating within coaching teams. Much of the North American literature on the high-school/collegiate coach could be relevant, in terms of recruitment, advancement, appraisal, role conflict, etc. Nevertheless, there is less evidence available on voluntary sector and professional sport sector organisational behaviours in the UK as they apply to coaches.

COMMENTARY

Sport coaching creates and is created by a social context of practice, and operates within a broader social and societal framework to which it contributes. It is a relational, dynamic social microcosm that needs to be understood not as a benign social space, or indeed a 'system', but as something that creates and recreates difference – a space where identities and hierarchies are formed and endlessly disputed and contested. In addition, coaching denotes doing – i.e. it is practical – but not just doing in and of itself, it is doing in a historical and social context that gives structure, and in this sense coaching practice is always social.

Conceiving a social structure such as coaching as the "mere aggregate of individual strategies and acts of classification makes it impossible to account for their resilience as well as for the emergent objective configurations these strategies perpetuate or challenge" (Bourdieu & Wacquant 1992, pp. 9–10). Hence, there is a set of social dynamics created by the coaching team, the performer–coach relationship and the organisational parameters of the coaching process. There are also social dynamics in sport and society more generally, and therefore issues about status, achievement, commercialisation, drugs in sport, etc. will impact on sport coaching and sport coaches. Yet understanding from a sociological perspective remains a missing cornerstone to conceptual development and in engaging practitioners. For example, how coaching impacts the subjectivities of those involved and how coaching is experienced as both a social space and a social structure offers fertile ground for conceptualising coaching. Against this backdrop, any consideration of interaction and discourse within the coaching process, and of the coaching process itself, devoid of context is both flawed and limited (Cushion & Lyle 2010). However, coaching researchers and research must also grasp the dual character of coaching practice with its subjective and objective aspects. The objective/subjective dichotomy as described earlier in the chapter is an enduring meta-theoretical dilemma and remains a significant obstacle to the construction of a total picture of coaching practice. However, a more sophisticated understanding of coaching practice is essential. As Marx argued:

> all social life is essentially practical. All the mysteries that lead theory toward mysticism find their rational solution in human practice and in the comprehension of this practice.
>
> (Cited in Bottomore & Rubel 1963, p. 84)

Analysis of coaching practice in real settings (in collaboration with coaches) provides the tools to better comprehend coaches' and athletes' individual and collective work. Indeed, paying attention to the detail of coaching practice, the social and other forces that shape coaching practice and the interconnections that run between them, has revealed much about the construction and complexity inherent in the coaching process. For example, sociological informed research is providing evidence that supports the notion that coaching is not something that is merely delivered, but a dynamic social activity that engages coach and athlete and is built upon a web of complex context and inter-dependent activities that come together to form a holistic process. This shows coaching is a remarkably intricate yet coherent process incorporating a myriad of individual variations that each coach, athlete and coaching context add to the blend. In this light, Cushion *et al.* (2006) outline five features of the coaching process that develop our understanding of coaching practice and the coaching process:

1. The social nature of the coaching process means it is not necessarily cyclical, but is continuous and interdependent.
2. This process (and practice) is continually structured and constrained by a range of 'objectives' that derive from the club, the coach and the athletes.
3. The process is a constantly dynamic set of intra- and inter-group interpersonal relationships. These relationships are locally dialectic between and among agent (coach, player) and structure (club, culture) and are subject to a wide range of pressures.

Coaching and social context

4. The coaching process is embedded within external constraints, only some of which are controllable.
5. A pervasive socio-cultural dimension infuses the coaching process through the coach, the club, the players and their interaction.

Despite these examples and others in the chapter, there is no doubt that the social of coaching is a very under-explored field, but with great potential. Sport coaching is slowly being subjected to sociological analysis, and this has the potential to contribute to a more complete understanding of the coaching process than is currently the case. Moreover, the preliminary sketch of the area given earlier in the chapter suggests that coaching would be richer for analysis from differing theoretical perspectives.

A 'holistic' appreciation of the coaching process will include all social contexts and part of the conceptual framework around which the coaching process is built should, therefore, comprise the social networks and values within which it is implemented. It is a plausible argument that coaches will be more effective if they take into account

---

 SUMMARY

This chapter should have familiarised you with the following:

- The social dimension to understanding sport and sport coaching.
- A brief account of sport sociology and the range of theoretical perspectives adopted.
- An overview of two social issues that currently influence sport coaching – and an indication of a 'social agenda' in understanding coaching.
- The potential of power analyses as a tool for understanding social interaction in sport coaching.
- The links between the conceptual framework and the development of a sociological 'reading' of coaching.

 PROJECTS

1. Carry out an analysis of a coach education curriculum. Select two NGBs and appraise their coach education materials for content relevant to the social dimension.
2. Identify the markers of a coaching domain culture – examine how they influence coach and athlete behaviour.
3. Interview six performance coaches. Construct a matrix of power/influence exercised by the coaches within their clubs/national governing bodies.

the social circumstances (at all levels) that are impacting on the coaching process. However, sociology and social awareness still remain the 'missing ingredient' in much coach education (Jones 2011). As for example Jarvie (1990) and Jones (2011) argue, the incorporation of sociological knowledge, social thought and social theory into coaching and coach education programmes will lead to a better understanding of interpersonal relationships, develop reflective practitioners, enhance personal development and improve awareness of social context.

READING

There is a growing body of literature on the sociology of sport coaching. Jones, Potrac, Denison and Cushion are all authors who have conducted sociological analysis of sport coaching. *The Sociology of Sport Coaching* (Jones *et al.* 2011) provides an overview of key social theorists and links sociology and sports coaching through discussions of power, interaction, knowledge and learning.

REFERENCES

Acker, J. (1990). Hierarchies, jobs, bodies: A theory of gendered organizations. *Gender & Society*, 4(2), 139–158.

Acosta, R. V., & Carpenter, L. J. (2012). Women in intercollegiate sport: A longitudinal, national study thirty-five year update 1922–2012. Unpublished manuscript, available at: www.acosacarpenter.org

Ball, D. W., & Loy, J. W. (1975). *Sport and the Social Order: Contributions to the Sociology of Sport*. Reading, MA: Addison-Wesley.

Bottomore, T. B., & Rubel, M. (Eds) (1963). *Karl Marx: Selected Writings in Sociology and Social Philosophy*. Harmondsworth: Pelican.

Bourdieu, P., & Wacquant, L. J. D. (Eds) (1992). *An Invitation to Reflexive Sociology*. Chicago, IL: University of Chicago Press.

Brohm, J. M. (1978). *Sport: A Prison of Measured Time*. London: Pluto.

Brookfield, S. D. (2009). *The Power of Critical Theory for Adult Learning and Teaching*. Berkshire: Open University Press.

Bush, A., Silk, M., Andrews, D., & Lauder, H. (2013). *Sports Coaching Research: Context, Consequence, and Consciousness*. London: Routledge.

Calhoun, C., Gerteis, J., Moody, S., Pfaff, P., & Virk, I. (Eds) (2012). *Classical Sociological Theory*. Chichester: Wiley & Sons.

Cassidy, T., Jones, R., & Potrac, P. (2009). *Understanding Sports Coaching: The Social, Cultural and Pedagogical Foundations of Sports Practice*. 2nd edition. London: Routledge.

Cushion, C. J. (2011a). Coach and athlete learning: A social approach. In R. Jones, P. Potrac, C. Cushion, & L. T. Ronglan (Eds) *The Sociology of Sports Coaching*. London: Routledge, 166–178.

Cushion, C. J. (2011b). Pierre Bourdieu: A theory of (coaching) practice. In R. L. Jones, P. Potrac, C. Cushion, & L. T. Ronglan (Eds) *The Sociology of Sports Coaching*. London: Routledge, 40–53.

228

Cushion, C. J. (2016). Reflection and reflective practice discourses in coaching: A critical analysis. *Sport, Education and Society*, doi.org/10.1080/13573322. 2016.1142961

Cushion, C. J., & Jones, R. L. (2014). A Bourdieusian analysis of cultural reproduction: Socialisation and the 'hidden curriculum' in professional football. *Sport, Education and Society*, 19(3), 276–298.

Cushion, C. J., & Lyle, J. (2010). Narrowing the field: Some key questions about sport coaching. In J. Lyle & C. J. Cushion (Eds) *Sports Coaching: Professionalization and Practice*. Edinburgh: Churchill Livingstone, 243–253.

Cushion, C. J., Armour, K. M., & Jones, R. L. (2006). Locating the coaching process in practice: Models 'for' and 'of' coaching. *Physical Education and Sport Pedagogy*, 11(1), 83–89.

Denison, J. (2011). Michael Foucault: Power and discourse – the loaded language of coaching. In R. L. Jones, P. Potrac, C. Cushion, & L. T. Ronglan (Eds) *The Sociology of Sports Coaching*. London: Routledge, 27–39.

Denison, J., Mills, J. P., & Konoval, T. (2015). Sports' disciplinary legacy and the challenge of coaching differently. *Sport Education and Society*, doi:10.1080/ 13573322.2015.1061986

Dewar, A. M. (1991). Incorporation or resistance? Towards an analysis of women's responses to sexual oppression in sport. *International Review for the Sociology of Sport*, 26(1), 15–22.

Donnelly, P. (Ed.) (2000). *Youth Sport in Canada: Problems and Resolutions*. Harlow: Pearson Education.

Elliot, A. (2008). *Contemporary Social Theory: An Introduction*. London: Routledge.

Ely, R. J., & Meyerson, D. E (2000). *Theories of Gender in Organisations: A New Approach to Organizational Analysis and Change*. Boston, MA: Centre for Gender in Organizations, Simmons School of Management.

Evans, J. & Davies, B. (2002). Theoretical background. In A. Laker (Ed.) *The Sociology of Sport and Physical Education*. London: Routledge, 15–35.

Fasting, K. & Pfister, G. (2000). Female and male coaches in the eyes of elite soccer players. *European Physical Education Review*, 6(1), 91–110.

Fernandez-Balboa, J.-M., & Muros, B. (2006). The hegemonic triumvirate-ideologies, discourses and habitus in sport and physical education: Implications and suggestions. *Quest*, 58, 197–221.

Foucault, M. (1972). *The Archaeology of Knowledge*. London: Tavistock Publications.

Foucault, M. (1979). *The History of Sexuality, Vol 1: An Introduction*. London: Allen Lane Penguin Press.

French, J. R. P., & Raven, B. (1959). The bases of social power. In D. Cartwright (Ed.) *Studies in Social Power*. Ann Arbor: University of Michigan Press, 150–167.

Giulianotti, R. (2005). *Sport: A Critical Sociology*. Cambridge: Polity.

Groom, R., Cushion, C. J., & Nelson, L. J. (2012). Analysing coach–athlete 'talk in interaction' within the delivery of video-based performance feedback in elite youth soccer. *Qualitative Research in Sport, Exercise and Health*, 4(3), 439–458.

Hall, A., Slack, T., Smith, G., & Whitson, D. (1991). *Sport in Canadian Society*. Toronto: McClelland & Stewart.

Hargreaves, J. (1994). *Sporting Females: Critical Issues in the History and Sociology of Women's Sport*. London: Routledge.

Harrington, A. (2005). Introduction: What is social theory. In A. Harrington (Ed.) *Modern Social Theory and Introduction*. Oxford: Oxford University Press, 1–15.

Jarvie, G. (1990). The sociological imagination. In F. Kew (Ed.) *Social Scientific Perspectives in Sport*. Leeds: NCF.

Joas, H., & Knobl, W. (2009). *Social Theory*. Cambridge: Cambridge University Press.

Johns, D. P., & Johns, J. (2000). Surveillance, subjectivism and technologies of power: An analysis of the discursive practice of high performance sport. *International Review for the Sociology of Sport, 35*, 219–234.

Jones, R. L. (2000). Towards a sociology of coaching. In R. L. Jones & K. M. Armour (Eds) *The Sociology of Sport: Theory and Practice*. London: Addison-Wesley Longman, 33–43.

Jones, R. L. (2011). Introduction. In R. L. Jones, P. Potrac, C. Cushion, & L. T. Ronglan (Eds) *The Sociology of Sports Coaching*. London: Routledge, 3–12.

Jones, R. L., & Corsby, C. (2015). A case for coach Garfinkel: Decision making and what we already know. *Quest, 67*, 439–449.

Jones, R. L., Armour, K. M., & Potrac, P. (2002). Understanding the coaching process: A framework for social analysis. *Quest, 54*(1), 34–48.

Jones, R. L., Armour, K. M., & Potrac, P. (2004). *Sport Coaching Cultures: From Practice to Theory*. London: Routledge.

Jones, R. L., Potrac, P., Cushion, C. J., & Ronglan, L. T. (Eds) (2011). *The Sociology of Sports Coaching*. London: Routledge.

Kincheloe, J. L. (2000). Making critical thinking critical. In D. Weil & H. K. Anderson (Eds) *Perspectives in Critical Thinking: Essays by Teachers in Theory and Practice*. New York: Peter Lang.

Lombardo, B. J. (1999). Coaching in the 21st Century: Issues, concerns and solutions. *Sociology of Sport On-line, 2*(1), www.physed.otago.ac.nz/sosol/v2i1/v2i1a4.htm

Loy, J. W., McPherson, B., & Kenyon, G. (1978). *Sport and Social Systems*. Reading, MA: Addison-Wesley.

Messner, M. (2011). Gender ideologies, youth sports, and the production of soft essentialism. *Sociology of Sport Journal, 7*(2), 151–170.

Moore, R. (2004). Cultural capital: Objectivity probability and cultural arbitrary. *British Journal of Sociology of Education, 25*(4), 445–456.

Murphy, M. (Ed.) (2013). *Social Theory and Education Research: Understanding Foucault, Habermas, Bourdieu and Derrida*. London: Routledge.

Norman, L. (2014). A crisis of confidence: Women coaches' response to their engagement in resistance. *Sport Education and Society, 5*, 532–551.

Norman, L. (2015). The impact of an equal opportunities ideological framework on coaches' knowledge and practice. *International Review for the Sociology of Sport*, DOI:10.1177/1012690214565377

Parsons, T. (1969). The distribution of power in American society. In T. Parsons (Ed.) *Politics and Social Structure*. New York: The Free Press, 185–203.

Popper, K. (1992). *The Logic of Scientific Discovery*. London: Routledge.

230

Potrac, P., & Jones, R. (2009). Micro-political workings in semi-professional football coaching. *Sociology of Sport Journal*, *26*, 557–577.

Potrac, P., & Jones, R. (2011). Power in coaching. In R. Jones, P. Potrac, C. Cushion, & L. T Ronglan (Eds) *The Sociology of Sports Coaching*. London: Routledge.

Purdy, L., Jones, R. L., & Cassidy, T. (2009). Negotiation and capital: Athletes' use of power in an elite men's rowing program. *Sport Education and Society*, *14*(3), 321–338.

Rail, G. (2002). Postmodernism and sport studies. In J. Maguire & K. Young (Eds) *Theory, Sport and Society*. London: Elsevier.

Ritzer, G. (2003). *Contemporary Sociological Theory and Its Classical Roots*. London: McGraw-Hill.

Shaw, S., & Slack, T. (2002). It's been like that for donkey's years: The construction of gender relations and cultures of sports organisations. *Culture, Sport & Society*, *5*(1), 86–106.

Snyder, M. & Kiviniemi, M. (2001). Getting what they came for: How power influences the dynamics and outcomes of interpersonal action. In A. Lee-Chai & J. Bargh (Eds) *The Use and Abuse of Power: Multiple Perspectives on the Causes of Corruption*. Philadelphia, PA: Taylor & Francis, 133–155.

sports coach UK (2011). *Sports Coaching in the UK III*. Leeds: sports coach UK.

Stones, R. (1998). Introduction. In R. Stones (Ed.) *Key Sociological Thinkers*. London: Macmillan, 1–18.

Westwood, S. (2002). *Power and the Social*. London: Routledge.

Wright Mills, C. (1959). *The Sociological Imagination*. Oxford: Oxford University Press.

CHAPTER 11

COACHING PHILOSOPHY

CHAPTER OUTLINE

- Introduction
- Current understanding of the term 'coaching philosophy'
- Current research: coaching philosophy – coaching rhetoric, ideology and discourse
- Issues with current conceptions of 'coaching philosophy'
- Philosophy of coaching: the role of philosophic enquiry
- Some conclusions
- Summary
- Projects
- Reading

INTRODUCTION

The assumption underlying this chapter is that coaching behaviour reflects a set of values about coaching, sport and human relationships more generally. This set of values or values framework has been termed a coaching philosophy and this, above all else, will inform coaching practice. Indeed, coaching philosophy is a central plank in understanding a coach's behaviour and forms a core aspect of coach education (e.g. Cassidy *et al.* 2009; Gilbert & Trudel 2005; Nelson & Cushion 2006). The articulation of a 'coaching philosophy' and reflecting on its attributes offers much for understanding and developing coaching practice (Cassidy *et al.* 2009; Jenkins 2010) – and it is important that the conceptual framework is able to account for the relationship between values and practice. However, in reality, there remains a lack of engagement with this process, and this is due, in part, to what Cassidy *et al.* (2009) describe as "superficial and simplistic assumptions about the value of establishing and locating definitive philosophies" (p. 56).

Understandably, coaches themselves get on with the business of coaching; one does not need to be a 'philosopher of coaching' in order to be a coach. Coaches often see little value in a philosophy as they attempt to cope with more tangible aspects of coaching practice, such as session content and organisation (Nash *et al.* 2008). Therefore, coaches tend to prefer to ground coaching in a 'common-sense view' (Carr & Kemmis 1986; Cushion 2013) of experience and practice. This has been conceptualised as coaches' 'practice theories' (Cassidy 2010), and we describe these as *coaching theories* (see Chapter 9); that is, experience and a body of informal knowledge and developed assumptions about coaching where these assumptions are viewed as 'taken-for granted' or 'normal' (Cassidy 2010), rather than *theories of coaching* which are grounded in empirical evidence. As a result, the impetus for studying the basis of coaching and coaching knowledge does not come from coaches but from researchers 'outside' coaching. Consequently, whatever the theoretical complexities of understanding coaching and coaching knowledge, many of the necessary intellectual questions are bound in personal research agendas, disciplinary outcomes and competition (Cushion & Lyle 2010; see also Chapter 15). Too frequently this has resulted in a fragmented field offering confusion, conflict and misdirection, and this is particularly the case when considering 'coaching philosophy'.

While 'philosophy' is complex, diverse and difficult to define, its central concerns, issues and concepts are less so (Morgan 2006). There are three themes that are central to philosophical enquiry (Hardman & Jones 2013; Morgan, 2006):

1   metaphysical questions that are concerned with the nature of reality (ontology);
2   questions concerning the nature of knowledge (epistemology); and
3   questions concerned with value (axiology), sub-divided into ethics and aesthetics.

However, the 'coaching philosophy' literature suffers from confusion, with a muddle of different languages used and a lack of consensus on the terms of reference. 'Coaching philosophy' is often defined in different ways without clear explanation of meaning or interpretation or without any explanation at all, assuming a shared common understanding of the term. A central issue, therefore, is not just the complexity of philosophy and its relationship to coaching practice, but also definitional and conceptual incoherence.

 KEY CONCEPT

There are three themes that are central to philosophical enquiry: metaphysical questions that are concerned with the nature of reality (ontology); questions concerning the nature of knowledge (epistemology); and questions concerned with value (axiology).

'Coaching philosophy' is currently grounded in, and reflective of, coaches' practice that, in turn, is primarily driven by self-referenced anecdotal approaches based on 'what works' and what is perceived to 'get results'. However, a coaching philosophy that is not derived from practice is merely a speculative set of intentions that have not been tested in implementation.

QUESTION BOX

It is not unusual for coaches to express statements about how behaviour and practice 'should be'. Is it possible to 'borrow' a philosophy from others or from education, or must it come from experience? Can a non-coach have a coaching philosophy?

In reality, coaches' 'coaching or practice theories' or 'philosophies' can be understood as a social system of beliefs, structures and practices; an ideology, a systemised influence on the social construction of knowledge (Cushion 2011; Devís-Devís 2006). This is important as it means that coaches' beliefs and justifications of existing and ongoing practice have not been subject to rational reconsideration, and instead there is a conflation of philosophies and ideologies. The outcome has been pseudo-principles and coaching rhetoric evidenced from coaching practice ideology described as 'coaching philosophies'. Consequently, 'philosophies' bear the hallmark of particular ideologies rather than philosophies in the truest sense (Green 2000), with "a conceptually incoherent smorgasbord of esoteric positions, methodologies, and ideologies" (Grant 2007, p. 24) that does little to help academics or practitioners make sense of what underpins actions in practice.

As a result, we need to differentiate between definitions of the nature and purpose of coaching *and* ideas about coaching held by coaches themselves, thus distinguishing between philosophical attempts to make sense of this nature and purpose (abstract, detached and rational conceptualisations) from ideologies and the discourse of coaching. Moreover, because definitions of coaching will depend on 'philosophy', and the landscape of coaching can be viewed through a variety of philosophical lenses, there remains a need to provide – for both practitioners and researchers – a conceptual framework and common vocabulary to interrogate 'coaching philosophies' and understanding and interpreting what is observable.

 KEY CONCEPT

There remains a need to differentiate definitions of the nature and purpose of coaching *and* ideas about coaching held by coaches themselves.

The purpose of this chapter is to provide an overview of 'coaching philosophy', allowing some of the gaps, problem areas and issues to be clearly identified and arguments developed. Such analysis provides a basis for understanding and disentangling some of the problems that have to-date plagued coaching philosophy, an area that remains haunted and hindered by fragmented and diverse approaches, unchallenged assumptions and often esoteric debates, and inconsistent theory-building based on a dearth of empirical research. There remains a need for meaningful empirical enquiry into coaches' philosophies, as this helps with developing the conceptual framework as well as informing coach education and coaching practice.

CURRENT UNDERSTANDING OF THE TERM 'COACHING PHILOSOPHY'

Attempting to establish and identify a clear understanding of what underpins coaches' actions allows a coach to utilise the practice activities that they believe are most effective for the learner in a complex coaching environment. This underpinning is defined as a 'coaching philosophy' made up of a collective of values, beliefs, assumptions, attitudes, principles and priorities.

 KEY CONCEPT

A coaching philosophy underpins practice and is made up of a collective of values, beliefs, assumptions, attitudes, principles and priorities.

It is this 'philosophy' that underpins everything a coach does and coaches' 'core values' purposefully and singularly drive coaching philosophies. Indeed, value frameworks may contain 'core' and 'peripheral' values, although this has not been subject to any depth of research (see Lyle 1999), and it will be obvious that values are subject to social construction where there will be an element of social acceptance, or otherwise, in individual values. Thus, what coaches do and how they behave is shaped by their individual coaching philosophy. However, despite us offering a definition here, the reality is that it is not, in fact, always clear what is meant by a 'coaching philosophy' – with an often assumed shared understanding – while research findings are frequently based on coaches' self-referenced perceptions of 'coaching philosophy'.

It is not uncommon for coaches (and the media) to discuss a particular 'philosophy' about a sport (which is really a technical/tactical model), and this should not be confused with a coaching philosophy. A coach's technical/tactical model might be based on a set of beliefs about the advantages and disadvantages of specific preparation methods, offensive/defence strategies or desirable performer qualities. However, this would be one element of the coach's knowledge structures and is probably based on the efficacy of the choice for performance achievement.

A coaching philosophy is a more comprehensive set of personal values and beliefs. While there seems to be consensus on these core elements, values and beliefs are frequently discussed but with no explanation of the terms. In defining a 'coaching philosophy' and its components, there appears only a loose consensus rather than conceptual clarity; and within the consensus, there are few clear definitions. This is not helped by different definitions of the same terms. For example, Rokeach (1973) suggested that a practice philosophy consists of:

- beliefs (defined as a proposition or premise to be true);
- values (defined as an underpinning view of importance or worth of an object);
- attitudes; and
- norms.

Burton and Raedeke (2008) suggest beliefs are "what dictate the way we view experiences in our lives" (p. 4) and values are what "we hold in our lives" (p. 4). To further muddy the waters, there is the consideration of the relationship between values and beliefs and how this is defined. For example, work on the nature of human values and beliefs suggest that a philosophy is a framework that clarifies the relationship *between* values and beliefs, where coaches' values are more deeply held and underpin their beliefs. For example, Lyle (1999) used content analysis to identify the coaching philosophies of 43 senior coaches, including 24 'values' common to all 43 coaches (for example, personal growth, respect for others and partnership). These, he argued, underpinned beliefs and behaviours that, in turn, characterised the coaches' practice. Conversely, other authors (e.g. Hardman & Jones 2013; Kidman & Hanrahan 2011) suggest that values and beliefs work *independently* of each other. In this case, a coach's values and beliefs are related yet separately organised into a hierarchy of importance, with personal or social values taking priority (Jenkins 2010), with variation according to the individual coach, their athletes and the social context.

Jenkins' (2010) analysis adopts Rokeach's (1973) description of values, where a human value system is an enduring organisation of three types of beliefs:

- descriptive or existential (i.e. capable of being true or false);
- evaluative (i.e. judged to be good or bad); and
- prescriptive or proscriptive (i.e. some means or end of action is judged to be desirable or undesirable).

These values are then split into personal and social values (self-centred or society-centred/intrapersonal or interpersonal in focus) or moral (refer mainly to modes of behaviour) and competence values.

 KEY CONCEPT

A 'coaching philosophy' is a value system made up of different types of beliefs (descriptive/existential, evaluative and proscriptive).

A recurrent theme in the literature and in coach education, then, is a failure to define clearly the terms used, whether that is of 'coaching philosophy' itself or the components thereof. Moreover, despite values and beliefs being identified as key parts of coaching 'philosophy', these terms are not defined clearly, nor the relationship between the two explicated. Furthermore, aside from Jenkins (2010), there is little insight into how values and beliefs might be categorised, or the characteristics of such categories. Lastly, despite a plethora of book chapters and position papers, there is limited empirical research investigating coaches' values and beliefs and how these may translate into practice – despite the repeated assertions of the importance of understanding coaching philosophy.

 QUESTION BOX

What are coaches' values and beliefs, and how is the relationship between them structured?

CURRENT RESEARCH: COACHING PHILOSOPHY – COACHING RHETORIC, IDEOLOGY AND DISCOURSE

When considering the existing research, a critical question we need to ask is the degree to which what is presented actually evidences a 'coaching philosophy'. The current crop of 'coaching philosophy' literature is largely descriptive rather than analytical; it is uncritically accepting and largely describes coaches' personal preferences (e.g. Burton & Raedeke 2008; Vealey 2005). In addition, although limited in number, empirical studies conducted in coaching (e.g. Nash *et al.* 2008; Robbins *et al.* 2010) tend to identify coaches' different perceptions of philosophies. Such findings are far from philosophical in nature, and instead are largely the reproduction of coaching rhetoric, truisms and value-laden ideologies (e.g. Bennie & O'Connor 2010; Collins *et al.* 2011; Schempp *et al.* 2006). This research has offered little in the way of critical, philosophical analysis and has even less to say about the complex production and reproduction of coaching practice and discourse.

As a system of ideas, beliefs, values, commitments, pattern of thought and social practice, ideology operates between individuals and structures dialectically to reproduce and maintain social characteristics (Devís-Devís 2006). Ideology is twofold; first, it functions as a shared system of symbols and social practice without which any social situation would be incomprehensible; and second, it functions as a system embedded in power relationships and sedimented forms of thought in everyday life that can distort communication and understanding (Devís-Devís 2006). Coaching is a social system of beliefs, structures and practices, and its ideologies – which appear natural, obvious and common sense – exercise a systemised influence on the social construction of knowledge of coaches to produce a particular coaching discourse. Discourses are shaped by "beliefs and commitments, explicit ideologies, tacit world views, linguistics and cultural systems, politics and economics, and power arrangements" (Cherryholmes 1988, p. 106). They are the prevailing "set of meanings, metaphors representations, images stories [and] statements that, in some way, together produce a particular version" of coaching (Burr 1995, p. 48). Coaching is an ideologically determined practice, and is perceived as universal, rational and obvious. Coaching thus retains a tacitly understood persistent and resilient culture in which ideology endures partly because it contains elements that both coaches and researchers recognise as accurate in their experience (Eagleton 1991). Against this backdrop, coaches are left to define their own 'coaching philosophy'. When this occurs it does so within coaching's culture, where coaches come to accept and value certain types of knowledge over others and perpetuate these perspectives through practice (Cushion *et al.* 2003).

Thus, the coaching process and coaching practice – and coaching research by reporting it – nourishes and maintains ideology through the imposition of language, meanings and symbolic systems that actually support certain segmented ways of understanding and ordering coaching. Both coaching and coaching research are guilty of 'mis-recognising' the arbitrary nature of coaching culture and instead serve to reproduce existing ideology while caught in its ideological web. Far from being benign activities, coaching practice, coach education and coaching research always contain and advance values and agendas. Indeed, rather than leading coaches and coach education in understanding underlying 'ideologies', existing research contributes to these issues through its perpetuation of existing coaching discourse and its lack of conceptual clarity. Consequently, the 'coaching philosophies' currently described are not philosophical in nature (in the sense of being abstract, detached and rational conceptualisations of coaching), but merely what Green (2002) calls "mythical ideas regarding the supposed worth of their subject" (p. 65).

ISSUES WITH CURRENT CONCEPTIONS OF 'COACHING PHILOSOPHY'

Up to now we have accepted to a lesser or greater degree the idea of 'coaching philosophy', the next thing to do is to examine this more closely – and problematise the term. There remains a dominant psychologism and individualism through humanistic discourse that runs through writing and talking about coaching. Such approaches or ideologies have implicit assumptions about coaches, coaching and therefore coaching philosophy that remain unchallenged. These include assumptions that:

- knowledge and skills are neutral rather than socially and culturally constructed;
- experience is seen as a given and the source of authentic knowledge, and not in any way problematic; and
- there is a true unitary self that exists independently of the social realm.

As a result, 'coaching philosophy' is presented as a "logical chain of propositions that can be developed into a system of knowledge" (Jones *et al.* 2014, p. 3) that, in turn, underpins and explains practice unproblematically. The growing corpus of writing concerning 'coaching philosophy' fails repeatedly to take any critical standpoint towards these assumptions, nor does it question or problematise the notion of a 'coaching philosophy', instead providing legitimacy to the concept and defending the grounds for developing and articulating it.

238

Coaching philosophy as an ideological structure?

Rather than just representing what coaches say about themselves and their practice as 'coaching ideology', the literature (and coach education) instead presents and perpetuates an ideology of coaching philosophy. This ideology acts as a structure for coaching identities and is legitimised as a valid explanation for coaches' thoughts and actions. As Althusser (1971) suggests, ideology enables coaches to reconstruct in an imaginary plane, a coherent discourse that can operate as the skyline of their lived experience, and gives shape to a social process that, in turn, helps place them in their particular social formation. Ideology has an opaque character; it impacts the rational perceptions of individuals regarding social practices and helps individual coaches articulate a normative framework and behaviour to orient their practices (Torres 1999). Coaching philosophy, then, is itself an ideological structure, "a system of representations by which social agents express a particular mode of appraising reality, codifying information and processing practical outcomes" (Torres 1999, p. 108).

Coaching philosophy ideology assumes reflexivity – the ability to see oneself as object – as a defining characteristic where this self-awareness can generate valid knowledge (Fendler 2003). In a scheme of self-awareness, the self plays simultaneously the role of subject-who-reflects and the object that is reflected upon (Nadler 1989). This notion of self-awareness in coaching philosophy ideology is extended to mean that this reflexive coach has agency, has the ability to make rational choices and assumes responsibility for decisions and actions; a 'coaching philosophy' becomes formalised in instrumental terms where everyone who goes through the steps will arrive at the same place. This construction is problematic as it ignores the social beyond the interactional (Jones *et al.* 2014) through not recognising the effects of socialisation, power, history and culture on subjectivity, and on the ways it is possible to be aware of ourselves as subjects and objects (Fendler 2003), while at the same time overemphasising coaches' agency, power and conscious action and reflexivity.

Rather than a meta-theoretical reflexivity on coaching practice, coaching philosophy is currently misunderstood as a constitutive part of the object; the ideology of coaching philosophy would have us believe that the subjective experience and practical knowledge at work in the mind of the coach is an objectified explanation of practice. However, subjective experience and knowledge have already been shaped by historical and cultural circumstances and ideology, and subjective perceptions are effects of historical contexts (Fendler 1999). The relationship between the social and the individual is therefore overlooked as coaching practice takes place in a given social context and coaches make meaning of their existence from the sporting cultures that they inhabit; they are part of the structure and the structure is part of them. Thus, the individual coach alone is an inadequate unit of analysis to understand coaching, and the ideology of coaching philosophy results in the true meaning of 'philosophy' and the connections with social structure being overlooked.

Coaching practice as entirely conscious?

The ideology of coaching philosophy also assumes that coaching practice is an entirely conscious activity and available for reflexive scrutiny. However, only a small part of human experience is retained in consciousness – experiences become sedimented (Berger & Luckmann 1966); coaching practices originally learned as part of a conscious process become remembered as a habitual response (Cushion & Jones 2014). Lessons are absorbed that become so ingrained they are forgotten in any conscious sense (Jarvie & Maguire 1994), and therefore coaches have learned and acquired a set of practical cultural competences, including a social identity. These are dispositions that operate "below the level of consciousness and language, beyond the reach of introspective scrutiny and control by the will" (Bourdieu 1984, p. 466). Coaching practice, therefore, is not *wholly* consciously organised or orchestrated, as Jenkins argues (2002); there is a practical sense and/or logic, "a mastery acquired by experience of the game, and one which works outside conscious control" (Bourdieu 1990, p. 13). Practical logic is fluid and indeterminate and not accomplished on the basis of normative models; coaching is therefore an improvisatory practice (Cushion & Jones 2014). As a result, it would be a mistake to see coaches' actions as entirely conscious. Moreover, as practice is rooted in both past and present positions and experience, as well as being located in social structure external to them, coaches' espoused values and beliefs are more likely simplified statements of interpretation rather than the actual cause of their thoughts and actions.

 KEY CONCEPT

As practice is rooted in both past and present positions and experience, as well as being located in social structure external to them, coaches' espoused values and beliefs are more likely simplified statements of interpretation rather than the actual cause of their thoughts and actions.

Yet, the 'coaching philosophy' literature is unanimous in agreeing that coaches possess the capacity to identify, understand and articulate the determinants of their practice in its entirety; that is, that coaches possess the capacity to function as entirely conscious and reflexive beings.

We need to remember, too, that the descriptive language of practice in coaching philosophies produced can act to normalise *how* a coach should be (e.g. Jenkins 2010). Culturally and ideologically driven descriptors correlate the ideology and culture with certain coaching activities and practices, the language sets up certain expectations about behaviour and practice, the descriptors connect coaching to identity, constructing language to understand and identify self; and the descriptors by omission obliterate alternative perceptions that are not based on prevailing dominant culture or ideology (Cushion, 2013). Thus, coaches state either:

240

1. what they perceive the demands of an employer or organisation to be; or
2. what the coach perceives 'should' be said – that is, commensurate with prevailing ideologies.

There is an obvious danger here of a mismatch between the coach's actual behaviour and practice and stated values. This will be most evident to the athletes. This supports the wider issue that coaching philosophies might become ideological (conforming) statements rather than guides to individuals' behaviour and preferred practice – and by implication are poor measures of coaching practice. Thus a situation arises in which coaches (and researchers through reporting) defend and promote the legitimacy of the ideology while offering little insight, either implicitly or empirically, into the objectivities and subjectivities that produce and reproduce coaching practice.

However, coaching philosophy, or rather, philosophical contemplation, provides coaches with the tools to deconstruct who they think they are and the social conditions that govern their development and existence. Such a reflexive process should expose the social and cultural embeddedness and taken-for-granted assumptions in which the coach is located, and encourage alternative readings of the text of experience (Tennant 1999). Philosophy and philosophic thinking, therefore, does offer a means of enlightening coaches about the ideology of 'coaching philosophy' and the limits on their thinking and practice.

PHILOSOPHY OF COACHING: THE ROLE OF PHILOSOPHIC ENQUIRY

All practical activities are guided by theory; coaching is a performed social practice that can only be understood by reference to the framework of thought in terms of which practitioners make sense of what they are doing (Carr & Kemmis 1986; Brockbank & Magill 2007). As Carr and Kemmis (1986) argue, "the assumption that all 'theory' is non-practical and all 'practice' is non-theoretical is entirely misguided" (p. 113). The coach's role is the product of existing and ongoing negotiations about coaching where coaching norms provide an overriding, powerful and historical view of what coaches *should* do and what coaching *should* look like (Cushion 2013). This results in the development of a set of beliefs, attitudes and expectations about coaching and the nature of a 'philosophy'. Though acquired through coaching practice and coaching experiences in a subconscious manner, this is still a prescribed way of thinking (Carr & Kemmis 1986) informed by assumptions that have axiological, ontological and epistemological underpinnings (see also Chapter 9). The adequacy of concepts, beliefs and assumptions about coaching incorporated within prevailing practice or coaching theories need to be subject to critical appraisal. Therefore, by subjecting beliefs and justifications of existing and ongoing practice to abstract rational and detached (i.e. philosophical) reconsideration, theory can in fact inform and transform practice by informing and transforming the ways in which practice is experienced and understood.

Rather than simply asking coaches to recite them, we should be helping them unpack assumptions and beliefs; this emancipates practitioners from their dependence on

By subjecting beliefs and justifications of existing and ongoing practice to abstract rational and detached (i.e. philosophical) reconsideration, theory can in fact inform and transform practice by informing and transforming the ways in which practice is experienced and understood.

habit and tradition by providing them with resources to enable reflection and to critically examine the inadequacies of different conceptions of practice (Carr & Kemmis 1986). However, this is largely beyond existing conceptions of coach education, which is additive (grafting new 'skills'/knowledge onto an existing repertoire) rather than critically transformative (deconstructing taken-for-granted beliefs, assumptions, knowledge and habits, and rebuilding practice) (Thompson & Zeuli 1999). Therefore, coaches are not engaged in meaningful reflection about their underlying beliefs, but instead evidence pragmatic practice utilitarianism (Grant 2007). Such an uncritical approach leaves coaching closed to objective enquiry around the outcomes (intended and unintended) of adopted methodologies. Moreover, coaches, coach educators and sports organisations have a tendency to 'cherry pick' ideas that fit these unchallenged 'beliefs', while rejecting or resisting others that are more challenging (Cushion 2013; Jones *et al.* 2014; Light & Evans 2010; Roberts 2011). The resulting application of pseudo-principles and coaching myths are not only evidenced in coaching practice ideology, but are also included in coach education ideologies and rhetoric (e.g. Roberts 2011), and become affirmed and reproduced through 'coaching philosophy'.

However, it could be suggested that this lack of work from researchers and in coach education is, in part, due to the difficulty of identifying the often implicit, ontological, epistemological beliefs and axiological, ethical values deeply embedded within coaches. However, rather than being comprehensive, the literature remains largely superficial and descriptive, while philosophical questions that can be the most "complex and frustrating of all" (Hardman & Jones 2013, p. 105) are just not posed. A more philosophical approach suggests more in-depth exploration relating to axiology, which includes values of importance; ethics which includes moral values; ontology which includes beliefs about the nature of existence, including a core set of features of coaching that provide personal significance and a central source of meaning, self-understanding, social expression and self-esteem to that person (Hardman & Jones 2013); and epistemological assumptions that include beliefs on the nature of knowledge (Light 2008). All coaches' practice narratives contain underpinning ontological and epistemological beliefs that inform their assumptions about learning that, in turn, influence the types of coaching methods and practice activities used (see Chapter 9).

We need an empirical philosophical understanding to support coach education and coaches (Collins *et al.* 2009; Hardman & Jones 2013; Jenkins 2010). Philosophical reflection can help establish a rationale for action and provide the tools to deal with questions in a clear and justified way (Drewe 2000). While recognising the problems with making the tacit explicit, coaches themselves can be encouraged to use philosophical 'tools' to develop a more coherent and sophisticated understanding of their own coaching and coaching in general (Hardman & Jones 2013).

 KEY CONCEPT

While recognising the problems with making the tacit explicit, coaches themselves can be encouraged to use philosophical 'tools' to develop a more coherent and sophisticated understanding of their own coaching and coaching in general.

The methodology used most frequently to attempt this process has been coach interviews (e.g. Bennie & O'Connor 2010; Camire *et al.* 2012; Jones *et al.* 2004; Macallister *et al.* 2000; Nash *et al.* 2008; Robbins *et al.* 2010) with the research tending to investigate elite coaches in performance contexts (e.g. Collins *et al.* 2009; Jones *et al.* 2004; Voight & Carroll 2006). Researchers have also utilised questionnaires (e.g. Debanne & Laffaye 2013) and document analysis of personal statements or reflective writing (e.g. Collins *et al.* 2011; Schempp *et al.* 2006) to attempt to understand coaches' perceptions of their practice and their 'philosophy'. In addition, in addressing its research questions the coaching philosophy research has tended to use single rather than multiple or mixed method research designs (e.g. Bennie & O'Connor 2010; Carless & Douglas 2011; Collins *et al.* 2011; Nash *et al.* 2008; Robbins *et al.* 2010).

Irrespective of methodology, however, all authors assume that coaches' values, beliefs and practices are entirely conscious entities and infer that coaches consciously construct and live out their philosophies, while elite coaches appear to be sampled on the inference (e.g. Cassidy *et al.* 2009; Nash *et al.* 2008) that more experience brings more capacity for reflexivity. While acknowledging that often coaches do not have sufficient philosophical understanding to articulate the values underpinning their thoughts and actions (Lyle 2002), researchers present a paradox, assuming that 'expert' coaches naturally become more reflexive but continue to stress the need to 'trigger' coaches' internal conversations through questioning (e.g. Cassidy *et al.* 2009; Nash *et al.* 2008) without articulating the assumptions underpinning such questions.

There is a recognition in the literature that beliefs are framed over time, often early in the life course, and are inextricably linked to biography (Armour 2004; Cassidy *et al.* 2009). As a result, linking practice to biography, which includes a temporal element, seems an important methodological step. To this end, the use of storytelling and the identification of critical incidents have been advocated (Carless & Douglas 2011; Jenkins 2010). Moreover, Bourdieu (2000, p. 50) insisted that in order to 'encounter' rather than reassemble the social, we need to move close to the site of practice and production; social practice cannot be understood without an appreciation of practice itself (Cushion & Jones 2014).

In teaching, Green (1998) argued that "if we wish to understand teachers' 'philosophies' of PE, then we must study them not as abstract philosophical systems of ideas, but rather as practical, everyday 'philosophies' which provide practical guides to action as well as a justification for those actions" (p. 141). Tsangaridou and O'Sullivan (2003) go on to suggest that "the only way to determine teacher's theories-in-use may be through observations of these professional practices" (p. 133). However, practice, as a visible social phenomenon, cannot be understood outside of time and any adequate analysis of practice must treat temporality as a central feature (Jenkins 2002). These arguments suggest that any consideration of philosophy must be conducted over time (i.e. longitudinally), be based *in situ* (grounded in practice) and use a range of methods to highlight and attempt to move beyond coaches' subjective perceptions. However, thus far we are no further forward in understanding, in a coaching context, of how values change over time or of how particular kinds of experience might impact on the coach's values framework. There is clearly a research agenda relating to the effects of education, maturity, responsibility, success, organisational authority and other factors on the development of values. Values do not change quickly and it seems unlikely that coaches can, or would want to, adapt these deeply held constructs in a superficial way. It may lead, however, to coaches' public pronouncements being different to their personal values. A process of self-reflection (which in practice may actually involve others) is necessary to identify a values framework and is a growing part of coach education. The framework is also an essential element in analysing practice, since it has an explanatory power. Coaches must, therefore, come to realise that a complete understanding of practice is not possible without identifying the coaching philosophy.

How should a coaching philosophy be constructed? Table 11.1 suggests a likely procedure.

SOME CONCLUSIONS

Hardman and Jones (2013) remain the only scholars to acknowledge and integrate legitimate philosophical thinking into a discussion concerning 'coaching philosophy'. They recognise that philosophy is more complex than a selection of statements concerning the circumstances and dilemmas of coaching practice (Hardman & Jones 2013). Through the portrayal of the objective nature of philosophical thought, the authors challenge the commonly accepted depiction of coaches' philosophies as entirely subjective and counter coaches' claims of 'exclusivity'. However, the authors paint a utopian picture of coaching philosophy that privileges the ideas of morality, and this work remains a philosophical discussion rather than empirical philosophical enquiry. Of the empirical work carried out, and as has been discussed in this chapter, there remains significant conceptual incoherence and confusion where "coaches notions of their philosophies appear more ideological than philosophical" (Cassidy *et al.* 2009, p. 58). In addition, we have tried to drive this important area forward and therefore have attempted to problematise the assumptions underlying coaching

244

Table 11.1 Steps to constructing a coaching philosophy

1. Provide an introduction that makes explicit the context within which the statement has been constructed or for which it is intended.

2. Describe motives for becoming a coach and whether or not this has changed. Identify core values and priorities.

3. Describe an interpretation of the role of the coach.

4. Focus on interpersonal relationships with performers. What is key about these relationships?

5. Describe developmental constructs that are intended to be fostered in athletes.

6. Derive a series of principles from a review of several critical incidents.

7. An 'operational' set of practices can be identified from reconstructing typical activities and how they are conducted.

8. Step outside the sporting context and review practice/relationships in the context of more generally held values about people and conduct.

9. Review values to decide whether there are any situational compromises in their application.

10. Review 'difficult' issues for all relationships – abuse of power, trust, harassment, discrimination. Firmed up positions should be reflected in statements.

11. Sport has an explicit set of rules and a less explicit set of expectations about conduct in relations to these. Clarify values in relation to these.

12. Consider professional context and expectations in relation to standards, education, development and conduct.

13. Review the statement made for the correspondence between practice and aspiration.

14. Consider the presentation of the framework in the light of the potential readership. Has the statement been amended to meet the expectations of the reader? Is the coach comfortable with this?

philosophy and instead argued that what is currently presented as coaching philosophy is itself an ideology. Coaching scholars are culpable in producing and reproducing this ideology as research repeatedly legitimises coaching philosophy as a valid unproblematised explanation of coaches' thoughts and action. There is a case

 SUMMARY

This chapter should have familiarised you with the following:

- A broad definition of coaching philosophy and the place of values in analysing and understanding a coaching philosophy.
- The relevant literature looking at coaching philosophy and some of the issues with this.
- A critique of the concept of coaching philosophy.
- The benefits of 'philosophic enquiry' to developing coaching practice and the conceptual framework.
- How to construct a coaching philosophy.

PROJECTS

1. Using the detail provided in this Chapter and the steps in Table 11.1, devise your own coaching philosophy. Enlist the help of an observer to evaluate whether your practice and philosophy are consonant.
2. Carry out a case study investigation of a coaching philosophy with one experienced performance coach. Try to elicit explanations and elaborations for their philosophy for which you have accumulated some observational evidence.
3. Analyse a selection of coaching philosophies. Choose your sample to facilitate an investigation into a particular variable – team/individual, novice/expert, etc.

that this ideology overemphasises coaches' agency and conscious action and reflexivity, while underestimating the significance of social structure on coaches' dispositions and the degree to which practice is unconscious.

READING

Hardman and Jones (2013) give a 'philosophical' overview of coaching philosophy, while Jenkin's (2010) chapter examines the nature of values of beliefs. Cushion and Partington (2014) conduct a critical review of the coaching philosophy literature

ACKNOWLEDGEMENT

This chapter is derived in part from an article, Cushion, C. J., & Partington, M. Critical analysis of the conceptualisation of 'coaching philosophy', published in *Sport Education and Society* (2014) copyright Taylor & Francis, available online: www. tandfonline.com/ DOI:10.1080/13573322.2014.958817.

REFERENCES

Althusser, L. (1971). Ideology and ideological state apparatuses. In B. Brewster (Ed.) *Lenin and Philosophy*. London: Monthly Review Press, 170–186.

Armour, K. M. (2004). Coaching pedagogy. In R. L. Jones, K. M. Armour, & P. Potrac (Eds) *Sports Coaching Cultures*. London: Routledge, 94–115.

Bennie, A., & O'Connor, D. (2010). Coaching philosophies: Perceptions from professional cricket, rugby league and rugby union players and coaches in Australia. *International Journal of Sports Science and Coaching*, 5, 309–320.

Berger, P., & Luckmann, T. (1966). *The Social Construction of Reality: A Treatise in the Sociology of Knowledge*. London: Penguin.

Bourdieu, P. (1984). *Distinction: A Social Critique of the Judgement of Taste.* Cambridge, MA: Harvard University Press.

Bourdieu, P. (1990). *The Logic of Practice.* Stanford, CA: Stanford University Press.

Bourdieu, P. (2000). *Pascalian Meditations.* Cambridge: Polity Press.

Brockbank, A., & Magill, I. (2007). *Facilitating Reflective Learning in Higher Education.* 2nd edition. London: Open University Press.

Burr, V. (1995). *An Introduction to Social Constructionism.* London: Routledge.

Burton, D., & Raedeke, T. D. (2008). *Sport Psychology for Coaches.* Champaign, IL: Human Kinetics.

Camire, M., Trudel, P., & Forneris, T. (2012). Coaching and transferring life skills: Philosophies and strategies used by model high school coaches. *The Sport Psychologist, 26,* 243–260.

Carless, D., & Douglas, K. (2011). Stories as personal coaching philosophy. *International Journal of Sports Science & Coaching, 6*(1), 1–12.

Carr, W., & Kemmis, S. (1986). *Becoming Critical: Education, Knowledge and Action Research.* London: Falmer Press.

Cassidy, T. (2010). Understanding athlete learning and coaching practice: Utilising 'practice theories' and 'theories of practice'. In J. Lyle & C. Cushion (Eds) *Sports Coaching Professionalisation and Practice.* Edinburgh: Churchill Livingstone, 177–192.

Cassidy, T., Jones, R., & Potrac, P. (2009). *Understanding Sports Coaching: The Social, Cultural and Pedagogical Foundations of Coaching Practice.* 2nd edition. London: Routledge.

Cherryholmes, C. (1988). *Power and Criticism: Post-structural Investigations in Education.* New York: Teachers College Press.

Collins, K., Gould, D., Lauer, L., & Yongchul, C. (2009). Coaching life skills through football: Philosophical beliefs of outstanding high school football coaches. *International Journal of Coaching Science, 3,* 1–26.

Collins, K., Barber, H., Moore, K., & Laws, A. (2011). The first step: Assessing the coaching philosophies of pre-service coaches. *Journal of Research in Health, Physical Education, Recreation, Sport & Dance, 6,* 21–29.

Cushion, C.J. (2011). Coach and athlete learning: A social approach. In R. Jones, P. Potrac, C. Cushion, & L.T. Ranglan (Eds) *The Sociology of Sports Coaching,* 166–178. London: Routledge.

Cushion, C. J. (2013). Applying game centred approaches in coaching: A critical analysis of the 'dilemmas of practice' impacting change. *Sports Coaching Review, 2*(1), 61–76.

Cushion, C. J., & Jones, R. L. (2014). A Bourdieusian analysis of cultural reproduction: Socialisation and the 'hidden curriculum' in professional football. *Sport, Education and Society, 19,* 276–298.

Cushion, C., & Lyle, J. (2010). Conceptual development in sports coaching. In J. Lyle & C. Cushion (Eds) *Sports Coaching: Professionalisation and Practice.* Edinburgh: Churchill Livingstone, 1–14.

Cushion, C. J., Armour, K. M., & Jones, R. L. (2003). Coach education and continuing professional development: Experience and learning to coach. *Quest, 55,* 215–230.

Debanne, T., & Laffaye, G. (2013). Coaches' beliefs and knowledge: Training programs used by French professional coaches to increase ball-throwing velocity in elite handball players. *International Journal of Sports Science & Coaching, 8,* 557–570.

Devís-Devís, J. (2006). Socially critical research perspectives in physical education. In D. Kirk, D. Macdonald, & M. O'Sullivan (Eds) *The Handbook in Physical Education.* London: Sage, 37–58.

Drewe, S. B. (2000). An examination of the relationship between coaching and teaching. *Quest, 52*(1), 79–88.

Eagleton, T. (1991). *Ideology: An Introduction.* London: Verso.

Fendler, L. (1999). Making trouble: Prediction, agency and critical intellectuals. In T. Popokewitz & L. Fendler (Eds), *Critical Theories in Education: Changing Terrains of Knowledge and Politics.* New York: Routledge, 169–190.

Fendler, L. (2003). Teacher reflection in a hall of mirrors: Historical influences and political reverberations. *Educational Researcher, 32*(3), 16–25.

Gilbert, W., & Trudel, P. (2005). Learning to coach through experience: Conditions that influence reflection. *Physical Educator, 62,* 32–43

Grant, A. M. (2007). Past, present, and future: The evolution of professional coaching and coaching psychology. In S. Palmer & A. Whybrow (Eds), *Handbook of Coaching Psychology.* London: Routledge, 23–39.

Green, K. (1998). Philosophies, ideologies and the practice of physical education. *Sport, Education and Society, 3,* 125–143.

Green, K. (2000). Exploring the everyday 'philosophies' of PE teachers from a sociological perspective. *Sport, Education and Society, 5*(2), 109–129.

Green, K. (2002). Physical education teachers in their figurations: A sociological analysis of everyday 'Philosophies'. *Sport, Education and Society, 7*(1), 65–83.

Hardman, A. R., & Jones, C. R. (2013). Ethics for coaches. In R. L. Jones, M. Hughes, & K. Kingston (Eds), *An Introduction for Sports Coaching: Connecting Theory to Practice.* London: Routledge, 113–130.

Jarvie, G., & Maguire, J. (1994). *Sport and Leisure in Social Thought.* London: Routledge.

Jenkins, R. (2002). *Pierre Bourdieu.* Revised edition. London: Routledge.

Jenkins, S. (2010). Coaching philosophy. In J. Lyle & C. Cushion (Eds) *Sports Coaching: Professionalisation and Practice.* Edinburgh: Churchill Livingstone, 233–242.

Jones, R. L., Armour, K., & Potrac, P. (2004). *Sports Coaching Cultures: From Practice to Theory.* London: Routledge.

Jones, R. L., Edwards, C., & Filho, I. A. T. V. (2014). Activity theory, complexity and sports coaching: An epistemology for a discipline. *Sport Education and Society.* http://dx.doi.org/ 10.1080/13573322.2014.895713

Kidman, L., & Hanrahan, S. J. (2011). *The Coaching Process.* 3rd edition. London: Routledge.

Light, R. (2008). Complex learning theory: Its epistemology and its assumptions about learning – implications for physical education. *Journal of Teaching in Physical Education, 27,* 21–37.

Light, R. L., & Evans, J. R. (2010). The impact of Game Sense pedagogy on Australian rugby coaches' practice: A question of pedagogy. *Physical Education and Sport Pedagogy, 15*(2), 103–115.

Lyle, J. (1999). Coaching philosophy and coaching behaviour. In N. Cross & J. Lyle (Eds) *The Coaching Process.* Oxford: Butterworth-Heinemann, 25–46.

Lyle, J. (2002). *Sports Coaching Concepts: A Framework for Coaches' Behaviour.* London: Routledge.

Macallister, S. G., Blinde, E. M., & Weiss, W. M. (2000). Teaching values and implementing philosophies: Dilemmas of the youth sport coach. *Physical Educator, 57,* 33–45.

Morgan, J. M. (2006). Philosophy and physical education. In D. Kirk, D. Macdonald, & M. O'Sullivan (Eds), *The Handbook in Physical Education.* London: Sage, 97–108.

Nadler, S. M. (1989). *Arnauld and the Cartesian Philosophy of Ideas.* Princeton, NJ: Princeton University Press.

Nash, C. S., Sproule, J., & Horton, P. (2008). Sport coaches' perceived role frames and philosophies. *International Journal of Sports Science & Coaching, 3,* 539–554.

Nelson, L. J., & Cushion, C. J. (2006). Reflection in coach education: The case of the national governing body coaching certificate. *Sport Psychologist, 20,* 174–183.

Robbins, J. E., Houston, E., & Dummer, G. M. (2010). Philosophies and expectations of wheelchair and stand-up collegiate basketball coaches. *Journal of Sport Behavior, 33,* 42–62.

Roberts, S. J. (2011). Teaching games for understanding: The difficulties and challenges experienced by participation cricket coaches. *Physical Education and Sport Pedagogy, 16*(1), 33–48.

Rokeach, M. (1973). *The Nature of Human Values.* New York: The Free Press.

Schempp, P. G., McCullick, B. A., Busch, C. A., Webster, C., & Mason, I. S. (2006). The self-monitoring of expert sport instructors. *International Journal of Sports Science and Coaching, 1*(1), 25–35.

Tennant, M. (1999). Lifelong learning as a technology of self. In K. Illeris (Ed.) *Contemporary Theories of Learning.* London: Routledge, 147–158.

Thompson, C., & Zeuli, J. (1999). The frame and the tapestry: Standards-based reform and professional development. In L. Darling-Hammond & G. Sykes (Eds) *Teaching as the Learning Profession: Handbook of Policy and Practice.* San Francisco, CA: Jossey-Bass, 341–375.

Torres, C. A. (1999). Critical theory and political sociology of education: Arguments. In T. Popkewitz & L. Fendler (Eds), *Critical Theories in Education: Changing Terrains of Knowledge and Politics.* New York: Routledge, 87–116.

Tsangaridou, N., & O'Sullivan, M. (2003). Physical education teachers' theories of action and theories-in-use. *Journal of Teaching in Physical Education, 22,* 132–153.

Vealey, R. (2005). *Coaching for the Inner Edge.* Morgantown, WV: Fitness Information Technology.

Voight, M., & Carroll, P. (2006). Applying sport psychology philosophies, principles, and practices onto the gridiron: An interview with USC football coach Pete Carroll. *International Journal of Sports Science & Coaching, 1,* 321–331.

CHAPTER 12

PEDAGOGY IN PRACTICE

CHAPTER OUTLINE

- Introduction
- What is pedagogy?
- Learning theories
- Learning environments
- Coaching style or strategy?
- Miscellaneous
- Case study
- Summary
- Projects

INTRODUCTION

There were elements of pedagogical practice throughout the 2002 edition of this book, but we felt that it was appropriate to provide a more specific and in-depth focus on pedagogy. There is a good deal of supporting literature (Jones 2006a; Cassidy *et al.* 2009; Lyle & Cushion 2010; Armour 2011) with excellent prescriptions for practice, but we stress that our approach is not simply to review the literature but to consider how coaching pedagogy impacts on the development of the conceptual framework. We have also drawn on our experience as coaches and coach developers, while attempting to situate pedagogical practice within the coaching process. The chapter is given its character by (1) focusing on the implications for the coach's practice behaviour; and (2) providing a case study on creating a performance sport learning environment.

Inevitably, we will deal with definitions and scope, but it is important to emphasise that one of the benefits of studying coaching pedagogy is that it refers directly to the practice of coaching, with implications for expertise and education. Coaching pedagogy has been adopted in the literature as a 'movement'. This emphasises its perceived importance, and reinforces its value as a lens through which to describe and understand sport coaching. It will become evident that it is not sufficient simply to view pedagogy as the 'teaching element' within sport coaching; learning, as both

250

concept and practice, is key. Even a superficial understanding of learning as a change in capacity highlights its role at the heart of coaching, whether that purpose is the holistic development of the individual or improvements in performance. It will also be obvious that there will be a pedagogical perspective to the coach's learning.

As an introduction it will be useful to summarise why a pedagogical lens has become a common mechanism for understanding sport coaching (Table 12.1).

Table 12.1 Rationale for adopting a pedagogical lens

Strong tradition of coaching as teaching	Although it is not a perspective that we endorse, traditionally there has been an analogy drawn between (physical education and sport) teaching and coaching in the UK. This may partly have been the result of the dual role practised by many teachers, but also reflected the simplistic notion that both roles involved teaching basic sport skills.
Participation coaching as the norm	Much the greater proportion of total coaching hours in the UK is devoted to the coaching of children and young people. Much of this is episodic in nature, and this emphasis on session delivery has reinforced the perception of coaching as teaching and teaching as pedagogy. There is also an instructor role that is conflated by some with the coaching role and this is also episodic in nature.
Reinforcement of complementary perspectives	It will be very clear that we emphasise the process nature of sport coaching and recognise the complex and multi-variable nature of sport performance. We also acknowledge a balance between performance goals and personal development goals. However, there are a number of perspectives common in the study of coaching that find the pedagogical lens to be an appropriate approach with which to highlight their concerns. Examples of this might be the centrality of skill development, the humanist developmental focus and those who emphasise the immediacy of delivery management over the application of planning.
Learning as a common purpose	Many, if not all, of the purposes and objectives in sport leadership roles can be reconceptualised as learning, and learning is central to pedagogy. This applies to the processes necessary to achieve the performance improvement aspect of coaching and to the betterment of more general characteristics of personal development.
Direct intervention as a key feature of expertise	No matter the perspective adopted, there is no doubt that coaches spend the greater proportion of their time in the direct intervention role. Although we often stress the wider and interdependent roles of the coach, it is understandable that a pedagogical emphasis on delivery should find fertile ground in the study of the coach's expertise.
Pedagogy as a convenient tool	As we have demonstrated, there are many different perspectives or lenses that can assist in describing and understanding coaching. Perhaps key to all is the way that the athlete, coach, context and purpose come together. Pedagogy is an excellent tool for demonstrating this interdependence.

The relationship between coaching and teaching is not unproblematic. Various authors (Bergmann Drewe 2000; Jones 2006b; Cassidy 2010) go to some lengths to stress the advantages of treating sport coaching as analogous to teaching and as an 'educational endeavour' in which these arguments reflect the self-evident case that sport coaching involves the teaching of skills. However, there is also an explicit and implicit criticism that 'coaching' is teacher-led, creates a dependency culture and disregards wider educational values. We (citing the earlier edition of this book) are criticised for an unnecessary distinction between teaching and coaching. The tone of the argument adopts the moral high ground, assuming that treating coaching as teaching will lead to the incorporation of all the positive aspects of teaching. We support the sentiments involved in the argument but we find it unnecessary (and inaccurate) to portray all (performance?) coaching as devoid of educational value or good practice. The analysis would benefit from a clearer distinction between role and process, and greater recognition of domain characteristics. Pedagogy is an extremely valuable lens for understanding sport coaching and the positive lessons that might be adopted using this stance should enhance coaching practice.

WHAT IS PEDAGOGY?

There is a common perception that pedagogy is simply another, perhaps more academic, word for teaching. Its derivation is rooted in the guidance of young people (andragogy applies to adults but is rarely used). Although we need not dwell too long on it, there is a need to define and examine the scope of pedagogy for coaching. Kirk (2010) uses the term to refer to what he terms the interdependence and irreducibility of subject matter, learning, instruction and context. Consideration of these factors in a cultural and social setting leads to the socio-pedagogy of coaching. You might note that the juxtaposition of athlete, coach, context and content is a common feature of recent conceptualisations of coaching (cf. Muir *et al.* 2011). In Table 12.2 we expand a little on these elements. Note that the emphasis is on pedagogy as a process rather than the actors involved. The principals – the athlete and the coach – are identified in the process. Kirk points to the evident interdependence of these elements, and implies that it is difficult to treat them individually for the purpose of analysis.

We have already noted that these elements are interdependent. Kirk (2010) highlights these inter-relationships and the potential impact that changes in one might have on the others. How might a change in delivery style influence the learning that takes place? Which environments are most likely to facilitate learning, and for which athletes? What would be the implications of different pedagogical settings (e.g. squad size, a team of coaches) on learning?

As a lens through which to understand coaching, pedagogy is a valuable tool. Proposing that pedagogy goes beyond teaching/coaching delivery and is characterised by an aggregation of the athlete's needs and wants, the coach's expertise and goals, the activity and tasks intended to bring about learning, and the context or environment within which it takes place is an unremarkable contention. Pedagogy is a socially and organisationally bounded learning process that in sport coaching finds

Table 12.2 Constituent elements of pedagogy

Subject matter	Refers to the body of knowledge or skill (perhaps expressed as performance-related content) that is both the medium for learning and the intended outcome. The subject matter will be specific (the activity in the pedagogic episode) and more general. The subject matter will be closely related to the purpose and goals established, and in a narrower sense may be interpreted as the 'task'.
Learning	This refers to both the purpose of the pedagogic episode (goals) and the process of bringing about a change in capacity (knowledge, skills, behaviour, attitudes). The athlete is actively engaged in learning – cognitively, physically and emotionally. Learning is active and involves immersion in practice, repetition, rehearsal, enquiry, problem solving and so on.
Instruction	This is not a helpful term, but you will recall that we have already discussed the distinctions between instructors and coaches. Most writers are at pains to stress that pedagogy should not be thought to be synonymous with teaching when interpreted as a one-way didactic process. Nevertheless, there is a process, and usually a person, that involves management, intervention or delivery of the learning experience, and/or provides guidance and structure to that process.
Context	Context, like goals, has a local or immediate set of factors and a more general set of factors with precedents, history and plans. It is difficult to summate the potential contextual factors that could impinge on a pedagogic episode; these ranging from resources, organisational goals and environmental factors to the expertise, expressed needs and wants and idiosyncrasies of the actors involved. Perhaps key is the quality of the learning environment created.

 QUESTION BOX

Consider your own coaching practice. Devise two examples of how the relationships between the four elements of pedagogy influence your 'direct intervention' behaviour.

expression in the behaviour of the principal actors, in play, practice and performance, in training and preparation, in the transmission of values, in the creation and management of the learning environment and in the myriad interpersonal interactions that bring this to life.

LEARNING THEORIES

Learning is at the centre of pedagogy and can be said to be the unifying goal of our coaching activity. We defined learning as a process of bringing about a change in

KEY CONCEPT

knowledge, skills, behaviour or attitudes). As with most constructs, the meaning attached to learning depends on the disciplinary lens adopted. Our purpose here is not to elaborate on learning theories, but merely to reinforce learning's important role in coaching pedagogy. We stress again, no one theory is correct. Your preference for any particular explanation of learning will depend on (1) your learning goals, (2) how you view the role of the learner and (3) your beliefs about social reality and the construction of knowledge. In other words, there will be an alignment between the 'type' of learning you wish to facilitate, how this is best explained and your particular perspective on 'how' change is brought about. The way you explain and justify your practice, and some of the key words, may be more evident from Table 12.3.

It would be valuable at this point to acknowledge the very useful notion of 'practice theories' (Cassidy 2010), or what we have called *coaching theories*. These are different to the more general theories of learning or practice, being developed by individual coaches over time and according to their particular beliefs about 'what works'. These practice theories may remain implicit because they are rarely articulated. Over time, coaches will have developed ideas about what is the best way to approach issues, which drills and exercises work best, how much to intervene, which performance component to emphasise, which training loadings to use, how

Table 12.3 Learning theories

Behaviourism	Individuals learn observable behaviour change by building a repertoire of stimulus–response linkages; there is a very strong reliance on positive and negative reinforcers; coaches pay particular attention to specific feedback and praise; the coach controls the transmission of knowledge by controlling the environment; the emphasis is on drills, repetition, learning by doing and internal and external feedback; it can be criticised for viewing the learner as 'passive'.
Cognitivism	Learning activity that is centred on the development of reasoning and decision making; the individual is viewed as an information-processing system; cognitive structures are developed via better knowledge structures, more efficient internal/mental processes, and effective access to memory structures; there is a move from the simple to the complex in tasks; coaches control the flow of information; development of declarative and propositional knowledge is crucial; management of the environment facilitates experiential decision making.
Constructivism	A reaction against the assumed passivity of behaviourism; there is an emphasis on how individuals construct their own 'meaning' in knowing and understanding; learning is greatly assisted by working with a knowledgeable 'expert'; coaching moments are constructed anew between coach and athlete; coaching activity involves a range of experiences, with an element of discovery encouraged; questioning to encourage athletes to address 'how' and 'why' for themselves is important.
Social theory	Centred on reinforcement of learning through observation and modelling; role models are important; self-regulation, self-setting of goals is important; coaches manage the social interaction; mentoring is an effective means of mediating the athlete's learning; coaches' learning can be thought of as an apprenticeship; establishing a facilitating community of practice provides a valuable learning environment.

Note
See Morgan (2008), Bush *et al.* (2012) and Cushion (2011) for useful summaries.

to use questions and, of course, how the sport/game should be played. The practice theory will be a combination of 'accepted wisdom' within the sport, interaction with other coaches and the coach's tried and tested interpretations through experience. There is an overlap here with what is often termed 'coaching philosophy' (see Chapter 11).

 QUESTION BOX

Are you able to articulate your 'practice theories'? Choose two or three features of your coaching (e.g. how to develop a skill, tactical decision making, planning phases). Discuss these with a colleague. Compare to each other and to recommendations in coach education and technical publications.

As you will have noted many times, the application of theories is not an either/or business. Your practice is likely to be an aggregation of interventions that owe something to each of these four major theory groups. You may combine repetition within drills with decision making, but attempt to emphasise athlete understanding and self-determination – all with a supportive interaction with others. The important objective is to create a learning environment and deploy coaching strategies that will enable the desired learning to take place. It would be helpful, therefore, if you (1) considered your 'practice theories' in the light of the major theories above; (2) became aware of any personal biases or predilections in the way you choose to structure your interventions; and (3) think of your own learning as an exemplar.

Learning principles

Improvement in performance is not accidental. What, therefore, are the conditions under which learning is likely to take place? There are a number of sets of principles that provide us with guidance on how to evaluate the conditions under which learning is more likely to be facilitated. A valuable repository of learning principles can be found in adult education. Rowntree (2000) identifies the characteristics of adults that impact on their learning. These learners are:

- rich in experience;
- goal oriented;
- driven by personal agendas;
- aware of the need for perspective (work/leisure balance); and
- interested in a 'return' for time and money invested.

Knowles (1990 p. 57) makes the assumptions about the self-directed learner shown in Table 12.4. This takes adult characteristics and applies them to the extent to which adults can take responsibility for their learning. You may rightly be saying 'but the great majority of the coached population are children and young people'. This is true (North 2009), and so you should compare these characteristics with the capabilities of those less mature young people and consider the impact on their learning.

Table 12.4 The self-directed learner

The need to know	Adult learners need to know why they need to learn something before undertaking to learn it.
Learner self-concept	Adults need to be responsible for their own decisions and to be treated as capable of self-direction.
Role of learners' experience	Adult learners have a variety of experiences of life that represent the richest resource for learning. These experiences, however, are imbued with bias and presupposition.
Readiness to learn	Adults are ready to learn those things they need to know in order to cope effectively with life situations.
Orientation to learning	Adults are motivated to learn to the extent that they perceive that it will help them perform tasks they confront in their life situations.

Pedagogy in practice

A practical set of principles can be gleaned from Race's (2005) conditions for effective learning. These are prescriptions that have been aggregated from asking adult learners about their experiences during professional education workshops. Learning is more likely to take place when individuals:

- *want to learn* (there is a degree of commitment to the learning process);
- *take ownership of the need to learn* (they realise that the learning is relevant to their needs);
- *learn by doing*;
- *learn through feedback*;
- *make sense of what has been learned* (they internalise the learning and relate it to what is already known);
- *verbalise orally* (perhaps not relevant to all learning, but this brings a useful level of consciousness to the process); and
- *evaluate their learning* (make judgements based on 'testing out' their learning).

If we think of these principles as precursors for 'learning readiness', they are extremely valuable as evaluation guidelines that can be applied to coaching interventions, and, particularly, as 'troubleshooting' questions when learning does not seem to be taking place.

 QUESTION BOX

1. The principles and characteristics are those of adult learners. Do you consider that they apply to learners of all ages and in all sporting domains?
2. Reflect on your own practice, either as a coach or athlete. Can you think of situations in which it became obvious that your learning was stifled by lack of attention to one or more of these principles?

LEARNING ENVIRONMENTS

One of the responsibilities of the coach is to provide a supportive learning environment. This might be described as one in which appropriate learning is likely to take place. As we have already noted, this could be conceptualised as a combination of physical features and resources, coach behaviour and a set of less easily defined characteristics of the environment that encourage or support learning. It does seem likely that distinctive coaching domains will adhere to the same principles, but that these will be operationalised differently to suit the specific needs of the domain population. The balance of priorities may differ across populations.

Putting together the principles that we have already identified with some of the implications for coach behaviour from learning theories, we can identify a framework of key features of the learning environment. Therefore, we argue that the desirable features of the environment are:

☆ KEY CONCEPT

A supportive learning environment might be described as one in which appropriate learning is likely to take place.

- stimulation;
- attractiveness;
- feedback loops;
- interactivity;
- progression; and
- reflection.

Most of these are self-explanatory. Feedback loops refer to the importance of feedback but implies that a degree of 're-visiting' is incorporated; in other words, repetition and variation in both activity and feedback. Interactivity refers to both an engagement in activity (not normally an issue in sport) and interaction with peers and coaches. Therefore, interventions should be (in the context of young people) relevant, attractive, meaningful, active, progressive and rich, with appropriate feedback. There will also be a link back to the coaching process boundaries that we established earlier. Variation in frequency, duration, intensity and stability of athlete groupings will clearly impact on the levels of progression, variety, constraints and so on that are experienced by the athlete. We counsel on two issues: first, it may be relatively easy to make individual sessions attractive and enjoyable, but progression and repetition under varying conditions are also needed; second, it is important to select appropriate activity. For example, children will enjoy learning through games, but the contextual understanding and inherent variation should be balanced by rehearsal and repetition, with time for reflection.

Another useful way to conceptualise the appropriateness of the learning environment is to ask whether a supportive learning climate has been created. If we combine this with the previous set of principles, a set of evaluative questions can be generated (Table 12.5).

The examples given have focused on training interventions, but it is important to remember that competitions (events, races, games and so on) are also a learning opportunity. However, it is also the case that overemphasis on competition outcomes and unrealistic expectations can create an atmosphere that is not conducive to learning, with inappropriate behaviour by coaches and parents. We stress, therefore, that the questions above can also be applied to participation in competition. Appropriate expectations, examples, expertise and education should be evident throughout.

Although the focus here is not on skill acquisition, some comment might be helpful on the alignment between intervention activity, learning, and performance outcomes. The purpose is to illustrate the linkage between intentions and how the learning

Table 12.5 Evaluation of the learning environment

Is learning the main goal of the session?	The coach manages the environment towards a specific learning purpose; clear goals set; relevance established; competition outcomes put into context
Is progress evident?	There are opportunities to test out progress made; targets established; modelling of desired behaviour
Is each athlete catered for?	There is an element of differentiation in activities and expectations; some specialisation depending on age and stage
Is 'failure' tolerated?	There is recognition that individuals learn from mistakes; effort is rewarded; the distinction between symptoms and causes of errors is acknowledged
Is there a supportive environment?	Coaches provide attention, communication, resources and feedback; goals are appropriate to age, stage and ability
Are 'steps' identified?	Manageable change is expected; skills are broken down into appropriate stages; key features are identified; challenge in the environment is gradual
Are role models/learning mentors provided?	Modelling is appropriate to age, stage and ability; the coach may have additional support to establish context and meaning; longer-term goals and requirements are discussed where appropriate
Is competition adapted to needs?	There is an appropriate level of challenge within interventions; adapted competition is used as a learning platform
Is there constructive alignment within the intervention?	There is an alignment between goals, activity, feedback and the coach's behaviour

environment is structured. Figure 12.1 demonstrates how the particulars of skill development must necessarily lead to a specific configuration of intervention activities to bring about the desired learning.

The lesson here is for you to consider how the learning environment would need to be structured to bring about these ends. There would be a need for specific combinations of whole–part–whole exercises (and variations on this), game-like activities, rehearsal and simulated competition and other forms of deliberate practice. Perhaps more important is that momentum and progression are maintained throughout.

The question was raised earlier about the application of learning principles and the creation of appropriate learning environments across coaching domains. Although it was suggested that the principles would apply more generally, the examples given have largely been drawn from coaching interventions with children and young people. It seems reasonable to assume that there would be some particular characteristics of the high-performance environment that would be specific to that domain and that would impact on learning. We would not claim that the list given (Table 12.6) of high-performance sport characteristics is exhaustive, but it will suffice to invite you to reflect on how learning environments might differ. This list was

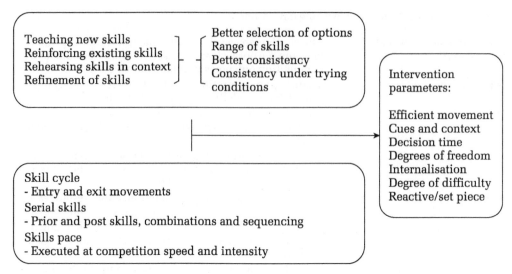

Figure 12.1 The link between skill development and intervention parameters.

compiled from the responses of high-performance rugby coaches during a workshop on coaching expertise.

We decided to bring this section on learning environments to a close with a set of practical recommendations for the delivery of coaching interventions. These arose from a coaching practice workshop in which coaches were asked to identify the practical lessons they had learned from the workshops, and that they could 'take away' and incorporate into their practice. The following list is derived from their responses:

- decide on (and communicate) the criteria for improvement (consistency, efficiency, range, difficulty, appropriateness);
- put interventions into appropriate skill cycles and sequences;
- technical knowledge required (analytics, cues, efficiency, personalisation, principles);
- structuring the practice is important (structure, progression, momentum, feedback);
- need to give athletes time for reinforcement and internalisation (more observation, less 'instruction');
- maintain progression, and accept incremental improvement;
- try to create 'tie in' to other learning;
- feedback is always the most important factor; reinforce good 'calls' and adherence to principles;
- all open skills need to have each skill parameter 'stretched' (varied routines);
- focus on the use of the skills (the 'why' element);
- initially, modify drills and exercises to exaggerate the principle (or cue), then reduce;

Pedagogy in practice

Table 12.6 Characteristics of high-performance sport

Characteristic	Implications
Fine margins in performance	Sports science, analysis, competition management
Accountability	Results oriented, evaluation/appraisal, multiple stakeholders
Technical dependence	Advanced knowledge and awareness, immersion in new developments
Intensity of process	Pedagogy, leadership, detailed loadings, longer-term planning, time for reinforcement and reflection
Use of support teams	Range of knowledge, leadership/influence
Performance management	Tournaments, schedule planning, specific preparation
Specialist roles of coaches	Specialist expertise, not full role
Sophistication	Detail, science, data-driven, innovation, knowledge structures
More interaction with other personnel	Leadership a priority for coaches
Contested	Public, contested goals, element of privacy
More use of data, analyses	CPD, science approach, target-driven
Highly structured and formalised environment	Hierarchical, resource-dependent
Aspirational goals	Contingency, management of outcome goals
Competition management emphasis	Game rehearsal, coach match management, decision making, importance of strategy and tactics
Considerable variation in roles	Sport-specific, head coach, expert performers
Smaller numbers	Greater individual attention, greater individualisation
Greater variety of activity	Modelling, repetition, rehearsal, conditioning, relaxation/recuperation

- use questioning to aid understanding (and check responses);
- keep drills and exercises to 'recognisable chunks' to aid repetition;
- implement a reflection exercise for individual decision making;
- create the learning experience for the athlete, don't just pass information;
- try to reduce coach-based feedback; increase self-assessment opportunities;
- create relevant, interesting, stimulating activity at all ages and stages.

COACHING STYLE OR STRATEGY?

Coaching style is a common term in the coaching literature (Nash 2015), but it is clear that the construct is a problematic one. Sproule (2015) and Høigaard *et al.* (2008) reduce the discussion to one of generic leadership styles; Morgan (2008) and Bush *et al.* (2012) reduce it to 'teaching styles'; and Cassidy *et al.* (2009) prefer to use the term 'method'. We do not find the latter an appropriate use of the word, believing that there is already a more common use of the term to denote particular (and contested) configurations of performance development strategies, having more to do with component training emphases than coaching behaviour. We remain unconvinced that the coaching styles construct has received sufficient conceptual attention. Nevertheless, the 2002 edition of this book gave considerable attention to coaching styles.

Our thinking has now moved on and we believe that coaching styles is a construct or descriptor that is problematic; we argue that this is not a useful way to describe coaching behaviour and that a more appropriate term would be 'coaching strategy'. In short, we are not convinced by the assumed flexibility of individual coaches to adopt different 'styles', by the quality of the research to support the, largely leadership, studies, or by the ideological prescriptions to adopt a particular approach. Consider, for example, the statement by Sproule (2015, p. 58) that "a coaching style is the way in which the coach delivers his or her coaching sessions, and this will vary depending on the situational context, the needs of the performers, the emotional intelligence of the coach and so forth". This appears to suggest that coaches have the capacity to be flexible or that coaches are deployed according to their 'style'. We believe that there is a perfectly adequate conceptual terminology available (e.g. delivery, intervention, role, practice, behaviour).

The interpersonal dimension

We begin with this because the interpersonal dimension can be ignored and we will suggest that it forms an important component of the coaching strategy. There is no doubt that sport coaches are conscious of the interpersonal dimension of the coaching process and that this interpersonal behaviour has the potential for a range of positive and negative effects on the performer. The length of time that coaches spend in interaction with performers makes it difficult to believe that coaches could be unaware of the human dimension to coaching, from both performer and coach perspectives, and within the dynamics of personal characteristics, values, aspirations, motives and achievement. Nevertheless, the danger of focusing on performance and performance outcomes, and the potential for emphasising organisational rewards and goals above individual interests, have highlighted the human and interpersonal aspects of coaching as areas of concern.

Performance can be thought of as consisting of stable and unstable elements. Stable elements are the developed and learned abilities associated with physical and technical capacities. However, performance, in training and competition, is also influenced by emotion, perception of effort, motivation/activation, identity, ownership and other social-psychological factors that constitute a less stable element. Managing these factors is part of reducing the unpredictability of performance, and they are influenced by the nature of the interpersonal behaviour between athlete and coach. It is not possible to adopt a completely value-free approach to any analysis of sport coaching. The value position adopted in this analysis is that:

- reducing sport performance to a mechanistic concept is inappropriate. It is simply wrong not to emphasise the interpersonal dimension in the coaching process

262

- added value is obtained from attending to interpersonal relationships in the coaching process.
- coaching practice may be accompanied by a set of goals, purposes and values that emphasise competition, achievement and external outcomes. However, these should not be achieved at the expense of the interests of the individual performer.

Before moving on to a consideration of 'coaching styles', Table 12.7 elaborates on a number of brief statements that set out the relationship of interpersonal exchanges to the conceptual framework.

Table 12.7 The relationship between the conceptual framework and the interpersonal dimension

Framework issues	The interpersonal dimension
Pervasiveness	The coaching process model deals with stages and sub-processes. It is assumed that the process is goal-directed and that attention to goals pervades the process. Similarly, the interpersonal relationship between performer(s) and coach is pervasive throughout the process; not only in direct intervention but also in recruitment, goal-setting, planning, etc. The interpersonal relationship can be thought of as the 'oil' that makes the process work.
Role	The role of the coach finds expression in interpersonal relationships. The extent of the athlete's engagement in a number of directional and decision-making functions is a question of role and style, and interpersonal behaviour reflects this.
Boundaries	Empathy (two-way) between coach and performers is often cited as a feature of performance coaching. However, the nature and strength of the interpersonal relationship can be based on a number of factors – personal liking, respect for knowledge and experience and organisational structure.
Individualisation	The individuality that the athlete and coach bring to a coaching context will shape the process and be visible in the interpersonal exchanges and other behaviours. This is not surprising and reflects personality, education, experience, values and the context within which they operate. However, 1. Interpersonal relationships are a means to an end in the performance domain in so far as they can be shown to impact on performance and preparation for performance. 2. Interpersonal relationships are also an end in themselves in so far as they represent an aspect of the personal growth and development that exemplify some motives and value frameworks in sport coaching.
Analysis and description	There is a tendency to portray interpersonal behaviours at either end of a continuum of 'person-centred' or 'performance-centred' modes. First, these extremes are unlikely to describe adequately the subtleties of interpersonal behaviour. Second, this perpetuates a dualism between performance and the person that is not reflected in the operationalisation of the coaching process.

(continued)

ASKHAM BRYAN
COLLEGE gy in practice
LEARNING RESOURCES

Table 12.7 The relationship between the conceptual framework and the interpersonal dimension *(continued)*

Framework issues	The interpersonal dimension
Recruitment	The emphasis is understandably often on direct intervention and other aspects of the coach's role and practice. However, it is important to acknowledge that interpersonal behaviour will impact on coach education, coach recruitment and selection and professional development.
Social context	Values have an element of context-specificity and the social and organisational context within which the coaching takes place will partly explain coaching practice. There is no attempt to separate individual and social context, merely to accord them sufficient depth of treatment.
Participation/ performance	It is tempting to distinguish between these two coaching domains on the basis of interpersonal behaviour – perhaps suggesting that there will be a qualitatively different person-orientation within participation coaching. This reflects differences in goal orientation and individual motives for coaching (Lyle *et al.* 1997). However, our own experience and many anecdotal accounts confirm that experienced and expert coaches can have a very athlete-centred approach to the role, and the distinctions, if any, are likely to be quite complex.

Coaching styles/strategies

We begin with the assertion that what has been termed 'coaching style' is either a useful mechanism for describing and analysing practice or a superficial way of caricaturing the most obvious elements of the coach's behaviour patterns. There is some truth in each of these positions. Variation in coaches' approaches to coaching is not simply about instructional behaviour, although the use of behavioural observation instruments to investigate leadership behaviour has focused attention on direct intervention. As an analytical tool, any relatively stable profile of behaviour would have the potential to offer an understanding of interpersonal relationships, social exchange, decision-making behaviour, communication, goal management and so on. For these reasons, 'coaching styles' should be part of the conceptual framework and certainly not treated in a trivial or superficial manner. First, we examine briefly the more common ways of categorising coaching styles.

Leadership studies

The debate about 'coaching styles' has often been polarised into a comparison between extreme, but simplified, conceptualisations of leadership styles. The contrast is generally between the more authoritarian/autocratic and the democratic/person-oriented styles (Figure 12.2). Clearly, these extreme positions have been exaggerated for effect. Given our conceptualisation of coaching as a continuous accommodation to a dynamic environment, it is difficult to imagine that stereotypical

Pedagogy in practice

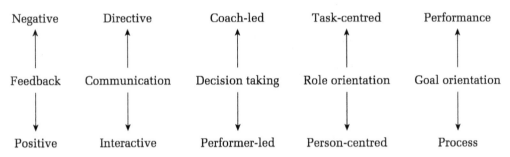

Keywords: performance-orientated; authoritarian; autocratic; directing; dictatorial

Coaching practice is characterised by:
- The primacy of the coach in decision taking
- A dominating, directive approach to IP-behaviour
- The transmission of knowledge, teaching and learning assumed to be one-way
- Coach determined rules, rewards, standards and application
- Rigidity and lack of personal empathy

Autocratic coaching practice

Negative	Directive	Coach-led	Task-centred	Performance
Feedback	Communication	Decision taking	Role orientation	Goal orientation
Positive	Interactive	Performer-led	Person-centred	Process

Democratic coaching practice

Coaching practice is characterised by:
- A participative decision-making style
- An interactive communication process
- Human values incorporated into goals and evaluation
- The active involvement of the athlete in the teaching – learning process
- Flexibility, empathy and support in personal relationships

Keywords: person-centred; humanistic; sharing; democratic; caring; interactive

Figure 12.2 The distinctions between autocratic and democratic coaching practice.

descriptions such as these are sufficiently refined as to capture the subtlety of coaching practice.

Leadership style has been a significant part of the coaching literature (Gilbert & Rangeon 2011). Much of this research has been carried out in North America and has given the area some academic credibility. However, the insight into and impact on sport coaching practice and coach development has been limited. The seminal work was carried out by Chelladurai (Chelladurai & Saleh 1980; Chelladurai 1984) and the resulting Leadership Scale for Sport has been used in countless investigations and studies, and continues to be used (Høigaard *et al.* 2008).

There is no doubt that some key variables have been identified and general preferences established for coaches and athletes in some domains. However, the positivistic survey paradigm, the lack of context specificity and opportunistic sampling has limited the richness of the data. The absence of control of contextual variables (performance level, experience, maturity, organisational role, reward environment, etc.) within and across studies has resulted in generally conflicting evidence. Few of the studies adopt a critical perspective in relation to coaching process boundaries and socially and organisationally determined power relationships. The factors that may prove insightful include reward dependency, coach outcome accountability, social cohesion and stability and the intensity of the coaching process. There is no doubt that identifying athlete satisfaction or preferred behaviours provides valuable information, but a simple catalogue of likes and dislikes does not delve deeply enough into important questions about coaching practice.

Figure 12.3 illustrates the factors involved in determining leadership practice. These factors are reconciled by individuals into a preferred leadership style. The styles can be categorised as humanistic, directive, instrumental, systematic or adaptable. Although providing a useful set of descriptors, the 'how' and 'why' of the reconciliation have yet to be fully determined.

Teaching styles

Another vehicle for explaining and categorising 'coaching styles' has been Mosston and Ashworth's (2008) spectrum of teaching styles (Bush *et al.* 2012; Morgan 2008). The spectrum categorises teacher intervention on a ten-point continuum from a more teacher-focused directive style to a more learner-focused self-determined style. Kirk *et al.* (1996) provides a more manageable interpretation of the spectrum:

Direct: (Command style)
Task: (Practice style)
Reciprocal: (Reciprocal style)
Guided discovery: (Guided discovery style)
Problem solving: (Convergent discovery style)

It will be obvious that the spectrum applies to intervention behaviour, although there is a useful distinction between practice and discovery styles. Once again, it is not clear that this conceptualisation has had a significant impact on coach education and development. In addition, there is maintenance of the assumption of teacher/coach flexibility: "to switch, adapt and blend a range of styles seamlessly to match a range of factors influencing the learning experience" (Bush *et al.* 2012, p. 71).

A humanistic approach to coaching

An extreme stance on 'democratic', athlete-centred coaching practice has been packaged as a 'humanistic approach to coaching' (Kidman 2005). This was described in some detail in the first edition of the book (Chapter 9) and is mentioned here

266

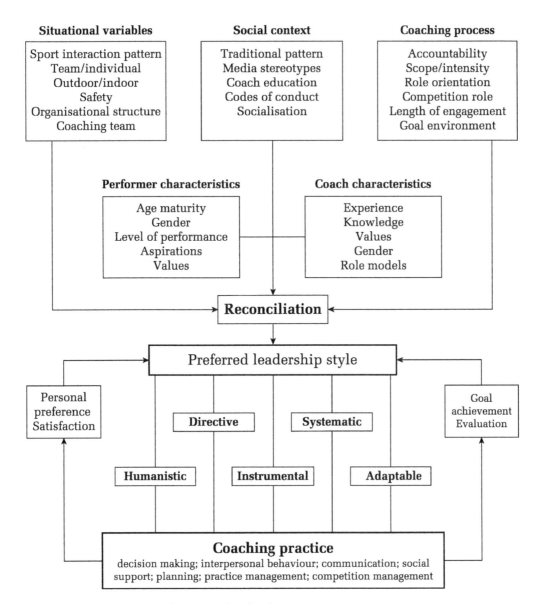

Figure 12.3 Factors influencing leadership practice.

because such practice is often conflated to a 'coaching style'. A more recent critique suggests that "the entirely laudable and eminently sensible enjoinders to greater individualisation, integrated interventions, the development of multiple talents, ownership by athletes, and non-authoritarian communication become mired in a discourse that resorts to generalisation and superficiality, is rarely ever related to coaching domains, and appears not to be susceptible to any level of verification"

(Lyle 2010, p. 449). The object here is not to describe in detail or to criticise such an approach; the first edition of the book was supportive although it raised many questions. It is recognised merely as a manifestation of the 'style' construct, and one that we now go on to review.

A review of issues

The potential adoption of coaching styles into the conceptual framework raises a number of issues:

- Is a 'style' a relatively stable group of behaviours or a more transient approach that can be assumed by coaches as the situation demands? Indeed, given the tacit nature of much of coaching practice, is coaching style a conscious aspect of practice? It cannot be assumed that, once identified as appropriate, coaching styles can be adopted readily by all coaches. However, we must assume that a degree of personal preference, idiosyncrasy and the diversity of prior experiences will mean that the coaching practice of all coaches will be recognisably different.
- The emphasis on social and personal values underpinning coaching behaviour raises the issue of coaching styles being defended on the basis of a prescriptive 'should' and 'ought' rather than a rational or empirical assessment of impact.
- Although much leadership style research has featured athlete satisfaction as the dependent variable, there has been little research into the effects on other athlete characteristics or performance. Coaches and athletes must surely have had successful performance outcomes with the full gamut of 'coaching styles'!
- An emphasis on direct intervention has focused attention onto observable behaviours. Given the scope of the coaching process, this may have considerably underestimated and under-reported behaviour in non-intervention contexts.
- Participation coaches may be more interested in immediate satisfaction and adherence, and the coach's communication and delivery style is likely to be much more influential in that context. More research is required across domains.

The unanswered questions are whether or not (1) the coach's characteristics, preferred behaviours and so on combine into a profile that is stable across circumstances; and (2) such a profile is a *predisposition*, behaviour *learned* from coach education, or *emergent* and based on experience – self-selection, gradual adoption or a means– ends computation. It seems unlikely that coach education will have a sufficiently strong impact. Many performance coaches rely heavily on their own experiences as performers, and are recruited directly from active participation. A 'social learning' process is a much more likely explanation for the way that coaches assimilate coaching style, often from other more expert and experienced coaches (Lave & Wenger 1991).

There may well be a link with the 'personal practice theories' discussed earlier. Another issue is that the vocabulary is not sufficiently role-specific and, although the reduction to parent categories (such as autocratic/democratic) may have some value for classifying coaches' practice, the descriptors might benefit from having multiple dimensions. The typology suggested previously – humanistic, directive, instrumental, systematic, adaptable – is merely a proposal, and more work is required in classifying behaviour, particularly in the performance sport context.

 QUESTION BOX

The capacity to assimilate 'style' options may be best achieved through social learning. This has implications for the selection of coaching mentors and for senior coaches more generally. Are 'coaching styles' adaptable, and have we considered this as a part of the formal training of coaches and mentors?

Style resolution

Our attempt to resolve the question of 'style' rests on an assertion that style is not a useful construct; its use is both ubiquitous and nebulous. Coaches' practice profiles are best conceived of as 'coaching strategies'. Our argument rests on the following points:

- Coaches will attempt a degree of instrumental congruence between a number of impacting factors (Figure 12.4).
- Coaching strategies will be both conscious and subconscious.

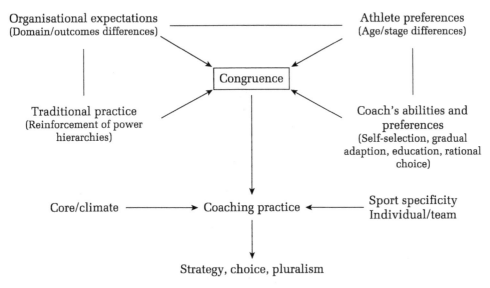

Figure 12.4 Attempted congruence in coaching strategies.

- Coaching strategies refer to not only intervention behaviour, but the full operationalisation of the coaching process.
- There is a degree of adaptability or flexibility, but it is likely that coaches will also have developed predispositions towards some practices.
- *Compensatory judgements* take place. Coaches and athletes will weigh up the advantages and disadvantages in the mix of strategies, preferences, goals and achievements. The absence of an overtly person-centred approach (if that was valued) might be compensated for by the coach's considerable experience and knowledge.
- Coaching strategies are subject to ideological influences and may be based on belief rather than evidential justification.
- We recognise the possibility of a distinction between core activity (impacting directly on performance), which may be more directive, and relationship climate, which may be less directive. (This explains much of the contradiction in leadership studies.)

There is a need for a new conceptual vocabulary: core/climate, instrumental congruence, compensation judgements, occupational socialisation, expertise-based coaching strategies and pluralistic delivery strategies. We, therefore, conceive of coaching strategies as not about 'style' but about expertise. They are context-dependent but the necessary situational strategic flexibility needs to be developed and may not always be done well or be ideologically satisfying for everyone. If we recognise some coaches as being more effective than others, we must also recognise that 'getting it right' is a demanding task. Even when reflected upon, coaches may perpetuate coaching practices that appear to maintain apparently taken-for-granted practices. The exhortations to select, adapt and align to contextual needs may yet be aspirational.

MISCELLANEOUS

There are a number of aspects of pedagogy that are more than adequately covered in the sport coaching literature; for example, communities of practice, reflection and mentoring (Cushion and Nelson 2013). Each of these is said to have an impact on the learning of both athletes and coaches. Our summary position is that:

- the arguments and anecdotal evidence are strong and that their use should have a positive impact on learning;
- there is no sound evidence, beyond prescription and satisfaction studies, to support their use;
- the absence of solid evidence is likely to be a result of difficulties in creating appropriate research designs rather than any lack of effectiveness (Cushion 2011);
- it might be argued that these features of pedagogy have been explored in coach learning rather than athlete learning;
- as with much of academic writing, we find that 'much is written but little is said'. However, their inclusion in athlete and coach learning has theoretical and implementation support and should therefore be encouraged.

270

Nevertheless, there are some comments that might provide some critical insight into these constructs. For these reasons, we will confine ourselves, at this point, to a few comments on each of these features of the learning environment. These are not designed to provide you with a complete background – these are readily available – but to enable you to read and interpret the literature with a critical eye.

Communities of practice

You should note the theory links between communities of practice and situated learning (Lave & Wenger 1991). This emphasises both learning as a social practice and the active role of the learner, and there are some useful sources that explore the implications for learning (Galipeau & Trudel 2006) and the theoretical background (Cushion & Denstone 2011). This is hardly surprising and we might expect imitation and facilitated learning to take place in close communities of common practice. Nevertheless, when reading the generally unquestioning accounts of the potential contribution of communities of practice, you might bear in mind:

1. It might be anticipated that there would be informal/incidental learning (see Mallett *et al.* 2009 for a review) within a community, but there could also be some non-formal learning, if it was purposefully structured (for example, within a coach education programme) and facilitated. For most athletes, learning is a social exercise but the difference in ages and stages, competitiveness and variations in ability might suggest that it would be performance-related factors (attitude to training, commitment and so on) rather than performance itself that would be most affected.
2. For coaches, learning within communities of practice will normally be combined with more formal processes. The most effective combination of learning modes has yet to be articulated.
3. The term 'legitimate peripheral participation' refers to the gradual adoption of tasks/roles within the community by taking part as a novice/beginner and learning from those around you (and becoming less peripheral). This is a useful way of conceptualising how athletes learn to become coaches before taking on the role. Consider whether or not there might be some 'downsides' to occupational socialisation in this way.
4. It is important to be critical of the 'boundaries' and nature of putative communities. Note the distinction between: (1) communities of practice (common sense of purpose, mutual engagement, shared resources); (2) networks of practice (looser, informal, accessed for specific purposes); and (3) specific mentoring or apprenticeship relationships (see Mallett 2010 for a critical review). Does a sports team constitute a community of practice? Note that there will very often be an 'organisational' layering to social engagement.
5. If a superficial definition is 'a group who share an interest in some activity and who learn to do it better through regular and purposeful interaction', is it possible for athletes to be a community of practice when coaches adopt a directive intervention role?

6. Communities of practice will be subject to differentiated power relationships, hierarchical roles, politics, jealousies and secrecies within relationships – and this cannot be considered unproblematic.
7. Mallett (2010) suggests that 'social networks' (informal knowledge networks) are more useful and more prevalent. These are looser in practice than communities of practice. He is keen to stress that many interactions in a professional context will be 'just a relationship' and not a sustained interaction that can be described as a learning context.

Reflective practice

Reflection or reflective practice is another ubiquitous feature of coaching pedagogy (Gilbert & Trudel 2006; Miles 2011). It is a generic term for internal cognitive processes that act as a bridge between experience and learning, and is a feature of coach education and professional education more widely. It is prevalent in the development processes of occupations in which practitioners rely on experiential decision making, and expertise is dependent on 'making sense' of an accumulation of previous events. Once again, there is a wealth of theoretical support and enormous amounts of practice; however, there is no strong evidence that unequivocally links reflective practice and the effectiveness of coaching practice or athlete performance. It would appear to be something that is 'good practice' by good practitioners (Cushion & Nelson 2013).

The intention of the many reflective practice prescriptions (see Martindale & Collins 2015 for an excellent example) is that information, feedback and experience are translated into personal insight and understanding. This is then fashioned into a retrievable form of expertise for future application. At face value this satisfies both the need to verbalise (even if internally) learning, and more common sense notions of simply 'thinking about what you have done'. Note, however, the advice that more instrumental and focused reflection is necessary to assimilate this into existing knowledge. Much is made in the literature of Schön's (1983) reflective practice metaphor. His reflection-in-action describes the likely cognitive processes involved in experiential decision making; whereas the reflection-on-action happens after the immediate 'direct action present'. This is an occasion for both deliberative and semi-deliberative cognitions, and is a useful way of conceptualising professional action in a serial, interdependent context. Retrospective reflection-on-action is a more apt descriptor for the use of reflective practice in education and development.

Figure 12.5 is a conceptual framework using constructs from the literature. We find that reflection is treated as a taken-for-granted process that will enhance learning and more effective practice. Despite the absence of direct evidence, we believe that this is likely to be the case. However, as with all aspects of the conceptual framework, we urge you to be critical in your interpretation of its value and application:

■   Reflective practices need to be as 'situated' as possible (real coaching events) and meaningful to you (catalysts for choosing particular actions are important).
■   'Making sense' is the key stage; it is very important that reflection is specific (see the 'reflective focus' in Figure 12.5).

272

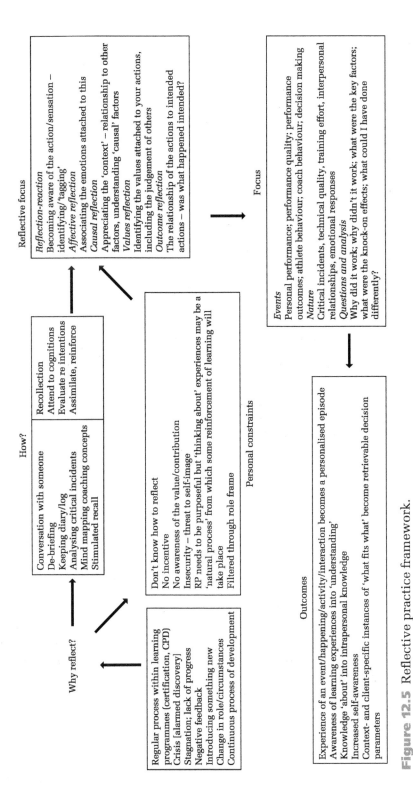

Reflective focus

Reflection-reaction
Becoming aware of the action/sensation – identifying/'tagging'
Affective reflection
Associating the emotions attached to this
Causal reflection
Appreciating the 'context' – relationship to other factors, understanding 'causal' factors
Values reflection
Identifying the values attached to your actions, including the judgement of others
Outcome reflection
The relationship of the actions to intended actions – was what happened intended?

How?

Conversation with someone	Recollection
De-briefing	Attend to cognitions
Keeping diary/log	Evaluate re intentions
Analysing critical incidents	Assimilate, reinforce
Mind mapping coaching concepts	
Stimulated recall	

Why reflect?

Regular process within learning programmes (certification, CPD)
Crisis [alarmed discovery]
Stagnation; lack of progress
Negative feedback
Introducing something new
Change in role/circumstances
Continuous process of development

Personal constraints

Don't know how to reflect
No incentive
No awareness of the value/contribution
Insecurity – threat to self-image
RP needs to be purposeful but 'thinking about' experiences may be a 'natural process' from which some reinforcement of learning will take place
Filtered through role frame

Focus

Events
Personal performance; performance quality; performance outcomes; athlete behaviour; coach behaviour; decision making
Nature
Critical incidents, technical quality, training effort, interpersonal relationships, emotional responses
Questions and analysis
Why did it work; why didn't it work; what were the key factors; what were the knock-on effects; what could I have done differently?

Outcomes

Experience of an event/happening/activity/interaction becomes a personalised episode
Awareness of learning experiences into 'understanding'
Knowledge 'about' into intrapersonal knowledge
Increased self-awareness
Context- and client-specific instances of 'what fits what' become retrievable decision parameters

Figure 12.5 Reflective practice framework.

- We speculate that a developed cognitive structure is necessary for instrumental reflection. Therefore, you need 'models' to provide a frame of reference. The implication is that reflective practice may be less useful for beginners.
- Be careful to structure reflection around a developmental programme, rather than being drawn (only) to critical incidents.
- Superficial reflection (mere description) is not effective as a means of learning – there needs to be a critical interpretation of meaningful actions.
- Reflective practice is a learned behaviour and is not without some potential for 'uncomfortable' insights. There are practical matters of support, collaborative approach, stimulation to recall, immediacy and follow-up that should be incorporated.

Mentoring

There is a substantial literature on mentoring in coaching education that will provide a background and bibliography (Cushion 2006; Jones *et al.* 2009; Bloom 2013; Nash & McQuade 2015). In particular, Nash and McQuade (2015) provide an excellent account of the concept itself and the variation in roles that it subsumes. There is a significant amount of both formal and informal mentoring in coach development, and we can assume that coaches play a variety of mentoring roles with their athletes. At this stage, we cannot do justice to the scale of the concept and offer just a few thoughts to stimulate your thinking.

The process is one in which a person of greater expertise or experience guides a less experienced or expert person in an occupational or professional context. This may involve acting as a learning facilitator, a role model, a guide or an expert in a master–apprentice relationship. A responsive mentor may be most suitable for experienced practitioners; a directive approach may suit the novice, but you should be aware of creating a dependency culture. The interactive style of mentoring emphasises openness between the parties, and the 'parity' within the relationship is valued by practitioners. The evidence of impact is scant, but those experiencing mentoring are generally positive about it.

There are a number of prescriptions for good practice that can be gleaned from the literature (see Jones *et al.* 2009; Nash & McQuade 2015).

- Recognise, develop and articulate knowledge about the learner's practice.
- Build on the knowledge and experience of the learner.
- It should be situated in meaningful practice, and a supportive (social) framework.
- Develop problem-solving strategies.
- Mentors should be trusted, respected, accessible and committed, and exercise a flexible approach.
- Recognise the unique personal, professional and contextual dynamic of each individual.
- Focus away from 'correct' and 'acceptable' responses to the development of a personal model of expertise and performance.

274

- Formalise the relationship and identify goals.
- This is a process that requires time and patience, and benefits from an element of challenge.

In addition to the above, we have listed some of the findings from a mentoring programme in which elite athletes and coaches mentored 'at risk' young people (this was a programme evaluation carried out by the author), using sport as a vehicle. These may provide a valuable set of evaluative tools:

- Willingness of participants to engage and readiness to change are crucial.
- Flexibility and contingency are important features (within a structured programme).
- Sustainable change in behaviour may need continued support.
- Training for mentors is vital, with clear objectives set.
- 'Supportive social scaffolding' around the relationship is important.
- A concentrated period of 'interaction' followed by a gradual 'release' process is more effective.

Once again, we urge you not to treat the concept as unproblematic. There are a number of implications for the operationalisation of the concept that may lessen or increase its effectiveness in facilitating learning. There is a need for extended duration, an active process, a meaningful relationship, common purpose, a compatible mentor and a willingness to exercise an 'objective' and challenging voice at appropriate times. In addition, there are limitations in much of the current provision (which we have learned from evaluating coach development programmes): lack of time to engage, lack of training, personal incompatibility, perceived lack of interest, problematic behaviours (e.g. being over-critical), absence of shared mental models and expectations and being expensive to provide – particularly in a volunteer context.

CASE STUDY

We thought that it would be interesting to end the chapter with a practical example of how an experienced and expert coach creates a performance sport learning environment, and to offer the key elements of his 'personal practice theory'. We have done this by providing a graphic (Figure 12.6) and an elaboration on some aspects of his ideas. We hope that there will be some 'nuggets' within this that will stimulate reflection on your own practice.

Thomas Dowens is head coach of a very successful volleyball club in Scotland, and head coach of the Scotland senior men's team. Previously, he was a coach with the Great Britain volleyball team in the preparations for the 2012 Olympic Games. Thomas was invited to give a presentation to postgraduate coaching students on 'building a learning environment', and what follows has been adapted from his presentation.

275

Key prerequisites	Complications
Coach's philosophy and knowledge infused throughout	Recognising symptoms, causes and flaws
Recognise the athlete's level of motivation	Dealing with emotion of winning and losing
Practice 'level' means more than quantifiable intensity	Monitoring activity levels from moderate to vigorous
Balance the process versus product issue	Acknowledging the priorities in learning
Consider the needs of the individual and the needs of the team	
The learning environment is dependent on the quality of the coach's intervention toolkit	

Consider your behaviour:	Key points in learning
Prioritise cue recognition	Set appropriate tasks (coach)
Recognise the importance of rhythm in performance	Patience – give time to learn (coach)
Analyse the product to identify the process	Communicate successfully at different levels (coach)
Analyse performance: basic movements include balance and coordination (balance 'goes' when tired, off form, stressed)	Understand the importance of being reflective (coach)
Base selection on personal qualities, thinking skills, physical skills, physical element	Have a robust set of personal qualities (athlete)
Modelling the game is vital	Acknowledge interim success (athlete)
Try not to intervene, give space	
Communicate at different levels	
If progression is poor, review what you are doing	

Figure 12.6 Building a learning environment.

What follows is an elaboration on some aspects of coach Dowens' personal practice theories:

1. If progress is slower than expected, have patience and work harder!
2. Your personal philosophy will include an attitude to risk. For example, what is your attitude to playing young players (risk) or relying on experienced players (safe)? Take a chance!
3. Rhythm is an overarching quality in performance and provides the context for the specific timing of skills. Recognise and reinforce it.
4. Smart athletes have better cue recognition and decision making.
5. It is important to assess 'mood'. Have three different warm ups depending on mood (if good – self warm up; if not good – cognitively demanding exercises to 'switch on'; occasionally warm up as a club to reinforce club ethos).

6. Evaluating practice levels involves feelings of intensity, levels of comedy/'banter', requirements for progressions, inclusion of physical training – not simply load factors.
7. The coach's role is to balance product versus process. If the process is right, the product will follow.
8. When analysing skill, technique is a specific action that rests on some other factors – balance and coordination. Use balance (management of foot and head position) as an indicator of good movement.
9. Moving to the 'next level' involves greater speed, greater power and smarter thinking.
10. Learning involves more than physical skills. Prioritise personal qualities (dealing with setbacks, showing confidence) and thinking skills (focusing attention, multi-processing, prioritising).
11. Learn to deal with winning, losing and making mistakes. It is important to recognise variation in performance as 'everyday'. Add value to mistakes by identifying what was done well.
12. Activity within the learning environment should be 'close' to the game. 'Modelling' is very important, and deliberate practice should reflect the conditions, timing and demands of game play.
13. Don't intervene if possible; speak to individuals and groups during exercises/drills. Learn to 'walk and talk'. Recognise 'leaders' and communicate through them.
14. If you've said it ten times and they're not 'getting it' – try the 11th!
15. Plan, communicate and care and be the best you can be. Try to influence players but acknowledge that you cannot take responsibility for the lives of adult performers. However, you need to understand them and recognise how their needs and wants impact on the learning environment that you provide.

⟳ SUMMARY

The chapter should have familiarised you with the following:

- The importance of pedagogy to sport coaching.
- A definitional framework for pedagogy.
- An overview of learning theories.
- The significance of coaches' personal practice theories.
- Race's (2005) learning principles.
- The key features of a supportive learning environment.
- An argument for conceptualising coaching styles as coaching strategies.
- An overview of communities of practice, reflective practice and mentoring.
- A case study of a performance sport learning environment.

PROJECTS

1. Interview two coaches. Discuss their 'personal practice theories' on a number of selected aspects of coaching intervention. Invite them to discuss how these ideas developed and compare this to evidence from the literature. Discuss any further changes to their practice as a result.
2. Apply Race's adult learning principles to your own practice and experience of coach education.
3. From the principles presented in the chapter, create an observation template and monitor the interventions of four coaches. Create a list of issues for discussion from any differences you have observed.
4. Create a case study of your own coaching practice.
5. Observe a coach working with at least three different groups/teams/squads. Identify any common and different features of practice and use them to discuss the stability of coaching strategies.

REFERENCES

Armour, K. (Ed.) (2011). *Sport Pedagogy: An Introduction for Teaching and Coaching.* London: Prentice Hall.

Bergmann Drewe, S. (2000). An examination of the relationship between coaching and teaching. *Quest, 52,* 79–88.

Bloom, G. A. (2013). Mentoring for sport coaches. In P. Potrac, W. Gilbert, & J. Denison (Eds) *Routledge Handbook of Sports Coaching.* London: Routledge, 476–485.

Bush, A., Brierley, J., Carr, S., Gledhill, A., Mackay, N., Manley, A., Morgan, H., Roberts, W., & Willsmer, N. (2012). *Foundations in Sports Coaching.* Harlow: Pearson Education.

Cassidy, T. (2010). Understanding athlete learning and coaching practice: Utilising 'practice theories' and 'theories of practice'. In J. Lyle & C. Cushion (Eds) *Sports Coaching: Professionalisation and Practice.* Edinburgh: Churchill Livingstone, 175–191.

Cassidy, T., Jones, R. L., & Potrac, P. (2009). *Understanding Sports Coaching: The Social, Cultural and Pedagogical Foundations of Coaching Practice.* 2nd edition. Abingdon: Routledge.

Chelladurai, P. (1984). Discrepancy between preferences and perceptions of leadership behavior and satisfaction of athletes in varying sports. *Journal of Sport Psychology, 2*(2), 14–29.

Chelladurai, P., & Saleh, S. D. (1980). Dimensions of leadership behavior in sports: Development of a leadership scale. *Journal of Sport Psychology, 2,* 34–45.

Cushion, C. J. (2006). Mentoring: Harnessing the power of experience. In R. L. Jones (Ed.) *The Sports Coach as Educator: Re-conceptualising Sports Coaching.* Abingdon: Routledge, 128–144.

Cushion, C. (2011). Coaches' learning and development. In I. Stafford (Ed.) *Coaching Children in Sport*. Abingdon: Routledge, 57–69.

Cushion, C. J. with Denstone, G. (2011). Etienne Wenger: Coaching and communities of practice. In R. L. Jones, P. Potrac, C. Cushion, & L. T. Ronglan (Eds) *The Sociology of Sports Coaching*. Abingdon: Routledge, 94–107.

Cushion, C. J., & Nelson, L. (2013). Coach education and learning: Developing the field. In P. Potrac, W. Gilbert, & J. Denison (Eds) *Routledge Handbook of Sports Coaching*. Abingdon: Routledge, 359–374.

Galipeau, J., & Trudel, P. (2006). Athlete learning in a community of practice: Is there a role for a coach? In R. L. Jones (Ed.) *The Sports Coach as Educator: Re-conceptualising Sports Coaching*. Abingdon: Routledge, 77–94.

Gilbert, W. D., & Rangeon, S. (2011). Current directions in coaching research. *Revista de Iberoamericana de Psicologia del Ejercicio y el Deporte*, 6(2), 217–236.

Gilbert, W. D., & Trudel, P. (2006). The coach as a reflective practitioner. In R. L. Jones (Ed.) *The Sports Coach as Educator: Re-conceptualising Sports Coaching*. Abingdon: Routledge, 113–127.

Høigaard, R., Jones, G., & Peters, D. (2008). Preferred coach leadership behaviour in elite soccer in relation to success and failure. In *International Journal of Sports Sciences & Coaching*, 3(2), 241–250.

Jones, R. L. (Ed.) (2006a). *The Sports Coach as Educator*. Abingdon: Routledge.

Jones, R. L. (2006b). How can educational concepts inform sports coaching. In R. L. Jones (Ed.) *The Sports Coach as Educator*. Abingdon: Routledge, 3–13.

Jones, R. L., Harris, R., & Miles, A. (2009). Mentoring in sports coaching: A review of the literature. *Physical Education and Sport Pedagogy*, 14(3), 267–284.

Kidman, L. (2005). *Athlete-Centred Coaching: Developing Inspired and Inspiring People*. Christchurch: Innovative Print Communications.

Kirk, D. (2010). Towards a socio-pedagogy of sports coaching. In J. Lyle & C. Cushion (Eds) *Sports Coaching: Professionalisation and Practice*. Edinburgh: Churchill Livingstone, 165–176.

Knowles, M. S. (1990). *The Adult Learner*. 4th edition. Houston: Gulf Publishing.

Lave, J., & Wenger, E. (1991). *Situated Learning: Legitimate Peripheral Participation*. Cambridge: Cambridge University Press.

Lyle, J. (2010). Holism in sports coaching: Beyond humanistic psychology – a commentary. *International Journal of Sports Sciences & Coaching*, 5(4), 449–452.

Lyle, J., & Cushion, C. (Eds) (2010). *Sports Coaching: Professionalisation and Practice*. Edinburgh: Churchill Livingstone.

Mallett, C. J. (2010). Becoming a high-performance coach: Pathways and communities. In J. Lyle & C. Cushion (Eds) *Sports Coaching: Professionalisation and Practice*. Edinburgh: Churchill Livingstone, 120–134.

Mallett, C. J., Trudel, P., Lyle, J., & Rynne, S. (2009). Formal vs informal coach education. *International Journal of Sports Science & Coaching*, 4(3), 325–334

Martindale, A., & Collins, D. (2015). Reflective practice. In C. Nash (Ed.) *Practical Sports Coaching*. Abingdon: London, 223–241.

Miles, A. (2011). The reflective coach. In I. Stafford (Ed.) *Coaching Children in Sport*. Abingdon: Routledge, 109–120.

Morgan, K. (2008). Pedagogy for coaches. In R. L. Jones, M. Hughes, & K. Kingston (Eds) *An Introduction to Sports Coaching*. Abingdon: Routledge, 3–17.

Mosston, M., & Ashworth, S. (2008). *Teaching Physical Education*. First online edition www.spectrumofteachingstyles.org/ebook.

Muir, B., Morgan, G., Abraham, A., & Morley, D. (2011). Developmentally appropriate approaches to coaching children. In I. Stafford (Ed.) *Coaching Children in Sport*. Abingdon: Routledge, 17–37.

Nash, C. (Ed.) (2015). *Practical Sports Coaching*. Abingdon: London.

Nash, C., & McQuade, S. (2015). Mentoring as a coach development tool. In C. Nash (Ed.) *Practical Sports Coaching*. Abingdon: London, 206–222.

North, J. (2009). *The Coaching Workforce 2009–2016*. Leeds: National Coaching Foundation.

Race, P. (2005). *Making Learning Happen: A Guide for Post-Compulsory Education*. London: Sage.

Rowntree, D. (2000). Who are your distance learners? http://iet.open.ac.uk/pp/D.G.F.Rowntree/distance_learners.htm.

Schön, D. A. (1983). *The Reflective Practitioner: How Professionals Think in Action*. New York: Basic Books.

Sproule, J. (2015). The importance of a coaching philosophy. In C. Nash (Ed.) *Practical Sports Coaching*. Abingdon: Routledge, 54–68.

CHAPTER 13

THE PROFESSIONALISATION OF SPORT COACHING

INTRODUCTION

The first edition of this text provided an evaluation of the potential for the professionalisation of sport coaching (Lyle 2002, p. 201). However, since that time critical appraisal of the potential for the professionalisation of sport coaching has been a recurring theme in academic writing in the United Kingdom (Lyle & Cushion 2010; Taylor & Garratt 2010a, 2013; Duffy *et al.* 2011), what Taylor and Garratt (2013) have called a "fractured and discontinuous call for the organisation and regulation of coaches" (p. 29). A substantial paper by Duffy *et al.* (2011) and a restatement of the principles therein by the International Council for Coaching Excellence (ICCE) (ICCE *et al.* 2013) appear to adopt what might be construed as a pragmatic but possibly optimistic interpretation of the process. In this chapter we offer a personal perspective on the issue – one that relies for an interpretation of the situation on our 40-year involvement as coach, coach educator, academic and policy maker; an interpretation that it is not intended to be negative, but a realistic evaluation of the potential for moving the debate forward. We have deliberately written the chapter to stimulate debate and discussion.

The basic premise is that the failure to address a number of conceptual issues, the need to understand the limited reach of coaching policy networks, and the omission of a more updated concept of professional behaviour help to explain the very limited scale of the professionalisation process over the past 40 years. We argue that the latent drive for external recognition should be couched in terms of ensuring that sport coaches operate in ways that are acknowledged to represent professional behaviour. There seems to be little doubt that sport coaching, at least in the UK, needs to move the professionalisation agenda towards professionalism rather than profession status. This, of course, will force us to consider what it means to act with professionalism.

 KEY CONCEPT

The failure to address a number of conceptual issues, the need to understand the limited reach of coaching policy networks and the omission of a more updated concept of professional behaviour help to explain the very limited scale of the professionalisation process over the past 40 years.

In relation to the modest progress towards professionalisation, it is necessary to consider whether or not there has been an implementation failure (lack of impetus, finance, collective authority, sufficiency of consensus) or some inherent limitations in the 'occupational space' that is sport coaching. We will argue that both are relevant. There is no evidence of a public clamour for a sport coaching profession. Governments can be impelled to act when confronted by disasters, scandals, ideology, evident benefits or public disquiet. Evidence of government intervention is made manifest in public scrutiny, training budgets, recruitment quotas, requirements to licence, performance targets in education and establishing (or at least endorsing) an at-arms-length agency with powers to sanction. It may seem surprising that the hype of the Olympic Games, the overwhelming proportion of coaches who work with young children and regular ethical misdemeanours by coaches have not raised public awareness. This may be the price of a 'hidden profession'. Nevertheless, it can clearly be argued that there is no practitioner demand. The policy network (see ICCE, sports coach UK, UK Sport) has professionalisation as an agenda item, but there is limited, if any, evidence that coaches themselves put this issue high on their agendas.

 QUESTION BOX

Consider your interaction with those around you who are coaches or involved in coaching in some way. Consider also parents and other 'stakeholders'. Do you perceive any latent demand for professionalisation?

282

BRIEF REVIEW AND CRITIQUE OF EXISTING WORK

Historical consideration of the issues has been more than adequately discussed by Taylor and Garratt (2013), and in their previous writings (2008, 2010a, 2010b). Most recently, Malcolm *et al.* (2014) have rehearsed a critical interpretation of the professionalisation process. This was accompanied by a commentary (Sheriden 2014) that provided a contemporary account of the professionalisation process in the US. We perhaps need to begin by acknowledging that much of the early discourse (Lyle 1986) and subsequent analyses (e.g. Duffy *et al.* 2011) have centred on what Malcolm *et al.* (2014) term the 'trait' approach: that is, identifying the system characteristics of traditional professions and comparing sport coaching to these. This is evident in Taylor and Garratt (2008) and Duffy *et al.* (2011), although there is something of a consensus that such an approach is unhelpful (Taylor & Garratt 2013; Malcolm *et al.* 2014), and there needs to be consideration of alternative approaches focused on the concept of professionalism (Evetts 2011a, 2011b, 2013), pragmatic responses to state managerialism (Taylor & Garratt 2013) or reconfiguring the occupational space. For example, Duffy *et al.* (2011) agreed that sport coaching demonstrates a weak profile when compared to traditional models of professions. However, the subsequent proposals (ICCE *et al.* 2013) to adopt a 'blended profession' approach appeared simply an attempt to mitigate the limiting factors. A policy principle of being 'inclusive' may bring a neatness of approach but changes none of the limiting factors.

In the first edition it was suggested that, despite some positive portents, the realisation of professionalisation was still some way off. More importantly, coaching expertise was identified as key to the professionalisation process – a matter that is clearly ongoing. In simple terms, 'how do we know that coaches are exhibiting professional behaviour if we can't identify what that behaviour should be'? Admittedly, some early work was intended to reflect a positive stance (Taylor & Garratt 2008). These authors identified a number of enablers to professionalisation (the development of the United Kingdom Coaching Certificate, the 2012 Olympics and the establishment of a professional body). However, their acknowledgement of several barriers (internal resistance, government priorities and limited employment/deployment opportunities) seemed to be a more convincing argument. Malcolm *et al.* (2014) also identify four drivers (greatly increased finance into sport, expansion of undergraduate provision, an element of payment for a greater number of coaches and recognition of coaching as a more generic process), but these are also unconvincing, failing as they do to explain how such factors might assist the professionalisation process. Nevertheless, the paper is valuable for being sceptical about the assumed value of this process. We tend to agree with Sheriden (2014) that acknowledging the practice of exercising power over knowledge, entry routes and deployment in order to build and maintain relative autonomy is an apt descriptor of some of the characteristics of professionalisation, but merely recognises the protection of boundaries that most occupations will attempt to establish. This attempt at legitimisation (knowledge, ideas and autonomy) may be evident to some extent in sport coaching, but an insufficiently distinct and diffuse understanding of expertise, role confusion, no evidence of coaches being held in high status, the huge proportion of unqualified coaches (North 2009) and a failure to agree on boundary markers have significantly limited its impact. Consider surveys using self-designation by coaches (Townend & North 2007), or a comment from a Sport England consultation paper: "if a participant feels that they are being coached, then we should consider that session leader as part of the coaching family" (Sport England 2014).

FACTORS THAT MITIGATE A PROFESSIONALISATION AGENDA

We will go on now to elaborate on what we consider to be a series of factors that limit the potential for professionalisation. We offer these as an interpretation of the current situation and invite you to support or refute these. They are not offered as fully sourced arguments, but are intended to stimulate debate. We then describe an alternative approach, a focus on professionalism, describe what that might look like for sport coaching, and propose the actions necessary to encourage such an approach.

1. Sport coaching can be described as a 'hidden occupation'. There are a number of factors that often keep coaches in the background, and provide few catalysts for public interest. Historically in the UK, traditional sports such as cricket, rugby union and hockey underplayed the role of the coach (compare to the more central role of the coach in baseball, American football and basketball in the USA). This was allied to amateurism and, although now no longer the case, the status of the coach was not held in high regard. In addition, the contested nature of sport means that there is often a deliberate obfuscation of the coach's approach to performance enhancement.

   Public interest may be stimulated by direct contact with coaches, a practice redolent of a 'service industry'. However, the majority of those deemed to be coaches, and who work with children (North 2009), are employed by schools and other organisations. Coaches in talent development and performance sport tend to be attached to particular teams, clubs, squads, groups or individuals. This limits the extent of the public's direct recourse to the coach's services.

2. Academics have failed to establish the precise nature of the link between coaches' behaviour and practice and athlete/team performance. This is not a criticism: the variability inherent in performance, its contested nature, the challenge of evaluating potential, the human/psychological element in preparation and performance, and the range of coaching philosophies available bedevil an obvious intervention–outcome equation. The result of this is that the field is replete with prescriptions for good practice (e.g. Côté et al. 2010), but few convincing measures of effectiveness. Sport coaches, particularly in high-performance and professional sport, are measured by their association with successful athletes/teams, and the resultant unsustainability of this leads to a high level of turnover.

3. There is no protection of boundary markers. Indeed, it is not too difficult to argue that there is little agreement as to what these should be. An extreme position would state that 'anyone can coach'. National surveys (North 2009) suggest that over 40 per cent of those who classify themselves as coaches are unqualified.

Even within the coaching workforce of sporting organisations, in work carried out by the authors, almost 20 per cent of the coaches were unqualified. It is perhaps understandable that policy makers should wish to be inclusive, but the resultant agglomeration of roles – sport leaders, instructors, PE teachers, coaches of children and performance coaches – has created an occupational landscape that is extremely diverse and difficult to regulate. The failure to adopt a national licensing system for the employment and deployment of coaches is an insurmountable barrier to professionalisation.

 KEY CONCEPT

The diverse occupational landscape reflects a failure to establish role boundaries. The absence of a national licensing system within this landscape is an insurmountable barrier to professionalisation.

4. The diversity of roles, qualifications and practices prevents any consensual attribution of occupational status. The predominance of part-time volunteer coaches, often with limited qualifications, attests to this. It is not surprising that the UK's Standard Occupational Classification (see www.ons.gov.uk), which classifies occupations according to skill level and content, says that there are no formal academic requirements for coaching, and links coaches with supervising recreational activities and officiating. It is difficult to envisage a professional grouping that has no entry standards, no qualifications threshold and only general role specificity.

5. Professionalisation will not move forward until there is recognition of the distinctive domains within sports leadership. These are not held together sufficiently and coherently by simply calling every sports leader a 'coach'. The term 'sport coaching' is simply not a useful construct. It collectivises those who engage in sports leadership but does not actually delimit an occupational grouping. It is a family term (Lyle 2011) that is too all-embracing. If the term is intended to encompass the practitioner who introduces an adapted form of a sport to primary school aged children over a few short sessions, the individual who leads national age-group squad preparations, the instructor who provides lessons to adults wishing to improve their recreational capacity, the 'club coach' of youth or adult participants in regular organised sport and the coach of individuals or squads in the midst of Olympic preparations, it is not difficult to appreciate why the distinctions in education and training, expertise, commitment, remuneration and deployment, and specificity of domain role and practice, create an amorphous social entity that is simply not susceptible of being treated as one occupational grouping.

6. A phenomenon in coaching termed 'coaching up' and 'coaching down' impacts on professionalisation. The former refers to coaches who work with athletes whose performance-related needs are beyond the coach's knowledge-based

285

education, training and experience. This is perhaps not very common as the coach's practice will not result in appropriate or expected progression. 'Coaching down' refers to situations in which individuals who normally work with more advanced performers operate with children or beginners. There are advantages and disadvantages in such circumstances. This issue has been raised as an example of limited mobility. Professions traditionally have established stages through which practitioners will progress, most often related to hierarchical occupational employment. These stages are acknowledged within the profession and often related to formal or informal recognition of professional status. It is simply not the case that a coherent developmental pathway exists in sport coaching and, we would argue more importantly, that the 'pathways' are too extended, do not restrict access based on expertise, do not have evident progression criteria and, in practice, are domain limited.

 QUESTION BOX

Reflect on the full list of factors being identified in this section. Which of these have their basis in a conceptual issue that we have raised in other chapters in the book? Can you think of any other factors?

---

7. Sport coaching is not sufficiently valued by society for the government to impose regulations on the education and training of coaches. We have failed to convince the wider society that coaching is a necessary underpinning for other sport-related policy objectives. The initial momentum achieved by the UK Coaching Framework (sports coach UK 2008) has been lost and the Framework has become a reference point rather than an active policy for reform and development. There is no political agenda related to the financing or recruitment of coaches. The absence of licensing and the difficulty in measuring supply and demand mean that there is no need for a quota process in allocating training places. It might be argued that some measure of public control (setting targets, per-formance indicators) would be expected and targets associated with the Olympic programme or National Sport Organisation five-year plans are a form of governmental control when dependent on grant funding. The absence of political interest and the diffuse nature of employment and deployment mean that the likelihood of occupational control lies solely within the centrally funded high-performance sector.
8. A corollary of the failure to demonstrate the value of, and necessity for, coaching is that there is no public clamour for professionalisation. The role of the coach may be hidden in much of high-performance sport, but in the context of the preponderance of children's coaching, a culture of accountability and issues of safeguarding, it is somewhat surprising that there is no external (the public) impetus for the professionalisation of sport coaching. However, neither is it evident that there is any 'internal' practitioner demand for professionalisation.

286

There is no evidence that practitioners perceive there to be a disadvantage in not being professionalised and it is more likely that the drive has been initiated by 'activists', that is, policy makers and academics.

 KEY CONCEPT

Sport coaching is not sufficiently valued by society for the government to impose regulations on the education and training of coaches. We have failed to convince the wider society that coaching is a necessary underpinning for other sport-related policy objectives.

9. It might be argued that internal standards of coaching practice do not stand up to scrutiny. We need more time to evaluate the evidence for this, but our immediate reaction would be to affirm that much of coaching practice, in all domains and at all levels, would be indefensible in terms of criteria associated with sound practice in areas such as preparation and planning practice, intervention based on individual performance needs, specificity of goal setting, levels of intensity of preparation, systematic training loads and management, good practice in interpersonal management, some elements of ethical practice, skill acquisition principles, use of advanced technology and performance data, evidence of continuous professional development and so on. However, if the response is to say that some of our best coaches or high-performance coaches exhibit good practice, this serves only to reinforce the notion that professionalism is characteristic of a relatively small sector of sports coaching.

10. There is limited consensus on coaching qualifications. The inception of the United Kingdom Coaching Certificate, although not universal, was an attempt to provide a measure of standardisation and greater consistency in outcomes and expectations, and should be applauded. However, without a licensing requirement, and with modest selection/recruitment barriers, it might be considered a line of least resistance. A sticking point is that coaching qualifications are often thought of as a coherent and self-referent 'ladder' of qualifications from entry awards with minimal requirements to more demanding higher-level awards. There would be no defence for the inclusion of such initial entry qualifications as a 'professional' qualification, and high-performance sport appointments attend to 'track record' rather than qualifications. This is not unreasonable, providing there is a threshold point that is considered to be an entry point to the 'profession'. The standard undergraduate degree plus a professional training qualification and period of probationary practice is absent, but not yet replaced by education and training expectations that confer a similar quality assurance.

11. In practice, there is no system of sanctionable membership of a recognised professional body. Although policy makers have toyed with registration and licensing schemes (often for commercial motives), there appears to be very

limited appetite for (a) firm markers of professional entry based on education, training and experience, and (b) correlation of the resultant professional status to employment or deployment (whether in the 'coaching' of beginners or high-performance athletes). Standards of ethical behaviour, and more serious criminal activity, are not tied to membership and consequent legitimacy to practise.

12. It is normal to have role models in professions, particularly at the 'pinnacle' of the profession. It is clear that we/the public are willing to accept practitioners who are unqualified, albeit usually experienced. This situation may be related to issues of accountability and consequence (cf. for example the unqualified surgeon or architect and the unqualified pastor). The question relates to entry to the profession. In most professions a commitment (presumably resulting from some prior consideration, career aspiration, family history or vocational calling) leads to a period of education, training and practice before the individual exercises an appropriate role. In sport coaching this nicety of progression is much less evident and there are fewer assessment stages at which the coach's expertise is assured.

13. There is an indisputable discontinuity between participation sport and high-performance sport. Although 'performance pathways' are in place and imply selection and development at a young age, there are enormous differences in culture, practices, expectations, finance and accountability for results. The absence of a smooth hierarchy in performance terms is matched by a similar domain-specific discontinuity in coaching practices – occasionally exacerbated by a form of occupational protectionism in some sports. There are a number of related issues that militate against professional recognition in high-performance sport: it is common for former and existing players in some sports to bypass any form of professional preparation prior to appointment; many individuals who are termed 'coaches' perform partial roles: and measures of expertise and effectiveness are secondary to performance outcomes (often expressed in relative terms).

14. There continues to be a need to define 'what it is that coaches can do that others cannot (or should not)' – what is it that coaches are said to profess? There are a number of issues: (1) the expertise demonstrated by coaches of young children is not evidently very different to that of other education specialists; (2) coaching practice in some domains is not evidently based on advanced education and training; (3) there are few, if any, selection criteria for entry to the profession; and (4) quality is perceived by many to be 'tainted' by being associated with untrained (or minimally trained) volunteers. Academic writing on expertise has most often been characterised by prescriptions for coaching practice or lists of necessary attributes, knowledge and competences. The widespread acceptance of apparently intuitive or experiential decision making and interaction that complement performance planning has not been translated into a clear model of how coaches make the subtle and nuanced decisions that characterise practice. The important issue is that this manifestation of advanced expertise has not been dealt with well in coach education and training, and therefore does not form the basis for a distinguishing measure of professional status.

These profession-related issues portray a landscape that is not, at first sight, conducive to either incidental or purposeful development. They lead us to ask the following questions. Within the broad occupational grouping that is sport coaching, can we distinguish:

1. those who are acting professionally from those who are not;
2. those who are bound by the formal or informal expectations of the profession and those who are not;
3. those who satisfy minimum criteria for professional status and those who do not;
4. those whose coaching interventions reflect a knowledge-based expertise and those whose interventions do not; and
5. those who have followed an acknowledged pathway with profession-related assessment stages and those who have not.

You may feel that these are rhetorical in that they merely highlight the absence of a professionalising agenda, and, further, that the absence of mechanisms for addressing such issues reinforces our professionally immature status.

However, becoming a profession is not a matter of self-determination. The public (again meaning the government apparatus) needs to see some benefit by more effectively achieving a service that the public values, reacting to and resolving crises of public disquiet when things go wrong, and consequently awarding a measure of esteemed and (relatively) unrestricted practice. This pre-requisite for professional recognition is not evident. The public needs to value and recognise the contribution of sport coaching as a specialist and knowledge-based occupation or vocation (and by implication, the education, training and experience required to underpin this) that merits the resultant elements of trust and discretion. Evetts (2011a) argues that the move towards the professionalisation of non-traditional knowledge-based occupations can largely be traced to the desire of the government apparatus to control public sector occupations in terms of training budgets, recruitment quotas, targets for performance and so on. However, for the reasons described above, this does not apply to sport coaching, and the demand for professionalisation is, at best, 'internal'.

In discussions with colleagues,[1] it was pointed out to us that our interpretation of the current 'landscape' was overly pessimistic. We acknowledged that our involvement in coaching development with high-performance coaches did confirm that there was much excellent practice. We also recognised that there had been some investment by government in sport provision, albeit with frequently changing policy goals and limited impact on coaching. Although there was common ground with much of our argument, we judged that the pace of professionalisation was much slower and less visible than our colleagues suggested.

OCCUPATIONAL PROFESSIONALISM: THE ARGUMENT

What, then, is the way forward? Much of the analysis that follows is influenced by the work of Julia Evetts (2009, 2011a, 2011b, 2013), whose expertise lies in the sociology of professions. Evetts has focused on knowledge-based occupations other than the traditional professions and she argues for a shift from the concept and pursuit of professions or professionalisation (that is, cultivating the 'enclosure' of the occupational group) to a focus on professionalism. Professionalism can be recognised in a number of ways:

1. as an occupational value – acting like a professional;
2. as an ideology – which can be turned to self-interest by linking it to rewards and protectionism; and
3. as the discourse of occupational change and managerial control (in which professionalism is used as a means to 'enforce' accountability).

In our analysis, the driver appears to be 'internal' and a loose form of protectionism, in that the practitioners – that is, the coaches – construct and promote an image and identity of professional behaviour that can be used as a 'bargaining chip'. However, the driver can also be 'from above', as a form of rationalisation leading to outcome targets and performance indicators. In this context, Evetts distinguishes, very usefully, between organisational professionalism (perhaps evident in the UK in the culture and climate of school teaching or the National Health Service), and occupational professionalism – high level of autonomy, lengthy system of education, strong occupational identity and work culture, codes of practice and professional institutions to support the professionalism agenda. The principal contention in this paper is that occupational professionalism, as described in the previous sentence, provides an appropriate agenda for sport coaching. The implications for sport coaching are considerable, if these features are to be realised:

- the distinctions between being a profession and a valued occupation are not worth pursuing;
- there is an urgent need to establish that sport coaching is a knowledge-based occupation based on tertiary education and an appropriate level of vocational training;
- the mechanisms need to be in place to encourage and monitor the diffusion of professionalism into coaching practice; and
- the criteria should be applied to a more restricted sub-set of the occupational space than is currently tagged as sport coaching.

 KEY CONCEPT

Occupational professionalism (high level of autonomy, lengthy system of education, strong occupational identity and work culture, codes of practice, and professional institutions to support the professionalism agenda) provides an appropriate agenda for sport coaching.

Before moving to an elaboration of the meaning of professionalism, we should note that the discourse on professions also recognises a loose association of agencies and practitioners that form an 'interacting network'. Our view is that the argument that there are sufficient commonalities across roles, deployment and employment in coaching to render it a recognisable occupational grouping is far from proven, and that the system requirements that provide cohesion (control mechanisms and strategy, shared practice and values, system mobility, occupational role grading, common education system, effective communication) do not stand up to scrutiny. Note that the 'loose association' is the ICCE approach, in which a 'blended profession' is serviced by a series of 'system enhancements' (Duffy *et al.* 2011). These measures are not incompatible with attempts to increase professionalism.

What might we mean by professionalism, and how can it help us to move forward? The Institute for Learning (2009) suggests that the meaning attached to the term has changed over time from the qualities associated with the traditional autonomous professions to those associated with the newer (often public sector) occupations. The traditional professions were imbued with positive (authoritative, altruistic, specialist expertise) and negative (arrogant, exclusive, elitist) qualities, but as the notion of professionalisation moved into a much broader range of occupations, qualities of accountability, competence and explicit standards became valued. The Institute for Learning looked to the future with a set of qualities, albeit aspirational, such as altruism, continuous learning and improvement, extending professional knowledge and skills, inclusivity, self-organisation, passion and trust (at face value, a set of qualities that might be immediately recognised by sport coaches!). We might argue, therefore, that professionalism becomes a 'marker' for professional status: 'I am a professional because my practice exhibits professionalism, and my profession reinforces this through mechanisms to encourage quality assurance and a measure of exclusivity.'

As suggested, the most appropriate option is to increase the level of professionalism within sport coaching. At a metastrategic level this could involve adopting very strict criteria of professional recognition (in order to pursue some of the benefits of professional privilege) with consequent restrictions on domain and context-specific deployment and employment. However, a more feasible and pragmatic alternative is a looser concept of a professional (and consequent distinctions in status, esteem and reward) in a number of domains – children's coaching, development sport, high-performance sport, participation/recreation instruction and community sport. If we pursue the 'professional' route – based on evidence of professionalism in practice – we forego the 'exclusive right to practice'. The client will have the responsibility of recognising when the service is provided by a chartered coach, qualified coach, experienced but unqualified coach or inexperienced helper. Where 'coaching' is treated as a marketplace (e.g. professional sport, recreational instruction) and government-recognised regulation is unlikely, the coach's expertise may be assessed differently (personal capacity, previous performer experience or record of outcome success).

QUESTION BOX

Is coaching currently treated like a market place in which it is difficult to evaluate coaches' qualifications, expertise, experience and, therefore, suitability for a role? Does this explain why results are used as a mechanism for judging coaches' performance?

IMPLICATIONS FOR MOVING FORWARD

Of course, we can adopt a number of specific actions that make professionalism in practice more likely. The first of these relates to limiting membership of the profession. For example, a useful debate should be initiated on the benefits of:

1. recognising national sports organisation (NSO) qualifications as preferring only quality-assured and recognised sport-specific status at a pre-coaching stage;
2. integrating NSO and higher education provision in coach education (perhaps at what we would currently recognise as a more demanding UKCC Level 3 and above);
3. being willing to set a limit at which 'chartered status' (implying wider public recognition) would be attainable (including tertiary education, vocational training and a period of probationary experience); and
4. acknowledging the distinction between sport coaching as extended preparation for performance in specific competitions within a contractual relationship (even if informal), and 'coaching' as teaching or introducing young people to a sport, or short-term instruction to improve technical competence.

We should note in passing that individual practitioners may operate across these domains and levels, if appropriately qualified (this might include evident and proven professionalism in the target context). We should be wary of having unreasonable expectations of modestly committed volunteer coaches if criteria of professionalism are applied.

Second, registration and licensing are essential within any professional occupational grouping. It is not defensible to say that coaches can operate outwith such a system of recognition (and monitoring). Sport coaching cannot claim public credibility until registration within a sport, and licensing within a professional body, are in place. Third, and in the context of encouraging professionalism in practice, professional bodies and authority regulators should focus less on exclusivity and more on the professionalism of member practitioners. (Note that this refers not only to an individual coach's professional capacity and behaviour, but to the conditions/ environment within which the coach operates.)

Even if the systems/mechanisms are not yet in place, and we lack an overall consensus or collective authority within sport coaching, it should still be possible to focus on occupational or practitioner professionalism. A crucial task for the 'profession',

A 'starter list' might consist of:

- demonstrable specialist expertise;
- application of advanced skills and knowledge;
- adherence to appropriate codes of practice;
- demonstrable concern for athletes' needs and preferences;
- accountable practice (clarity of roles and responsibilities);
- regular assessment of competence to practice;
- evidence of continuous learning and improvement;
- maintenance of awareness of technical developments in the sport;
- operating within collegial expectations;
- public recruitment and selection policies;
- evident standards of integrity;
- creation of positive learning environments;
- principled pedagogical or andragogical practice;
- performance planning that encompasses up-to-date knowledge;
- decision making based on the application of performance analysis data, performance science, behavioural sciences and other relevant disciplines;
- goal-directed intervention behaviour;
- crisis and coping strategies being available;
- aligning behavioural strategies to support the meaningful development of the athlete.

therefore, is to determine what would constitute professional behaviour and practice.

This is an example of how professionalism might be recognised in the individual coach, but recognising that these criteria need to be translated into threshold statements that define appropriate levels of practice and behaviour. However, it would also be necessary for policy makers and the coaching systems networks to implement development agendas designed to encourage greater professionalism.

Our judgement is that sport coaching has made relatively few steps forward in relation to its professional status. We have argued that the nature of sport coaching makes it unlikely that any pursuit of traditional profession-recognition criteria would be worthwhile. We should learn from a conceptualisation that values 'acting as a professional' as the mark of practitioners within a mature occupation. The currency of this new order is that of occupational professionalism. Those involved in furthering the 'profession' need to adopt a consensual position on what constitutes the desired and valued qualities of professionalism in sport coaching behaviour and practice, and create a development agenda that will promote, encourage, monitor and provide opportunities to develop these qualities. Some of the necessary actions are not dissimilar to current agendas, but others require a refocusing of priorities and attention to difficult issues around entry criteria, educational standards, accountability and expectations.

This might begin with:

- tighter boundaries on membership, including registration and licensing;
- more demanding coach education;
- increased expectations about matching qualifications/status to deployment/ employment;
- stronger occupational identities and role models;
- clearer expectations of workplace practice;
- coaching practice that is more evidently knowledge-based;
- mechanisms for more accountable practice;
- more detailed and accessible accounts of 'normal states of athlete engagement' for all levels of performance;
- increased opportunities and expectations for continuing professional development
- clear criteria of acceptable practice;
- stronger advocacy based on all of the above.

 SUMMARY

This chapter will have familiarised you with the following:

- An introduction to the academic treatment of professionalisation in sport coaching.
- A review and critique of the recent literature.
- A catalogue of factors that hinder the professionalisation of sport coaching.
- An outline of occupational professionalism as an appropriate agenda for sport coaching.
- An indication of the behaviour and practice that might constitute professionalism.
- The actions necessary to secure a suitable environment in which to promote professionalism in coaching practice.

NOTE

1 We are grateful to Bob Muir and Julian North of Leeds Beckett University for their helpful insights on an early draft of this chapter.

PROJECTS

1. Conduct a survey of public opinion (taking care with your selection of interviewees). Canvass opinion on coaches' esteem, qualifications, remuneration, and licensing. Evaluate the climate for the professionalisation of sport coaching.
2. Using the tentative proposals for criteria of professionalism, employ survey methods to reduce or expand the list, based on a survey of coaches.
3. Choose one of the criteria for system coherence; gather evidence to support or refute the assertion that there is little commonality across domains to support the contention that 'coaching' is a cohesive system.
4. Consider how the conditions necessary for establishing professionalism in practice might be put in place. Select three or four features and draw up a list of development steps, with appropriate evaluation criteria. Identify the opportunities and threats to establishing your list.

REFERENCES

Côté, J., Bruner, M., Erickson, K., Strachan, L., & Fraser-Thomas, J. (2010). Athlete development and coaching. In J. Lyle & C. Cushion (Eds) *Sports Coaching: Professionalisation and Practice*. Edinburgh: Churchill Livingston, 63–83.

Duffy, P., Hartley, H., Bales, J., Crespo, M., Dick, F., Vardham, D., Nordmann, L., & Curado, J. (2011). Sports coaching as a 'profession': Challenges and future directions. *International Journal of Coaching Science, 5*(2), 93–123.

Evetts, J. (2009). The management of professionalism: A contemporary paradox. In S. Gewirtz, P. Mahony, I. Hextall, & A. Cribb (Eds) *Changing Teacher Professionalism: International Trends, Challenges and Ways Forward*. London: Routledge, 19–30.

Evetts, J. (2011a). Sociological analysis of professionalism: Past, present and future. *Comparative Sociology, 10*(1), 1–37.

Evetts, J. (2011b). A new professionalisation? Challenges and opportunities. *Current Sociology, 59*, 406–422.

Evetts, J. (2013). Professionalism: Value and ideology. *Current Sociology, 61*, 778–796.

ICCE, ASOIF, and Leeds Metropolitan University (2013). *International Sports Coaching Framework: Version 1.2*. Champaign, IL: Human Kinetics.

Institute for Learning (2009). Professionalism and the role of professional bodies: A stimulus paper from the Institute for Learning. www.ifl.ac.uk/_data/assets/pdf_file/0005/5981/Professionalism-and-Prof-Bodies.pdf, accessed 2 July 2010.

Lyle, J. (1986). Coach education: Preparation for a profession (Paradigm Paper). In *Coach Education: Preparation for a Profession*. Proceedings of the VIII Commonwealth and International Conference in Sport, PE, Dance, Recreation and Health. London: E & FN Spon, 1–25.

Lyle, J. (2002). *Sports Coaching Concepts: A Framework for Coaches' Behaviour.* London: Routledge.

Lyle, J. (2011). What is a coach and what is coaching? In I. Stafford (Ed.) *Coaching Children in Sport.* London: Routledge, 5–16.

Lyle, J., & Cushion, C. (Eds) (2010). *Sports Coaching: Professionalisation and Practice.* Edinburgh: Churchill Livingstone.

Malcolm, D., Pinheiro, C., & Pimenta, N. (2014). Could and should sport coaching become a profession? Some sociological reflections. *International Sports Coaching Journal,* 1(1), 42–45.

North, J. (2009). *The Coaching Workforce 2009–2016.* Leeds: Coachwise.

Sheriden, M. P. (2014). 'Could and should sport coaching become a profession? Some sociological reflections.' A commentary. *International Sports Coaching Journal,* 1(1), 46–49.

Sport England (2014). *Coaching Plan for England – Survey Consultation.* www.sportengland.org/media/376783/coaching-plan-for-england.pdf

sports coach UK (2008). *The UK Coaching Framework.* Leeds: sports coach UK.

Taylor, W. G. & Garratt, D. (2008). *The Professionalisation of Sports Coaching in the UK: Issues and Conceptualisation.* Leeds: sports coach UK.

Taylor, W. G., & Garratt, D. (2010a). The professionalisation of sports coaching: Definitions, challenges and critique. In J. Lyle & C. Cushion (Eds) *Sports Coaching: Professionalisation and Practice.* Edinburgh: Churchill Livingstone, 99–117.

Taylor, W. G., & Garratt, D. (2010b). The professionalisation of sports coaching: Relations of power, resistance and compliance. *Sport, Education & Society,* 15(1), 121–139.

Taylor, W. G., & Garratt, D. (2013). Coaching and professionalisation. In P. Potrac, W. Gilbert, & J. Denison (Eds) *Routledge Handbook of Sports Coaching.* Routledge: London, 27–39.

Townend, R., & North, J. (2007). *Sports Coaching in the UK 11.* Leeds: sports coach UK.

CHAPTER 14

COACH EDUCATION AND COACHING PRACTICE

CHAPTER OUTLINE

- Introduction
- Coach education, training and learning: an overview
- Evaluating the impact of coach education
- Conceptual lessons
- Coach learning and coaching practice
- A contemporary theory of coaches' learning
- Delivery issues and enhancing meaningful learning
- Concluding thoughts
- Summary
- Projects
- Reading

INTRODUCTION

The purpose of this chapter is to examine the potential impact of the conceptual framework on coach education and to examine the progress of coach education since the first edition of the book. It is less about the nuts and bolts of coach education programmes and more about how the principles on which coach education is based need to be informed by a conceptual understanding of the coaching process and to what extent this has been achieved. The ongoing professionalisation of sport coaching is particularly influenced by a developed appreciation of the coaching process – and in particular developments in coach education, its evaluation and effectiveness.

Coach education should be based on a clear set of intentions about what the trainees/learners are expected to achieve. Any prescription for education and training will be centred on producing effective practice, and establishing this requires the analytical framework being developed throughout. A judicious blend of models *for* coaching (to provide a template for education) and models *of* coaching (to understand the implementation of the template) is required by coach educators; therefore there remains a need for greater conceptual clarity in order to inform education and training.

A number of examples will serve as reminders of the elements of the conceptual framework that are likely to have an impact on coach education: the process nature of coaching, the need for underlying knowledge, the distinction between participation and performance coaching, decision making and cognitive models as mechanisms for professional practice, and the regulation of activity through thresholds and contingency planning. However, this is not a 'how to' chapter on coach education and training; the purpose is to provide a critical conceptual analysis of coach education and consideration of its underpinning literature and evidence. Since the first edition of this book, the field in relation to coach education has developed and there are now numerous prescriptions *for* coach learning, but the evidence *of* coach learning is still limited. Therefore, the chapter argues for a more comprehensive understanding of coach learning and its development supported by empirical research.

COACH EDUCATION, TRAINING AND LEARNING: AN OVERVIEW

Education, training and learning (in the context of a specialised field such as sport coaching) serve the function of preparing individuals for occupational practice. However, the range of purposes stretches from specialist technical skills to personal development and socialisation into the field. The socialisation element also includes values and ethical practice. There are, therefore, a number of both formal and informal processes that characterise this preparation. These can be summarised as:

- teaching and learning of specialised knowledge, values and understanding that underpin the activity;
- training and practice in the skills-based implementation of practice; and
- initiation/induction into the social and professional mores of the occupation.

The importance of education and training cannot be overstated. For any occupation, the quality of future practice is a central concern and, to some extent, shapes the development and success of the profession. Indeed, issues of professional status rest on the nature of formal qualifications and the extent to which these are regulated. Thus, educational programmes serve as quality assurance mechanisms by regulating recruitment and by standardising delivery and expectations. The accreditation and 'kitemarking' of educational courses, and the licensing of practitioners through these courses, is an indicator of professional development. Certification, therefore, is important to a profession. Individuals progress through structured and standardised levels of award that are related to occupational requirements. Certification of coaches is not universal, however, with data from the UK suggesting that about 68 per cent of coaches or head coaches hold some form of governing body qualification, and that this figure is 36 per cent among coaching assistants (North 2009). The emphasis on certification of coaches shown by coach education demonstrates that coaches have satisfied sports governing bodies' quality assurance criteria by acquiring and displaying a desired minimum level of competency. Thus, an assumption is made that coaches will leave a given coach education episode having the requisite

Coach education and coaching practice

knowledge, and a battery of strategies, to work effectively as coaches at the level for which they have been prepared (Cushion *et al.* 2010). This process suggests an emphasis on learning in 'formal' situations.

For the most part, certification acts as a gatekeeper to the profession and ensures, therefore, that the competence of the practitioner can be assured. However, the absence of certification in recruitment to some professional sports, and the consequent lack of quality assurance, is a difficult issue for the sport coaching profession. Coach education provision will have a range of activities, from award courses and programmes of seminars, workshops and conferences to publications, visiting and mentor coaches, and a variety of structured forms of experience. However, education and training depends on a mix of formal, informal and non-formal provision, and understanding how learning and preparation is taking place is important in analysing practice. Research has shown consistently over the last 30 years that knowledge developed through experience forms the basis of expertise in coaching. Experience plays a central role, but at the same time the preparation of the practitioner cannot be left to experience alone. Even without formal training provision, novices have a structured initiation into an occupation, though just accumulating experiences is not enough as not every experienced coach is deemed to be effective. In addition, it has been suggested that idiosyncrasies in coaches' learning (and the relative success of coach education) originate with each individual's past experiences and networks of existing knowledge, beliefs and emotions (Cushion *et al.* 2003; Stodter & Cushion 2014, 2016; Werthner & Trudel 2009). Coaches' knowledge and experiential foundations act like a filter through which new situations will pass, exerting a continuing influence over the way they see and interpret them, and thus their learning and behaviour (Cushion *et al.* 2003). Therefore, the same coach education opportunity will have a different impact on the individual coaches that experience it, depending on their unique starting points and approaches to the situation (Griffiths & Armour 2013; Stodter & Cushion 2016).

 KEY CONCEPT

The same coach education opportunity will have a different impact on the individual coaches that experience it, depending on their unique starting points and approaches to the situation.

Coaches that consistently outperform others and reach the pinnacle of their profession seem to be united by a common characteristic – 'always learning' and 'always thinking', they have effectively mastered the skill of learning from the multitude of experiences they encounter (Stodter & Cushion 2016; Schempp & McCullick 2010). Ideas about effective coaching rely on the assumption that the coach will be able to draw on a base of applied knowledge relevant to sports performance, learning, the technical and tactical aspects of the sport, understanding interaction and appreciating the consequences of one's own behaviours in achieving desired ends (Stodter & Cushion 2016; Cushion *et al.* 2010). It seems clear that the learning experiences that enable effective coaching are gained in a variety of situations, from day-to-day episodes of coaching practice, observing and working with other coaches, to coach education programmes, workshops and reading. The idea that coaches make use of a complex mix of different learning experiences is nothing new, and has been reiterated in the literature for over a decade. However, it is important to acknowledge that these more informal aspects of provision are not merely intended to be opportunities for enhancing the formal certification process. These activities both complement the formal programme and constitute an essential element of coaches' education. Education accelerates the learning that takes place from experience and helps to differentiate between good and bad experience (although learning takes place from both). Experience may be rather narrowly focused and may not, of itself, provide the necessary preparation for adaptation and mobility within the occupation.

 KEY CONCEPT

Education accelerates the learning that takes place from experience and helps to differentiate between good and bad experience (although learning takes place from both). Experience may be rather narrowly focused and may not, of itself, provide the necessary preparation for adaptation and mobility within an occupation.

Treating different 'categories' of learning situations as stand-alone concepts, investigating the chosen source or situation without reference to other ways of learning or the coach's development as a whole means that we are unable to explain how different experiences combine to bring about the development of effective practitioners. In reality, coaches develop through a complex blend of different opportunities, yet identifying coaches' learning sources tells us very little about *what works* in these particular situations, *how, why,* and *for whom* (Stodter & Cushion 2016). Although formal–informal, acquisition–participation and mediated–unmediated frameworks are often used to delineate the various learning situations, coaches in reality utilise multiple sources that are interconnected modes of learning and each situation a coach encounters can comprise of a blend of more than one mode of learning existing simultaneously, and it is this blending rather than separation that is key to learning (Cushion *et al.* 2010). This suggests that any one learning situation or type of learning cannot be understood in isolation and the development of each coach is unique, with individuals encountering and using different situations and sources of information in diverse ways (Stodter & Cushion 2014; Werthner & Trudel 2009). As a result, the processes involved and the impact of different learning experiences on coaches' holistic knowledge and practice are not yet well understood (Stodter & Cushion 2016).

In undertaking further analysis, a problem in consideration of coach education, training and learning is a lack of definitional clarity. This is well illustrated by the wide range of terminology employed, at times uncritically, to describe coach preparation, learning and development (Cushion *et al.* 2010). Examples to illustrate this include: coach learning, coach education, coach training, coach development, continuing professional development, plus coaching and sport instructor certification, among others. These terms are often used interchangeably and inconsistently. Coach learning has only recently been presented as a term that brings together research into, and understanding about, the broader learning of coaches. Learning is an important term as it places the emphasis on the person rather than on a system or curricula. Learning can happen through a number of means; for example, through experience, reflection, study or instruction, and can embrace all of the mechanisms through which coaches acquire the knowledge that informs their professional practice (Cushion & Nelson 2013). The recognition and use of coach learning as a term enables a view that "extends far beyond any formal training program" (Côté 2006, p. 221). Coach learning therefore not only occurs inside, but also outside of educational settings. Consequently, while the coach learner is the essential element in the learning process, the coach educator is not, as learning often occurs without teaching (Cushion & Nelson 2013). Nevertheless, the coach educator still plays a central role in coach learning, contributing to efforts to raise coaching standards and develop coaching as a profession.

The operationalisation of educational provision provides an enormous range of implementation issues: content, assessment, training of educators, the delivery system, levels of award, genericism versus specialisation, training 'on the job' versus courses and so on. One particular issue is the distinction between education and training. Anything with 'educational value' will contribute to the development of knowledge and understanding – examples might be: enhanced personal skills, a capacity for critical analysis and reflection, decision making and problem solving, appreciation of values and ethics and flexibility/adaptability. Obviously, educational outcomes are to be valued, particularly for future practice and developing individual capacities, but there must also be a balance between vocational skills training sufficient to fulfil the role functions and vocational/professional education. Recently, there have been questions about the 'education' within coach education and whether it is appropriate that provision of this nature is conceived of as an educational endeavour (see Nelson *et al.* 2006; Cushion & Nelson 2013). 'Coach education' is the terminology most frequently employed to describe formalised provision. Despite this, developmental courses could, perhaps even should, be more appropriately labelled coach training or even indoctrination in some cases. Dearden (1984) suggests that training is narrower, more structured and more directly related to vocations; according to Buckley and Caple (2000), education and training have a number of significant conceptual differences, with training more job-oriented because it focuses on the acquisition of the knowledge, behaviour and skills specific to a profession. Training, therefore, "tends to be a more mechanistic process which emphasises uniform and predictable responses to standard guidance and instruction reinforced by practice and repetition" (p. 2). Education, on the other hand, is viewed as being more person-oriented, focusing on providing "more theoretical and conceptual frameworks designed to stimulate an individual's analytical and critical abilities" (p. 2). While training promotes uniformity of knowledge and practices, education attempts to increase variability by emphasising and explicating individual differences (Nelson *et al.* 2006; Cushion & Nelson 2013).

 QUESTION BOX

There is no doubt that, traditionally, coach education has emphasised the training and technical elements. Has the absence of an 'educational' element been a contributory factor to the slow development of the profession?

Much of the research critiquing formal provision seems to locate it as training rather than education. In this respect, coaches are frequently subjected to a standardised curriculum privileging a technocratic rationality through a 'tool box' of professional knowledge and a 'gold standard' of coaching (Abraham & Collins 1998; Cushion & Nelson 2013). This approach is aimed at developing coaches with standardised knowledge and a battery of strategies to overcome perceived typical coaching dilemmas in their domain, suggesting that much of coach education provision could in fact be labelled as coach training (Cushion & Nelson 2013). Viewed in this way, coach training is arguably effective in achieving its desired learning objectives, with the gaining of certification providing evidence that many practitioners have satisfied the governing bodies' criteria by acquiring and displaying desired minimum levels of coaching competency (Cushion & Nelson 2013).

Some provision in formal situations could perhaps even be described as indoctrination, which can be defined as "activities that set out to convince us that there is a 'right' way of thinking and feeling and behaving" (Rogers 2002, p. 53; Cushion & Nelson 2013). Indeed, Chesterfield *et al.* (2010) provided evidence supporting the claim that coach education can be appropriately considered indoctrination where the learner is denied choice, instead being exposed to a single set of expected values and attitudes. This might include indoctrinating a prescribed method of delivery, feedback sequence, coaching philosophy or tactical and technical approach (Nelson *et al.* 2006; Cushion *et al.* 2010; Cushion & Nelson 2013). Currently, coach learning in formal situations defines what knowledge is necessary for coaches to practice and how that knowledge can 'best' be transmitted, and certification requires coaches to structure sessions, deliver information to athletes, and provide feedback in a prescribed manner to be deemed competent (Nelson *et al.* 2006; Cushion *et al.* 2010; Cushion & Nelson 2013). With this in mind, coach education might be appropriately described as training or even indoctrination in certain instances.

Coach education and coaching practice

EVALUATING THE IMPACT OF COACH EDUCATION

Coach learning typically involves activities that are packaged as large-scale coach certification programmes developed by the national governing bodies of sport and higher education courses relating to coaching and the sport sciences (Nelson *et al.* 2006). Such formal coach education has attracted considerable attention, with numerous scholars having researched and specifically written about this topic. Despite a seemingly large body of work, closer inspection reveals that, to date, there have been few studies that have attempted to directly investigate and evaluate coach education programmes (Cushion & Nelson 2013; Cushion *et al.* 2010; McCullick *et al.* 2009). As a result, there remains no evidence to link coach education certification with coaching competency or developments in practice, despite many courses being competency-based (Cushion & Nelson 2013). In other words, it cannot be said that the competency achieved has been as a result of the programme.

Evidence over time has suggested that coaches have tended to attach much less importance to formal coach education for acquiring knowledge. When asked to comment on their experiences, coaches have suggested that:

1. courses often give little more than a basic understanding, but offer a starting point;
2. they often arrive already knowing about, and putting into practice, much of what is covered, meaning that little new knowledge is gained;
3. some of the theoretical material covered is considered too abstract from everyday practice to be considered worthwhile;
4. courses can be guilty of trying to cram too much information into a relatively short period of time; and
5. they have come to question much of the information acquired during courses later in their careers.

As a result of such experiences, some coaches admit to attending later awards because of their being a compulsory requirement only. The element of compulsion and the need for certification means that coaches are unlikely to directly contest the programme or coach educator, rather giving an outward appearance of acceptance while still harbouring and hiding their disagreement with, and rejection of, the official coaching orientation (Cushion *et al.* 2003; Chesterfield *et al.* 2010).

Importantly, research investigating coach learning has yet to provide specific, structured, evidence-based suggestions that coaches can use to enhance their learning and effectiveness. Indeed, formal coach education programmes, thought of as key to coaches' development, have been criticised as a low-impact endeavour with a number of failings linked to a lack of concern for how coaches learn. Following a review, Lyle (2007) identified four key themes from recommendations that coaching scholars have put forward as changes to bring about 'better' coach education.

1. designs more closely linked to the perceived demands of coaching;
2. development of personal models of coaching;
3. use of learning theories; and
4. more attention towards the cognitive skills underlying desirable practice.

In the same review, however, Lyle (2007) noted that such ideas are rarely properly evidenced or transferred into practice, while coach educators are often unaware of the multitude of frameworks that could underpin and guide their practices. Generally, although many scholars have made idealistic prescriptions *for* coach learning, the underpinning evidence *of* coach learning remains scant. The coaching literature has been quick to offer solutions to problems that are poorly understood, and there is a need for more robust empirical research that can explain how coaches' learning works, allowing the development of pertinent frameworks that can improve learning and practice within different populations of coaches.

CONCEPTUAL LESSONS

An important distinction is that between coach education systems (the structures, levels and delivery issues) and coach learning (the processes, content and mechanisms through which the coach's behaviour comes to be changed). The latter is often subsumed by the former but there is a danger that it is given less attention. A good exemplar is the design, initiation and development of the National Vocational Qualification (NVQ) and National Standards approach to coach education in the UK. The structures and delivery system, and the basic elements and their associated competences, have been identified, but the individual's means of enhancing their capacities are no further forward. This overstates the case, since there have been advances in the use of supervised experience, mentors and logbooks as elements of good practice have infiltrated the system. Nevertheless, the principle of questioning macro-level decisions put into practice without evidence of micro-level implementation is sound.

The potential benefits of education over the extended trial and error and imitation characteristic of unstructured experience have already been noted. The coach receives the benefit of the wisdom of expert practitioners as their experience is distilled and packaged into coach education. However, this assumes that coach education is based on the practice of experts. Perhaps just as important is the emancipatory and developmental aspect of education. Structured education should provide an opportunity for developing capacities that will enable the coach to move beyond existing practice, to innovate, to experiment, to adapt, to reflect, and build underpinning knowledge and skills for the requirements of 'higher levels' of coaching. Expressed in the language of effectiveness, coaches need to develop a capacity for competent and effective (future) practice, and not merely to polish their existing practice.

The capabilities of the coach have to be matched against the requirements of practice. Put another way, it is not sufficient for coach education and training to produce generic capabilities. There should be a complementarity between the skills and knowledge being developed and the roles that the coaches will fulfil. This has been one of the issues in harmonising levels of award across sports and across countries. What does club coach, senior coach, etc. imply? Numbering, for example levels 1–5, achieves nothing if not related to a meaningful role in practice. Harmonisation is

KEY CONCEPT

Structured education should provide an opportunity for developing capacities that will enable the coach to move beyond existing practice, to innovate, to experiment, to adapt, to reflect and to build underpinning knowledge and skills for the requirements of 'higher levels' of coaching. Coaches need to develop a capacity for competent and effective (future) practice, and not merely to polish their existing practice.

essential for professionalisation, but it and the systems it represents must be based on a sound conceptual understanding of sport coaching, the coaching role and the coaching process. In the UK, the UK Coaching Certificate and a number of governing bodies have attempted to address this with 'Coach Development Models' based on a 4 × 4 approach – four domains of coaching with four levels. Despite the separation of participation and performance coaching in such models, many coaches still conceive of a continuum of coaching where the skills and knowledge requirements necessarily build from one domain to the other.

One issue that has been given some attention is that of the educational 'level' of coach education. A number of factors combine to suggest that performance sport coaching should be a practice that requires a significant level of developed intellect:

- Much of the professional's competence is cognitive.
- Many coaches have experienced higher education.
- The sub-discipline knowledge on which principles of practice are based requires an understanding at an advanced level.
- Coach education materials have been successfully incorporated in undergraduate and postgraduate degrees in the UK.
- There now exists some alignment of coaching qualifications with 'advanced'/ performance coaching awards (UKCC Level 4) at postgraduate degree level.

Nevertheless, this remains a tricky conceptual issue. Anecdotal evidence suggests that the performance-coaching role can be fulfilled without recourse to the kind of developed intellectual activity required for analysis and synthesis of knowledge. Coaches can work from common sense, experiential recipes and prescriptions without testing these from first principles. Because practice is cognitive and the knowledge base and skills are tacit, practice may not be reflective of the adjustment to the complexity and dynamism of the coaching process that is assumed throughout the book. Raising issues such as these points to the importance of research into coaching practice and reinforces many of the, as yet unanswered, questions about the coach's contribution to athlete performance, the difference between success and effectiveness and, very importantly, the extent to which coaching process competences are actually assessed during education and training.

305

COACH LEARNING AND COACHING PRACTICE

The question for this section is whether there is anything about coaching practice to suggest that there is a conceptualisation of coach education that would be the most appropriate. How should the coach learning process be structured? In addition to the specificity of the sport coaching process and the sport within which they operate, coaches require a particular configuration of skills and knowledge to cope with a complex and multi-variable process, with multiple goals and a very dynamic environment. Coaches exhibit process-related skills of planning, monitoring and regulating. At the same time, coaching is an interpersonal activity and much of the day-to-day activity of the coach is characterised by a variety of face-to-face encounters. The outcome of much of performance coaching is in the public domain and there are accountability, ethical and moral dilemmas to be resolved.

The breadth of the coaching role is demonstrated by the generic coaching competences identified: training programme delivery and management, competition management, strategic planning, personnel management, athlete support, human resource management, organisation and administration, material resource management, extended role fulfilment and contingency management. When focusing more on the operationalisation of the coach's role, the place of recipe planning, contingency planning, threshold regulation, mental models of performance and strategic coordination of progress and goal attainment were identified. Coaches also have social and organisational responsibilities and personal development to consider.

The purpose of the previous two paragraphs is to add to the discussion of the basis on which coach education should be structured and fashioned. Coaches need: to gain experience at the higher levels; to be mentored by a more experienced coach; to learn from others; to balance personal and professional priorities; and to obtain cutting-edge technical information. The inference to be taken here is that these requirements do not consistently and evenly form the basis of current coach education. The issue is not the sub-division into the categories of educational experiences outlined above, but the nature of the coach learning experience that characterises it. A review of these requirements provides the following principles for coach education and training: role-related competences; usable competences; cognitive organisation; process management skills; capacity for performance; progression; interpersonal skills; sport specificity; management; practice/experience based; and research-based education and training.

1. Role-related competences

The competences identified for coaches need to be role-related and this requires a sound appreciation of the coaching process. The range of role-related competences was illustrated above – competition management, strategic planning, programme delivery, etc. A key factor here is the requirement not to focus solely on direct intervention, although, even in this set of competences, the appropriate performance sport intervention management role has to be recognised.

2. Usable competences

One of the terms that emerges from a discussion of coaching effectiveness is 'application': because of the dynamics of the coaching process, the coach must be able to apply the principles of good practice and other sub-discipline knowledge. In other words, the coach must be able to translate knowledge into effective behaviour. This has two elements. First, the presentation of knowledge needs to acknowledge the distinctions between procedural and propositional knowledge (Abraham & Collins 1998), and second, the integration of theory and practice should not be left to the coach. All education programmes struggle with the need to integrate theory and practice, but innovative ways of developing these links must be found. At the same time, there must be sufficient underpinning sub-discipline knowledge to allow coaches to apply theoretical principles to novel situations and to analyse the prescriptions of others.

3. Cognitive organisation

The role of the coach is sufficiently well understood for the significance of cognitive processes to the coach's day-to-day activities to be appreciated. An absolutely vital part of the coach's skills are the decision making and modelling skills that have been given considerable attention throughout the chapters. Decision making is a capacity that changes as the coach moves from novice to expert: the deliberative problem-solving skills using recipes and routines are very different from the non-deliberative contest management skills of some sport coaches and the crisis management decision making required to cope with the dynamics of the coaching process. The use of mental models to 'manage' and regulate progress and the use of threshold values to minimise derailed regulation is insufficiently understood, but needs to be acknowledged. An example of the emphasis on cognitive skills is the nature of the relationship between mentor and coach. The real benefit to the trainee coach is not the principles on which decisions are based (albeit very useful), but how these are translated into decisions. This is required to assist the trainee to make the next difficult decision.

4. Process management skills

These have been emphasised throughout the book, but it is worth repeating their importance. Performance sport coaching is a process and the educated, effective and expert coach must be able to manage the process. This requires skills of planning, monitoring, regulating and evaluating. As described above, these process skills can be most effective when integrated into role-related competences. Note, however, that many of the process skills require cognitive organisation. A balance has to be struck between learning the professional shortcuts used by the experts and building this competence on a foundation of deliberative knowledge and analysis. Despite the many advantages, one of the potential dangers of moving too directly from performer to coach is that of acquiring some of the professional practice without the foundation to adapt, apply and contextualise as necessary.

5. Capacity for performance

Once again, this principle overlaps with some already identified. The effective coach is one who has the capacity for effective performance. The education and training process should create that capacity for performance. The capacity will be created best by:

- focusing on process-related skills;
- ensuring the development of theory into practice;
- emphasising the contextualisation and adaptation of knowledge and principles; and
- pursuing an element of individualisation within the programme (clearly there has to be a degree of standardisation of delivery and assessment; however, minimum competency can be extended by an education programme designed to fit the needs of individual performance coaches).

6. Progression

There is an assumption that education programmes will have a progressive and cumulative effect. However, what is it that is becoming more advanced? It is not simply more technical knowledge (although that is vital). Lessons have to be learned from novice–expert differences. The coach's competences have to be improved by dealing with more challenging problems, applying more advanced knowledge, dealing with more difficult 'cases'. Building more complex solutions – prescriptions, scenarios, schemata, scripts, increasing interpersonal skills, presenting more challenging contest management patterns. At the same time, the coach's learning and experience have been building through coaching practice – the more advanced levels of coach education will adapt and apply that knowledge and experience. However, further clarity is required on the stages or levels of professional development through which the coach will progress. These have to integrate novice–expert levels, role descriptors within coaching practice and skills and knowledge expectations at each level.

7. Interpersonal skills

Coaching is an interpersonal activity and the implications of good/bad relationships can be felt in athlete satisfaction, motivation, dealing with problem solving, athlete support and development and the interpersonal climate that characterises day-to-day coaching activity. It is also key in the coach's adherence to a code of ethics. Although the early stages of certification include some simplistic relationship principles, coach education programmes have not been characterised by attention to this aspect of practice; nor can recruitment gateways have been said to sift on the basis of suitability for a positive disposition towards interpersonal skills. This could

Coach education and coaching practice

be thought to be surprising given the intensity of relationships in performance sport but, more realistically, it reinforces the lack of sophistication of some aspects of current provision. Although this element of coaching competence and effectiveness has been left to in-role socialisation and personal dispositions, future education and training ought to accord it a much higher priority.

8. Sport specificity

The earlier chapter dealing with the implementation of the coaching process identified a number of factors that suggest that coach education programmes will be distinctive and sport-specific. The technique and training dominating individual power sports and interactive team sports will shape differently the coach education requirements of their sports. One very important element of the coach's role is 'match-coaching' (in some sports) and a more general contest-management role in others. Match-coaching has not been given sufficient attention in coach education and appears to be left to 'experience' and trial and error for coaches to establish good practice.

9. Management

A cursory review of the suggested coaching process competences will show that many of them are characterised as 'management' functions. This has a number of implications. First, there may be some potential for teaching basic management principles (while acknowledging the above plea for role-related competences). Second, there is sufficient genericism for the role of the coach to be portrayed as that of a manager – particularly in the more complex context of high-level performance sport. The management element of the coaching role demonstrates why there has been an entrepreneurial transition into 'management education' by using the principles of coaching and team building.

10. Practice/experience based

This may seem an obvious suggestion when coach education now generally requires a period of supervised experience involving a mentor, the completion of logbooks, a period of experience before moving to the next level of award and the inclusion of exemplar sessions and practice-based teaching. However, these have been fairly recent developments for most sports. Two issues are important:

1. The role of the mentor is very important.
2. The value to the trainee coach of transiting to coaching from a performance sport background becomes obvious.

Most writers in the field advocate coaching apprenticeship schemes in various forms, and these have been built into the structure of coach education and training for performance sport (for example in the UK the 'Elite Coach Apprenticeship Schemes' (ECAP) run by UK Sport and the Premier League in football).

11. Research-based education and training

It is hardly novel to suggest that education should be based on research. However, despite a growing research base into coach education – and, indeed, into some aspects of coaching practice – as has already been suggested, research providing evidence of 'what works' is limited. It should be made very clear to trainee coaches that the prescriptions and principles of good practice to which they are exposed have been derived from research on expert coaches. Part of the education process should be to make the coaches aware of the research that has been conducted. Clearly, and given that the principle is not contentious, the exhortation is for more research into coaching practice and coach education.

The limited amount of time that coaches have to invest in their preparation has been noted (Abraham & Collins 1998), and the appropriateness of 'weekend education programmes' is questionable if we want to facilitate coach learning and development by taking experience into account (Trudel & Gilbert 2006). These reservations notwithstanding, any learning method in addition to the principles outlined also needs clear tutor/facilitator training and support, and needs a well-planned curriculum with clear learning objectives (Cushion *et al.* 2010). In light of what has been discussed so far in the chapter, the following need to be addressed:

1. The issues already identified from existing research of current formal provision need to be addressed.
2. Longitudinal research is required, examining how existing formal learning impacts coaches' knowledge, practice and athlete learning.
3. Research is required that compares different approaches to coach learning and their impact on coaches' knowledge, practice and athlete learning.

A CONTEMPORARY THEORY OF COACHES' LEARNING

This leads us to present some recent empirical research (Stodter & Cushion 2016) that resulted in a substantive model of the processes of coaches' learning, highlighting 'what works' and why. Based on a longitudinal project that collected data from twenty-five English youth soccer coaches taking part in formal and informal learning alongside their regular coaching practice, a grounded theory was developed (see Figure 14.1; also see Stodter & Cushion 2014, 2016). This framework shows the mechanisms involved in the cognitive filter process described above, where coaches' existing biography (experiences, knowledge, beliefs and practice) forms a screen through which all future events will pass. As a result, apparently similar learning situations can result in entirely different outcomes for individual coaches (Stodter & Cushion 2016). The learning filter process (Figure 14.1) shows how coaches approach and learn from different coach education and practice-related experiences. Actions, conditions and consequences are shown in boxes, while arrows represent the links between these, depicting directional processes. Knowledge and practice, as well as beliefs about coaching and 'what works', are closely intertwined, framing coach learning where different elements play roles in all stages of the learning process.

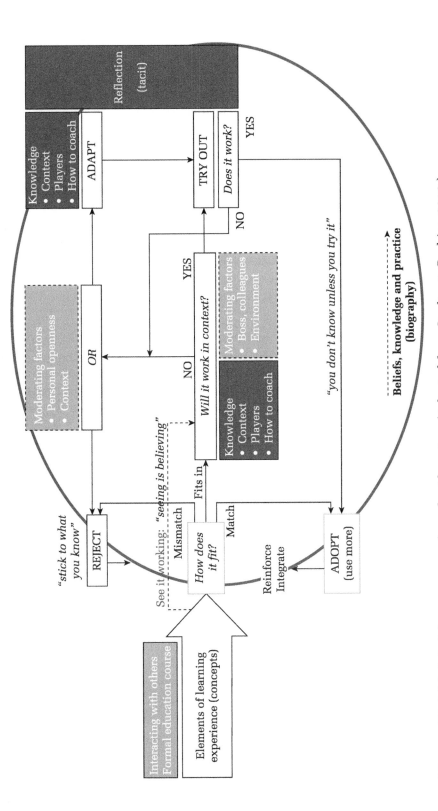

Figure 14.1 Model of the processes of coaches' learning. (Adapted from Stodter & Cushion 2016.)

The model illustrates the individual focus of cognitive behavioural approaches, but places the individual as an active agent in the process, which takes place in interaction with others in wider contexts.

The multi-level approach has two central elements that make up a double-loop filter process (Stodter & Cushion 2014). The coach's knowledge, beliefs and practice at the individual level precede a secondary level contextual filter. The elements of any learning experience engaged in by the coach must therefore pass through these two levels before new knowledge can be translated into practice and 'tried out', for potential full integration to the coach's repertoire. Thus new concepts move through the process from beliefs and knowledge towards practice. In addition, reflective processes also have a role in the adaptation of constructed knowledge. A significant element in coach learning is a pragmatic desire for relevant, practical knowledge that 'works', leading to enhanced coaching ability.

Coaches perceive wider learning experiences in terms of the various ideas, or 'bits' of knowledge available (i.e. knowledge concepts (Entwistle *et al.* 2000; Abraham *et al.* 2006)). Often encountered through formal education, concepts have a shared rather than personal meaning characterised by specific procedural knowledge, and underpinned by associated declarative knowledge (Abraham *et al.* 2006). Stodter and Cushion (2016) describe an initial cognitive filter process taking place at the individual level, with coaches identifying new knowledge concepts as matching, mismatching or fitting in with their personal existing knowledge, beliefs and practice. Each of these alternatives has different consequences for actions further down the process chain, and therefore for subsequent implementation and behaviour. While matching concepts lead to confirmation and reinforcement, or non-reflective assimilation, mismatching concepts are 'filtered out' and rejected. This process of collecting evidence to confirm pre-existing knowledge, while rejecting concepts that are more challenging, has been labelled 'safe simulation' (cf. Cushion, 2013) and is relatively commonly reported. Concepts that are new to coaches, yet fit in with their biography, are tried out *if* the coach believes they would work in context. Coaches describe this as experiential, trial and error learning, regardless of the original source of the ideas being tested. Abraham *et al.* (2006), for example, explained this process as the internalisation of concepts, which become conceptions as they are applied to a particular context meaningful to the practitioner. With the addition of the 'try out' reflective loop in the current model, each particular conception becomes available for use in the same type of situation it was implemented in, with its meaning embedded in experiences of using it. Consequently, coaches put great emphasis on 'what works' in practice, with the judgements of and consequent rejections or adaptations, based on a feedback-loop process. When coaches perceive that the new learning does not work in practice, having tried it out, they progress to either reject it or enter into a cycle of continuous adaptation and experimentation, akin to Schön's (1987) 'reflective conversation' (see also Gilbert & Trudel 2001). If the outcome of using the new knowledge in context is satisfactory, the individual adopts it as part of their 'tried and tested' practice repertoire for sustained use, integrating it into their coaching biography. In this way, coaches are constantly working through a cycle of constructing and linking new knowledge, tightly bound to context-specific practice,

Coach education and coaching practice

into their existing knowledge structures. Newly updated biography in turn acts as a filter for the next learning experience engaged in, meaning that the coach's knowledge, beliefs and practice are in a constantly dynamic state of flux.

 KEY CONCEPT

Coaches are constantly working through a cycle of constructing and linking new knowledge, tightly bound to context-specific practice, into their existing knowledge structures. Newly updated biography in turn acts as a filter for the next learning experience engaged in, meaning that the coach's knowledge, beliefs and practice are in a constantly dynamic state of flux.

Stodter and Cushion (2016) go on to explain the choice between rejecting and adapting conceptions as part of the reflective feedback loop, which is identified as a significant feature of the learning process. Coaches refer to their own personal openness and contextual factors when discussing this (often tacit) reflective practice. Since coaching and management are often strongly associated with maximising performance success and winning (inside and outside of the performance domain), with practitioners accountable for and dependent on achievement of such outcomes, it is perhaps understandable that they "are reluctant to take risks or depart too far from the status quo of accepted practice" (Light & Robert 2010, p. 113). Coaches' reflective cycles of learning are bound up with coaching practice that often takes place in contexts subject to power relationships and deeply held anti-intellectual beliefs. Consequently, while learning situated in everyday practice is essential, coaching environments are not often conducive to generating new ideas, supporting active experimentation or facilitating transfer from knowledge to implementation (Stodter & Cushion 2016). These contexts, combined with personal openness, impinge on coaches' reflective feedback cycles and the overall 'quality' of learning. Individual subscription to 'right' and 'wrong' ways of coaching underpinned by legitimate knowledge provided by authorities, such as club bosses, follows a dualistic assumption about knowledge (Entwistle & Peterson 2004). Individuals holding these more absolute, closed ideas about knowledge tend to also approach learning as simple reproduction of the accepted norm (Entwistle & Peterson 2004; Piggott 2013). As people begin to recognise knowledge as provisional and relative, evidence is used to reason among alternatives (Entwistle & Peterson 2004); in other words, experimenting with and critically evaluating new conceptions in practice based on 'what works'. Abraham et al. (2009) compared such practitioners to chefs who use in-depth knowledge of ingredients to develop new ideas and orchestrate successful outcomes, as opposed to 'cooks' who live by other people's tried-and-tested recipes as safe simulators (Cushion 2013). Alongside an appreciation of the relative nature of coaching knowledge, learning is said to become more reliant on individuals' efforts to fully understand ideas for themselves, by relating them to previous knowledge and experiences, thereby seeing things in a different light. Thus the idea of meaningful, transformative learning (Mezirow 2009) rests on the open-minded transformation and implementation of conceptions in practice, through reflective linkage with existing knowledge as presented in the model (Figure 14.1; Stodter & Cushion 2016).

DELIVERY ISSUES AND ENHANCING MEANINGFUL LEARNING

The work of Stodter and Cushion (2016) usefully re-affirms that two prominent variables must be considered and accounted for in the design and delivery of coach learning opportunities: namely individuals' biographies and coaching contexts. This is not a new idea, as it has been accepted for some time that coaches' belief systems exert a huge influence in constructing coaching practice. Nevertheless, the design and provision of coach learning has consistently failed to accommodate this. Individualised, contextually and practically relevant learning opportunities are most valuable for coaches in any learning situation, and therefore 'one size does not fit all' in coach education. Coaches' 'filter' and reflective processes are often uncritical and inadvertent, based on tacit understanding of how to implement concepts in context and implicit judgements of 'what works'. These processes could usefully be targeted to enhance the impact of learning situations.

Reflective practice

Ideas about reflection have spread across a range of domains, including nursing, healthcare and teaching. However, across these practice fields there remain concerns about the relationship between reflection and effective behaviour. That said, reflective practice is particularly relevant in situations such as sport coaching, in which practice is complex, applied and contextualised, and in which learning therefore requires a degree of introspection. Reflection allows this introspection most significantly into professional practice that is characterised, as sport coaching is, by tacit knowledge, cognitive professional shortcuts (recipes, routines, mental models) and non-deliberative and contingent decision making. In order to learn from experience, it is necessary to generate an understanding and appreciation of practice for subsequent analysis. The various elements of practice can then be examined against established principles and goals, and behaviour either reinforced or amended. While reflection may be useful for monitoring and evaluating procedures such as analysis of planning decisions, it is perhaps most beneficial in 'behavioural role activity'. In sport coaching, examples of this might be interpersonal relationship interaction between athlete and coach, directing drills/exercises, or competition management behaviour by a coach during a match. Hence, reflection appears to offer a great deal for understanding about how coaches learn experientially, but a caveat is that these arguments tend not to be supported empirically.

What is clear is that a sound understanding of the coaching process is required for successful reflection on coaching experiences. Arguably, the best theoretically

314

KEY CONCEPT

Reflection appears to offer a great deal for understanding about how coaches learn experientially, but a caveat is that these arguments tend not to be supported empirically.

framed explanation for how coaches learn experientially, through the process of reflection, has come from Gilbert and Trudel's (2001) experiential learning model. The authors demonstrate how coaches learned by engaging in three forms of reflective practice:

1. reflection-in-action (i.e. during the action present);
2. reflection-on-action (i.e. within the action present but not in the midst of activity);
3. retrospective reflection-on-action (i.e. outside of the action present).

In so doing, Gilbert and Trudel (2001, 2004, 2005) presented evidence that Schön's (1983) theory of reflective practice provides an effective framework for analysing and explaining how coaches frame their knowledge and learn from practical coaching experiences. While Gilbert and Trudel's work has provided great insight into how coaches engaged in the process of reflection, there remain concerns about the relationship between reflection and effective coaching behaviour and practice (Cushion *et al.* 2010). Related to this is an awareness of a 'depth dimension' to reflection and a recognition that superficial reflection may not be effective as a means of learning (Cushion & Nelson 2013). Much activity is performed in the name of reflection because it is in fact largely non-critical and non-reflective, suggesting therefore that reflection has a range of applications, with a continuum from shallow description at one end to deep critical reflection at the other (Cushion *et al.* 2010; Cushion & Nelson 2013). The key to this process is learning the skill of reflection and allowing enough time for the skill to be developed and supported. Indeed, the "development of reflective skills is not a simplistic process even with structured support. Coach educators cannot therefore assume that development of reflective skills will be a naturally occurring phenomena that runs parallel to increasing coaching experience" (Knowles *et al.* 2001, p. 204). Reflective strategies can be used in coach learning, but these approaches also require time, commitment and programmatic effort (Trudel & Gilbert 2006). The question therefore remains, how much might learning to reflect on a course be used in actual coaching practice? A similar issue can be found in the education domain, where "educators seem to assume that reflective thinking learned via reflective practice would be retained, generalised and or transferred to ordinary settings. No evidence exists to support this assumption" (Tsangaridou & Siedentop 1995, p. 228).

While reflective practice is often identified as beneficial for coaches' development, formal education provision fails to provide adequate support for the process (Cushion & Nelson 2013; Knowles *et al.* 2001). Coach educators should not continue to assume that explicit reflection will 'just happen' as a naturally occurring phenomenon (Knowles *et al.* 2001). Coaches need more support to uncover and link their underlying reasoning, assumptions and values to disjunctive concepts, transforming them for integration into biography, thus deepening meaningful learning (Stodter & Cushion 2016). Reflection involves a structured approach and makes use of procedures such as journals/diaries, stimulated recall, de-briefings, reflective conversations and analysis of critical incidents. The 'analysis' of questioning must also be structured. Ghaye and Lillyman (2000) suggest a series of 'frames' through which events can be re-evaluated:

- *Role framing*: was the role exercised appropriately? How might it have been done differently?
- *Temporal framing*: was the sequence of events appropriate? Were any of the decisions too soon or too late? Why?
- *Problem framing*: what was the problem? Was it identified appropriately? Did everyone involved perceive the problem in the same way?
- *Value framing*: were any value-positions evident during the experiential events? Were there any value conflicts?
- *Parallel process framing*: could the outcomes have been different? Construct an alternative sequence of events and behaviours with a different outcome.

This could be achieved through a number of avenues. First, reflection should be structured around coaches' existing authentic practice. It is suggested that an emphasis on drawing links between new concepts and tacit knowledge for implementation, as well as live experimentation and adaptation, would be effective in terms of impact on learning. Linked to this, the notion of 'what works' is significant in coaches' choices to implement and adopt certain conceptions over others. Educators could help individuals examine and challenge what practice that 'works' looks like in context, deconstructing 'assumed know-how' and demonstrating how it may constitute a limited base for practice.

Learning can also be enhanced through specifically designed teaching methods and products. Perhaps the most important of these products are those that engage the coach actively with realistic exemplars that are designed to illustrate particular principles 'that work'. Obvious examples are

- detailed case studies for planning and inter-personal skills;
- interactive video scenarios for decision making; and
- problem-solving exercises.

Video can be a powerful and flexible tool to facilitate judgements of 'what really works' and reflective practice more generally. Stodter and Cushion (2016) suggest a number of ways that video could usefully be employed; for example:

1. Coaches could be supported to cultivate their own peer video reflection groups while coach educators could facilitate coaches' deep learning by using video to explicate tacit cognitive processes vital for the implementation of knowledge (see Partington *et al.* 2015).

316

2. Video could also quite straightforwardly enhance the impact of coach educators on coaches' learning by helping to construct their own knowledge of learners' individual biographies.
3. Videos of candidates' pre-course coaching sessions or even meetings of a format similar to the stimulated recall protocol could help coach educators understand and work with the starting points and 'frames of reference' of individual learners.

In developing reflective feedback loop mechanisms, coaches need opportunities to experiment with implementing new knowledge in contexts that are highly realistic, yet open to innovation and occasional failure. Realism is vital to allow practitioners to make valid links between concepts and implementation, since conceptions are understood and linked primarily to the types of situations in which they are learned. Thus, there are a number of conceptual caveats to be addressed:

- Reflection must be complemented by an understanding of coaching practice as a cognitive activity.
- Reflection is not a 'process for its own sake' and the coach must, therefore, have knowledge of principles of good practice and prescriptions in order to inform the analysis and evaluate solutions.
- Reflection would appear to be a particularly useful procedure with mentoring (discussed below). However, the shared reflection process depends on a shared vocabulary and understanding of the coaching process in addition to a developed and developing schemata and scripts for performance sport.
- Reflection on emotion-laden activity is acknowledged to be difficult. The win–lose, contested nature of sport activity is often tinged with emotion, of coach and athletes, and this will bring additional challenges.
- Participation coaching is episodic in nature. Reflection may be valuable for analysing the coach's behaviour in such circumstances. Nevertheless, the performance coach has a more strategic, metacognitive overview of a complex, dynamic and more long-term process. Reflecting on either isolated incidents within the 'bigger picture' or reflecting on more extended processes will also bring particular challenges.
- Reflection is part of a broader learning process and ought, therefore, to be integrated into its other stages. In other words, reflection should not be solely a summative activity. This has been described as pre-flecting (anticipation, goal-setting, scenario building), in-flecting (Schön's (1983) reflection-in-action) and re-flecting.

Mentoring

Mentoring has been identified as offering both structured and unstructured support for coach learning, and several authors have outlined the pervasiveness and impact of mentoring in coaching. Indeed, influencing the experiences and interactions of coaches is widely suggested where mentoring is conceived as bringing an increasing formalisation of a practice that is inherently informal (Cushion & Nelson 2013). The issue, therefore, is not that it should be part of the delivery system, but how coach learning can be better enhanced by its practice.

Colley *et al.* (2003) strike a cautionary note concerning problems with formalising mentoring as 'fervour without infrastructure' (Freedman 1999, p. 2). They argue that the perception of mentoring as inherently informal means minimal training and support for mentors. Formal mentoring can expose the frailty of dyadic models of mentoring relationships and introduces the triadic element of external interests pursued by dominant groupings (Colley *et al.* 2003; Jones *et al.* 2009). The findings from the reviews and research into mentoring suggest that there can be unthinking assumptions that such transference is straightforward (Cushion *et al.* 2010). In fact, the mentoring process changes as it becomes applied through planned programmes in formalised situations (Cushion & Nelson 2013). The success of learning will be dependent upon the quality of the relationship between mentor and protégé. Indeed, there are common issues identified that negatively impact mentoring, including:

■ lack of time and training;
■ personal or professional compatibility;
■ undesirable attitudes or behaviours; and
■ unnoticed workloads.

Mentees were concerned with a lack of mentor interest and training, and problematic behaviours (overly critical, defensive and controlling) (Cushion *et al.* 2010). In addition, Jones *et al.* (2009) highlight 'toxic mentoring' with asymmetric power relationships shaping both the mentoring experience and the learning that takes place. An important distinction is that between the mentor's supervisory and monitoring role and the master–apprentice role. It is a structured approach to this function that is required. The coach must have available a number of procedures for interrogating practice – stimulated recall, question and answer, critical analysis of practice, simulated examples and joint reflection. This is, of course, in addition to the 'situated learning' (see below for a discussion of situated learning) that occurs from interaction and observation. Through this experience, the coach is building the mental models required for professional practice. Of course, the mentor must be trained to allow the trainee 'space' to build individualised models, and to recognise the importance of adaptation, application and contextualisation of the mentor's own practice.

"Mentoring is a highly complex dynamic and interpersonal relationship that requires at the very least, time, interest and commitment of mentors and mentees and strong support from educational or organisational leaders responsible for overseeing programmes" (Ehrich *et al.* 2004, p. 533). Much of the wider mentoring literature and coaching-related work offers theories and ideas '*for*' mentoring, rather than evidence '*of*' mentoring. This is a perspective reiterated by Jones *et al.* (2009), who suggest that many of the claims about mentoring are largely unfounded. These authors cite Colley *et al.* (2003, p. 1), who conclude that "existing research evidence scarcely justifies [mentoring's] use on such a massive scale, [while] the movement has not yet developed a sound theoretical base to underpin policy or practice".

318

Coach education tutors

Many of these implications rely on the skills of coach educators to be able to facilitate learning through active listening and effective questioning, and to build reflective partnerships free from micro-political manoeuvrings. Hence coach education tutors must be trained to deliver coach education. It can be assumed that some teaching skills are required, but the role of the tutor may be more appropriately conceived as that of facilitator. Key to this is a capacity to analyse performance, simulate practice, employ supporting knowledge products and demonstrate application. It seems unlikely that this role (unlike the specialist delivery of technical sub-discipline knowledge) could be achieved by other than an individual with considerable coaching experience and a very sound appreciation of the coaching process. Tutors can support practitioners integrating new ideas into situated action by scaffolding the reflection and adaptation process, but more challenging performance contexts may require further strategies. A possible strategy in this respect could be using evidence to persuade stakeholders that the desired practices work. Since for practitioners, "seeing is believing" (Nelson *et al.* 2012, p. 7), as Stodter and Cushion (2016) suggest, coach education tutors can provide clear demonstrations of the worth of different approaches, and ways to apply them in specific contexts, rather than attempting to initiate change through shifting deeply ingrained values and cultures.

Situated learning

Situated learning is a theory that has been offered as having utility to explain and frame learning within the coaching domain. First conceptualised by Lave and Wenger (1991), who were unhappy with overly simplistic views of learning 'by doing', they argue instead for learning to be conceived as a complex, relational and situated endeavour. This required a conceptual shift from the traditional view of "the individual as learner to learning as participation in the social world, and from the concept of cognitive process to the more-encompassing view of social practice" (Lave & Wenger 1991, p. 43). They argue that social practice is the primary, generative phenomenon, and learning is one of its characteristics, and as such should be analysed as an integral part of social practice. This view seems to be analogous with the evidence from coaching on how knowledge evolves from practice (Cushion & Nelson 2013; Cushion *et al.* 2010).

Through situated learning, coaches progress towards crucial 'core' tasks, thus moving from peripheral to full or central participation, with understanding unfolding as the learner develops a view of what the activity entails (Cushion & Nelson 2013). This process ensures that learning is an improvised practice in which the 'curriculum' unfolds in opportunities for engaging in practice and the individual is located within a community of practice that facilitates learning through mutual engagement in an activity that is defined by negotiations of meaning both inside and outside the community. As communities are social structures, they involve power relations, and the way power is exercised can make legitimate peripheral participation empowering or disempowering. Examples from coaching are presented by Culver and Trudel (2006) and Culver *et al.* (2009), who cultivated coaching communities of practice (CCoPs). The results of these studies suggested that a facilitator played an important role in the group learning process, adding a certain amount of structure to the learning (Culver & Trudel 2008). However, it is the processes, relationships and experiences that constitute the participants' sense of belonging that underpin the character and extent of subsequent learning. Therefore, it could be argued that the nature of 'manufactured' or 'facilitated' CCoPs do not engage the coaches' sense of belonging, existing only in a superficial sense and thus inhibiting any meaningful learning (Cushion & Nelson 2013).

Innovation

It is important that coach developers consider innovative ways of maximising the coach's operational behaviour. An example might be the mechanisms for improving coaches' decision making in order to micro-manage the flow of intervention. The coach's association of problem and potential solution is enhanced when the developer is able to create educational opportunities that 'prime' the coach's decision making through realistic scenarios, identification of cues, initial structure and increasing accountability. In reality, the coach's real-time practice may not allow this to take place, and it is therefore necessary to be innovative in creating a development programme to engage coaches' thinking within a realistic practice intervention. There is a wealth of literature on the importance of mental models and cognitive organisation, but little about how they might be enhanced. The following example has been adapted from ideas by Shadrick and Lussier (2009), and we present it as an example of innovative practice.

Hence, there is a need to situate coaches' learning in the practical experience of coaching in an appropriate and supportive 'natural' and not manufactured context. Such practical experience elements of education and training have a number of purposes and each of these indicates the need for a supportive environment:

- Practice allows an element of trial and error, and the 'practice of changed behaviour'. This needs a supportive environment.
- Changed behaviour needs time and reinforcement to take effect. This cannot be done without practice.
- A practicum also allows for an element of assessment and monitoring to take place.
- The delivery aspect of coaching requires attention and practice. However, many of the process elements of coaching (planning, monitoring and regulating) can only appropriately be enacted over a period of time.
- Decision making often requires an appreciation of the context within which the decision must be taken – an understanding of the contributory factors. This can best be achieved using experiential practice.
- The practice element creates a real-life context in which adaptation, resolution of ethical issues and problem solving are required.

TRAINING ADAPTIVE DECISION MAKING: A PRACTICE SCENARIO IN VOLLEYBALL

Approach

- Break the role into (problematic) functions.
- Construct model themes/questions.
- Create a series of highly complex and unpredictable (tactical) situations or vignettes (typical and challenging).
- Initially the coach developer is employed, but assistant coaches can be used during games, or video of games can be reviewed.

Example of prompt questions (for game activity, but amended for training sessions)

- Why did the other coach do that?
- Why are the opposition playing like that?
- Are my players performing as expected?
- Is this (action) helping to achieve my goal?
- What is the balance of strengths and weaknesses on each side?
- Are we still on course for achieving our goal/target?
- What is the current balance of momentum?
- What is the big strategic picture?

Development process

- The intention is to develop 'thought habits'.
- Coaches engage in their practice, but this is halted after, say, ten minutes. Coaches are then led through some of the questions over a period of two minutes. This is continued.
- There is particular attention to 'triggers' for action (this may be structured to some extent by the developer).
- Coaches are encouraged to defend decisions and identify implications.
- The time given for the coaches to reflect on the questions is gradually reduced over time (many sessions); the ultimate aim is that coaches attend to these questions without conscious thought – but this is checked through reflective practices.
- Coaches move from a conscious focus on problem areas, areas of weakness or key aspects of expertise to a more semi-deliberate decision making.
- Developers give feedback, manage scenarios, engage in reflection with coaches and may encourage attention to new knowledge.
- Progress is measured by success in dealing with problematic issues.

- It is important that the coach has some responsibility and accountability for the results of the experiential period. This again needs a supportive environment.
- Socialisation into the role of the coach and an appreciation of the organisational management issues can best be appreciated through situated experience.

Given these demands, the most appropriate solution would be a practicum in the coach's own situation, and preferably working with a more experienced mentor from within that organisation. This is one of the reasons that assistant coach positions are important in performance sport.

CONCLUDING THOUGHTS

We have demonstrated that there are a number of issues with the effectiveness of coach education systems:

- the absence of a consensual model of development;
- the absence of a clear and consensual understanding of coaches' expertise;
- the perception of a lack of direct relevance to coaching roles;
- a concern that coach education may reinforce existing values, without an opportunity for emancipatory innovation; and
- practical issues of standardisation across multi-site delivery, minimal time demands, and validity of assessments.

This means we have to be realistic about what can be achieved (and perhaps 'tone down' a number of our criticisms) in the context of formal education at the early stages of certification and in a mass-delivery format. Nevertheless, formal education is an important milestone in coaches' career development (Erickson *et al.* 2007), and we have suggested a number of mechanisms by which it might be improved. We emphasise strongly that formal coach education cannot encompass all of the experiential learning required to 'embed' learning, and the potential disadvantages of informal educational opportunities can be ameliorated by elements of structured mentoring and learning contracts.

We tentatively propose that there might be a two-tier education system for sport coaches to address issues of practicality, motive and conceptual difference between distinctive roles within the 'family of sport coaching'. Rewards mechanisms are not in place for the majority of those who begin the certification pathway; it is not possible to encourage these 'starters' to a more demanding, expensive and lengthy education and training. Indeed, a task for those who are critical of certification is to compare provision to occupational groupings in which there is a mixture of volunteer and professional roles. There would be merit in viewing these initial certification stages as an entry-level pathway, particularly for participation coaching. A second stage of entry to 'chartered' status where demands and expectations would be greater, and coaches are able to benefit from existing practice, would have the potential to create the intellectual and reality-based learning that would contribute more directly to advanced expertise and professionalisation.

Coach education and coaching practice

 **SUMMARY**

This chapter should have familiarised you with the following:

- The nature of education and training and their importance for sport coaching.
- Major developments in coach education and a review of its impact, highlighting perceived shortcomings in current provision.
- The relationship between coach education and a number of conceptual issues: experience, role specificity, intellectual focus and participation/performance coaching differences.
- The structure and delivery of coach education in relation to appropriate learning opportunities.
- Principles for coach education and training.
- A range of delivery issues.
- An insight into reflective practice and some relevant conceptual concerns.

 PROJECTS

1. Select six coaches. Chart all of their education and training courses/workshops, etc. in relation to changes in their coaching roles. Try to compare their perceptions of role-demand with the nature of the courses/workshops, etc. attended.
2. Work with one coach in a longitudinal study. Carry out a needs analysis and agree criteria for improved practice. Monitor changes in practice and the coach's diary of events. Report on your analysis of the nature of learning.
3. Identify criteria for assessing competence in one or more aspect of the coaching process. Investigate coaches' degree of competence at three levels of coaching practice (six coaches in each). Relate this to role-demands and stages in professional development.
4. Select a case study sport with which to work. Collate information on its coach education programme (including content analyses and interviews) and analyse using the eleven principles of coach education and training.
5. Identify a mentor and mentee with whom to work. Ask each of them to maintain a diary and engage in a joint reflection exercise with each of them. Attempt to establish some principles of good practice.

READING

For a comprehensive review of coach learning and development, see Cushion *et al.* (2010) *Coach Learning and Development: A Review of Literature*. This work is summarised and updated in Cushion and Nelson (2013), while Lyle (2007) offers a review of the 'impact' of coach education.

REFERENCES

Abraham, A., & Collins, D. (1998). Examining and extending research in coach development. *Quest, 50*, 59–79.

Abraham, A., Collins, D., & Martindale, R. (2006). The coaching schematic: Validation through expert coach consensus. *Journal of Sports Sciences, 24*(6), 549–564.

Abraham, A., Collins, D., Morgan, G., & Muir, B. (2009). Developing expert coaches requires expert coach development: Replacing serendipity with orchestration. In A. Lorenzo, S. J. Ibanez, & E. Ortega (Eds) *Aportaciones Teoricas Y Practicas Para El Baloncesto Del Futuro*. Sevilla: Wanceulen Editorial Deportiva.

Buckley, R., & Caple, J., (2000). *The Theory and Practice of Training*. 4th edition. London: Kogan Page.

Chesterfield, G., Potrac, P., & Jones, R. L. (2010). 'Studentship' and 'impression management': Coaches' experiences of an advanced soccer coach education award. *Sport, Education and Society, 15*(3), 299–314.

Colley, H., Hodkinson, P., & Malcolm, J. (2003). *Informality and Formality in Learning: A Report for the Learning Skills Research Centre*. London: Learning and Skills Research Centre.

Côté, J. (2006). The development of coaching knowledge. *International Journal of Sports Science & Coaching, 1*(3), 217–222.

Culver, D., & Trudel, P. (2006). Cultivating coaches' communities of practice. In R. L. Jones (Ed.) *The Sports Coach as Educator: Reconceptualising Sports Coaching*. London: Routledge, 113–127.

Culver, D., & Trudel, P. (2008). Clarifying the concept of communities of practice in sport. *International Journal of Sports Science & Coaching, 3*(1), 1–10.

Culver, D., Trudel, P., & Werthner, P. (2009). A sport leader's attempt to foster a coaches' community of practice. *International Journal of Sports Science & Coaching, 4*(3), 365–383.

Cushion, C. J. (2013). Applying game centred approaches in coaching: A critical analysis of the 'dilemmas of practice' impacting change. *Sports Coaching Review, 2*(1), 61–76.

Cushion, C. J., & Nelson, L. (2013). Coach education and learning: Developing the field. In P. Potrac, W. Gilbert, & J. Denison (Eds.) *Routledge Handbook of Sports Coaching*. Abingdon: Routledge, 359–374.

Cushion, C. J., Armour, K. M., & Jones, R. L. (2003). Coach education and continuing professional development: Experience and learning to coach. *Quest, 55*, 215–230.

Cushion, C. J., Nelson, L., Armour, K., Lyle, J., Jones R. L., Sandford, R., & O'Callaghan, C. (2010). *Coach Learning and Development: A Review of Literature*. Leeds: sports coach UK.

Dearden, R. F. (1984). *Theory and Practice in Education.* London: Routledge.

Ehrich, L., Hansford, B., & Tennent, L. (2004). Formal mentoring programs in education and other professions: A review of the literature. *Educational Administration Quarterly, 40*(4), 518–540.

Entwistle, N. J., & Peterson, E. R. (2004). Conceptions of learning and knowledge in higher education: Relationships with study behavior and influences of learning environments. *International Journal of Educational Research, 41,* 407–428.

Entwistle, N., Skinner, D., Entwistle, D., & Orr, S. (2000). Conceptions and beliefs about 'good teaching': An integration of contrasting research areas. *Higher Education Research and Development, 19*(1), 5–26.

Erickson, K., Côté, J., & Fraser-Thomas, J. (2007). Sport experiences, milestones, and educational activities associated with high performance coaches' development. *The Sport Psychologist, 21,* 302–316.

Freedman, M. (1999). *The Kindness of Strangers: Adult Mentors, Urban Youth and the New Voluntarism.* Cambridge: Cambridge University Press.

Ghaye, T., & Lillyman, S. (2000). *Reflection: Principles and Practice for Healthcare Professionals.* Salisbury: Quay Books, Mark Allen Pub.

Gilbert, W. D., & Trudel, P. (2001). Learning to coach through experience: Reflection in model youth sport coaches. *Journal of Teaching in Physical Education, 21,* 16–34.

Gilbert, W. D., & Trudel, P. (2004). Role of the coach: How model youth team sport coaches frame their roles. *The Sport Psychologist, 18,* 21–43.

Gilbert, W. D., & Trudel, P. (2005). Learning to coach through experience: Conditions that influence reflection. *Physical Educator, 61*(1) 32–45.

Griffiths, M. A., & Armour, K. M. (2013). Volunteer sport coaches and their learning dispositions in coach education. *International Journal of Sports Science & Coaching, 8*(4), 677–688.

Jones, R. L., Harris, R. A., & Miles, A. (2009). Mentoring in sports coaching: A review of the literature. *Physical Education and Sport Pedagogy, 14*(3), 267–284.

Knowles, Z., Gilbourne, D., Borrie, A., & Nevill, A. (2001). Developing the reflective sports coach: A study exploring the processes of reflective practice within a higher education coaching programme. *Reflective Practice, 2*(2), 185–207.

Lave, J., & Wenger, E. (1991). *Situated Learning: Legitimate Peripheral Participation.* Cambridge: Cambridge University Press.

Light, R., & Robert, J. E. (2010). The impact of Game Sense pedagogy on Australian rugby coaches' practice: A question of pedagogy. *Physical Education and Sport Pedagogy, 15*(2), 103–115.

Lyle, J. (2007). A review of the research evidence for the impact of coach education. *International Journal of Coaching Science, 1*(1), 17–34.

McCullick, B. A., Schempp, P., Mason, I., Foo, C., Vickers, B., & Connolly, G. (2009). A scrutiny of the coaching education program scholarship since 1995. *Quest, 61,* 322–335.

Mezirow, J. (2009). An overview on transformative learning. In K. Illeris (Ed.) *Contemporary Theories of Learning.* Abingdon: Routledge, 90–105.

North, J. (2009). *Coaching Workforce 2009–2016.* sports coach UK: Leeds.

Nelson, L. J., Cushion, C. J., & Potrac, P. (2006). Formal, nonformal and informal coach learning: A holistic conceptualisation. *International Journal of Sports Science & Coaching, 1*(3), 247–259.

Nelson, L., Cushion, C., & Potrac, P. (2012). Enhancing the provision of coach education: The recommendations of UK coaching practitioners. *Physical Education and Sport Pedagogy*, DOI:10.1080/17408989.2011.649725

Partington, M., Cushion, C., Cope, E., & Harvey, S. (2015). The impact of video feedback on professional youth football coaches' reflection and practice behaviour: A longitudinal investigation of behaviour change. *Reflective Practice, 16*(5), 700–716.

Piggott, D. (2013). The Open Society and coach education: A philosophical agenda for policy reform and future sociological research. *Physical Education and Sport Pedagogy*. DOI: 10.1080/17408383.2013.837435

Rogers, A. (2002). *Teaching Adults* (3rd edn). Buckingham: Open University Press.

Schempp, P. G., & McCullick, B. (2010). Coaches' expertise. In J. Lyle & C. Cushion (Eds) *Sports Coaching: Professionalisation and Practice*. Edinburgh: Churchill Livingstone, 221–231.

Schön, D. A. (1983). *The Reflective Practitioner: How Professionals Think in Action*. New York: Basic Books.

Schön, D. A. (1987). *Educating the Reflective Practitioner*. San Francisco, CA: Jossey-Bass.

Shadrick, S. B., & Lussier, J. W. (2009). Training complex cognitive skills: A theme-based approach to the development of battlefield skills. In K. A. Ericsson (Ed.) *The Development of Professional Expertise: Toward Measurement of Expert Performance and Design of Optimal Learning Environments*. New York: Cambridge University Press, 286–311.

Stodter, A., & Cushion, C. J. (2014). Coaches' learning and education: A case study of cultures in conflict. *Sports Coaching Review, 3*(1), 63–79.

Stodter, A., & Cushion, C. J. (2016). Effective coach learning and processes of coaches' knowledge development: What works? In P. A. Davis (Ed.) *The Psychology of Effective Coaching and Management*. New York: Nova Science Publishers, 35–52.

Trudel, P., & Gilbert, W. (2006). Coaching and coach education. In D. Kirk, M. O'Sullivan, & D. McDonald (Eds) *Handbook of Research in Physical Education*. London: Sage, 516–539.

Tsangaridou, N., & Siedentop, D. (1995). Reflective teaching: A literature review. *Quest, 47*(2), 212–237.

Werthner, P., & Trudel, P. (2009). Investigating the idiosyncratic learning paths of elite Canadian coaches. *International Journal of Sports Science & Coaching, 4*, 433–449.

CHAPTER 15

SETTING A RESEARCH AGENDA

CHAPTER OUTLINE

- Introduction
- An overview of existing research
- The research process
- The coaching process and research issues
- Suggestions for a research agenda
- Implications for coaching researchers
- Summary
- Reading

INTRODUCTION

Interest in sport coaching has grown significantly in the new millennium in line with coaching being perceived as a legitimate profession around the world, and an emerging field of academic study. These factors have resulted in an increase in the volume and scope of scholarly activity related to it (Rangeon *et al.* 2012; Lyle & Cushion 2010). In a recent review and citation network analysis of coaching research that included 3,891 references, Rangeon *et al.* (2012) found that:

- some of the most prominent sport coaching research articles have been traced back to the early 1970s;
- the yearly publication rate of coaching related research has increased dramatically;
- there are over 1,000 research studies on sport coaching published in peer-reviewed English-language journals;
- forty-one publications were identified as 'key publications' – the top three being a book (*Sports Coaching Concepts: A Framework for Coaches' Behaviour* (Lyle 2002)) and two research papers (Cushion *et al.*'s (2003) article on coach education; and the 'coaching model', published by Côté *et al.* (1995));
- numerous overviews of the 'coaching science' literature are now available (e.g. Côté & Gilbert 2009; Gilbert & Trudel 2004; Horn 2008; Lyle & Cushion 2010); and
- "coaching science is highly influenced by a small set of key publications and researchers" (p. 103).

From this work, and as we have previously suggested (see Lyle & Cushion 2010; Cushion & Lyle 2010), there is now a considerable landscape of coaching research with a bewildering range of theoretical and empirical perspectives and insights into coaching. Despite this apparent depth of empirical work, we remain surprised that there is still a lack of in-depth understanding of coaching and a clear conceptual underpinning with which to inform coaching practice and coach education. Despite our research efforts, and a degree of 'clustering' of ideas around, for example, 'coach effectiveness' and 'decision making', these remain contested notions, leaving us with little consensus or clarity about the nature of coaching.

Cited in our earlier review of the 'state of the field' (Lyle & Cushion 2010), but still useful, is Ward and Barrett's (2002) test of the utility and value of research to a practice community, which asks the extent to which its findings are (a) used as recommended practices in the preparation of practitioners; and (b) incorporated by practitioners in everyday practice. There are positive research examples to be found of interventions in coach education and coaching practice – but no evidence for the systematic application of these, or any other findings, in the development of coaching practice or coach education in terms of either methodology or results. As a result, the increased research attention devoted to coaching, with its considerable weight of research studies and the level of conceptual and theoretical development in coaching, has had little apparent impact on coaching practice or coach education and a somewhat disheartening picture of the 'effectiveness' of coaching research to impact practice can be drawn – we have yet to distinguish between our knowledge of how coaches operate and our capacity to describe this, or indeed how we educate and develop coaches.

 KEY CONCEPT

There is a lack of in-depth understanding of coaching and a clear conceptual underpinning with which to inform coaching practice and coach education.

There are positive research examples to be found of interventions in coach education and coaching practice – but no evidence for the systematic application of these, or any other findings, in the development of coaching practice or coach education in terms of either methodology or results.

The purpose of this chapter is to give some consideration to why research is a low-impact endeavour when it comes to influencing coach education and coaching practice. It is not to conduct a 'review of literature' as such, but to provide some insight to, and suggest possible reasons for, the current impotence of coaching research in generating impact on practice. The chapter then goes on to develop a research agenda for coaching and considers the research process pertaining to coaching, the nature of the coaching process and assertions about coaching from which to demonstrate the generation of research questions.

AN OVERVIEW OF EXISTING RESEARCH

Coaching research has its own history and character. The early systematic observation studies (e.g. Lacy & Darst 1985) and leadership model (Chelladurai & Saleh 1980) were influential in the devising of coaching behaviour frameworks. It is not surprising, therefore, that Gilbert and Trudel's (2004) review identified that 'coaches' behaviours' were the main research interest from 1970 to 2001. These gave way to the interview and observation approaches of, for example, Salmela (1995), Gould *et al.* (1990), Gilbert (Gilbert & Trudel 2004) and Côté (Côté *et al.* 1995). In the last 10–15 years, the acknowledgement of a coaching *process* has spawned a search for the most appropriate means to represent and understand it (see Lyle 2002 and review by Cushion *et al.* 2006). While Rangeon *et al.*'s (2012) review showed this focus had shifted to research considering 'coach development', with 25 per cent of the most cited publications in their analysis directly dealing with this topic (a focus on coach education, learning and related developmental issues for coaches). They suggest that this shift is due to a growing field moving beyond description to understanding in terms of coach development and learning.

However, Cushion *et al.* (2010), in their review, point out that this area of coaching research suffers from a number of issues:

- being of mixed quality;
- often lacking a developed theoretical position;
- approaches coaching with implicit assumptions;
- research is from educational contexts with students, rather than with coaches;
- research is often cross-sectional perception/satisfaction studies;
- the research rarely sets a conceptual boundary for coaching or the domain under study;
- the findings are stretched in some way to fit all coaching domains, or are highly context-specific;
- meaningful research is often precisely that, namely highly context-specific; and
- it is difficult to find longitudinal, empirical evaluation.

While taken specifically from the coach learning and development research, we would contend that these issues would apply when considering the wider coaching research field. Importantly, as we have suggested previously (Lyle & Cushion 2010; Cushion & Lyle 2010), coaching research itself may be a misnomer, and we may be guilty of perpetuating here the concept of a unified field or consensual purpose that we argue does not exist currently. Without wishing to offer a taxonomy of research, we can point to the following areas of research interest, in addition to coach education and development:

- coaching practice, both environment and career;
- coaches' behaviours, both intervention/delivery and interpersonal;
- coaches' cognitions, both decision policies and decision making; and
- coaches' expertise.

Rangeon *et al.* (2012) also identified the following research areas as 'hotbeds' of publication and citation – in order of 'importance' in their analysis:

1. coach development
2. sport coaching – 'general'
3. qualitative research
4. coach–athlete relationship
5. coaching efficacy
6. coach knowledge
7. general talent development
8. coaching behaviours
9. general self-efficacy
10. quantitative data analysis
11. coach leadership
12. professional development.

While giving a flavour of the broad areas of coaching research, these lists taken together give some insight to the 'research agenda' in coaching over the last decade. We now turn to a consideration of this agenda, why it has emerged in this way and, importantly, what this means for coaching as we develop the conceptual framework.

Coaching as a research area, while still emerging, has a research agenda that has largely developed serendipitously, and is driven by individual research interests; such work often cites 'in-vogue' theories or has a particular theoretical agenda, with coaches and coaching a convenient data set for some other issue (Cushion & Lyle 2010). Moreover, coaching does not yet have a 'professional body' nor an obvious source of research funding to impact or drive focused research. As a result, a diverse research community or 'schools' have developed that are seldom coaching-specific, but instead tend to be driven by disciplinary or sub-disciplinary outcomes. Too often, this means that the 'coaching' within the research is superficial or secondary. In addition, subservience to disciplinary outcomes means that 'new' theories brought to coaching are, in fact, re-cycled approaches and theories from other domains. This brings with it the danger of simply compounding perhaps already limited thinking, while recourse to models and theories from other fields has limited value in building a coherent conceptual or theoretical body of knowledge (Lyle & Cushion 2010; Cushion 2007b). So despite a seemingly comprehensive list of research areas, coaching and coaching practice unfortunately remains, relatively speaking, under-researched with the breadth of research meaning the field is in fact "sparse, unfocussed and subjective" (LeUnes 2007, p. 403; Lyle & Cushion 2010). As a result, coaching practice and its process have received considerably less attention than other outcomes. Importantly, our recent review of coaching research (Lyle & Cushion 2010) could find few, if any, links between coaching practice and performance outcomes, limited attention to intervention research and performance outcomes that were rarely the dependent variables in such research. There is little evidence to suggest that this situation has changed in the interim.

These limitations notwithstanding, the literature has broadly come to acknowledge to various degrees that coaching is a social activity built on a web of complex,

330

context-dependent, and interdependent activities that come together to form a holistic process – a key premise of the book. It is a remarkably complex, intricate yet coherent process incorporating myriad individual variations that each coach, player and environment add to the blend and, as we have previously alluded to, perhaps it is this very complexity that has resulted in a dearth of "research that has explored the conceptual development of the coaching process", possibly because it is too complex to research neatly or about which to draw straightforward conclusions (Lyle 1999, p. 13; Lyle & Cushion 2010). Put simply, coaching is complex, not linear, and it is difficult to quantify and as such there are myriad variables that impact it that can make 'measuring' in experimental or causal studies problematic.

 KEY CONCEPT

Coaching is complex, not linear; it is difficult to quantify and as such there are myriad variables that impact it, which can make 'measuring' in experimental or causal studies problematic.

Despite coaching being understood as often ambiguous, complex and having a social nature, the tendency in research has been to treat complex issues in coaching (e.g. practice, learning, knowledge, delivery, curriculum) as solvable by a narrow focus on quick-fix data, with coaching assumed as unproblematic and as a generic identifiable phenomenon. As a result, there has been scant systematic research on improvements in coaching practice or on athlete outcomes. In addition, coaching research by and large remains largely descriptive in nature and offers little in the way of 'why', while having even less to say about the complex relations between, and influence of, coaching, coaches, athletes and contexts. Hence, we would argue that this is a significant reason why coaching, inclusive of values, beliefs and practice, has remained largely unchanged by the findings of coaching research over the last 35 years.

As discussed in Chapter 9, coaching always has, as Rink (2001) contends, its "roots in particular theory" (p. 112). Theoretical perspectives and perceptions of coaching together will impact approaches to researching it. To a large extent, then, coaching research is dependent on, and characterised by, design, and ultimately our research designs are hostage to our understanding, perspectives and theories (Lyle & Cushion 2010; Cushion 2007b). For example, as Cushion and Nelson (2013) point out, research methodology will likely be different if one assumes that coaching is stable, consistent and identical across and between contexts, with the aim of generating best practice models – versus an assumption that coaching is individual, has its own contextual make-up, is in constant flux and where the aim is understanding these inherent complexities and diversities, and assisting coaches in becoming capable of adapting to contextual demands. In Chapter 9 we highlighted the dominance of psychology's influence on coaching, and Rangeon *et al.* (2012) also note the 'tight link' between coaching science and sport psychology, reporting that half of the journals appearing in their key publications list are sport psychology journals. As a result, despite more qualitative research methodologies with marked changes into interview-based and observation-based research away from questionnaire studies, and compelling arguments for a 'paradigm shift' in coaching research (see for example, Lyle 2002; Cushion *et al.* 2006; Jones 2006), perhaps reflecting the wider sport science and particularly sport psychology research field, there remains a predominantly narrow, reductionist, rationalistic or positivistic approach to coaching research.

 QUESTION BOX

The extreme positions of more stable to more complex may not reflect the realities of a 'middle ground'. Do you think that there may be sport-specific differences in how a sport coaching intervention is conceived?

As we have argued for some time, the questions posed in coaching research have to date by and large been shaped by the methods and assumptions of the positivist paradigm (Cushion & Lyle 2010; Lyle & Cushion 2010; Lyle 1999) (see Chapter 9 for a further discussion of this issue). Underpinned by positivist assumptions, 'coaching' research becomes characterised by distinct and fragmented categories and coaching itself is reduced in scale and scope, often viewed as unproblematic and portrayed as a matter of simplistic technical 'transfer'. Even in circumstances in which there has been an attempt to investigate the 'how' of delivery – for example, through issues such as motivational climate, feedback, coach behaviour and communication – a singular focus does not have the capacity to capture sufficiently the dynamic and complex nature of coaching (Cushion & Lyle 2010). Furthermore, research topics such as the coach–athlete relationship and decision making are self-evidently important to coaching but the most-often used methodologies are limited in the extent to which they are able to embrace the wider coaching context. These issues typically are considered devoid of context and not placed in their socio-historical and cultural moment. In addition, although an integral part of coaching practice, they alone do not account sufficiently in their resultant prescriptions for the breadth of coaching expertise. From a practitioner's perspective, the impact of what we've described as this 'competition of importances' has been confusion and, not unsurprisingly, a perception of much of the majority of research as being irrelevant, of not being linked to the real world (Lyle & Cushion 2010; Cushion *et al.* 2006).

It is important at this stage to strike a cautionary note, and we have to be careful about generalising across *all* coaching research, and about criticising research for not being something that it did not set out to be. Therefore, we might be critical of coaching research for paying less attention to the complexity of the coaching milieu, but we also need to address the methodological challenges that this brings. However, the overall outcome is a body of work that is in some part useful, but ultimately limited in developing our understanding of all aspects of coaching. Coaching research consistently, and frustratingly, reduces the complexity of practice by presenting coaching in overly systematic and unproblematic ways (Lyle & Cushion 2010; Jones 2006). More seriously, perhaps, there persists a fundamentally flawed assumption that a positivist science, with a sub-disciplinary focus, inevitably reducing coaching to episodes of neat dependent and independent variables, can account fully for what coaching practice actually entails (Lyle & Cushion 2010; Cushion 2007a). Indeed, the process of separating and specialising components of real-life coaching and feeding them back to coaches in order to enhance understanding or prescribe practice results in abstractions that clearly fail to substitute for real-life derived intuitions about coaching (Lyle & Cushion 2010; Cushion 2007a). Viewed from this perspective, coaches are considered to be motivated solely by narrow reductionist logic, and this reinforces the concept of coaching as simply efficient technical transfer. As we have been at pains to stress, these arguments are not designed to claim superiority of one method or paradigm over another, but suggest that making a reductionist approach central to understanding practice is problematic in that it serves only to define coaching both narrowly and unilaterally (Lyle & Cushion 2010; Cushion 2007a). As Cushion (2007a) argues, it is these representations that produce, on one hand, the illusion of a 'complete' understanding but in reality are weak and limited; while on the other hand, are viewed with irony and even cynicism by practitioners and hence fail to impact the practice realm, to the disadvantage of coaching and its professional standing.

 QUESTION BOX

There may be some value in research within a positivistic paradigm; after all, it does not suggest that coaches themselves think or act in such a reductionist way – merely that such research fails to capture the 'messiness' of real practice. What would coaching research need to look like to be able to capture these dynamics, to impact practitioners and lead to changes in coaching practice?

Our critical appraisal here of the positivist paradigm is neither new nor exclusive to coaching. Nevertheless, we suggest that it continues to contribute significantly to the failure of coach research to impact on coach education (Lyle & Cushion, 2010). Indeed, this also raises the issue of how much coaching research is 'used' by coaches, performers or coach educators, what is 'used' and in what circumstances. Although we point to the link between the dominant research paradigm and a narrow concept of coaching, the dominance of psychologically driven research is apparent here with simple and seductive concepts that appear readily applicable but contribute to the narrowing of the coaching concept. We also suggest that the problem lies as much with the absence of other competing paradigms and the positioning of these as 'alternative', rather than the overstated claims of positivist research. The criticism that positivism is reductionist and attempts to reduce 'interference' (for example, systematic observation of coaching behaviours) is apt; more interpretive method-ologies are able to identify the complex interweaving of personal, performance and environmental factors, but have not, as yet, contributed substantively to coaching-specific theory building or practice prescriptions. We are also careful to acknowledge that some practitioner cynicism is attributable to both a residual 'anti-intellectualism' and a disregard for any non-self-experiential research, rather than the limitations of particular paradigms.

Lastly, a close examination of the existing body of research reveals that among the insightful empirical work there is arguably also a large amount of what MacDonald *et al.* (2002) describe as "waving theory from the balcony" (p. 194) (Lyle & Cushion 2010). That is, too many researchers are not immersed in coaching and are guilty of speaking seemingly authoritatively about an aspect of coach education or coaching practice based solely on the production of a well-argued but ultimately arbitrary theory (perhaps derived from their own research agenda, or through spotting a perceived gap, rather than driven by the needs of coaching) (Lyle & Cushion 2010). Theory is necessary to act as a signpost to new ways of seeing and understanding coaching, and in its conceptual development, not as convenient scaffolding for isolated and unintegrated enquiry.

 KEY CONCEPT

Theory is necessary to act as a signpost to new ways of seeing and understanding coaching, and in its conceptual development, not as convenient scaffolding for isolated and unintegrated enquiry.

This overview (in addition to previous chapters) has recognised that sport coaching is a problematic and contested activity, has a high level of uncertainty of practice and outcome, remains significantly under-theorised, has both conscious and unconscious elements in its professional practice, has a high level of complexity and even uniqueness, and is widely varied in its scale, form and practice. There is not as yet a consensual conceptual framework that recognises and embraces the scale, scope and complexity of this practice, nor is there a consensual body of knowledge that has informed policy and practice.

THE RESEARCH PROCESS

Generally, research is targeted at the resolution of problematic – often contemporary – issues, the improvement of current practice or the testing of theoretical propositions, or occasionally genuinely exploring innovative ideas. In addition, research problems in a particular field may have more specific purposes: the need to apply theoretical understandings into demanding and untested contexts; to stop occasionally and review and synthesise the received wisdom in an area; and the need to base education and training on a rigorously achieved understanding of professional practice. There seems to be a lack of clarity as to the explicit scientific approach underpinning coaching research undertaken, i.e. whether the research aligns itself with basic science or applied science principles. For example, the purpose of basic science is to discover new knowledge and information, often without the primary concern of how the knowledge created might be used. However, it is common for coaching researchers to attempt to draw applied science conclusions from their work, thus inferring that the research is aligned with applied science principles. Basic science approaches appear to be adopted to establish causal relationships between isolated performance variables in an attempt to predict outcomes, yet authors are then drawing applied conclusions from their data. Therefore, researchers arguably are currently investigating coaching from a basic science approach, but attempt to make applied claims from the research. This leads to a lack of conceptual clarity about the scientific origins of the work and its desired outcome.

Therefore, there is a need to address the purpose of coaching research based on a classification or typology of research forms. Figure 15.1 suggests not that sport performance research be replaced with coaching research, but that research into coaching is complementary (perhaps essential) if the full picture is to be achieved. Perhaps it would be better to say that performance sport research is incomplete without much greater attention to sport coaching research. It is certainly incomplete if implementation in a naturalistic coaching setting has not been taken into account.

What really happens to hard-won scientific knowledge at the implementation stage? Can it be applied? What really happens? Does it work in practice? And does it have an impact? There is no question about the centrality of fundamental or applied research on sport performance, just that there are also other questions to ask.

■ The fundamental scientist asks '*What* makes performance better?'
■ The applied scientist asks '*How* can performance be made better?'
■ The contextual scientist asks '*In which circumstances* can performance be made better?' or 'What will improve (or sustain) the performance of that performer at that time and in those circumstances?'

The last question, for example, is remarkably similar to the question that all coaches constantly have in their minds! These questions apply whether the focus is on, for example, biochemistry, physiology, psychology, coach behaviour or strategy. Not all of the sections in Figure 15.1 have been attended to by the research community on a satisfactorily equal basis. If it is caricatured, rather simplistically, as an issue of performance versus coaching, lessons might be learned from a similar model of enquiry into the balance of research between learning and teaching. School performance, league tables, multiple social deprivation and parental expectations, etc. is a similarly difficult context within which to apply and implement learning theories.

There can be little doubt that the sport science research community has focused on athlete performance, although perhaps less so on athletes performing. In the goal of improving sports performance, the coach, the coach's behaviour and the coach's

Research model		Balance of research focus			Scientist
Forms	Terminology	Sport performance ←——→ Coaching process			
Basic research	Fundamental research	Performance components		(The coach)	Fundamental scientist
Applied research	Ecologically valid research	Applied performance components	Training theory	The coach	Applied scientist
Application research	Applied research		Integrated training programmes	The coaching process	Contextual scientist
Implementation research				The coaching process	Contextual scientist

Figure 15.1 A research typology related to the coaching process.

intervention programme and impact have not purposefully been treated as unproblematic variables. The research community needs to address a holistic set of questions. How has this research influenced coaching practice? How sure are you that the performer is receiving the benefit of the application of new knowledge? Has it made a difference to performance outcomes? The answers to these questions depend on an increased attention to the coach and the coaching process.

 KEY CONCEPT

In the goal of improving sports performance, the coach, the coach's behaviour and the coach's intervention programme and impact have not purposefully been treated as unproblematic variables.

The benefits of interdisciplinary and cross-disciplinary research are incontrovertible given the complexity of both performance and the coaching process. Some issues, such as overtraining that undoubtedly benefit from a multidisciplinary approach would further benefit from being investigated as coaching process issues.

THE COACHING PROCESS AND RESEARCH ISSUES

A key element in discussing coaching research is to revisit some previous insights into sport coaching and the coaching process. This is necessary because it is these assumptions about the coaching process that will significantly shape the research agenda and identify the difficulties of research design. These ideas were discussed in some length in earlier chapters and are summarised rather than elaborated.

As a starting point, it may be instructive to reinforce the central purpose of sport coaching. Coaching is about improving or sustaining performance towards identified goals, through a structured intervention programme, and delivering within constraints of time, place and resource. This suggests that the outcomes of coaching are measurable – but not easily. The phrase 'reducing the unpredictability of performance' is a useful one to describe the coaching role. Whatever the definition, the contextual nature of both the performance and the intervention programme present problems of using simple outcome measures of athlete performance as a mark of coaching performance. The most immediate issue, therefore, is that simplistic assessment of athlete performance is a poor measure of the quality of the coaching process.

 KEY CONCEPT

Coaching is about improving or sustaining performance towards identified goals, through a structured intervention programme, and delivering within constraints of time, place and resource.

The contextual nature of performance and the intervention programme mean that simplistic assessment of athlete performance is a poor measure of the quality of the coaching process.

Furthermore, it should also be noted that this is to be accomplished within a contested terrain. Improvement is not only constrained by the limitations of the performer (and the coach), leaving aside the issue of how much value-added is acceptable, but by the deliberate and purposeful intentions of other competitors and coaches. Much of sport involves relative achievement – this makes it difficult to attain and to measure. The issue here is not that the performance of the player or athlete cannot be assessed, whether in output or outcome measures, but that ascribing improvement or success within such a complex process is fraught with difficulty.

The coaching process was shown to have a number of important characteristics. The passage that follows identifies six of these characteristics and their attendant research implications.

1. *Coaching is a process.* It is serial; it has inter-dependent and inter-related elements and stages; it has sub-processes and stages designed to contribute to an overall goal, and it is incremental and accumulative in its effect.

    Research issue. It is difficult to carry out research into processes. Controlling the input variables is very demanding and the confounding environmental variables are difficult to control and almost impossible to replicate. The key elements of processes are planning, regulating and monitoring. Of themselves these are not difficult to address, but they are longitudinal in nature and not informed by rigorously evaluated exemplars of good practice to the extent that would be beneficial.

2. *There is a deep-seated genericism and commonality about the process, but it is characterised by apparent uniqueness and variety.* The process varies in scale and in the extent of the control exercised over the variables that influence performance. The process varies by the intensity of the involvement (duration, frequency, continuity, stability), by the coach's role in competition, by the degree of responsibility exercised by the athlete, by the contribution of other individuals to the implementation of the process and by the requirement/constraints/resources of the organisation within which the coach operates.

    Research issue. It is difficult to effect research designs from which generalisations might be drawn.

3. *Performance and participation coaching.* This distinction was described in an earlier chapter, but deserves more attention because it is at the root of much of the irrelevant research carried out under the banner of coaching. Participation coaching is characterised by being less intensive, often not about competition goals, usually not systematic, more about immediate satisfactions and not all of the performance elements are attended to. It is largely 'episodic' in nature. Performance coaching has competition goals, longer-term horizons, significant athlete commitment and an attempted control of contributory variables – hence lifestyle management as a current buzzword. Performance coaching is 'processual'.

    The implications of this distinction are really quite important, and a failure to appreciate the implications bedevils the literature.

    ■ The skills and knowledge requirement are different. One emphasises instructional, pedagogic and motivational skills; the other planning, monitoring, decision making and management skills.
    ■ The two forms of coaching are not on a continuum. Understanding this would greatly assist coach education and recruitment. The participation coach is not necessarily a beginner performance coach.
    ■ (Without going into details, which would be unfair), in an often-cited piece of research from the US, the implications for coaching were derived from four 'coaches' teaching a 'give-and-go' in basketball to young children. In another, otherwise admirable, piece of research on gender issues in coaching, there was clearly some significant doubt about the intensity of involvement of the subjects in the coaching process. In addition, larger-scale surveys of coaches have not distinguished in their summaries the findings as they apply to participation and performance coaches.

    Research issue. The subjects and contexts used in research must match the intended goals. All of the research is valuable but researchers must make clear the context within which they are operating and their assumptions about coaching.

4. *Coaching is a cognitive activity within a social context,* although there are craft elements related to the management of the training environment, interpersonal behaviour and the competition environment, and often some sports-specific expertise. We conceive of the operationalisation of the coaching intervention as a decision-making process, characterised variously as deliberative, semi-

deliberative and non-deliberative in nature. Deliberative or classical decision making is evident in the construction of training schedules and tactical plans, whereas semi-deliberative decisions are evident in the micro-management of the flow of momentum and progression in training drills and activities, in addition to crisis management of interpersonal tensions. Much of the coaches' cognitive activity is tacit and apparently intuitive. However, this form of experiential decision making is a means of responding to issues in time-pressured and uncertain contexts and is a mark of professional behaviour.

Research issue. The coach's overt behaviour is more visible, more accessible and more easily measured. There is a danger of researching what can be researched rather than what needs to be researched. Coaching behaviour is emphasised but coaching practice is sadly under-researched. To understand this better, it is valuable to conceive of coaching practice in four parts: direct intervention (directing the training session, counselling, match coaching); intervention support (planning, monitoring, etc.); external constraints management (handling the resources, facilities, equipment, finance, etc.); and strategic coordination (metacognitive management of variables). This is complicated by the fact that these roles are not necessarily all handled by one person. In summary, investigating coaching practice is not easily captured by behavioural analysis alone.

5. *Coaching is a social process.* It is not merely a technical exercise. It almost goes without saying that coaching is a form of interpersonal activity and this brings with it issues of power relationships, ethical behaviours, personal aspirations, emotional highs and lows and compatibilities. There is also a factor called 'performer variability', which recognises that performers do not always produce their best performances on each occasion (and are not expected to), but it does provide a significant source of difficulty for monitoring and regulating progress.

Research issue. Research into this aspect of the coaching process is complicated by a complex matrix of personal characteristics, individualisation/uniqueness, specificity of context, coaching philosophies and a dearth of solid evidence on the relationships between these factors and performance.

6. *The coach is a manager.* There are two levels to this. The coach can be conceived of as a manager of the coaching process or as a part of a larger system. A simple input–treatment–output model would help to identify key parts of the coaching process, from talent identification and recruitment, to programme management. However, the interesting questions are process ones. For example, what does the coach do when the outputs are not being achieved – re-set goals, recruit new performers, modify the intensity of the programme, modify the quality of the programme, ascribe it to injury, illness, etc.?

Research issue. There would be some value in using soft systems methodology (Wilson & van Haperen 2015) to examine performance coaching, particularly when teams of coaches and support personnel are involved. This is a valuable, problem-focused mechanism for understanding messy and untidy processes such as coaching. This would be one approach for identifying critical paths or models for different coaching contexts.

SUGGESTIONS FOR A RESEARCH AGENDA

Constructing a research agenda forces us to consider the limitations of existing research, but also to recognise the barriers to more ecologically valid research. The very factors inherent in the coaching process that we identify as necessary to an appropriate description of coaching are those that present considerable challenges to future research. Perhaps we might ask if this is the reason for more writing *about* the shortcomings of current research than remedial contributions (Lyle & Cushion 2010).

One of the most obvious first steps is to bridge the gap between relevance and feasibility, to site coaching research within practice and the practice community. Coaching practice, however, is not a construct that is in some way subordinate to the needs of empirical work (Lyle & Cushion 2010; Cushion 2007b). As we have previously suggested, the relationship between research and practice, and researchers and practitioners, needs to be better established and further developed – this may seem self-evident but so far has proven elusive:

- We need to strike up a dialogue with practitioners and demonstrate an engagement and collaboration with coaching practice.
- Research questions should arise from practice and practice issues.
- Research needs to be relevant to the problems and challenges of the day-to-day work of the coach.
- Research needs an appropriate level of utility for coach education and development, improved practice and more effective coaching.

Much of coaching research and researchers have yet to face up to and grasp the dual character of coaching practice, with its subjective and objective aspects – the currently overly polarised (and psychologically 'heavy') research field has led to a reductionist and misleading (or perhaps simply 'less helpful' and 'less useful') portrayal of practice and research approaches. This issue is a considerable obstacle to the development of a meaningful portrayal of coaching practice.

Focusing on explicit features of the coaching process and at the same time arguing for engagement with practice that is neither episodic or reductionist may seem somewhat paradoxical or even contradictory (Lyle & Cushion 2010; Cushion & Lyle 2010; Cushion 2007b). The episodic concept may result in a profile of behaviour and expertise that negates, or at best fails to capture, the very coordination and management of the coaching process that the emerging complexity, inter-relatedness and inter-dependence imply. Alternatively, a focus on the social and contextual character of coaching practice may provide a perspective that can appear relativist and unable, and indeed unwilling, to capture any 'generic' features of practice.[1] As we have previously argued (Lyle & Cushion 2010), framing an analysis to focus on coaching practice in the social world will provide a conceptualisation with the potential to capture specific practice in specific circumstances, thus doing justice to the multiple relations through which practice is defined and which seems so necessary for sport-specific analysis. Such an approach perhaps offers the potential to transcend some of the 'oppositions' outlined in this chapter, while integrating them into a broader knowledge framework.

How, then, can coaching practice be best described and analysed? The following description of how coaches operate is summarised from earlier chapters. These are presented as an outline research agenda on coaching practice. *Each of these statements should be interpreted as a tentative hypothesis.*

 QUESTION BOX

We have deliberately reproduced this (slightly updated) list from the previous edition of the book, and we invite you to update this in the light of your reading of previous chapters.

Performance coaches:

- operate within an umbrella of detailed planning, but implement this with a high degree of contingency;
- implement more systematic interventions in target/physical sports and less systematic interventions in more cyclical/team sports;
- play a central role in directing intervention and (often) competition management;
- constantly balance priorities between performance components (technical, tactical, physical, etc.) and relatively imprecise workload management;
- rely on extensive use of mental models of day-to-day expectations about athlete performance in both training and competition;
- exhibit expertise in the form of accommodating and aligning goals, activities and context on a continuous basis;
- develop sport-specific, personal cognitive knowledge structures, which are derived from experience and facilitate decision making;
- exercise what appears to be intuitive decision making, but is simply an efficient mechanism for reducing decision options;
- supplement subjective data gathering by objective testing and monitoring at selected times in the programme;
- use contingency planning as a normal and expected part of coaching practice – operationalisation demands a constant fine-tuning of schedules and major adjustments to accommodate injury, illness and recruitment changes;
- operate a system of crisis thresholds; that is, they recognise and deal with problems only when they reach a threshold of under-achievement or threaten longer-term goals – this takes into account fluctuations in athlete performance;
- devise coaching strategies (content, delivery and personal behaviour) to address the needs of immediate and future interventions;
- have a bank of stored and retrievable coping strategies to deal with common short- and long-term problems; and
- integrate the contributions of a team of professionals on a complementary and substitution basis.

Not only do these assertions suggest many research questions, particularly when considered in a sport-specific context, but they also raise similar questions about coach education.

In the previous edition, an example was given of research into coaches' decision making (Lyle 1999). The interest had been developed from personal experience as a volleyball coach and a curiosity about how coaches coped with the need for speedy decision making during the game itself. Coaches had to deal with the difficulty of decomposing the messages from a game sport. Even expert coaches will have some margin for error in their interpretation and diagnosis. Therefore, they had to deal with the dilemma of either acting very quickly, but with uncertainty, or delaying action and being ineffective (but sure that the problem is identified correctly). The coach will therefore have coping mechanisms to reduce uncertainty. One of these is a loss-minimisation heuristic. Coaches choose options based on conservatism – begin diagnosis early, don't get panicked into action and try not to reduce options too much. They appeared to use 'anticipatory reflection' to be prepared for contingencies. In other words, they model potential variations with the likely solutions available (perhaps tacit and pre-programmed), and again tempered by the resources available.

In order to illustrate the complexities involved in the coaches' thinking, and, by implication, a potential research framework, we imagine that the coaching moment is conceived of in this way: "I understand the problem at the moment, but how serious is it in relation to problems that might arise later? Is the problem likely to impact significantly on the target performance? The solution is obvious but will it work if I do it now? If I make changes, will this restrict my freedom and flexibility to make more important changes later on? If I don't change now, will this problem continue to grow and become insurmountable? Do I have any other strategic/ developmental plans in mind, which might supersede my interpretation of the current situation?" (Lyle 1999, p. 224). It is easy to see why the coach needs a decision-making model with shortcuts, and why researchers might find it difficult to model such behaviour.

IMPLICATIONS FOR COACHING RESEARCHERS

From what has been argued thus far, there are a number of implications for the researcher. Coaching practice can only be understood and appreciated when there is an understanding of the conceptual framework that constitutes the coaching process. This provides immediate insights into the shortcomings of a good deal of so-called coaching research, and reinforces the need for conceptual clarity. There are, as we have discussed here, pockets of empirical research that are contributing to the conceptual and intellectual development of coaching that force us to go back and question earlier perspectives and help us form new understandings of coaching practice. This research, and the debate it engenders, has great potential to develop coaching's conceptual base and add meaningfully to coach education and development. Yet our vocabulary for communicating about the coaching process remains somewhat under-developed.

342

Despite a body of 'behavioural' research, we are a good way from being replete with descriptive accounts of coaching practice. Attempts to measure coaching effectiveness have not been successful. Researchers have resorted to athlete satisfaction measures and few, if any, studies have come to grips with the issue of 'value-added' as a concept. Often, concepts come from outside the coaching field. There is, of course, a utility in drawing on relevant theoretical resources and learning from other, perhaps 'similar', fields. However, pre-constructed theories with limited empirical evidence or basis in coaching can produce a representation that is a fiction obscuring true meaning and understanding (Lyle & Cushion 2010; Cushion 2007b). Empirical objects appear to 'emerge' from coaching and become the focus of research; yet they are ultimately arbitrary. Somehow the discourse of the moment becomes deemed important by researchers and research agendas, but not always of interest or value to the coaching field. Because coaching research is still immature, there is therefore a need to access and investigate the practice of our expert coaches. However, there is a danger that coaching research pays inadequate attention to the issues of importance to coaching and coaching practice. Clearly to establish coaching as an autonomous field there is an overwhelming need for our own evidence-based theories and concepts. Indeed, regardless of the method or approach adopted to engage with coaching and coaching practice, conceptual development and understanding needs to be grounded in coaching practice and empirically supported.

Moreover, as our understanding of coaching becomes more sophisticated and a shift in the nature of coaching research occurs, we should not disregard existing accumulated knowledge, but rather consider ways to integrate new knowledge with what is already known (Lyle & Cushion 2010; Cushion 2007b). It is not in the interests of coaching and its development to block or delay integrating existing contributions or ideas in establishing a more sophisticated knowledge base – the challenge, therefore, lies in not only looking for new ways to understand coaching but also to build on existing work. Thus, the research community must begin to ask the important albeit difficult questions and address difficult issues.

1. Meaningful forms of replication and reduction are very difficult because of the complexity of the coaching process. More naturalistic, field-based studies are required; of course this brings with it significant challenges for research design and data collection.
2. Far greater empirical work is required on the coach's cognitive processes – mental models, thresholds, action triggers, heuristics, for example. Performance-enhancement research cannot be complete without attention to the coach's application, integration and delivery of coaching interventions.
3. Context is paramount and coaching can only be fully understood in the particular. Therefore, knowledge construed in general must inevitably fall short of offering a full understanding of coaching expertise.
4. Subtle judgements in particular contexts derive from the accommodation and alignment necessary to 'do the right thing at the right time to address the goals and needs of the athlete'. This capacity has been identified in coaches' expertise but is not yet evident in research.

343

5. We have been at pains to emphasise the aggregation of roles, domains and specific sports that constitute sport coaching. This is rarely recognised in coaching research, but, in our view, should overlie the coaching agenda.
6. There may be some interesting issues about coaching 'styles', or better expressed as coaching strategies. However, the significant issue is the effect of different strategies on the coach's intentions and capacity to effectively deliver, monitor and regulate the process – not on measures of athlete satisfaction. This is a not-too-thinly veiled criticism of many studies.
7. There are some really key questions related to implementation or application research. An example of this is the (surprising) dearth of research on planning the intervention programme. How can we investigate the effectiveness of planning decisions? How should processes be amended to account for illness, injury and weather? How accurate and individualised are workload measurements?

The complexity of the coaching process makes it difficult for the researcher. However, investigating how the coach copes with this complexity provides a most exciting challenge for the research community. The difficulties involved should not prevent researchers from attempting to control some of the variables in naturalistic research through inventive design, using more action-research based on attempts to improve cognitive processes over time, recognising the value of ethnographic enquiry and case studies, attempting to unravel the coach's cognitive processes, in particular the professional shortcuts employed, and appreciating the potential of systems analysis for an alternative approach to studying the coaching process.

There are a number of reasons why coaching research should become more widespread. A desire to enhance the coach education of our aspiring performance coaches should be sufficient reason for the research policy community to expand its interest in coaches and the coaching process. A more pragmatic reason is that much more funding is being invested in coaches and coaching. There are legitimate doubts that the knowledge exists on which to base accountability – other than in purely

---

 SUMMARY

This chapter should have familiarised you with the following:

- An overview and critique of research in coaching.
- The purpose of research and the status of research in sport coaching.
- A research typology that emphasises application and implementation, and an emphasis on the coaching process.
- Six characteristics of the coaching process and their attendant research implications.
- Issues from coaching contributing to generating a research agenda; hypotheses created from a description of coaching practice.
- A summary of questions to be addressed by the research community.

344

results-based terms. A more scholarly reason is that the research cycle is not being completed without attention to the application and implementation stages. Answering the 'how' questions about coaching practice will require recourse to supporting disciplines. However, in time, sufficient weight of evidence will be generated to create a coaching-specific family of theories.

READING

Although published in 2004, Gilbert and Trudel's review is a comprehensive overview that shows the evolution of coaching research since the 1970s – read in conjunction with Rangeon *et al.*'s (2012) citation analysis, it provides a comprehensive look at the direction of travel for coaching research. Our recent review and commentary (Cushion & Lyle 2010) gives a critical take on the issues further developed in the chapter. Lastly, Cushion *et al.* (2010) offer a systematic review of the literature examining research in coach education and learning.

NOTE

1 There have to be some generic features of coaching practice to enable us to recognise coaching as coaching. As has been argued elsewhere, there is a 'sameness' about our uniqueness; not all coaching practice is the same, but it is nonetheless coaching practice. The continuous adjustment inherent in practice captures the meeting place of object and subject and forces a consideration of the degree of predictability and control within practice, the *how* and *why*, rather than the *what*.

REFERENCES

Chelladurai, P., & Saleh, S. D. (1980). Dimensions of leader behavior in sports: Development of a leadership scale. *Journal of Sport Psychology*, 2, 34–45.

Côté, J., & Gilbert, W. (2009). An integrative definition of coaching effectiveness and expertise. *International Journal of Sports Science & Coaching*, 4(3), 307–323.

Côté, J., Salmela, J., Trudel, P., Baria, A., & Russell, S. (1995). The Coaching Model: A grounded assessment of expert gymnastic coaches' knowledge. *Journal of Sport and Exercise Psychology*, 17(1), 1–17.

Cushion, C. J. (2007a). Modelling the complexity of the coaching process. *International Journal of Sport Science & Coaching*, 2(4), 395–401.

Cushion, C. J. (2007b). Modelling the complexity of the coaching process: A response to commentaries. *International Journal of Sport Science & Coaching*, 2(4), 427–433.

Cushion, C. J., & Lyle, J. (2010). Conceptual development. In J. Lyle & C. J. Cushion (Eds) *Sports Coaching: Professionalisation and Practice*. Edinburgh: Churchill Livingstone, 1–14.

Cushion, C. J., & Nelson, L. (2013). Coach education and learning: Developing the field. In P. Potrac, W. Gilbert & J. Denison (Eds) *Routledge Handbook of Sports Coaching*. Abingdon: Routledge, 359–374.

Cushion, C. J., Armour, K. M., & Jones, R. L. (2003). Coach education and continuing professional development: Experience and learning to coach. *Quest, 55*, 215–230.

Cushion, C. J., Armour, K. M., & Jones, R. L. (2006). Locating the coaching process in practice: Models 'for' and 'of' coaching. *Physical Education and Sport Pedagogy, 11*(1), 83–89.

Cushion, C. J., Nelson, L., Armour, K., Lyle, J., Jones, R. L., Sandford, R., & O'Callaghan, C. (2010). *Coach Learning and Development: A Review of Literature*. Leeds: sports coach UK.

Gilbert, W., & Trudel, P. (2004). Analysis of coaching science research published from 1970–2001. *Research Quarterly for Exercise & Sport, 75*(4), 388–399.

Gould, D., Giannini, J., Krane, K., & Hodge, K. (1990). Educational needs of elite US national team, Pan American and Olympic coaches. *Journal of Teaching Physical Education, 9*, 332–334.

Horn, T. S. (2008). Coaching effectiveness in the sport domain. In T. S. Horn (Ed.), *Advances in Sport Psychology*. 3rd edition. Champaign, IL: Human Kinetics, 239–267.

Jones, R. L. (2006). How can educational concepts inform sports coaching? In: R. L. Jones (Ed.) *The Sports Coach as Educator: Re-conceptualising Sports Coaching*. Routledge: London, 3–13.

Lacy, A. C., & Darst. P. W. (1985). Systematic observation of behaviours of winning high school head football coaches. *Journal of Teaching in Physical Education, 4*, 256–270.

LeUnes, A. (2007). Modelling the complexity of the coaching process: A commentary. *International Journal of Sport Science & Coaching, 2*(4), 403–406.

Lyle, J. (1999). The coaching process: An overview. In N. Cross & J. Lyle (Eds) *The Coaching Process: Principles and Practice for Sport*. Oxford: Butterworth-Heinemann, 3–24.

Lyle, J. (2002). *Sports Coaching Concepts: A Framework for Coaches' Behaviour*. London: Routledge.

Lyle, J. (2007). A review of the research evidence for the impact of coach education. *International Journal of Coaching Science, 1*(1), 17–34.

Lyle, J., & Cushion, C. J. (2010). Narrowing the field: Some key questions about sport coaching. In J. Lyle & C. J. Cushion (Eds) *Sports Coaching: Professionalisation and Practice*. Edinburgh: Churchill Livingstone, 243–253.

Macdonald, D., Kirk. D., Metzler, M., Nilges, L. M., Schempp, P., & Wright, J. (2002). It's all very well in theory: Theoretical perspectives and their applications in contemporary pedagogical research. *Quest, 54*,133–156.

Rangeon, S., Gilbert, W., & Bruner, M. (2012). Mapping the world of coaching science: A citation network analysis. *Journal of Coaching Education, 5*(1), 83–108.

Rink, J. (2001). Investigating the assumptions of pedagogy. *Journal of Teaching Physical Education, 20*, 112–128.

Salmela, J. H. (1995). Learning from the development of expert coaches. *Coaching and Sports Science Journal, 2*(2), 3–13.

Ward, P., & Barrett, T. (2002). A review of behavior analysis research in physical education. *Journal of Teaching in Physical Education, 22*, 242–266.

Wilson, B., & van Haperen, K. (2015). *Soft Systems Methodology and the Management of Change*. London: Palgrave Macmillan.

INDEX

Page numbers in italics refer to figures. Page numbers in bold refer to tables.

coaching constructs, generic 49–51
coaching context 98, 103–4; *see also* alignment
    skills
coaching domains: about 71–2, 74, 76; boundary
    criteria and 74; categories of 76–8, **78**; criteria
    for 75; implications in recognition of 73
'coaching down' *see* 'coaching up' versus
    'coaching down'
coaching effectiveness 30
coaching expertise: capacity and performance in
    107; coaching practice and 164–5; as coaching
    process building block 136–7; conceptual
    framework 95, *106*, *109*; interpretation of
    104–5, *106–9*, 110–12; overview of 96–9,
    99; UKCC Level 4 competencies *108*;
    see also high-performance coaching expertise
coaching forms 61–2, *62*, 64–5; *see also specific
    types of coaches*
coaching intervention 29–30; *see also* decision
    making
coaching philosophy 233–44, **245**
coaching practice: about 29, 48–9, 164–5, 183–4;
    autocratic versus democratic *265*; belief
    systems and 183–4, 237, 242, 310, 312–13;
    coach learning and 304–5, 306–10, 312–13;
    as conscious versus reflexive behavior 240–1,
    243; decision making in 169–75, *175*; process
    characteristics and **52**; social issues in 209–12,
    218–27; sport specificity and 148–9, **149–50**;
    see also coaching philosophy; systematic
    practice
coaching practice theory and paradigms
    185–204, **203**
coaching process: authors' experiences of 131;
    boundary criteria and 53–6, **54–5**; building
    blocks identification 134–43, *135*; control box
    166–9, *166*, **168**; misrepresentations of 132;
    operationalisation of 48; overview of 46–8, 51,
    52, 53, 146, 162–4; process skills 58–60, *59*,
    121–2, 307–8; research issues about 336–9;
    research typology related to *336*; role conflicts
    within 88–9; skills in 58–60, *59*; as a social
    process 209–12, 225–7; visual representation
    of 143, *144–5*, 146; *see also* operationalisation;
    proposed models; roles of coaches
coaching researchers 342–5
coaching schematic 123–4
coaching strategies: attempted congruence in
    269; autocratic versus democratic coaching
    practice *265*; conceptual framework versus
    interpersonal dimension **263–4**; factors
    influencing leadership *267*; learning
    environments *276*; overview of 261–70;
    reflective practice framework *273*; *see also*
    coaching expertise

coaching style resolution 269–70, *269*
coaching styles 264, 268–9; *see also* coaching
    strategies; leadership practice; teaching styles
coaching theories 187, 188, 192; *see also* learning
    theories
'coaching up' versus 'coaching down' 285–6
Cobb, P. 198
cognitive constructivism 198–200
cognitive organisation 307
cognitivism 8–10, 196–7
Colley, H. 318
Collin, A. 201
Collins, D. 13
communities of practice 271–2; *see also* coaching
    communities of practice (CCoPs)
competences *108*, 303, 306, 307; *see also*
    coaching expertise; roles of coaches
competition cycles **148**
competition management 112; *see also* learning
    environments
competition phases models *157*
competition programmes 142
complexity approaches overview 10–11
conceptual appreciation and issues 23–7, 34,
    35–7
conceptual approaches overview 13
conceptual framework: application issues
    and elements of *30*; coaching expertise 95,
    106, *108*, *109*; complexity issues 31, *31*;
    interpersonal dimension versus **263–4**;
    overview of 27–31, **28**; *see also* boundary
    criteria; coaching domains; coaching practice
    theory and paradigms; definition framework;
    proposed models
conflict theory 216
constraints management 84, 85–6
constructivist approaches 184–5; *see also* cognitive
    constructivism; social constructionism
consultants 87; *see also* specialist coaches
context *see* coaching context; learning
    environments
control box 166–9, *166*, **168**
Côté and colleagues model 123, 327
Côté, J. 116, 329
Côté's Development Framework 77
craft skills 111, 176, *177*; *see also* pedagogy
critical theory 216
Cross, N. 154–5
Culver, D. 320
Cushion, C. 11, 36, 220, 226, 312, 313, 314,
    319, 329, 331, 333

d'Arripe-Longueville, F. 10
Dearden, R. 301
decision making: evolution in 307; factors

influencing 171–2; heuristics 171; importance of 162, 163; mental models 123, 172–5, *175*; NDM model 9, 169, 170, 172; stages of 170–1; types of 169–70
definition framework 42–4, 45–7; *see also* conceptual framework
development coaching 62–3, 64
Dewar, A. 222
direct intervention 83–5
domain specificity 100–1
Downey, M. 176
Duffy, P. 47, 98, 281, 283
Durand, M. 10, 132

effectiveness *see* coaching expertise; competences
Ely, R. 223
epistemology *see* ontology and epistemology
Ericsson, K. 96
European Coaching Council 47
Evetts, Julia 289–90
expert coaches 166; *see also* high-performance coaching expertise
expertise 96; *see also* coaching expertise

Fairs model 122–3
Fasting, K. 223
feminism 217–18; *see also* women coaches
Foucault, Michel 211, 217, 219, 220
frame of reference *see* boundary criteria; coaching context; domain specificity; roles of coaches
Franks and colleagues model 122
French, J. 220
functional skills 102; *see also* sport-specific knowledge
functionalism 214

Garfinkel, Harold 211
Garratt, D. 281, 283
gender issues *see* feminism; inequality and inclusion
generic coaching constructs 49–51
Ghaye, T. 316
Giddens, Anthony 211
Gilbert, W. 7, 315, 329
Giulianotti, R. 213, 214, 217
goal mental models 174
goal-setting 140
Goffman, Erving 211, 214, 215, 217
Gould, D. 329
Green, K. 244
Groom, R. 220

Hagger, H. 132, 164, 178
Hall, A. 223
Hardman, A. 244

Hargreaves, J. 222
Harvey, S. 170
head coaches 86, 99, 111
hegemony 216
heuristics 171
high-performance coaching expertise 99–104
high-performance sports **261**
Høigaard, R. 261
humanistic approach to coaching 266–8

ICCE *see* International Council for Coaching Excellence (ICCE)
ideology *see* coaching philosophy
inclusion *see* inequality and inclusion
individualisation 137, 142
indoctrination 302
inequality and inclusion 221–5
information platform 136; *see also* monitoring procedures
innovation 320, 322
Institute for Learning 291
instrumental rationality 193–4
intellect and knowledge 103; *see also* sport-specific knowledge
interactive coaching 132
International Council for Coaching Excellence (ICCE) 90, 281, 291
interpersonal dimension 262–4, **263–4**, 308–9
interpretive sociology 214–15
intervention parameters 259–61
intervention parameters, skill development and *260*
intervention support 84, 85, 112

Jenkins, R. 240
Jenkins, S. 236, 237
Jones, C. 244
Jones, Robyn 10, 11, 36, 50, 210, 211, 212, 214, 217, 219, 220, 221, 318

Kahneman, D. 172
Kemmis, S. 187, 241
Kincheloe, J. 216
Kirk, D. 252, 266
Klein, G. 172
knowledge categories 136; *see also* intellect and knowledge
Knowles, M. 256

Lave, J. 201, 319
leadership practice 264–6, *267*
Leadership Scale for Sport 265
learning environments 257–61, *259*, 260, 275–7, *276*, 300–1
learning principles 256–7, **256**

player coaches 89
positivism 192–3
postmodernism/poststructuralism 216–17
Potrac, P. 11, 219, 220, 221
power 219–21
practice theories *see* coaching theories
preparation and training programmes 141–2
professional club coaches 89
professional development *see* coach education and
    professional development
professionalisation 29, 281–94
progress monitoring *see* monitoring procedures
proposed models: adaptation of 156, *157*, 158;
    building blocks identification 134–43, *135*,
    147; extension of *151*, *152*, **153**, **155**; ideal
    coaching process 143, *144–5*, 146; limitations
    of 147–9, **148**, **149–50**, 158–9; prior
    assumptions for 133–4; research using 146–7;
    systematic practice 150–6, *150*, *152*, **153**, **155**

qualifications *see* professionalisation
quality control stages *152*

Race, P. 257
Raedeke, T. 236
Rail, G. 216
Rangeon, S. 7, 327, 329, 330, 331
Raven, B. 220
Recognition Primed Decision model 172
reflection-in-action 179
reflective practice 309, 312, 313, 314–17
reflective practice framework 272, *273*, 274, 316,
    317
regulation procedures 140–1, 154; *see also* control
    box; planning; professionalisation
relationships *see* interpersonal dimension
replacement roles 87
representative team coaches 65, 89
research: assistant coaches 90; coach education
    and professional development 303–4, 310;
    coaching philosophy 237–8; coaching practice
    184; coaching process 43, 51, 146–7, 336–9;
    model building 125, 126; overview of 30,
    327–34; shortfallings of 72; *see also* academic
    literature; coaching researchers
research agenda suggestions 340–2
research process 334–6, *336*
Rink, J, 331
Ritzer, G. 214
Rokeach, M. 236
role concepts 81–2
role frames 76
roles of coaches: about 79–81, 97; cognitive
    organisation 307; concepts regarding 81–2;
    organisational impact on 89–92;

professionalisation and 285; purpose and
    function of 82–6, *83*; role of support
    personnel versus 86–9, *87*; *see also* coaching
    process; competences
roles of support personnel 86–9, *87*
routine versus adaptive expertise 111
Rowntree, D. 256

Salmela, J. 329
Saury, J. 10, 132
Schön, D. 179, 272, 312, 315
Schuh, K. 185, 189, 195, 197
Schunk, D. 195
self-coached athletes 85
self-directed learner **256**
senior coaches *see* advanced/senior coaches
Shadrick, S. 320
Sheriden, M. 283
Sherman and colleagues model 123
simulation mental models 174–5
situated learning 319–20
skill development 259–61, *260*
social approaches 11–13
social constructionism 200–3
social process of coaching 209–12, 225–7;
    see also interpersonal dimension
social theory 212–18
sociology 210
The Sociology of Sport Coaching (Jones) 212
specialist coaches 65, 88; *see also* consultants
sport, as a concept 37–8
sport coaching: commonalities in 16; definition
    and definition issues 15, 42–4, 47–9, 173;
    definition framework 45–7; demographics 222;
    as a hidden profession 284; human element
    versus 27; as a multi-dimensional construct
    163–4; professionalisation of 281–94; reasons
    for studying role of 22–3; typology **57**; as a
    unidimensional construct 1–2; *see also* sport
    performance coaching
Sport England 284
sport participation coaching 63; *see also*
    participation coaching
sport performance coaching 63–4, 90, *108*, 121,
    305; *see also* performance coaching
sport performance factors 138, 262
sport scientists 88
sport-specific knowledge 103; *see also* functional
    skills
sport specificity 147–9, **149–50**, 309, 312–13
sports coach UK 43
sports instructors 65; *see also* sport participation
    coaching
Sproule, J. 261, 262
Stafford, I. 176